Pāli

The grammar presents a full description of Pāli, the language used in the Theravāda Buddhist canon, which is still alive in Ceylon and Southeast Asia. The development of its phonological and morphological systems is traced in detail from Old Indic. Comprehensive references to comparable features and phenomena from other Middle Indic languages mean that this grammar can also be used to study the literature of Jainism.

Pāli

A Grammar of the Language of the Theravāda *Tipiṭaka*

Thomas Oberlies

With a Concordance to

Pischel's *Grammatik der Prakrit-Sprachen*

MUNSHIRAM MANOHARLAL

Munshiram Manoharlal Publishers Pvt. Ltd.

ISBN 978-81-215-1234-3
First Indian edition 2012

Originally published by Walter de Gruyter GmbH & Co., Berlin, 2001

PRINTED IN INDIA
Published by Vikram Jain *for*
Munshiram Manoharlal Publishers Pvt. Ltd.
PO Box 5715, 54 Rani Jhansi Road, New Delhi 110 055, INDIA

www.mrmlbooks.com

To the memory of
HELMER SMITH
(1882-1956)

Preface
by A. Wezler

It is merely a coincidence that after Oskar von Hinüber's *A Handbook of Pāli Literature* we now have Thomas Oberlies' *Pāli. A Grammar of the Language of the Theravāda Tipiṭaka*. But this coincidence is not by any means unwelcome in that it once more underlines an important turning point in the development of Indian philology (in the continental sense of the word), viz. the breaking away from one-sided concentration on Sanskrit and Sanskrit literature alone and the extension of Indological studies to Middle Indo-Aryan languages, and the literature written in them. This 'change-of-paradigm' is not, as is well-known, a recent event; but in spite of the, indeed, already long tradition of Pāli and Prakrit studies it is not yet possible to say that they are on a par with Sanskrit studies and have fully caught up with them.

The general significance of Dr. Oberlies' Pāli grammar, which we are most happy to be able to publish in our series, is therefore a twofold one: Firstly, it is an attempt, and in my view a highly successful one, to bring together, analyse critically and utilize for his new handbook of the Pāli language all that has been achieved by scholars working almost exclusively or mainly or even sporadically on problems connected with this language, in the last eighty years, i.e. since the publication in 1916 Wilhelm Geiger's *Pāli Literatur und Sprache* as part of the predecessor of the JPSAS, the old *Grundriss der Indo-Arischen Philologie und Altertumskunde*. And this part of our Indological knowledge has indeed grown in a most impressive manner thanks to the scholarly endeavours of not a few Indologists like e.g. L. Alsdorf, N. Balbir, H. Bechert, H. Berger, W. B. Bollée, C. Caillat, T. J. Elizarenkova, O. von Hinüber, St. Insler, K. R. Norman, O. Pind, J. Sakamoto-Gotō, and Th. Oberlies himself, and, of course, also Indo-Europeanists like e.g. K. Hoffmann and C. Haebler. But, secondly, this new grammar of Pāli will promote no less the study of this language and the vast literature composed in it. It is meant not only for fellow-scholars as a work of reference but also for students as an indispensable tool. Indeed, it is primarily for their benefit that all Pāli elements are also translated.

Yet this new grammar is not, of course, just the outcome of an intelligent, diligent and comprehensive gathering of relevant materials. In reality it is the original work of a young scholar, and close friend of mine, who after his doctorate familiarized himself systematically with Pāli philology, his first two articles in this field of studies being devoted, significantly enough, to problems of the language and to a Jātaka story from the famous collection. The continuation of this twofold interest is further attested in his list of publications if one goes through it from 1989/90 to the last entry (of the year 2000). Yet another feature of Oberlies' involvement with Pāli studies becomes evident when one reads this list: Studies of individual problems, linguistic, text-critical or literary, lead finally to a comprehensive and fundamental discussion of the overarching problems. Thus his meticulous examination of various Jātakas – which shows how much Oberlies was able to learn from Alsdorf – are crowned by his two articles of 1993 and 1997 "Der Text der Jātaka-Gāthās in Fausbølls Ausgabe (Stand und Aufgaben der Jātaka-Forschung I)" and id. "II". Similarly, he winds up his studies on problems of the grammar of the Pāli language in the article "Stray remarks on Pāli phonology, morphology, and vocabulary. Addenda et corrigenda to Geiger's Pāli Grammar" of 1996. And yet, reading this article again one realizes that even this was no more than a prelude to the much more comprehensive, original and also ambitious undertaking of writing himself a new grammar of Pāli, offering a synthesis of the present state of our knowledge, on the one hand, and of his own opinions, observations and conclusions, on the other.

The result is in my view a big step forward in Pāli philology, and Middle Indo-Aryan philology at the same time. I hope that this new handbook will be well received by all those who already know this language as also by those who wish to learn it and to thus gain access to the marvellous and highly fascinating world of Theravāda Buddhist thought.

Hamburg, February 2001

Foreword

WILHELM GEIGER's *Pāli Literature and Language* is truly a *monumentum aere perennius* – one of the great achievements of Indology. Since its publication in 1916, however, much water has flowed down the Rhine and a great number of scholars have added to our knowledge of Pāli, in particular the 'Northern' school of Pāli philology as represented by e.g. DINES ANDERSEN and HELMER SMITH. And "however valuable as a descriptive grammar and as collection of material ... the *Pāli – Literatur und Sprache* of Wilhem Geiger ... undoubtedly is, it is far from linguistic in purpose" (LOUIS H. GRAY, *BSOS* 8 [1935/37] 563). And so the fact that this grammar published so long ago has been "reprinted only slightly modified as a handbook and an introduction for beginners is truly remarkable. This is exactly what happened to GEIGER's Pāli grammar ... when it was republished by the Pāli Text Society as 'A Grammar of Pāli by WILHELM GEIGER, translated into English by BATAKRISHNA GHOSH, revised and edited by K. R. NORMAN'" (VON HINÜBER 1999: 148). This publication should therefore not be regarded as a new Pāli grammar, which is still a desideratum. What a pity HELMER SMITH declined when asked by WILHELM GEIGER to prepare a second edition of his grammar!

When towards the end of 1997 Professor Dr. GEORGE CARDONA asked me to write the chapter on *Aśokan Prakrit and Pāli* for *The Indo-Aryan Languages* (ed. by GEORGE CARDONA and DHANESH JAIN) I was obliged to bring together and sift through my Pāli *collectanea*. During 1998 I prepared a draft Pāli grammar in order to have a solid base for my contribution to CARDONA's and JAIN's handbook (to be published by Curzon Press). Since then I have continually reworked my Pāli grammar, included references therein to secondary literature covering research done down to the year 2000; and I have prepared extensive indexes. The result now lies before you. But restricted as it is to the language of the canonical Pāli texts – despite some exceptions (e.g. Dīp, Mhv, Mil) – this grammar can be regarded only as a complement to 'Geiger', and like 'Geiger' it lacks a chapter on Pāli syntax. To make a long story short: a new 'Geiger' comprising all stages of Pāli, registering all forms with their references and giving an up-to-date description of the Pāli syntax has yet to be written. That this grammar may prove helpful for such an enterprise, I have taken the step of adding meanings to all words and references if such cannot be found with the help of CPD or PED; and I have appended concordances of the present grammar to 'Geiger' and von Hinüber's *Überblick* (see p. 356-360) and to Richard Pischel's *Grammatik der Prakrit-Sprachen* (see p. 361-380). As the phonological development of Pāli in the main runs strictly parallel to that of the various Prakrits, this Pāli grammar might be of some help for the study of Prakrit as well. And as it is unlikely – to the best of my knowledge – that a new 'Pischel' will be published in the near future, I have decided to include a short summary of the paragraphs of 'Pischel' and to add a number of *addenda et corrigenda* pertaining to particular problems.

Many thanks for advice and criticism go to my friend Dr. Chlodwig H. Werba, whose keen eye and great expertise spared me many an embarrasment, to Professor Dr. Oscar von Hinüber for numerous and pertinent discussions of individual problems and for loans of books and articles, and to Professor Dr. Lambert Schmithausen for valuable suggestions on an earlier version of this grammar. Professors Dr. Nalini Balbir and Dr. Junko Sakamoto-Goto, though not directly involved in this project, were over the years always helpful when I consulted them on problems of Middle Indo-Aryan grammar and metrics. My thanks are also due to Professor Dr. Colette Caillat for 'kind exhortations' given when I first took up Pāli – and of course for her exemplification of scholarly excellence. Peter Delion, a former student of mine, kindly searched the libraries of Tübingen for many an article not available in Freiburg, and Professors Dr. Saroja Bhate, Dr. S. D. Laddu (both Poona) and the late Dr. H. C. Bhayani (Ahmedabad) were kind enough to forward copies of articles not (readily) available in Europe. My sincerest thanks go to Dr. Anne MacDonald for having vetted my English – this despite much pressure of work – and to Jörn Peter Michels, a student of mine here in Freiburg, for having checked most of the text references. Naturally I alone am responsible for any remaining errors. I trust only they will not prove numerous. Not least I wish to thank Professors Dr. Albrecht Wezler and Dr. Michael Witzel for accepting this Pāli grammar for their series *Indian Philology and South Asian Studies* – and the former for kindly writing the preface – and the *Deutsche Forschungsgemeinschaft* for awarding a *Heisenberg Stipendium* (1994 - 2000) which enabled me to persue my researches.

Gundelfingen (Hochschwarzwald), 18th of March 2001

Table of contents

1. Introduction

§ 1. Pāli and the Middle Indo-Aryan languages

Pāli is the language of the texts of the Theravādins, an ancient school of Hīnayāna Buddhism. The Theravāda tradition has always claimed that the language the Buddha spoke was Māgadhī – i.e. an eastern language – and that this language was the same as that of its canonical texts, a language now called Pāli (a designation which originally meant 'text' and whose use as the name of a particular language seems not to antedate the 18th century[1]). And indeed we might expect that the language early Buddhism made use of was essentially an eastern one, current in the Gangetic basin in the 5th century B.C.[2] Pāli, however, as we have it, is basically a language of western India, as the edicts of Aśoka clearly show. Some of its salient features it shares with the western edicts (especially that of Girnār), e.g.

> the retention of both *r* and *l* (see § 14.10; Aś G *karoti*, *rāja(n)-*, *likhita-*, *sīla-*), the distinction of palatal, dental and cerebral nasal (see § 13; Aś G *p(r)āṇa-*, *ñātika-*, *Taṃbapaṃṇi*, *añña-*, *maṃñate*), *-cch-* < *-kṣ-* (see § 18.2; Aś G *vra[c]cha-*), the assimilation of consonant clusters (see § 16.1; Aś G *rā[ñ]ño*, *āra[b]bhare*, Brahmagiri *a[y]ya-*)[3], the non-cerebralisation of *t(h)* following *ṛ/r* (see § 14.5; Aś G *a[t]thāya*, *kata-*), the nominative sg. of the masculine *a*-stems in *-o*, that of the neuter in *-aṃ* (see § 30.1; Aś G *°piyo* –

---

[1] See VON HINÜBER (1994: 76-90).

[2] On the language of the earliest Buddhist tradition see BECHERT 1980.

[3] See ALSDORF, *Kleine Schriften* p. 440, and VON HINÜBER § 153. On the treatment of clusters with final *y* in (Aśokan) Prakrit see PISCHEL § 335 and ALSDORF, *Kleine Schriften* p. 451-452.

dānaṃ, *mūlaṃ*), the locative of the masc. and ntr. *a*-stems in *-e* or *-amhi* (see § 30.4; Aś G *vijite*, *dhaṃmamhi*) and the accusative plural of the *a*-stems in *-e* (see § 30.7; Aś G *yute*).

But sporadically it presents features that belong to the eastern part of the linguistic area of India[1], as evidenced by the Aśoka edicts of (e.g.) Kālsī, Dhauli and of *all* pillars[2], e.g.

the substitution of *l* for *r* (see § 14.10; Aś K *kaleti*, *lāja(n)-*), the merger of the palatal, dental and cerebral nasal into the dental one (see § 16.3; Aś K *pāna-*, *nātik[y]a-*, *Taṃbapaṃni*, *aṃna-*, *mannati*)[3], *-kkh-* < *-kṣ-* (see § 18.2; Aś K *lu[k]kha-*), the anaptyctical splitting of conjuncts (see § 21; Aś *lājine*, *alabhiyaṃti*, Bairāṭ *aliya-*)[4], the cerebralisation of *t(h)* following *ṛ/r* (see § 14.5; Aś K *aṭhāya*, *kaṭa-*)[5], the nominative sg. of the masculine and neuter *a*-stems in *-e* (see § 30.1/10; Aś K *°piye* – *dāne*, *mule*), the locative of the masc./ntr. *a*-stems in *-asi* (see § 30.4; Aś K *vijitasi*, *dhaṃma-*

---

1 On these see BLOCH, *Recueiḷ d'Articles* p. 404-405.

2 See ALSDORF, *Kleine Schriften* p. 450 n. 6.

3 See LÜDERS, *Kleine Schriften* p. 48, ALSDORF, *Kleine Schriften* p. 429, VON HINÜBER § 204 and TEDESCO, *JAOS* 80 (1960) 362. TEDESCO, l.c., maintained that "Eastern *nn* no doubt had also passed through the stages **ññ* and **ṇṇ*, attested in the West" (see also VON HINÜBER, in: *Sprachen des Buddhismus in Zentralasien*. Wiesbaden 1983, 31, who reconstructs **paṇṇā-* < *prajñā-* for "the older eastern Middle Indo-Aryan").

Does *panāyati* 'recognizes', D II 21,2/3, belong here? It looks like a derivation from *pra-√jñā*: (pass.) *paññāyate* > (act.) *pan[n]āyati*.

4 See LÜDERS (1954: 129 n. 2) and ALSDORF, *Kleine Schriften* p. 292.

5 See BLOCH (1965: 58-59), LÜDERS (1954: 128 n. 1). ALSDORF, *Kleine Schriften* p. 428, and VON HINÜBER § 195.

si)[1] and the accusative plural of the masc. *a*-stems in *-āni* (see § 30.6; Aś K *yutāni*), the lengthening of a vowel before the suffix °*ka-*[2] (cf. *āyatīkaṃ*, S I 142,2*[3], *apatīkā kumārikā*, Ja V 103,22* [so read against Ee *āyatikaṃ* and *apatikā*, see § 2][4]; Aś Dh *cilaṭhitīkā*[5]), the sandhi *-aṃ-m-eva / -ām-eva* (see § 26; Aś PE III *kayānaṃ-m-eva*[6]) and forms like *siyā* (see p. 207; Aś Dh *siyā* [vs. G *a(s)sa*]).

Many Pāli words and forms – "with 'frozen' phonetics", as RICHARD GOMBRICH aptly characterised them (in: GEIGER 1994: XXVII) – are relics from an earlier eastern dialect in which the 'texts' of early Buddhism were (orally) handed down. This proto-canonical language (which HEINRICH LÜDERS called *Alt-Ardhamāgadhī*[7]) – akin to the administrative language

---

[1] See LÜDERS, *Philologica Indica* p. 275-276. This locative (i.e. *-aṃsi*) is characteristic of Ardhamāgadhī (see PISCHEL § 366[a], ALSDORF, *Kleine Schriften* p. 65, SCHWARZSCHILD 1991: 177, and BALBIR, in: *Dialectes dans les littératures indo-aryennes* [édité par COLETTE CAILLAT]. Paris 1989, 506-507).

[2] See BALBIR, in: *Dialectes dans les littératures indo-aryennes* (édité par COLETTE CAILLAT). Paris 1989, 506.

[3] See Sadd V 1242.

[4] On the other hand, *taḷāka-* in the Apadāna (always) scans ⏑⏑x: *sobhayanti taḷākaṃ* (ə: *taḷakaṃ*) *tadā* (⏑-⏑-), Ap 16,14 (see SMITH *apud* BLOCH 1965: 46).

[5] For AMg. see PISCHEL § 70/73.

[6] See LÜDERS, *Philologica Indica* p. 573.

[7] See, e.g., *Philologica Indica* p. 280 (cf. ALSDORF, *Kleine Schriften* p. 824-830). On LÜDERS' terminology see VON HINÜBER, in: *Buddhism in Ceylon and Studies on Religious Syncretism in Buddhist Countries* (ed. by H. BECHERT). Göttingen 1978, 49 n. 8.

of the Maurya king Aśoka (268-232 B.C.) and based on an artistic MIA 'Dichtersprache' which was in use long before the time of the Buddha – was in many ways, when compared with OIA, further advanced than the western dialects of its time[1]: Internal voiced occlusives had been lost, while the surds were voiced (*-p-* to *-v-*), original initial *y-* had (at least in some words) already become *j-*[2], and the gender distinction was about to break down (etc.). That meant that the 'texts' were transformed into a more archaic language (unless the words were taken over unaltered) as Buddhism spread westward[3]. And that process over-reached itself in not a few instances, i.e. hyper-forms like *Isipatana* (*Ṛśyavṛjana)[4] were created (see § 12 rem. f., 14.4/10, 16.9). In that way Pāli originated as a mixture of different dialects, as a kind of *lingua franca* (see VON HINÜBER § 39). From the west of mainland India, where the Buddhist communities using Pāli as their sacred language settled, the 'texts' were brought to Ceylon during the reign of Aśoka. In the monasteries of that island they were handed down orally until they were committed to writing during the council of Mātalē, held under the auspices of king Vaṭṭagāmaṇī Abhaya (27-19 B.C.)[5]. The main part in the tradition of the *Tripiṭaka* and its commenta-

---

1 See VON HINÜBER, in: *The Dating of the Historical Buddha. Part I* (ed. by H. BECHERT). Göttingen 1991, 183-193.

2 See BERGER (1956: 103) and BROUGH, *Collected Papers* p. 468: "The mere existence of the form *Yamataggi* then forces upon us the conclusion that parts at least of the Pali canon were translated from a Middle Indian dialect in which original initial *y-* had already become *j-*" (cf. NORMAN, *JPTS* 20 [1994] 224, and id. 1992: 177 [ad Sn 149]). For this development in Prakrit see PISCHEL § 252.

3 See VON HINÜBER, *Untersuchungen zur Mündlichkeit früher mittelindischer Texte der Buddhisten*. AWLM 1994.5, p. 14.

4 On this word see CAILLAT, *JAs* 1968, 177-183, and VON HINÜBER (1999: 150).

5 See BECHERT, *WZKS* 36 (1992) 45-53.

ries[1] was played by the Mahāvihāra of Anurādhapura (for which a peculiar – though faulty – pronunciation [*-c- ~ -j-*, *-t- ~ -d-*, *-p- ~ -v-*, *-k- ~ -y-*] is recorded; cf. § 14.2 rem. a)[2]; this fundament of the Theravāda school was so dominant that another Pāli tradition independent of it is now documentable only in traces[3]. The Pāli of the 'Mahāvihāra'-texts has phonetic features which it shares with no other form of MIA and which strongly suggest Sanskritisation (see § 3.2, 16.9 rem. a, 18.3 rem.)[4]. This is the result of the great influence Sanskrit exercised on Pāli, notably in the 12th century when the texts were revised on the basis of (the Burmese) Pāli grammars (e.g. the Saddanīti) which were heavily influenced by the works of Pāṇini and other Sanskrit grammarians[5].

---

[1] On this literature see VON HINÜBER, *A Handbook of Pāli Literature*, Berlin – New York 1996, and OBERLIES, Die heiligen Texte des Buddhismus, in: UDO TWORUSCHKA (Ed.). *Heilige Schriften*. Darmstadt 2000, 174-176.

[2] See SMITH, *Orientalia suecana* 4 (1955) 113, id. *Analecta rhythmica* (Studia Orientalia XIX:7, Helsinki 1954), p. 15 n. 1, and VON HINÜBER (1994: 225).

[3] See VON HINÜBER, *Die Sprachgeschichte des Pāli im Spiegel der südostasiatischen Handschriftenüberlieferung*. AWLM 1988.8, p. 27 with n. 90 (*chaḷā*, Ja VI 238,32* [B^d], *subbhamu*, Ja IV 19,29* [B^d]).

[4] See VON HINÜBER (1982); cf. GEIGER § 7.

[5] In its vocabulary, Pāli is mostly dependent on Vedic and Sanskrit. And the portion of words borrowed – or reborrowed (*raṇa-* 'wound' < Tamil *iraṇam* < Skt. *vraṇa-* [see BARNETT, *JRAS* 1925, 187 n. 1]) – from non-Aryan language families such as Dravidian or Austro-Asiatic is not greater than in Sanskrit: Some loan-words found in Sanskrit are unknown to Pāli and *vice versa* (e.g. [2]*aṭṭa-* 'law-suit' [see p. 111], *cāṭi-* 'vessel' [CDIAL 4736], *cumbaṭa-* 'pad of cloth' [CDIAL 4869], *piṅka-* 'sprout' [Sadd V 1606], *māla-/māḷa-* '[some sort of] building' [see KIEFFER-PÜLZ, *Centenaire de Louis Renou*. Paris 1996, 285-325], *velli-* 'silver' [see KATRE, *Calcutta Oriental Journal* 1 (1934) 221-223]). And like Sanskrit Pāli knows some (originally) Greek words (*suruṅga-* 'underground passage' [see OBERLIES 1993: 165], *horā-*

Pāli as a MIA language is different from Sanskrit not so much with regard to the time of its origin than as to its dialectal base, since a number of its morphonological and lexical features betray the fact that it is not a direct continuation of Ṛgvedic Sanskrit; rather it descends from a dialect (or a number of dialects) which was (/were), despite many similarities, different from Ṛgvedic[1]. Some examples may help to illustrate this point[2]: (1) *(ug-/pag)gharati* 'oozes' points back to a form * *°gž^{h}arati* (from PII *√*gž^{h}ar*, see Avestan √*γžar*) which reflects the *voiced* cluster of PIE *√*d^{h}g^{uh}er* 'to flow, move forcefully' as against Vedic *kṣárati* and Greek *φθείρω*; **(2)** we meet with the same difference of voiced and surd consonant in ^{1}*jhāyati* 'burns, is on fire' (and *jhāna-* 'fire', *jhāpaka-* 'incendiary', *jhāpana-* 'setting on fire', *jhāpeti* 'sets on fire', *jhāma-* 'on fire') and ^{1}*ghāyati* 'is burnt, is tormented', on the one hand, and OIA √*kṣā* on the other, continuations of PIE *√*d^{h}g^{uh}eH*; **(3)** *(anupa/ano/uj)jagghati* 'laughs at' – as well as the Ṛgvedic hapax *jájhjhatī-* 'laughing' (5.52.6) – is a dialectical variant from Indo-Iranian **ǰ$^{(h)}$agž^{h}ati* as against RV(+) *jakṣa °* (< **ǰ^{h}a-g^{h}s-a °*)[3].

This base dialect (or dialects) of Pāli was (/were) in several points more archaic than Ṛgvedic Sanskrit: **(1)** *(i)dha* 'here'[4] (see p. 91) directly con-

---

'hour'). See also § 5 rem. d.

[1] But as in Ṛgvedic intervocalic *-ḍ(h)-* is represented by *-ḷ(h)-* (see BLOCH 1965: 57).

[2] A detailed analysis can be found in OBERLIES (1999). See also VON HINÜBER § 10-11.

[3] See (already) LEUMANN *apud* WOGIHARA, *Asanga's Bodhisattvabhūmi. Ein dogmatischer Text der Nordbuddhisten nach dem Unikum von Cambridge im allgemeinen und lexikalisch untersucht*. Leipzig 1908, 43.

[4] See also *kudha* 'where?' (< *ku[tra] x [i]dha*), Ja V 485,15*, and *sabbadhi* 'everywhere' (< PIE **°d^{h}i*).

tinues – other than Ṛgvedic *ihá* – PIE * *°dʰe* (see Greek *ἔνερθε*)[1], and (**2**) *kiṇāti* 'buys' has preserved – other than Ṛgvedic *krīṇāti* (with the *-ī-* from *krītá-* < **kᵘrih₂tó-*) – the original short *-ĭ-* of the present stem **kᵘrinéh₂-*. One of the dialects on which Pāli rests seems to have had affinities with the language of the holy texts of Zarathustrism, the Avesta: (**1**) *nhāru-* 'sinew' (< **snārut-* < **snāu̯r̥t-*) agrees with Avestan *snāuuarə* against Vedic (AV+) *snā́van-*[2]; (**2**) *(a)sāta-* '(mis)fortune, (un)pleasant'[3] is a continuation of **śāta-*, which belongs to PII **či̯ātá-* (< PIE **kᵘi̯eh₁tó-* [see Latin *quietus*]). Since (OIA) **cyāta-* and (Pāli) **cāta-* are to be expected, Yāska's and Patañjali's records, that the Kambojas of eastern Iran had a word *śavati* 'to go' (Nirukta II 2, Mahābhāṣya I 9,25-26) which answers to Avestan *š́(ii)auua(itē)* and not to the OIA *pendant cyáva(ti)*, is of particular interest[4].

Pāli is by no means younger than ('classical') Sanskrit as archaisms prove[5]: (**1**) The endings of the nom. and instr. pl. m. and ntr. of the *a*-stems (*°āse/°āso*, *°ā* and *°ehi*) and of the acc. sg. of the *ī*-stems (*°iyaṃ*) continue

---

[1] See BLOCH (1965: 23) and PISCHEL § 266 (diff. LUBOTSKY, in: *Sthāpakaśrāddham – Professor G.A. Zograph Commemorative Volume*. St. Petersburg 1995, 129).

[2] See Sadd V 1516. For Prakrit see PISCHEL § 255.

[3] On this word see NAKAMURA, in: *Buddhist Studies in honour of Walpola Rahula*. London 1980, 172 n. 10.

[4] On the preservation of original *-r̥̄- see p. 56 n. 2.

[5] See BAPAT, Vedicism in Pali, in: *Siddha-Bhāratī* ... Papers ... in Honour of ... Dr. Siddheshwar Varma. Hoshiarpur 1950, I/74-88, VON HINÜBER § 9 and – for Prakrit – PISCHEL § 6 (cf. CHILDERS, *A Dictionary of the Pāli Language*, Preface p. XII-XIII n. 2, and BLOCH 1965: 23-24).

Vedic °*āsaḥ*[1], °*ā*, °*ebhiḥ* and °*ịyam*, which are not retained in Sanskrit (see § 30.6, 30.10, 30.8 and 36.2)[2]; (**2**) the dative/genitive sg. of the personal pronouns and the locative sg. of the pronoun *ta(d)-* without final *anusvāra*, *mayha*, *tuyha* (see § 4.1) and *tamhi* (see § 42), correspond to RV *máhya*, *túbhya* and *yásmi*, *sásmi* (see Av. *yahmī*) as against Skt. *mahyam*, *tubhyam* and *tasmin*[3]; (**3**) the use of the aorist as *the* preterite presents it as vigorously alive, and this was the case in Vedic Sanskrit but not in (the dia- or sociolect[s] which determined the development of) Classical Sanskrit; (**4**) *uggahāyati*, Sn 791, corresponds to Vedic °*gṛbhāyati*[4], *aggahesuṃ*, Sn 847, to (AB 6,24) *(pary)agrahaiṣam*[5], *akā* is a continuation of the old root aorist /*akar*/, which was replaced in Sanskrit by the *s*-aorist *akārṣīt*, and the suppletion of OIA *adarśam* and *adrāk* is reflected in Pāli by 1sg. *ad(d)assaṃ* and 3sg. *addā*[6]; (**5**) some suffixes are preserved which Sanskrit no longer knows: The infinitive in °*tave* (°tavái; see p. 264), (probably) the absolutive in °*yā* (see p. 270), the participle in °*āvi(n)-* (see p. 263), the

---

[1] Diff. WITZEL, in: *Dialectes dans les littératures indo-aryennes* (édité par COLETTE CAILLAT). Paris 1989, 212-213 (§ 9.2).

[2] On *gonaṃ* / *gunnaṃ* (< RV *gónām*) see § 37.1, on the numeral *ti* see p. 193.

[3] See SCHELLER (1967: 2 n. 1), THIEME, *HS* 105 (1992) 13 with n. 1, and VON HINÜBER § 366 (cf. AiGr. III § 226a).

[4] See GEIGER § 186.5. The *-h-* of the Pāli form is due to the present *gaṇhāti* and the verbal adjective *gahita-*.

[5] See EDGERTON, *JAOS* 57 (1937) 28, and VON HINÜBER (1994: 144).

[6] See HOFFMANN, *Aufsätze zur Indoiranistik* I,147.

It is most difficult to decide whether the greater frequency of the ending °*are* in Pāli (*dicchare*, *udicchare*) as compared with Sanskrit is a relic from Vedic times (see VON HINÜBER § 425) or only a secondary extension (note Pāli *-are* vs. Vedic *-ire* [!]). What we can say is that it is a 'western' feature (see p. 219).

suffix °*ttana-* forming abstract nouns[1], which lives on in Apabhraṃśa °*ppaṇa* and Hindi °*pā* (e.g. *buṛhāpā*)[2]; (**6**) quite a number of words, unknown to classical Sanskrit, are used in Pāli[3]:

(**1**) *akkhaṇa(vedhin)-* '(hitting) the target' (Śrautasūtra+ *ākhaṇa-*)[4], (**2**) (°)*ajati* 'drives' (RV+ √*aj*)[5], (**3**) *addhā* 'certainly' (RV+ *addhā́*)[6], (**4**) *anti(ṃ)* 'before, in the presence of' (RV+ *ánti*), (**5**) *apiratte* 'early in the morning' (cf. RV+ *apiśarvaré*), (**6**) *abhijīhanā-* 'strong effort' (RV √*jeh*), (**7**) *amājāta-*[7] 'born at home' (RV+ *amā́*), (**8**) *amhasi* 'we are' (RV *smasi*)[8], (**9**) *asita-* 'sickle' (ĀpŚS

---

[1] E.g. *devattana-*, Th 1127, *dāmarikattana-*, Mhv LXI 71, *petattana-*, Th 1128, *purisattana-*, Mil 171,14 (see AiGr. II.2 § 530, PISCHEL § 6, 597, TRENCKNER 1908: 122 n.). On the archaic shortening of long vowels in *hiatus* see p. 63-64 and 68-69.

[2] See BLOCH (1965: 88).

[3] What follows is only a first attempt to collect Vedic-Pāli isoglosses (see OBERLIES 1999a: 170-171); a detailed study of the vocabulary of both languages is urgently needed (see VON HINÜBER, *IF* 88 [1983] 308-309). Not included are syntactic archaisms of Pāli (see e.g. CAILLAT, *Kratylos* 79 [1974] 251, on *iti*).

RV (etc.) means that the Vedic word is attested *only* in the Ṛgveda (etc.), *RV+* (etc.) that it is *also* found in younger parts of the Veda.

[4] See BHSD akṣaṇa-vedha and OBERLIES (1995: 106).

[5] See VON HINÜBER, *Ludwik Sternbach Felicitation Volume*. Lucknow 1981, 819-822, and id., *Zur Schulzugehörigkeit von Werken der Hīnayāna-Literatur*. Erster Teil (hrsg. von H. BECHERT). Göttingen 1985, 62 with n. 14.

[6] See RUEGG, *JAs* 1955, 163-170.

[7] This word is handed down as *āmajāta-* (Ja I 226,2*) but it scans ⏑--x, i.e. *amājāto* (see KERN, Toev. I,71, and CPD s.v. amā).

[8] For this ending which lives on in Nūristānī languages (see BLOCH 1965: 235) see § 46.1.

1,3.1 *asida-*, cf. Pkt. *asiya-*)[1], (**10**) *assa-* 'ashes'[2] (AV 9,8.10 *ā́sa-* [see § 5.2a]), (**11**) *ādīnavadassāvi(n)-* 'seeing the danger' (*ādinavadarśá-*, VS 30,18)[3], (**12**) *ādu* 'or' (RV 3,54.7 *ā́d u*)[4], (**13**) *āviñjati* 'pulls' (RV+ *ā-√vṛj*)[5], (**14**) *āsīvisa-* 'serpent' (AB 6,1 *āśiviṣa-*)[6], (**15**) *iñjati* 'moves, is disturbed' (RV+ *√ṛj*)[7], (**16**) *ibhiya-*, *ibbha-* 'vassal; rich' (RV+ *íbhya-*)[8], (**17**) *isikā-* 'reed' (AV+ *iṣī́kā-*), (**18**) *udda-* 'water' (cf. RV+ *anudrá-*, *udrín-*)[9], (**19**) *upacikā-* 'white ant' (upajīkā-)[10], (**20**) *uposatha-* 'day on which the *saṅgha* assembles to recite the *pātimokkha*' (ŚB+ *upavasathá-*), (**21**) *ussaṅkha-* 'curvature' (ŚB+ *ucchvaṅká-*)[11], (**22**) *ettaka-*

---

[1] The 'Vedic' word seems to be a 'Prakritism' for *asita-* 'black' (cf. *asi-* 'sword' ← 'the black one', see THIEME, *Kleine Schriften* p. 768).

[2] See KERN, Toev. I,91, CPD s.v. [1]assapuṭa and OBERLIES, *OLZ* 94 (1999) 390.

[3] See RENOU, *JAs* 1965, 20.

[4] See, however, PISCHEL § 155 n. 4.

[5] See HAEBLER, *MSS* 45 (1985) 85 with n. 17.

[6] See COOMARASWAMY, *Selected Papers* II,277.

[7] See HAEBLER, in: *Pratidānam. Indian, Iranian and Indo-European Studies Presented to F.B.J. Kuiper*. The Hague – Paris 1968, 283-298.

[8] See CAILLAT, in: *Buddhist Studies in Honour of I.B. Horner*. Dordrecht 1974, 41-49.

[9] On Pkt. *ulla-* (< *udra-) see PISCHEL § 111, SCHWARZSCHILD (1991: 53) and OBERLIES (1993: 40 [s.v. ullei]).

[10] See EWAia s.v. upajíhvikā- (cf. Sadd V 1268 s.v. upacikā: "≠ upadikā x upacinoti (PED)").

[11] See HOFFMANN, *Aufsätze zur Indoiranistik* I,138-145.

'this much' (RV+ iyattaká-)[1], (**23**) *kakkara-* 'partridge' (YV+ *kakkaṭá-*), (**24**) *kacchāvana-* 'thicket' (JB *vanākakṣa-*)[2], (**25**) *kaṇhavattani-* 'having a black trail' (RV+ *kṛṣṇávartani-*), (**26**) *kasambu-* 'refuse' (AVŚ 18,4.37 *kásāmbu-*)[3], (**27**) *kūṭa-* 'not horned' (AV+ *kūṭá-*), (**28**) *khambheti* 'props' / *chambhita-* 'made firm' (RV+ √*skambh*), (**29**) *khila-* 'fallow land' (AV+ *khilá-*, RV+ *khilyá-*)[4], (**30**) *gaddūla-* 'leather strap' (Vādhūlasūtra *gardūla-*)[5], (**31**) *gandhana-* 'destroying' (RV+ √*gandh*)[6], (**32**) *(tag)gha, (iṃ)gha, (yag)ghe* (RV+ *gha*), (**33**) *ca* 'if' (RV+ *ca*)[7], (**34**) *chakaṇa-* 'excrement' (RV+ *śakṛt*[8] ~ *śakn°*), (**35**) *chamā* 'on the ground' (RV+ *kṣamā́*)[9], (**36**) *janitta-* 'birth-place' (RV+ *janítra-*), (**37/38**) *jināti* 'deprives' / *jāni-* 'loss' (RV+ *jinā́ti*, Kāṭh+ *jyāní-*)[10], (**39**) *tapanī-* 'cooking

---

[1] See WACKERNAGEL, *Kleine Schriften* p. 372, and CDIAL 1589. On *ogaṇa-* (~ *ogaṇá-*, RV 10.89.15) see CPD s.v. and Sadd V 1289 s.v.

[2] See VON HINÜBER, *IF* 88 (1983) 309.

[3] See KERN, Toev. I,17, and WEBER, *Indische Streifen* I,150.

[4] See VON HINÜBER, in: *Sprachen des Buddhismus in Zentralasien*. Wiesbaden 1983, 29 (on the Vedic word see LOMMEL, *Kleine Schriften* p. 366-371).

[5] See CALAND, *Kleine Schriften* p. 359 (cf. BHSD s.v. gardula).

[6] See PISCHEL, *ZvS* 41 (1908) 181, FRANKE, *Kleine Schriften* p. 262, ALSDORF, *Kleine Schriften* p. 180-182, and OBERLIES (1995a: 130 [s.v. (kula)gandhin(ī)-]); cf. CALAND, *Kleine Schriften* p. 298, and WERBA, *Verba Indoarica*. I. Wien 1997, 346.

[7] See PED s.v. (3. *conditional*), OBERLIES (1995a: 134 [s.v. ce]), id. (1997: 17-18) and id. (1999a). On *candimā-* see p. 45 (*rem.* b).

[8] This nominative lives on in *saki*, Thī 466 (see CPD s.v. asuci in cpds).

[9] See § 18.2.

[10] See OBERLIES, *OLZ* 94 (1999) 390-392.

vessel', Ja V 201,23* (TS/Kāṭh+ *tapaní-*)[1], (**40**) *(abhit)tharati* 'draws near' (RV+ √*tsar*)[2], (**41**) *dubbhati/dūbhati* 'deceives' (RV+ *dabhnoti* [x *druhyati*])[3], (**42**) *dussa-* 'cloth' (AV+ *dūrśá-*), (**43**) *nahuta-* 'a high number' (Br+ *niyúta-*), (**44**) *nivāt(ak)e* 'in a place where there is no wind' (ŚB+ *nivāté*)[4], (**45**) *(a)pabbhāra-* '(not) steep' (JB I 278 *prahvāra-*), (**46**) *(indriya)paropariy(att)a-* 'higher and lower state' (Br *parovarīyáṃs-*), (**47**) *palāpa-* 'chaff' (AV+ *palā́va-*)[5], (**48**) *pisīla-* 'cup' (ŚB+ *piśī́la-*), (**49**) *phusāyati* / (pass.) *anuphusīyati* 'sprinkles; (pass.) is sprinkled' (RV+ *pruṣāyati*), (**50**) *maṅku-* 'staggering' (ŚB 5,5.4.11 *maṅkú-*), (**51**) *(su)mati-kata-* 'well harrowed' (Br+ *matī-√kr̥*)[6], (**52**) *masiṃ karoti* 'reduces to powder' (ŚāṅkhGS 1,24.7 *maṣiṃ kārayitvā*), (**53**) *mahasāla-* 'having great halls' (Br+ *mahā́śāla-*)[7], (**54**) *medhaga-* 'quarrel' (RV+ √*mith*)[8], (**55**) *ruppati* 'suffers a violent pain in the belly' (Kāṭh+ *rúpyati*), (**56**) *vana-* 'desire' (RV *vánas-*)[9], (**57**) *viddha-* 'blue sky' (AV+ *vīdhrá-*), (**58**) *vegha-*

---

[1] See OBERLIES (1995a: 136 with n. 28).

[2] See RAU, *Jñānamuktāvalī: Commemoration Volume in Honour of Johannes Nobel*. New Delhi 1959, 73 (ad Dhp 116), pointing to RV 8.2.6, Kāṭh 27.9 (: 149.5) and JB II 158 (: 228.16). Diff. CPD s.v. and VON HINÜBER § 135 who correct Dhp 116 to *abhittaretha*.

[3] See SAKAMOTO-GOTO (1987/88: 356).

[4] See MORRIS, *JPTS* 1887, 166-167, and VON HINÜBER (1994: 9-16).

[5] On *Māro Pāpimā* ~ (Atharvaveda / Brāhmaṇa) *pāpmā́ mr̥tyúḥ* see WINDISCH, *Māra und Buddha*. Leipzig 1895, 192-195.

[6] On the Vedic word see SCHNEIDER, *Wörter und Sachen* 21 (1940) 165-166.

[7] WITZEL, *Tracing the Vedic Dialects*, in: *Dialectes dans les littératures indo-aryennes* (édité par C. CAILLAT). Paris 1989, 221 with n. 314.

[8] On *middha-* see p. 124 n. 4.

[9] See EWAia s.v. and OBERLIES (1995: 135).

'loop' (MS *vleṣka-*)[1], (**59**) *saddhiṃ* 'in company with' (RV+ *sadhryàk*)[2], (**60**) *saṃdeha-* 'body', Dhp 148 (*sandehá-*, ChU 5,15.2, BĀU 4,4.13), (**61**) *sanna-* 'sunk', Dhp 327 (AV+ *sanná-*), (**62**) *samala-* 'impure' (AV+ *śámala-*)[3], (**63**) *siṅghāṇikā-* 'snot' (ĀpDhS *śṛṅkhāṇikā-*), (**64**) *simbala/i-* 'silk-cotton tree' (RV+ *śimbalá-*)[4], (**65**) *sumbhati* 'hits' (Kāṭh √*subh*)[5], (**66**) *seyyathā* ~ *sayathā* 'like' (Br+ *sá yáthā*)[6], (**67**) *harāyati* 'detests, loathes' (cf. RV *háras-* 'grudge' [?])[7], (**68**) *hi ssa*, Th 146, ~ *hi so*, Th 238 (RV *hi ṣma* [as against Br *ha vai*])[8], (**69/70**)

---

1 See § 11 rem. e.

2 See § 4.5 (p. 27-28).

3 See also *sāmā ca soṇā sabalā ca*, Ja V 268,15* (so read), VI 106,21*, strongly reminiscent of RV 10,14.10 (... *śvā́nau* ... *śabálau* ...) and AVŚ 8,1.9 (*śyāmáś ca tvā mā śabálaś ca* ... *śvā́nau*).

4 See GEIGER § 34 and PISCHEL § 109.

5 See OBERLIES, *MSS* 53 (1992) 125 n. 32.

6 See WITZEL, *Tracing the Vedic Dialects*, in: *Dialectes dans les littératures indo-aryennes* (édité par C. CAILLAT). Paris 1989, 221 with n. 313 (with literature).

7 It does not belong to *hirī-* as the semantics clearly shows (FRANKE, *Ostasiatische Zeitschrift* 6 [1917] 118 [*pace* GEIGER § 31.1 and 186.2]). BURROW, *The Sanskrit Language*. London 1955, p. 46, assumed that *harāyati* stands in the same relation to **hṛṇā́ti* as *gṛbhāyáti* to *gṛhṇā́ti* (for Avestan cognates see KELLENS, *Le Verbe Avestique*. Wiesbaden 1984, 134).

8 See BROUGH (1962: 228-229) – pointing to Gāndharī *hi ṣa* –, CAILLAT (1980: 56 n. 64) and WITZEL, *Tracing the Vedic Dialects*, in: *Dialectes dans les littératures indo-aryennes* (édité par C. CAILLAT). Paris 1989, 220 (cf. NORMAN 1969: 168).

But also (Br+) *ha vai* lives on in Pāli (to the references of the PED s.v. *have* add Ja VI 322,24* if ALSDORF's conjecture *paññā* + *ha* + *ve hadayaṃ paṇḍitānaṃ* [see *Kleine Schriften* p. 402 with n. 43] is acceptable).

vihesati 'injures', *heṭheti* 'hurts' (RV+ √*hiṣ*)[1], (**71**) *hurāhuraṃ* 'from rebirth to rebirth' (RV *huráḥ*, see § 4.5)[2]

(7) A couple of words has a meaning which is attested in Vedic but not (or: not any longer) in (Classical) Sanskrit: *avañcana-* 'not able to go' (√*vañc*), *kasati* 'ploughs' *vs.* *kassati* 'pulls, drags' (OIA *kṛṣáti* 'ploughs' *vs.* *kárṣati* 'pulls, drags')[3], *ñatta-* 'public reputation for skill' (TS+ *jñātra-*)[4], *panna-* 'fallen (down)' (RV+ *panná-*)[5], *siloka-* 'fame' (RV+ *ślóka-*)[6], *senā-* 'weapon, missile', Ja VI 448,28* (RV+ *sénā-*).

§ 2. The orthography of the Pāli texts

The orthography of our texts reflects the rules of the Pāli grammarians of the 12th century (see p. 5 and SMITH, Sadd p. VI). The discrepancy between this orthography, which is "historical and not phonetical" (CAIL-

---

[1] See LÜDERS, *Philologica Indica* p. 775 (and cf. p. 22 n. [8]).

[2] As OIA has no ind. pres. *yamate* (*yamate*, RV 1.127.3, is subj. of the root aorist) the present stem *yama-* (in: *yamāmase*, Th 275 = Dhp 6, *saṃyamāmase*, S I 209,27) cannot be an archaism of Pāli (*pace* GEIGER § 133). It is a denominative of *yama-* 'restraint' (see § 51[a]).

[3] See GOTO, *Die 'I. Präsensklasse' im Vedischen*. Wien 1987, 112-113.

[4] See BHSG s.v. jñātra und EDGERTON, *JAOS* 75 (1955) 63.

[5] See NORMAN (1991:125-126) and VON HINÜBER, *IF* 88 (1983) 308-309.
On *siñcati* 'bales (a boat)' (Sn 771, Dhp 369) see NORMAN (1992: 298 [ad Sn 771]) and BHSD s.v. *utsicati*, on *asecanaka-* 'irresistible' see BAILEY, *BSOAS* 21 (1958) 530, and BROUGH (1962: 193).

[6] See BLOCH (1965: 15).

LAT, *IF* 88 [1983] 315), and the phonology of the original language of the Canonical texts is considerable[1]. Thus the anaptyctic vowels (see § 21) – to give just one example – often do not count as far as the metre is concerned[2]. We even have to assume that there was something like an 'orthographical reform' (see OBERLIES 1996: 94). (Almost) throughout (e.g.) *par*$_{i}$*yaya-* (-˘x)[3], *pāmado* (-˘-), *mahisī-* (˘˘-)[4] and *°īka*-derivations (see § 1) were replaced by *pariyāya-* (> *peyyāla-* [see § 11.5]) 'succession, order, method' (Ja III 140,24*, V 367,2*, S I 24,10*), *(mā) pamādo* '(do not) be indolent' (Th 119, Dhp 371, Ja VI 94,30*), *mahesī-* 'the king's chief wife' (Thī 520, Ja V 45,10*, VI 421,20*) and *°īka*-forms[5]. We have then to look

---

1 And it should be kept in mind that "a wavering between *i* and *ī* and *u* and *ū* is widely spread within the whole Pāli text tradition" (VON HINÜBER 1994: 223; cf. id. § 160); cf., e.g., the confusion of *khila-* and *khīla-* (see OBERLIES 1995a: 132).

2 See GEIGER § 29, WARDER (1967: 29-36), NORMAN (1969: § 51), id. (1971: § 75) and OBERLIES (1993/94: 155). For Prakrit see JACOBI, *Kleine Schriften* p. 101-102, and PISCHEL § 131.

3 Cf. Pkt. *pajjava-* < paryaya- (BERGER 1955: 54 *pace* PISCHEL § 81 / 254).

4 But sometimes (e.g. Ja II 395,3*, VI 425,2* and 483,6*) *mahesī-* scans ˘-x (see Sadd V 1684 [s.v. mahesī]).

5 See VON HINÜBER § 488 (*pace* BROUGH 1962: 194) and SAKAMOTO-GOTO, *WZKS* 28 (1984) 53-54 n. 39 (both: *pāmado*), OLDENBERG, *Kleine Schriften* p. 1084 n. 1, SMITH, *BSL* 34 (1933) 217, id. Sadd 196 n. 2 / Sadd V 1684, ALSDORF, *Les Études Jaina*. Paris 1965, 59, CAILLAT (1970: 6-7), OBERLIES (1993/94: 150) and VON HINÜBER § 119 (all: *mahisī-*), OBERLIES (1993/94: 153, 1995a: 148 [*par*$_{i}$*yaya-*]), SMITH, *Analecta rhythmica* (Studia Orientalia XIX:7, Helsinki 1954), p. 12, OBERLIES (1993/94: 159 n.54), id. (1996: 109) and BECHERT, *'Alte Veḍhas' im Pāli-Kanon. NAWG* 1988.4, p. 10 (all: *°īka-*). On *Bhāradvāja* instead of (expected) *Bharadvāja*, *evam-eva* 'in this way, so' instead of *em-eva*, *anīgha-* 'not depressed' instead of *anigha-* and *ariya-* 'noble' instead of *ār(i)ya-* see OBERLIES (1993/94: 152-153).

behind the wording as handed down to us if we are to arrive at the old forms. This can be achieved by a strict philological interpretation of the texts; in this respect the use of metrical criteria has proved especially helpful[1].

---

[1] See ALSDORF (1968), BECHERT (1961) and CAILLAT (1970). OBERLIES (1993/94, 1995/96) is a *conspectus metrorum* of the Pāli texts to be supplemented by Sadd IV 8 (p. 1148-1172) and NORMAN (1992a: 45-59, 1994: 119-131).

There are, indeed, differing views about the value of metre for the restoration of a(n apparently) corrupt text. BROUGH (1962: 194) pointed out that "there is no reason to suppose that the compilers of the Pali canon were particularly sensitive to metrical minutiae", whereas KÖLVER maintained – though with reference to (Buddhist Hybrid) Sanskrit – that "for the vast majority of metres, a deviation from prescribed quantities is a downright mistake, and a rare one at that. I have always admired Edgerton for giving this principle its due weight and using it as a tool for textual criticism in Buddhist Hybrid Sanskrit" (in: *Sauhṛdayamaṅgalam. Studies in Honour of Siegfried Lienhard* .... Stockholm 1995, 192).

2. Phonology

2.1. Vowel quantity, word finals and word rhythm

§ 3. 1. The vowel system of Pāli consists of the following sounds: *a*, *ā*, *i*, *ī*, *u*, *ū*, *e* and *o* (see Sadd IV 1.1.2)[1]. Compared with OIA/Sanskrit, Pāli has lost the vowels (**a**) *ṛ*, *ṝ*, *ḷ* and the diphthongs (**b**) *ai* and (**c**) *au* which were replaced by (**a**) *a*, *i*, *u*, (**b**) *i*, *e* and (**c**) *u*, *o* (see § 5, 7, 9, 11-12)[2]. It gained, however, an 'umlaut' *-aï-* (written *-ăyi-* or *-e-*), medially due to the metathesis of *-ar(i)y-* and *-ah(i)y-* (see § 22.3), in *sandhi* due to the contact of *-ă* and *ĭ-*[3]. – **2.** Due to the law of *mora*[4], which rules that a syllable must not contain more than two *morae* (one *mora* [*mātrā*] is the length of time of a short vowel or of two consonants[5]), the OIA long vowels – as such count also a short vowel *plus anusvāra* (*aṃ*, *iṃ*, *uṃ*)[6], even if a vowel

---

1 See GEIGER § 2.1 and VON HINÜBER § 107. For Prakrit see PISCHEL § 45 and JACOBI § 1-2.

2 The OIA accent is – to the best of our knowledge – irrelevant for the explanation of MIA phonology (see VON HINÜBER § 159).

3 See CPD, *Epilegomena* 23* (s.v. *diphth.*), VON HINÜBER § 147-150 and OBERLIES (1995/96: 270).

This sound is to be distinguished from that *-ai-* which is retained in some Prakrit words (on which see PISCHEL § 61-61[a]).

4 See GEIGER § 5 and VON HINÜBER § 108-109. For Prakrit see PISCHEL § 83-84 and JACOBI § 11.

5 See Sadd IV 1.1.2 and 1.1.3.

6 We have to distinguish between (final) vowels followed by an *anusvāra* – a pure nasal sound following a vowel, which, however, is *not* nasalised – and nasalised

follows (*sappaṃ ghoravisaṃ iva* 'like a very poisonous snake' ⏑-⏑-, Ja V 18,4*, *puttaṃ anomavaṇṇaṃ* 'a son of beautiful appearance' --|⏑-⏑|--, Ja V 182,1*) – were (**a**) shortened before two or more consonants (*e* to *ĕ* and *o* to *ŏ*, written *e* or *i* and *o* or *u*; see § 7.4-5, 9.5-7) or else (**b**) the consonants (mainly *y*, *r* and sibilants) were reduced to one (partly due to quantitative metathesis)[1] – possibly an eastern feature of Pāli (see TURNER 1975: 430-432): (**a**) *atta(n)-* 'self, soul' (ātman-), *nananda(r)-* 'husband's sister' (nanāndṛ-), *maṃsa-* 'flesh' (māṃsa-), *jiṇṇa-* 'old' (jīrṇa-), *puṇṇa-* 'full' (pūrṇa-), *pārijuñña-* 'decay' (* °*jūrṇya-*[2] ← *jūrṇá-*), *upekkhā-* 'indifference' (upekṣā-), [1]*oṭṭha-* 'lip' (oṣṭha-); (**b**) *samīrate* 'is moved' (°īryate), *(saṃ)kīyati* 'is impaired' (°kīryate), *jīrati/* [2]*jīyati* 'grows old' (jīryate)[3],

---

vowels (*sânunāsika* [see Sadd IV 1.1.2]), i.e. between *aṃ, iṃ, uṃ* on the one hand and *aṁ̆, iṁ̆, uṁ̆* on the other. (In defiance of the mss.) the former should be reserved for *long* syllables, the latter (in case a consonant follows) for *short* (see EDGERTON, *JAOS* 66 [1946] 199 [§ 19] and 202 [§ 50], SMITH 1950: 3 and BECHERT 1961: 19; cf. PISCHEL § 178-179) while before a vowel *-Vm* should be used if the syllable is metrically *short* (see § 24 *rem.* [p. 121]). As the different scripts of the Pāli textual tradition have no sign for *ṁ̆* there is some confusion in the PTS text editions between final *-ṃ* and final *-ṁ̆* before consonants – as well as between *-Vm V-* and *-Vṃ V-* (see also § 4.1).

[1] See GEIGER § 6, BLOCH (1965: 41/92) and VON HINÜBER § 110. For Prakrit see PISCHEL § 87 / 89 / 284, JACOBI § 12.1, SCHULZE, *Kleine Schriften – Nachträge*. Göttingen 1966, p. 792-793, and ALSDORF, *Kleine Schriften* p. 69.

[2] See Sadd V 1602 and VON HINÜBER § 10. It cannot, however, be ruled out that the vocalism of (*juṇṇa-* 'old' – not attested in Pāli – and consequently of) °*juñña-* is not inherited from Vedic but that it is due to a contamination of *jiṇṇa-* (jīrṇá-) and *vuḍḍha-/vuddha-*, the regular outcome of *vṛddha-* 'old'. Both words are often met with together (cf. the formula *jiṇṇo vuḍḍho/vuddho mahallako*, D II 100,12, M II 66,14).

[3] See GEIGER § 138.

sīsa(ka)- ‘head’ (śīrṣan- / śīrṣaka-), *(anāva)sūraṃ* ‘(as long as) the sun (does not set)’ ([adv.] *anavasūryam)[1], *dīgha-* ‘long’ (dīrgha-), *([a]hattha)pāsa-* ‘side (of the hand [*loc.* = nearby])’ (°pārśva-)[2], *sīgha-* ‘swift’ (śīghra-), *lākhā-* ‘lac, red dye’ (lākṣā-), *apekhā-* ‘regard, longing for’ (apekṣā-), *vimokha-* ‘release’ (vimokṣa-), *paliveṭheti* ‘wraps up’ (°veṣṭayati), *heṭheti* ‘injures’ (*heṣṭati)[3], *(a)sekha-* ‘(not) to be trained’ ([a]śaikṣa-)[4]. In this way Pāli gets doublets such as *ummī-/ūmī-* ‘wave’ (ūrmi-) or [1]*patta-/pātī-* ‘bowl’ (pātra-/°ī-)[5] which occasionally give rise to unetymological quantitative metathesis (see 3 below). The shortening due to the law of *mora* even occurs when the geminate consonant is split by a vowel[6] (*apilapati* ‘floats’ < āplavate, *ācariya-* ‘teacher’ < ācārya-, *iriyā-* ‘behaviour’ < īryā-, *bhariyā-* ‘wife’ < bhāryā-[7], *sukhuma-* ‘minute, fine’ < sūkṣma- [see § 17]), but not so in (e.g.) *rājinā* ‘by the king’ (rājñā) and *Sākiya* (Śākya). Words like *dātta-* ‘sickle’ (Mil 33,3)[8], *brāhmaṇa-* ‘brahmin’, *bhasmācchanno* ‘covered by ashes’ (Dhp 71), *sāttha-* ‘meaningful’

---

1 On the rhythmically lengthened *-ā-* see § 6.3c.

2 Cf. *kuṭhārīpāsa-* ‘the side of the axe’, A IV 171,6.

3 See LÜDERS, *Philologica Indica* p. 775.

4 The same holds good if the long vowel is MIA: *ajjhosa* ‘having grasped’ (adhyavasya).

5 Cf. Pkt. *patta-* ~ *pāya-/pāī-* ‘bowl’.

6 See GEIGER § 8 and CAILLAT (1970: 8). For Prakrit see PISCHEL § 131.

7 *bhariyā-* (⏑⏑- [Ja V 170,27*]) scans -⏑- (i.e. *bhāriyā-*) at Ja V 448,19* and VI 265,25* (cf. CPD s.v. assasati), at Ja VI 434,20* and Sn 290 / 314 (as often) -- (i.e. *bhăr̯yā-*).

8 On this word see SCHELLER, ZvS 79 (1965) 236 n. 3, and TURNER (1975: 432-435).

(Vin III 1,19) or *svākkhāta*- 'well-preached' violating this law are Sanskritisms (see § 1). – **3.** A further effect of this law is the exchange of vocalic and consonantal length (*metathesis quantitatum* [see below § 5.2a])[1]: *jaṇ-ṇu(ka)-/jannu(ka)-* 'knee' (~ *jānu-*)[2], *samajja-* 'festive gathering' (samāja-)[3], *khiḍḍā-* 'play, amusement' (~ *kīḷā-* < krīḍā- [see also § 14.1]), *niḍḍa-* 'nest' (~ *nīḷa-* < nīḍa-)[4], Dhp 148, *niyyati* 'is led' (nīyati), Sn 851, *parijunna-* 'miserable', Ud 15,2* (paridyūna-)[5], *kubbara-* 'board of a car'[6] (kūbara-), *thulla-* 'gross' (~ *thūla-* < sthūla-)[7], *jessati* 'roams' (jeṣate)[8], *seyyo* 'better' (śreyaḥ), *yobbana-* 'youth' (yauvana- [see § 14.9]). – **4.** Compensatory lengthening of a vowel as a rule only occurs in connection with *liquids*, *-ṃ[s]-* (< -rś-, -rṣ-, -ṃś-, -ṃṣ-) and *-ṃh-*[9] and at the seam of

---

[1] See GEIGER § 6.1-2 and VON HINÜBER § 109-110. For Prakrit see JACOBI § 21.1, PISCHEL § 90 / 194 and BHAYANI (1997: 30-31).

[2] See BLOCH (1965: 95). On *jannutaggha-* 'reaching up to the knees', Ja VI 534,32*, see OBERLIES (1995: 121).

[3] On *bhaṭ(h)a-* 'wages', Ja IV 261,4*, < **bhāṭa-* (← *bhaṭa-* 'servant' < bhṛta-) see KERN, *Toev.* I,103, and OBERLIES (1995a: 152).

[4] That means that *niḍḍa-* does *not* continue PII **niždá-* from PIE **nisdó-* as maintained by AiGr. I § 236a (p. 272). See VON HINÜBER § 110.

[5] See BHSD s.v. parijūna.

[6] See JOHNSTON, *JRAS* 1931, 577-581.

[7] The ending of *bahunnaṃ* 'of many' (beside *bahūnaṃ* and *bahuna[ṃ]*, D III 169,2*, 170,4* [*metre*: Sadd V 1636]) is not due to this *metathesis quantitatum* but is taken from the gen. pl. of the numerals (see BARTHOLOMAE 1916: 10).

[8] See OBERLIES (1995: 122).

[9] See GEIGER § 6.3, BERGER (1955: 68-70) – ibid. 69 on the age of the loss of the *anusvāra* –, TURNER (1975: 421-429) and VON HINÜBER § 111-112 (cf. MALLIK,

prefix and root (in order not to obscure the root-initial sound, see § 20): *cūḷa-* 'small' (kṣudra-)[1], *kātuṃ* 'to make' (kartum), *mātiya-* 'mortal' (martya-), Ja VI 100,10* (*hi mātiyā* ⏑-⏑-), *paṭimāse* 'you should control' (pratimarśeḥ), Dhp 379, *sāsapa-* 'mustard' (sarṣapa-)[2], *(aṅgāra)kāsu-* '(charcoal) pit' (karṣū-)[3], *jūhato* 'of one who sacrifices' (juhvataḥ)[4], *uttāseti* 'impales' (uttaṃsayati)[5], *dāṭhā-* 'fang; row of teeth' (~ *daṭṭhā-*[6] < daṃṣṭrā-)[7], *vīsati-* 'twenty' (viṃśati-)[8], *sīha-* 'lion' (siṃha-)[9]. – **5.** Due to

Vishveshvaranand Indological Journal 30 [1992] 51-54). For Prakrit see PISCHEL § 62-66 / 76 and JACOBI § 12.2.

JOHANSSON, *Monde Oriental* 2 (1907/08) 106-107, explained *svātanāya* 'on the following day' *not* as derived from *śvastanāya* (*pace* GEIGER § 6 n.) but as formed analogical to *purātana-*, *sanātana-* and other such words.

[1] On this word see § 16.7. The same *metathesis quantitatum* is assumed by the PED for *saṃkāpeti*, Vin I 137,12 (saṃkalpayati).

[2] Differently on this word TURNER, who maintains that compensatory lengthening of a vowel followed by *-ss-* does not occur in Pāli (proper) (1975: 421-422; cf. ibid. 405-406 n. 8).

[3] On *hāsa-* 'joy', Dhp 146, (probably) from (OIA) *harṣa-* see BROUGH (1962: 217).

[4] On this word (Ja V 399,7*, Sn 428) and on *+jūha(n)ti* 'they sacrifice' (Sn 1046 [cf. SAKAMOTO-GOTO 1987/88: 357 and NORMAN 1992: 369]) see TURNER (1975: 429).

[5] See CHARPENTIER, *IL* 2 (1932) 48-49.

[6] In: *daṭṭhavisa-*, Mil 150,8/11 (see TRENCKNER's note *ad loc.*). As to the shortening of the final *ā* cf. *dāṭhabala-*, Ja II 409,15*, and *dāṭhabali(n)-*, Sn 72 (see OBERLIES 1995: 138).

[7] See LÜDERS, *Philologica Indica* p. 558, and OBERLIES (1993: 91 [s.v. dāḍhā-]).

[8] See TEDESCO, *Monde Oriental* 15 (1921) 223 n. 1. Here belongs *mahīsa-* ~ *mahiṃsa-* 'buffalo' (← mahiṣa-) 'buffalo' (Ja III 368,25* [read m.c. °*mahiṃso*], VI 110,30* [Ee

the similar pronounciation of both long vowel and short vowel followed by -*ṃ*-[1], a long vowel, irrespective of whether primary or due to compensatory lengthening (mainly < -*Vr/lC*-), could be replaced before a single consonant by a vowel *plus -ṃ-* (and *vice versa*, see 4, above)[2]: *sanantana*- 'eternal' (sanātana-), *niraṃkaroti* 'despises' (nirākaroti)[3], *jigiṃsati* 'desires to win' (~ *jigīsati*, Th 1110 [< jigīṣati]), *bhiṃsana(ka)*- 'dreadful' (bhīṣaṇa[ka]-)[4], *saṃvarī*- 'night' (śarvarī-), *(upa)daṃseti* 'points out' (°darśayati), *ukkaṃsati* 'raises; praises' (utkarṣati)[5], *ghaṃsati* 'rubs' (ghar-

mahīsaṃ, B[s] *mahiṃsaṃ* (see Sadd V 1684)], 111,13* [*mahīsaṃ*]). The form with -*iṃs*- is continued by different modern Indian languages (see CDIAL 9964).

vihesā- 'injury, annoyance', M I 510,34, Sn 247, and *vihesati* 'injures, insults', Ud 44,30, 45,8, however, seem to be remodellings of *vihiṃsā*- and *vihiṃsati* after *viheṭh°* (and not – *pace* GEIGER § 10 – their direct continuations).

9 *vācanaṃ*, Ja I 295,12*, should be corrected to *vañcanaṃ* 'deception' (corr. = Ja V 448,30*); see OBERLIES (1995/96: 289).

1 See BLOCH (1965: 48) and TURNER (1975: 99); cf. AiGr. III § 187b *rem.* (p. 366).

2 See GEIGER § 6.3, FRANKE, *Literarisches Zentralblatt* 1917, p. 1157, LÜDERS, *Philologica Indica* p. 93, BLOCH (1965: 48), BERGER (1955: 39, 65-71), TURNER (1977: 406 n.) and VON HINÜBER § 111. For Prakrit see PISCHEL § 74 / 86, JACOBI § 13 and BHAYANI (1997: 24-26).

Of a completely different kind – despite THIEME, *Kleine Schriften* p. 711 – is the -'*ṃ*'- of (e.g.) *siṅgāla*- 'jackal' (śṛgāla-) and *suṃsumāra*- 'dolphin; crocodile' (a continuation of RV *śiṁśumāra*-) – the latter probably due to 'regressive infiltration' of the following -*m*- (see THIEME, l.c.).

3 But cf. Sadd V 1503 and OBERLIES (1995: 126).

4 Cf. *ālimpeti* 'kindles' (ādīpayati [see § 14.14b.2 (p. 88)]).

5 See BERGER (1955: 46).

ṣati)[1], *(loma)haṃsa(na)-* 'excitement' (harṣa[ṇa]-), *suṅka-* 'tax' (śulka-), *°kampati* 'imagines' (°kalpate)[2], *vaṅka-* 'crooked' (vakra-)[3], *aṃsi- ~ (aṭ-ṭh)aṃsa-* 'edge, corner' (aśri-).

rem. **ad 2.** The different way of splitting up *V̄CC*-syllables was one of the metrical licences the poetic language made use of[4]. Thus, one and the same OIA word may appear in different guises (see WARDER 1967: 32-36): *suriyo* 'sun' (--), Ja VI 201,25*[5], Th 477, Sn 687, *suriyamhi* (◡◡-x), Ja VI 136,4* (Āryā), IV 61,1*, VI 263,12* (both Vait.), *(canda)sūriye*, Ja IV 61,8* (Vait.)[6]; **ad 4.** TURNER restricts compensatory lengthening to vowels followed by *ṃ+h/r/S*; all other cases are explained as due to analogy or replacement of a simple noun by its *vṛddhi*-derivative (1975: 405-406 n. 8; cf. ibid. 421-429); **ad 5.** The Ceylonese scribes tended to write 'unetymological' nasality: *naṃgara-* 'town' (~ *nagara-*), Ap 34,18, 61,10 (the readings

---

1 *ghaṃsanti*, Ja IV 56,26*, is not a by-form of *haṃsanti* (< harṣanti) but should be corrected to *ghasanti* 'they eat' (Sadd V 1365 *pace* PED s.v.).

If GEIGER's explanation (§ 184) were correct, *siṃsati* 'moves', Vv 1015-1016, 1181 ([si]sīrṣati [√sṛ]) would belong here. But it seems to mean 'neighs' (see CPD s.v. abhisiṃsati), and hence another derivation is called for (CPD l.c. points to "hasati, hiṃsati *or* hesati, sa. √h(r)eṣ" what I fail to understand).

2 See OBERLIES (1996: 120-121).

3 On *saṃpavaṅka-* 'intimate / good friend' (< *sampravakra- [?]) see DHADPHALE, *Synonoymic Collocations in the Tipiṭaka: A Study*. Poona 1980, 47.

4 See OBERLIES (1993/94: 155).

5 On Ja I 89,24* see OBERLIES (1995/96: 288).

6 See GEIGER § 29.

of Ee![1]), *nāṃga-* 'snake' (~ *nāga-*), S V 351,14 v.l.[2].

§ 4. 1. Except for *-(V)m* and *-(V)n*, which both resulted in *-(V)ṃ* (for the metrical value of *-Vṃ≠* see § 3.2 with p. 17 n. 6)[3], Pāli has lost all final consonants unless they were retained in sandhi clusters (see § 25)[4]. But due to analogies even *-ṃ* is dropped, in (e.g.) *āyasmā* 'venerable one' (āyasmān) and *vidvā* 'wise' (vidvān) after *rājā* 'king'[5], in *tuṇhī* 'silently' (tūṣṇīm) after *cvi*-forms[6] and in *(i)dāni* 'now' (idānīm) after temporal adverbs like *kadāci* 'at some time or another' (kadācit) or *sampati* 'just, now' (saṃprati). Due to strong metrical pressure *-Vṃ* was shortened to *-Vm̆*, i.e. a short nasalised vowel (*nāhesum̆ bhante* -⏑--, Pv 98, *alattham̆ bhante* -⏑--, Pv 566, *tathāham̆* ⏑-⏑, Pv 554, *pāpunim̆ cetaso* ⏑-⏑-, Thī 91), and the nasality of the vowel became so feebly pronounced that it could be lost completely[7] (note the fact that there was no sign to denote such a short nasal vowel[8]): *aṭṭhāna* '[it is an] impossibility', Sn 54, *dīgham addhāna*

---

1 See Ee of Ap, part II p. VII.

2 See GEIGER § 6 n. 3, VON HINÜBER § 113, THOMAS, *IHQ* 13 (1937) 498-499, and BECHERT, *MSS* 10 (1957) 56. On the alternation between nasalised and non-nasalised forms in loan-words see BERGER (1955: 66).

3 For Prakrit see PISCHEL § 183 / 348.

4 See GEIGER § 66.2 and VON HINÜBER § 168. For Prakrit see PISCHEL § 339 and JACOBI § 24.

5 See VON HINÜBER § 313.

6 See BECHERT (1955: 17 n. 41).

7 See GEIGER § 32.2, NORMAN (1994: 116) and OBERLIES (1993/94: 154 [point I]). For Prakrit see PISCHEL § 350.

8 See BECHERT (1955: 17 n. 41). For Prakrit see PISCHEL § 179.

'for a long time', Dhp 207, Sn 740, *paraloka gamya* 'having gone to the other world', Ja V 31,8* (B^d *°kaṃ*), *paresa pāvā* 'tells others' (-⏑--), Sn 782, *na mayha ruccasi* 'I do not like you' (-⏑-⏑-), Ja V 399,28*, *ārogā tuyha mātaro* 'your mothers are well' (⏑-⏑-), Ja VI 23,6*[1], *uttattarūpo bhusa dassanīyo* 'you have a splendid appearance and are a wondrous sight' (--⏑--/⏑⏑-⏑--), Pv 439, *Tārukkhass' aya(ṁ) māṇavo* 'this one is the pupil of Tārukkha' (⏑-⏑-), Sn 594, *ajānantā ta(ṁ) pucchāma* 'not knowing we ask you' (⏑---), D II 240,11*[2], *karohi Pañcāla mam' eta vākyaṃ* 'do, Pañcāla, what I say' (-⏑--), Ja IV 398,16*, *pañha pucchituṃ* 'to ask a question' (-⏑-⏑-), Ja V 139,19*, *abbhuṃ me* (|⏑⏑-|) 'woe is me', Ja V 178,11*, *brāhmaṇā upagañchu maṃ* 'brahmins approached me' (⏑-⏑-), Cp 21 (on denasalisation in *sandhi* see § 23). – **2.** Final *-aḥ* (< -as/-ar) developed almost throughout to *-o*, this sandhi form having been generalised (*putto* 'son' [putraḥ], *tato* 'then' [tataḥ], *pāto* 'early in the morning' [prātar])[3]; only in some words containing *-u-* or *-v-* was this *-o* dissimilated to *-e*, an (essentially) eastern feature[4]: *chave* 'corpse' (śavaḥ), *bhikkhave* 'monks!' (bhikṣavaḥ), *antepura-* 'a king's harem' (antaḥpura-), *pure* 'in

---

[1] On *mayha* and *tuyha* see BECHERT (1961: 17).

[2] See BECHERT (1961: 16 n. 1).

[3] See GEIGER § 66.2 and VON HINÜBER § 169. On the development of *-ar* and *-as* in Prakrit see PISCHEL § 342-347 and JACOBI § 24.

[4] See OBERLIES (1992) and id. (1996: 107-108 [with reference to TRENCKNER 1908: 134 n. 4]).

front; formerly' (puraḥ)[1], *s(u)ve* 'tomorrow' (śvaḥ)[2]. After vowels other than *°a-* the *visarga* is entirely lost (*jātī* 'births' < jātīḥ). – **3.** Hence all words end in (short or long) vowels or else (due to the law of *mora*) in *short* vowels *plus -ṃ/m̐* (see p. 17 n. 6): *puttā* 'sons' (putrāḥ), *kaññā* 'girls' (kanyāḥ), *aggi* 'fire' (agniḥ), *bhikkhu* 'monk' (bhikṣuḥ), *dhĭ* 'shame on' (dhik), *Assaji* (°jit), *assā* 'from the horse' (aśvāt), *samantā* 'on all sides' (samantāt), *kaññaṃ* 'girl' (kanyām), *mayhaṁ* 'me, my' (mahyam). – **4.** A long final vowel became shortened in polysyllabic words if the penultimate syllable was long whereas long finals remained in disyllabic words as well as in polysyllabic words possessing a short penult: *kaññāya* 'of the girl' (kanyāyāḥ), *tassā* 'her' (tasyāḥ), *deviyā* 'of the queen' (dev$_i$yāḥ), *sīlavatā* 'by the virtuous' (śīlavatā), *abravī* 'he said' (abravīt), *atāri* 'he crossed' (atārīt). This accounts also for the sporadic absolutives in *-tva* (see § 58). But possible unique forms, which this rhythmic law would have produced within a paradigm, were eliminated, e.g. *nattāro* 'grandsons' (naptāraḥ) and *sakhāro* 'friends' (see § 33) on the model of *pitaro* 'fathers' (pitaraḥ); and a number of levellings (e.g. due to the frequent use of augment and preverb) affected this rule also in the verbal inflection. At some stage this rule ceased to operate; subsequently, new forms were created and redactional modernisations removed the old ones (see INSLER 1994). That is the reason why the opposition of brevity and length seems to be neutralised in final vowels (see VON HINÜBER § 168 and BLOCH 1965: 229). – **5.** Final vowels may be 'nasalised' even after loss of a following

---

[1] Cf., however, Sadd V 1620 s.v. pure ('*pure* ≠ puraḥ x agge'), BERGER (1955: 15 n. 5) and BECHERT (1980: 30-31).

[2] Can Prakrit forms such as *bahave* (< *bahavo* < bahavaḥ) be explained in the same way? On *bahave* see PISCHEL § 380 and ALSDORF, *Kleine Schriften* p. 67.

consonant; this 'nasalisation' occurs sometimes analogically[1]: *cirassaṃ* 'after a long time, at last' (cirasya), *tiriyaṃ* 'transversely' (tiryak), *manaṃ* 'almost' (manāk), *īsaṃ* 'slightly' (īṣat), *pātaṃ* 'early in the morning' (prātar), *puna-p-punaṃ* 'again and again' (punar), *yāvaṃ* 'up to' (yāvat)[2], *huraṃ* 'on a wrong path, in another existence' (huraḥ)[3] – all of these analogical to adverbs in *-aṃ* –, *aduṃ/assosuṃ* 'they gave / heard' (aduḥ/aśrauṣuḥ :: [OIA] abharan), *yaṃ* 'which' (yat :: [ntr. in] °am), *aduṃ* 'that' (adaḥ :: tam)[4], *°khattuṃ* '-times' (°kṛtvaḥ :: prathamam/ekavāram)[5], *parisatiṃ* 'in the assembly' (°sati :: loc. in *-ṃ*), *peccaṃ* 'having died' (pretya), Ja VI 360,23*, 361,13*, *(a)sakkaccaṃ* 'with(out) care' ([a]sat-kṛtya), *sakiṃ* 'once' (sakṛt), *visuṃ* 'separately' (viṣvak), *saddhiṃ* 'together

---

[1] See GEIGER § 66.2, VON HINÜBER § 113 and BERGER (1955: 50-51). For Prakrit see PISCHEL § 114 and 181-182.

[2] See OBERLIES (1995: 155 [s.v. yāva]).

[3] See HOFFMANN, *Aufsätze zur Indoiranistik* I,118-119.

[4] Cf. TEDESCO, *Language* 21 (1945) 132. On the *-u-* of *aduṃ* see below, § 42.6.

[5] See BERGER (1955: 51, 61) and SAKAMOTO-GOTO (1988: 106 n. 5 [II]).

with' (sadhryak)[1]. – **6.** Final *-aṃ* may interchange with *-ā* (see § 3.5)[2]: (instr. sg.) *lapataṃ* (ə: *lapatā*) 'by one who talks', Ja IV 126,27*, (3sg. opt.) *kayiraṃ* (ə: *kayirā*) 'he should make', Dhp 313 = S I 49,10* (= *kareyya*, ct.s), (3sg. pret.) *akaraṃ* (ə: *akarā*) 'he made', Ja V 70,17* (*akaraṃ mayi*), (abs.) *kattaṃ* (ə: **kattā* < *katvā* < [Skt.] kṛtvā[3]) 'having made', Ja IV 98,4*, *nibbijjāpema Gotamaṃ* '... becoming despondent, we will go away from Gotama', Sn 448, ~ ... *Gotamā*, S I 124,8 ~ 127,17 (cf. CPD I,296a and NORMAN 1992: 231 [ad Sn 448])[4]. Here also analogy played a role: *sammā* 'in the right way' (< *sammaṃ [< samyak] :: *micchā*[5]). This feature accounts – among other factors – for the (**a**) abl. and (**b**) voc. sg. of

---

[1] See OBERLIES (1995: 138 [s.v. *saddhiṃ*]). For Prakrit see PISCHEL § 103 (whose explanation, however, is not correct).

Here belong also *saṇiṃ* 'gently, softly', which does not go back to a postulated **śanam* (*pace* GEIGER § 22) but to *śanaiḥ* (see LÜDERS, *Philologica Indica* p. 494-495 n. 1; cf. MATSUMURA, *JIBS* 32 [1983] 545) – on the *-ṇ-* see § 14.7 (according to TRENCKNER, Ee of M Vol. I, p. 540, the mss. write indiscriminately *-ṇ-* and *-n-*) –, and *sakkhiṃ(-karoti)* 'sees with his own eyes', which is a transformation of *sākṣāt(-karoti)* after the type *°iṃ-karoti* – a contamination of the *cvi*-formation with the periphrastic syntagmas *°ālayaṃ karoti* 'pretends', *kodhaṃ karoti* 'is angry', *corikaṃ karoti* 'robs' (cf. BERGER 1955: 48). The sequence *kkh__k* was also dissimilated to *cch__k*: *sacchi-karoti*.

[2] See VON HINÜBER § 113 / 304 and id. (1994: 224). For Prakrit see PISCHEL § 75 / 181 and CHANDRA, *A Critical Study of the Paumacariyaṁ*. Vaishali 1970, 567.

[3] See CPD s.v. *kattaṃ* (cf. PIND, *Bauddhavidyāsudhākaraḥ. Studies in Honour of Heinz Bechert on the Occasion of His 65th Birthday*. Swisttal-Odendorf 1997, 535 with n. 63).

[4] And *vice versa*: *Vajja-bhūmiyā* (ə: [= v.l.] *°iyaṃ*), S I 199,20*.

[5] See CPD s.v. *asammā*. Cf. *ivaṃ* 'like' (Vv 1225) < *ivā* (Ja III 530,12*, V 400,16*) ~ *vā* (iva :: yathā); On *vā* 'like' see p. 129 n. 3.

a-stems and (**c**) the 2sg. imp. in *-aṃ* ([**a**] < -ā < -āt / [**b/c**] < -ā [pluti] ← -a): (**a**) see § 30.4, (**b**) *Mahosadhaṃ*, Ja VI 363,17* (see § 30.5), and (**c**) *(so 'mhi raññā samijjhiṭṭho puttaṃ me) nikhaṇaṃ (vane)* 'I am commanded by the king: "Bury my son in the forest"', Ja VI 12,25* (see p. 257-258).

2.2. The vowels

§ 5. P. *a* generally goes back to OIA(**1**) *a*, to *ā* (**2a**) followed by one (see § 3.3 and § 5.4 [below]) or (**2b**) more than one consonant (see § 3.2), (**2c**) at the seam of a compound or at morpheme boundaries[1] or (**2d**) in word-final position, particularly in polysyllabic words whose penultimate is long (see § 4.4), and (**3**) (normally) to context-free *ṛ* (i.e. not preceded or followed by a palatal or labial; see § 7.3 and 9.3)[2]:

(**1**) *apagacchati* 'goes away' (apagacchati), *abhiharati* 'brings, offers' (abhiharati)

(**2a**) *assa(puṭa)-* '(a bag containing) ashes' (āsa- [see p. 10]), [1]*kapalla-* 'bowl' (kapāla-), *jaṇṇu(ka)- / jannu(ka)-* 'knee' (jānu-)[3], *vassita-* 'howl, cry' (vāśita-)[4]

---

[1] Seams of compounds (see OBERLIES 1993/94: 154-155) and morpheme boundaries are preferred places for rhythmic shortening / lengthening (see WACKERNAGEL, *Kleine Schriften* p. 897-961). For Prakrit see PISCHEL § 97.

[2] See BERGER (1955: 28), GEIGER § 12, VON HINÜBER § 122-126 and WERBA, *WZKS* 36 (1992) 13 n. 9 (cf. TEDESCO, *Language* 32 [1956] 498-501, and KATRE, *ABORI* 16 [1934/35] 189-201). For Prakrit see PISCHEL § 49/52-53/57.

[3] On GEIGER's example *abbahati* 'pulls out' see CPD s.v.: "*sa.* ā-bṛhati ... *with* -bb- *by influence of* nibbahati" (diff. TURNER [1975: 423] who derives *abbahati* from **ābrahati* < *ābṛhati*).

[4] *allāpa-* 'addressing' (ālāpa-), however, seems to be influenced by *sallāpa-* 'conversation' (saṃlāpa-) with which it often forms a compound (see CPD s.v.).

(**2b**) *aññā-* 'liberating insight' (ājñā-)[1], *kaṃsa-* 'metallic' (kāṃsya-)
(**2c**) *Māya-nāmā* 'whose name is Māyā', Th 533, *iṭṭhaka+rajata-* 'bricks and silver' (: *iṭṭhakā-*), Thūp 71,1, *mattika+thūpa-* 'tumulus made of clay' (: *mattikā-*), Ja III 156,22* = Pv 49[2], *(°)māla+bhāri(n)-* 'wearing a wreath' (: *mālā-*), *pañña+va(nt)-* 'wise' (: *paññā-*), *parikkha+va(nt)-* 'having examined' (: *parikkhā-*), Ja III 114,14*[3], *paccha+to* 'behind' (~ *pacchā*), Dhp 348 (see also § 31.2)
(**2d**) *yatha* 'like' (yathā)[4], [1]*va* 'or' (vā)[5], *kaññāya* 'of the girl' (kanyāyāḥ), (absol.) *°tva* (resulting in [e.g.] *chettu* and *daṭṭhu*[6], see p. 265)

---

[1] On the differentiation of the Skt. word into *āṇā-* 'order, command' and *aññā-* 'liberating insight' (cf. SCHMITHAUSEN, *Gedenkschrift für Ludwig Alsdorf*. Wiesbaden 1981, 199ff.) see § 16.8.

[2] On this word see SMITH, *Orientalia Suecana* 2 (1953) 126 n. 1. Such 'χρυσόθρονος'-compounds are rather common in Pāli (see e.g. *mattikāpattaṃ* 'an earthen bowl', Th 862).

[3] See OBERLIES (1995/96: 272).

[4] Ja II 217,15*, V 276,20* (see OBERLIES 1995/96: 275 / 278), Th 357-358, 1152 (cf. Ee, App. II p. 236f.), Thī 264, 267, 517 (cf. BOLLÉE, *IIJ* 11 [1968/69] 148-149), S I 197,19* (Vait.), 233,35* (cf. ALSDORF 1968: 55). Cf. *tathatā-* (lit.) 'the state of being so', S II 26,5, and *tada* 'then', Ja IV 404,11* (see ALSDORF, *Kleine Schriften* p. 365 n. 2 and OBERLIES 1995/96: 276). For *-a* < *-ā* in adverbs in Prakrit see PISCHEL § 113.

Obviously, *yathā* and *(i)va* influenced each other so that the final of the one was lengthened (*vā* [see p. 28 n. 5]) and that of the other one was shortened (*yatha*).

[5] Ja IV 107,7*, Th 1105, Dhp 139, Dhp-a I 31,12* (cf. CPD s.v. appa), Sn 222, 249, 773, 793, 795. For Prakrit see PISCHEL § 113.

[6] See SAKAMOTO-GOTO (1988: 107 n. 13).

(**3**) *ghat(āsan)a-* '(eating) ghee' (ghṛt[āśan]a-)[1], *hadaya-* 'heart' (hṛdaya-)[2].

As a result of an exchange of length *aCCV* develops from *āCV* (see **2a**). Sometimes, however, *a(C)* corresponds (due in part to rhythmical shortening or normalisation of suffix) to (**4**) OIA *ā(C)*[3]: *ajjhogahitvā* 'having plunged into' (*adhyavagāhitvā)[4], *nijjhapayati* 'makes someone reflect, has someone pardoned' (nidhyāpayati [cf. Skt. jñapayati])[5], *paccakkhata-* 'rejected' (pratyākhyāta-), Ja IV 108,9*[6], *bimbohana-* 'pillow' (<

---

1 On *ghaṭa-* (with 'eastern' *-ṭ-*) see ALSDORF, *Kleine Schriften* p. 788 n. 15, and OBERLIES (1995: 134 [s.v.]).

2 Cf. also *vaddha-* 'glad', Ja V 6,13*, and *vaddha-* 'old' (both < vṛddha-). On *saṭhila-*, Dhp 313, see TEDESCO, *Language* 32 (1956) 499 (cf. TURNER 1975: 374-375).

3 For Prakrit see PISCHEL § 80-82.

4 This absolutive is probably influenced by *gahetvā* 'having grasped' (cf. CPD s.v. ajjhogāhati).

5 On this meaning of *nijjhapayati* see LÜDERS, *Philologica Indica* p. 307. On the *-a-* cf. LEUMANN (1940: 226-227 [= *Kleine Schriften* p. 319-320]).

6 The *-a-* of *saṃkhata(dhammānaṃ)* '(for whom the doctrine is) well-taught', Dhp 70 (~ *sakkhāyadhammassa*, Uttarajjhayaṇasutta IX 44 [< svākhyāta°]), Sn 70, seems to be due to a confusion of (original) **sakkhāta-* / **sākhāta°* < svākhyāta- and *saṃkhata-* < saṃskṛta- (on *saṃ°* < *sakkh°* / *sākh°* see VON HINÜBER 1994: 224-225; cf. DHADPHALE, *PAIOC Thirtieth Session*. Poona 1982, p. 65). Is Pāli *(°)khata-* 'dug' (*parikkhatā ca sā bhūmi*, Ja II 242,11*, *palikhata-*, S IV 83,5* [cf. Sadd V 1578]) – besides *(°)khāta-* – due to a similar confusion of two verbs – viz. *khata-* 'hurt' (kṣata-) and *khāta-* 'dug' (khāta-)? The geminate of *(pari)kkh(atā)* seems to confirm this presumption (cf. OBERLIES 1993: 59 [s.v. khaiya-]).

bimbū[d]hāna*- ← bimbopadhāna-)[1]. (5**) *-i-* between *-r-* and a cerebral is lowered to *-a-* (see BERGER 1955: 38, 54): *khīraṇikā*- 'milk-giving cow' (*kṣīriṇikā-), *gharaṇī*- '*mater familias*' (*ghariṇī- [cf. Skt. gṛhiṇī-]), *pokkharaṇī*- 'lotus pond' (puṣkariṇī-). In the vicinity of palatals (*c*, *j*, *ñ*, *y*, *l*, *h*) the palatal colouring of the vowels *ĭ ŭ* was only optionally expressed in writing (i.e. as *ĭ* or *e*); instead (**6**) the vowel *a* was used[2]: *ānañja*- 'imperturbability' (*āniñjya-), *Koṇḍañña* (Kauṇḍinya), *kolañña*- 'born in a (good) family' (kaulīnya-), *kosajja*- 'idleness' (kausīdya-), *porohacca*- 'office of family priest' (*paurohitya-)[3], *Mucalinda* (Mucilinda)[4], *sākhalya*- 'friendship' (: *sakhila*-)[5], *āyasma(nt)*- 'venerable' (āyuṣmant-), *bāhusacca*- 'profound knowledge' (bāhuśrutya-). As a result of (**7**) assimilation[6] and (**8**) dissimilation/differentiation[7], *a* develops from *ĭ* and *ŭ*[8]:

---

[1] See LÜDERS, *Kleine Schriften* p. 446 n. 2. Cf. *(aṭṭhi-)kaṅkala*- 'skeleton' ~ (Skt.) *(asthi-)kaṅkāla*-, *uddhana*- 'cooking stove' ~ (Skt. [lex.]) *uddhāna*- (cf. Pkt. *uddāṇa*-, Deśīnāmamālā I 87).

[2] See TRENCKNER (1908: 128), GEIGER § 17 and BERGER (1955a).

[3] Sn 618 has *porohiccena* (v.l. *°haccena*) as B^{m} has *porohicce* at D II 243,20* (Ee *porohacce* which scans - - ⏑ -; cf. Sadd V 1628).

[4] On *rohañña*- 'red (cow)' see PED s.v.

[5] On this word see OBERLIES (1995: 137).

[6] See TRENCKNER (1908: 128-130) and GEIGER § 16d. For Prakrit see PISCHEL § 177.

[7] See GEIGER § 17b/c. For Prakrit see PISCHEL § 115 / 123 / 177.

[8] One of the rare cases of *e__e*-dissimilation is *meraya*- 'liquor' (< *mereya- < *madireya-): CHARPENTIER *ad* Utt XXXIV 14. On this word see WACKERNAGEL, *Kleine Schriften* p. 1487, and VON HINÜBER § 170.

(**7**) *ñātaka*-'relative' (jñāti[ka]-)[1], *sakkhali*- 'orifice of the ear' (śaṣkulī-), *pharati* 'pervades' (sphurati), *kappara*- 'elbow' (kūrpara-)
(**8**) *tad-aminā* 'by this' (iminā), Sn 137[2], *dakkhita*- 'consecrated' (dīkṣita-), *garu*- 'heavy' (guru-)[3], *makula*- 'bud' (mukula-).

As a (**9**) split vowel *a* appears between two consonants (at least) one of which contains an *ā̆* (see § 21)[4]: *garahati* 'reproaches' (garhati), *palavatī* 'floats, swims' (plavate)[5], *ratana*- 'gem, jewel' (ratna-), *nahāpeti* 'washes' (snāpayati), *pāsaṇī(ka)*- 'heel' (pārṣṇi-), D III 150,22* (so read[6]). It functions as (**10**) prothetic vowel in the emphatic particle *assu(daṃ)* (< sudaṃ < sma taṃ) originally abstracted from sandhi collocations such as *tayas-su* (see § 24, end).

rem. (**a**) The rules governing the substitution of OIA *ṛ* are interfered with by numerous analogies (see VON HINÜBER § 123). And due to semantic differentiation *ṛ* can be represented in two different ways in one and the same OIA word (see BERGER 1955: 40 / 55 and VON HINÜBER § 124):

---

1 See TRENCKNER (1908: 129).

2 As this word is attested only after *tad* Sadd V 1410 (s.v. tad-) suggests that we have to do with a haplology: *tada<m-i>minā* (see also BLOCH, *Recueil d'Articles* p. 410, and VON HINÜBER § 384). But what about *tad-iminā*, M II 239,23, 240,8?

3 This dissimilation was certainly supported by forms like (OIA) *garīyas*- and *gariṣṭha*- (see OBERLIES 1993: 66 n. 85). For Prakrit see PISCHEL § 123.

4 See GEIGER § 31.1, BERGER (1955: 29) and VON HINÜBER § 154. For Prakrit see PISCHEL § 132.

5 Th 399 = Dhp 334 (cf. *pilavati*, Th 104). On the *-ī* see § 8.4.

6 See Sadd V 1604 (cf. NORMAN 1993: 40).

maga- 'wild beast' , *miga-* 'gazelle', both < mṛga-, *vaḍḍhi-* 'profit, interest; welfare', *vuḍḍhi-* 'growth', both < vṛddhi-[1], *vaṭṭati* 'is proper', *vattati* 'becomes', both < vartate; (**b**) Such a differentiation of meaning (see also § 18.2) has favoured vowel assimilation in OIA *punar* (cf. 8, above): *pana* 'but', *puna* 'moreover'[2]; (**c**) The change of *ṛ* to *a*, *i* and *u* led to new analogical *vṛddhi* formations (see § 6.6, 11.14, 12.16)[3]; (**d**) Changing vowel quantity and quality often occur in foreign and onomatopoetic words (*avāka-* 'Blyxa octandra' [Skt. avakă-], *kākaṇikā-* 'a small coin' [Skt. kākiṇī(ka)-], *papphāsa-* 'the lungs' [Skt. pupphusa-][4], *mutiṅga-* 'drum' [Skt. mṛdaṅga-], *kukkusa-* 'the red powder of rice husks' [Skt. kiknasa-], *māsalu-* 'period of time' [Skt. māsala-][5], *sajju[lasa]-* 'resin' [Skt. sarja-])[6]. They are, as a rule, not taken into account in the following *conspectus*.

§ 6. P. *ā* continues OIA *ā*, followed normally (**1**) by one, but sometimes (**2**) by more than one consonant (see § 3.2b):
(**1**) *ājānīya-* 'of good breed' (ājāney[y]a-), *āḷārika-* 'cook' (ārālika-), *kaññā* 'girl(s)' (kanyā[ḥ])
(**2**) *(a)kāsi* 'did' ([a]kārṣīt)

---

1 On these four words see also FRANKE, *Literarisches Zentralblatt* 1917, p. 1040. For Prakrit see PISCHEL § 52 (end).

2 See MICHELSON, *IF* 23 (1908/09) 258 n. 1, LÜDERS, *Philologica Indica* p. 573-574, GEIGER § 34, BLOCH (1965: 310) and OBERLIES (1993: 120 [s.v. puṇo]).

3 See TURNER (1975: 173-180).

4 *papphāsassa*, Ja I 146,18* and Sn 195, scans ⏑--x (see Sadd V 1555).

5 On this word see, however, KERN, *Toev.* I/7.

6 See CPD, *Epilegomena* 27* (s.v. *lw.*), and MALLIK, *ABORI* 51 (1970) 77-82 (cf. GEIGER § 16.1 [*kukkusa-*], 17 [*kākaṇikā-*], 19.2 [*sajjulasa-*], 23 [*mutiṅga-*], 34 [*papphāsa-*]).

(**3a**) At the seam of stem and suffix or of compounds and due to (**3b**) *pluti*[1], (**3c**) rhythmical (◡|ā|◡x < ◡|a|◡x)[2] or (**3d**) compensatory lengthening, especially when followed by *-rC-* or *-ṃr/h-*[3] (see § 3.4) it corresponds to *a*:

(**3a**) *abbhā+matta-* '(of) the size of a cloud' (: *abbha-*), *ratanā-maya-* 'made of jewels' (°[a]maya-)[4]

(**3b**) see § 30.5 and 46.2

(**3c**) *anānugiddha-* 'free from greed', *anānupuṭṭha-/ °yāyi(n)-/ °rud-dha-* 'not asked / following / taking anyone's part' (ananu°), *anā-para-* 'matchless' (ana°), *anāvasūraṃ* 'as long as the sun does not set' (anavasūryam; see § 3.2b)[5]

(**3d**) *vilāka-* 'slender' (*vilāga- < vilagna-)[6], *kātuṃ* 'to make, to do' (kartum), *sāsapa-* 'mustard (seed)' (sarṣapa-), *avisāhāra-* 'absence of distraction' (~ *avisaṃhāra-*), *sāratta-* 'impassioned' (saṃrakta-), *sārakkhati* 'guards' (saṃrakṣati), *sārambha-* 'quarrel, anger' (saṃrambha-)[7], *udāheyyuṃ* 'they could eat up' (*udañh° < udaśn[ī-

---

1 For Prakrit see PISCHEL § 71.

2 (Old) Pāli tends to avoid a sequence of three short syllables ('law of de Saussure / Wackernagel'): CPD, *Epilegomena* 31* (s.v. *rhythm. length.*), SMITH (1950: 9), CAILLAT (1970: 8), (1980: 56) and ea., *BSL* 63 (1968) 52-53 (comptes rendus).

3 See GEIGER § 6.3. For Prakrit see PISCHEL § 76.

4 See OBERLIES (1995: 136 [s.v. *veḷuriyāmaya*]) and id. (1996: 109 n. 114 [add: Ja VI 279,16*, Bv I 12, Cp 24 = 86]). For Prakrit see PISCHEL § 70. On the abl. of the *a*-stems in *°āto* see § 30.4.

5 See CPD, *Epilegomena* 31* (s.v. *rhythm. length.*) and *Additional Abbreviations (1933)* p. XXVI (s.v. *rhythm.-length.*); cf. OBERLIES (1995/96: 271).

6 On this word see LÜDERS (1954: 106-107).

7 See TURNER (1975: 425).

yuḥ]), M I 306,12[1].

And it may represent (**4**) *a* in word-initial position (especially in the preverbs *pā* °< *pa* °, *pāṭi* °< *prati* °, *pāri* °< *pari* °[2], sometimes used as 'metrical doublets' [SMITH 1950: 11])[3]: *ādīna-* (~ *adīna-*) 'not depressed', *ānubhāva-* 'power, might' (anubhāva-), *ābhijeti* (~ *abhijeti*) 'conquers, wins', *ābhirucchi* 'ascended' (: *abhirūhati*)[4], *pāricariyā-* (~ *paricaryā-*) 'service', *pāriṇāmita-* (~ *pariṇāmita-*), 'bent down', Ja VI 269,17*[5], *pākaṭa-* 'not controlled; familiar' (prakṛta-), *pākāsiya-* 'evident' (prakāśya-), *pāvacana-* 'saying' (pravacana-), *pāṭikaṅkha-* 'to be desired' (*pratikāṅkṣya-), *pāṭidesanīya-* 'to be confessed' (pratideśanīya-)[6]. Moreover, we have (**5**) *ā* for *a* owing to a wrong resolution of compounds and (**6**) as the *vṛddhi* of (MIA) *a*:

(**5**) *āgāra-* 'house' (← *°âgāra-*)

(**6**) *sākhalya-* 'friendship' (← *sakhila-* [sakhi- x akhila-], see § 5.6),

---

[1] See VON HINÜBER, *Die Sprachgeschichte des Pāli im Spiegel der südostasiatischen Handschriftenüberlieferung*. AWLM 1988.8, p. 25-26, id. (1994: 157-158), and NORMAN, *IIJ* 34 (1991) 204. See also p. 103 n. 4.

[2] See GEIGER § 24 / 33.1 (cf. VON HINÜBER § 160). For Prakrit see PISCHEL § 70 / 77.

[3] See CAILLAT, *IF* 71 (1966) 309, and OBERLIES (1995/96: 271).

[4] *aroga-* 'healthy' is often spelled *āroga-* by confusion with *ārogya-* (see CPD s.v. aroga and ALSDORF, *Kleine Schriften* p. 307).

[5] So read m.c. (see SAKAMOTO-GOTO, *Buddhist Studies* 7 [1978] 170 <49>). On *pariṇāmitā-* 'the law of change', Ja VI 189,29*, see OBERLIES (1996: 147).

[6] See Sadd s.vv. It is interesting that SMITH (Sadd V 1602) explains *pārisuddhī-* 'purity' in a different way (*pārisuddhī- : parisuddha- = pāramī- : parama-*).

(ab)bhākuṭika- '(not) frowning' (← *bhakuṭi-* [bhṛkuṭi-])[1].

It is also the result of various contractions, (7) *-ayā-*, (**8**) *-āya-* (especially after palatals and *-y-* and analogically to that kind of haplological contraction[2]; see also § 31.1) and (**9**) *-avā-*[3]:

(7) *katipāhaṃ* 'for a few days' (katipayâham)

(**8**) *(ap)paṭisaṃkhā* 'with(out) reflecting' (°khyāya)[4], *Kaccāna* (Kātyāyana), *pajjhāti* 'muses' (~ *pajjhāyati* < pradhyāyati[5]), *pariyāgata-* 'had one's turn' (pariyāyagata-)[6], *Moggallāna* (Maudgalyāyana), *vesiyāna-* 'trader' (*vaiśyāyana-)[7], *sampāyati* 'replies' (*sampāyayati < sampādayati[8]), *anādā* 'not having taken' (anādāya), *anupādā* (~ *anupādāya*) 'without clinging', *(agg')upaṭṭhāka-*

---

1 See GEIGER § 3 and (for Prakrit) PISCHEL § 78 (cf. VON HINÜBER § 116).

2 See CPD, *Epilegomena* 25* (s.v. *hapl(ol)*), CAILLAT, *IF* 88 (1983) 315, and VON HINÜBER § 143.

3 See GEIGER § 27 and VON HINÜBER § 142 / 145.

4 On *°aññā°*, *ajjhā-*, *upajjhā-* and *sajjhā-* (< [°]adhyāya-) see CPD s.v. ²ajjhā and ²upajjhā (cf. also TRENCKNER 1908: 116 n. 23).

5 The derivation of the PED (< pra-√kṣā) is certainly wrong (see also Sadd V 1527). It is, however, possible to derive *pajjhāti* directly from *pradhyāti* (see OBERLIES 1995a: 145). On ⁽²⁾*jhāyāmi*, Vin I 359,9* (read m.c. *jhāmi* [?]), see CPD s.v. anāsava.

6 Or else we have to do with a haplology: *pariyā<ya>gata-* (see Sadd V 1571).

7 See LÜDERS, *Philologica Indica* p. 283-284 n. 3. On Ja VI 208,11* (Ee *vessā*) which ALSDORF, *Kleine Schriften* p. 811 with n. 65, wrongly emended to (nom. [!]) *vessāna* see FALK, *Festschrift Klaus Bruhn*, Reinbek 1994, 317 n. 16.

8 See LÜDERS (1954: 91-92).

'chief attendant' (°sthāyaka-), *vehāsa-* 'open air' (vaihāyasa-)[1] (**9**) *yāgu-* 'rice-gruel' (yavāgū-)[2].

rem. *-aya-* is never contracted to *-ā-* (*pace* GEIGER § 27): *paṭisallāṇa-* 'seclusion' (also *paṭi°* and *°sallāna-*) is an analogical formation (*°lāna-* : *°līna-* = *hāna-* : *hīna-*[3]), and *sotthāna-* 'well-fare' is a contracted form of **sotthāyana-*, which goes back to **sotthi-ayana-* (< svastiyayana-) as *paccāmitta-* 'enemy' to (OIA) *pratiy-amitra-* (see § 23, end)[4].

§ 7. P. *i* continues OIA (**1**) *i*, (**2a**) *ī* followed by one or more than one consonant, (**2b**) at the seam of a compound or of a stem and a suffix[5], (**3**) *ṛ* in the neighbourhood of a palatal, as word initial or with *i* following in the next syllable[6] and (**4**) *e* and (**5**) *ai* before a palatal that closes the

---

[1] Beside *vehāyasa-* (see PED s.v. and OBERLIES 1995: 136 [s.v.]).

[2] Is the *-ā-* of *kāyūra-* 'bracelet' (~ *keyūra-* < id.) due to the influence of *kāya-* 'body'? Or is the adaptation of a foreign word (see MAYRHOFER, EWAia III,122 [s.v. keyūra-]) the reason for the different vocalism of the Skt. and the Pāli word? It is to be noted that in Pāli *kāyūra-* is attested earlier than *keyūra-* (cf. also OBERLIES 1995a: 129 [s.v. kāyūrin-]).

[3] See Sadd V 1540 (s.v. paṭisalyāṇa).

[4] See LÜDERS, *Philologica Indica* p. 283-284 n. 3 (LÜDERS' explanation is misquoted by NORMAN 1992a: 171), and VON HINÜBER § 141 (diff. BERGER 1955: 54 n. 106). On *sotthayana-* (Ja IV 75,8* / 23*, V 29,2*/ 3* [so read *m.c.*]) see OBERLIES (1995/96: 272).

[5] See GEIGER § 32.2 and 33.2. For Prakrit see PISCHEL § 97-98.

[6] See BERGER (1955: 28-33, 35, 40), GEIGER § 12 and VON HINÜBER § 122-123. For Prakrit see PISCHEL § 50/52-53/57.

syllable (here *i* represents *ĕ*)[1]:

(**1**) *tiṭṭhati* 'stands' (tiṣṭhati)

(**2a**) *ciṇṇa-* 'practised' (cīrṇa-), *tikkha-* 'sharp' (tīkṣṇa-), *niḍḍa-* 'nest' (nīḍa- [see § 3.3])

(**2b**) *itthi+ratana-* 'ideal woman' (: *itthī-*), *siri/hiri+ma(nt)-* 'possessing fortune / modesty' (: *sirī-/hirī-*), *Bārāṇasi+to* 'from Benares' (: °sī-)

(**3**) *kicca-* 'duty' (kṛtya-), *siṅga-* 'horn' (śṛṅga-), *iñjati* 'moves; (intr.) stirs, is disturbed' (ṛñjate)[2], *iṇa-* 'debt' (ṛṇa-), *isabha-* 'bull' (ṛṣabha-), *gihi(n)-* 'householder' (gṛhin-)

(**4**) *ānissāmi* 'I shall bring' (*āneśyāmi < āneṣyāmi), *paṭivissaka-* 'neighbour' (prativeśya[ka]-), [1]*vissa-* 'dwelling' (veśman- [see § 16.6])[3]

(**5**) *issariya-* 'dominion' (aiśvarya-).

It also goes back to (**6**) *ĭC* or (**7**) *eC* in word-final position (see § 4.4): (**6**) *aggi* 'fire' (agniḥ), *āsi* 'he was' (āsīt), (7) *uppajji* 'might arise' (utpadyet), Ja IV 225,23*[4]. (**8**) Adjustments to (**a**) a regular form of suffix (*°ika-* /

---

[1] See BERGER (1955: 33/63); cf. GEIGER § 15.1-2 and PISCHEL § 84. Problematic is *khitta-* < kṣetra-, Th 1104 (see BERGER l.c. 64; for Prakrit *khitta-* see PISCHEL § 84 and JACOBI § 11).

[2] On this word see HAEBLER, *Pratidānam ... presented to Franciscus Bernardus Jacobus Kuiper* ... Den Haag – Paris 1968, 283-298.

[3] Such a *vi-* was often written *vya-* (*vyamha-* < veśman- [see OBERLIES 1989/90: 172-174]).

[4] See VON HINÜBER § 115.

°ita- / *°iya-*)[1] and (**b**) formations with new suffixes (*°ima-* ['quasi-ordinal'][2] / *-ima(nt)-*[3]) are the reason for the development *i* < (OIA) *a* / *ī*[4]:

(**a**) *alika-* 'lie' (alīka-), *paccanika-* 'enemy' (pratyanīka-), Cp 216, *vammika-* 'ant-hill' (valmīka-)[5], *gahita-* 'grasped' ([~ *(dug)gahīta-*,

---

1 See PISANI (1952: 280 [§ 2]) and OBERLIES (1996: 94 n. 19) *pace* GEIGER § 23 / 32.2. For Prakrit see PISCHEL § 80-82 (most of his examples belong here) and JACOBI § 14.2.

2 See CAILLAT, *Mélanges d'Indianisme à la mémoire de L. Renou*. Paris 1968, 187-204, ea. (1970: 9) and BHSG § 22.15-16 (cf. CPD s.v. ²-ima).

(A) different *°ima*-suffix(es) (cf. PISCHEL § 602, CAILLAT, *JAs* 1965, 289-308, ea., *IF* 78 [1973] 248 and AiGr. II,2 § 226b) is/are that/those of *avāyima-* 'not woven', *āharima-* 'charming', *(a)saṃhārima-* '(not) movable', *ugghāṭima-* 'being removed', Vism 113,4, *ghātima-* 'able to pierce', Ja III 282,23*, *pāliguṇṭhima-* 'covered round (of sandals)', Vin I 186,10, *(a)ropima-* 'what has (not) been planted', Vin IV 267,2, Vv 736, *pākima-* 'made by cooking', Anāg 27, and *kāṭhima-* 'boiling hot', Ja V 268,11* (so read; cf. Sadd V 1519 [s.v. pakkaṭhita] and VON HINÜBER 1994: 108 n. 3).

3 On this suffix – a blending of *°in-* and *°mant-* – (*arūpima[nt]-* 'ugly', Ja V 399,22*, *dhanima[nt]-* 'rich', Ja VI 221,12*, *pakkhima[nt]-* 'winged', Ja V 339,22*, *pāpima[nt]-* 'malicious', Th 1213, Sn 430, *puttima[nt]-* 'having sons', Sn 33, *phalima[nt]-* 'bearing fruit', Ja III 493,15*, *bhāgima[nt]-* 'sharing in', Thī 204) see LÜDERS, *Philologica Indica* p. 558, CAILLAT (1970: 9-10) and OBERLIES (1995a: 140 [s.v. dhanimat-]). A similar crossing of suffixes is found in *yasassima[nt]-* 'full of splendour', Ja IV 321,24* (*khattiyo ... abhijāto yasassimā* [~ *khattiyā abhijātā yasassino*, V 319,5*]; *yasasampannena parivārena samannāgato* [!], ct.), V 63,17* (*pāvako ... accimālī yasassimā* [*tejasampattiyā yasassimīhi accīhi yutto* [!], ct.]).

4 See PISANI (1952: 280) and CAILLAT (1970: 9-10) *pace* GEIGER § 19.1 / 23.

5 On *°ika-* < *°īka-* see § 2.

Dhp 311] < gṛhīta-)[1], *khādaniya-* 'solid food' (~ *khādanīya-*, M II 146,5), *dosaniya-* 'hateful' (dveṣanīya- [x doṣa-])[2], *pāniya-* 'water' (pānīya-)[3], *dutiya-* 'second' / *tatiya-* 'third' ([~ *dutīya-* / *tatīya-*[4]] < *dvatīya- ~ dvitīya- / tṛtīya-)[5]

(**b**) *carim(ak)a-* 'last' (≠ carama-), *parima-* 'best' (≠ parama-), *puttima(nt)-* 'having sons' (≠ putravant-).

(**9**) *a* could be assimilated to a neighbouring *ī̆* [6], while (**10**) *u__u* can be

---

[1] See TEDESCO, *JAOS* 43 (1923) 389 n. 48, TURNER, *BSOAS* 8 (1935/37) 204, and BERGER (1955: 46). Cf. also *(gambhīra)sita-* '(having a deep furrow =) well-founded' (°sīta-), A IV 237,8-9 (see OBERLIES 1995: 120).

[2] See GEIGER § 25.3 and SAKAMOTO-GOTO (1987/88: 356). The same contamination is to be met with in Prakrit (see PISCHEL § 129).

[3] See OBERLIES (1995a: 149). For the Prakrit word see PISCHEL § 91 (with a wrong explanation).

[4] For the most part the *°īya*-forms (*dutīya-*, Ja V 400,17*/27*, VI 285,23*, Sn 884, *tatīya-*, Dhp 309) were replaced by the more common *°iya*-forms: *dutiyāsi* (⏑--⏑), Ja VI 420,5*, *adutiyo* (⏑⏑--), Ja VI 51,13* (cf. Sn 49, 450, 740). Sometimes *dutiya-* and *tatiya-* scan -x (Ja VI 99,19* [read: *ye ve adutiyā*], Sn 1116), i.e. *dut̯ya-* and *tat̯ya-*. On these disyllabic forms and their Vedic forerunners (and their continuations in Prakrit) see DEBRUNNER, *Archiv Orientální* 17 (1949) 110-111 (cf. PISCHEL § 82 and JACOBI § 14.1).

[5] See EDGERTON, *JAOS* 75 (1955) 63 (cf. SMITH 1950: 33, BERGER 1955: 61, SAKAMOTO-GOTO 1988: 92). LÜDERS (1954: 137-138) regards *(dut/tat)īya-* as a peculiarity of the 'eastern' language (cf. VON HINÜBER § 411 [2.]).

[6] See GEIGER § 16c /17d and THIEME, *Kleine Schriften* p. 976, for Prakrit PISCHEL § 102.

dissimilated to *i*__*u*[1]: **(9)** *timissā-* ~ *timīsikā-* 'darkness' (tamisrā-)[2], *siriṃsapa-* 'snake' (sarīsṛpa-)[3], **(10)** *purisa-* 'man' (puruṣa-[4]). **(11)** *a* and – though to a lesser degree – *ŭ* had a tendency to become palatalised to *i* in the vicinity of palatal sounds[5]: *āsiṃsati* 'hopes for' (āśaṃsati)[6], *dighañña-*

---

[1] See GEIGER § 19.3 and LÜDERS (1954: 38), for Prakrit see PISCHEL § 124.

[2] Also *timisā-* is attested (D II 175,17, III 85,5, M III 174,26, S V 442,25). It seems to go back to **tamiṣā-*, a blending of *tamisrā-* and *tamas-* (cf. Pkt. *tamisă-* ~ *tamissā-* [see PSM s.v., PISCHEL § 315]). Somewhat differently NORMAN (1992: 272 [ad Sn 669]).

[3] *nisinna-* 'sitting' (≠ niṣanna-) shows the /i/ of the present *nisīdati* (see Sadd V 1508).

[4] On such *u_u_a* > *u_i_a*-dissimilations see LÜDERS (1954: 37-38), as to Prakrit see PISCHEL § 124.

muditā- (allegedly) "abstr. fr. mudu, for the usual *mudutā*" does not belong here (*pace* GEIGER § 19.3 and PED s.v. muditā). EDGERTON, *JAOS* 73 (1953) 118, rightly emphasizes that "it is at least very doubtful whether Pali ... *muditā* ... has anything to do with Skt. *mṛdu*; it means 'joy' ... and is standardly associated with forms of the Skt. root *mud*". That means: *mudutā-* (< mṛdutā-) is an altogether different word.

[5] See GEIGER § 18.2. For Prakrit (*asina-* < aśana-, *miṃjā-* < majjā-, *sijjā-* < śayyā-) see PISCHEL § 101-103 (these paragraphs are, however, an omnium-gatherum of words whose *i*-vocalism is due to altogether different causes [see JACOBI, *Kleine Schriften* p. 82-83, and BHAYANI 1997: 19-23]).

[6] *(°)ācikkhati* 'states, points out' owes its *-i-* to a contamination of *ā-√cakṣ* with *ā-√diś* and *√siks* (see EMENEAU, *IL* 29 [1968] 32). Such root blendings are not unknown to Pāli: *°nandhati* 'binds' (°nahyati x °bandhati [see § 14.15 *rem.* d and OBERLIES 1996: 96 n. 29]), *vijjotalati* 'shines forth', M I 87,1, Vin II 131,18 (*vijjotati x [uj]jalati* [see CPD I 507a (*pace* GEIGER § 188.1)]), *nirassajati* 'lets go', Sn 791 (nirasyati x niḥsṛjati [see Sadd V 1503 s.v. ²nirasana and CPD s.v. ²a- rem. b.]), *upa-siṅghāyati* 'gives a sniff-kiss' (*°gghāyati* x *°siṅghati*), *hassati* 'rejoices, is excited' (hasati x hṛṣyati), cf. *dhāta-* 'fed' (*dhita- x psāta- [see Sadd V 1665]), *parigghāsa-* 'fodder', Ja II 289,15* [m.c.] (√gras x √ghas [see OBERLIES 1995a: 147]).

'low, last' (jaghanya-), *miñjā-* 'marrow' (majjan-/°ā-), *tissā* 'her' (tasyāḥ), *rajassira-* 'dirty, polluted' (*rajassila- < rajasvala-)[1], *samijjhiṭṭha-* 'ordered' (~ *ajjhiṭṭha-*), Ja VI 12,25*, *jigucchati* 'is disgusted, detests' (jugupsate)[2], *vālikā-* 'sand' (vālukā-)[3], *bhiyyo* ~ *bhīyo* 'more' (bhūyaḥ)[4]. It resulted (**12**) by (so-called) *samprasāraṇa*[5] from *(C)ya* in open and closed syllables (> **(C)yi* > *(CC)i*)[6], a process partly favoured by analogies[7] and folk-

---

[1] On this word (which has a doublet *rajissara-*, Dhp-a III 231,21, 233,3) see CHARPENTIER, *IL* 2 (1932) 57-60, and ALSDORF, *Kleine Schriften* p. 289-290.

[2] According to BERGER (1955: 52) *jigucchati* has its *i* from desideratives like *jighacchati* 'desires to eat' and *pipāsati** 'desires to drink'. And it is also quite possible that the pre-form of *jigucchati* was **jigupsate*, as was pointed out by BIRWÉ, *ZDMG* 109 (1959) 223-224 (cf. CHARPENTIER, *Die Desiderativbildungen der indoiranischen Sprachen*. Uppsala 1912, 45 n. 2, and BURROW, *The Sanskrit Language*. London 1955, p. 46). Given that one of these explanations is right the above example should be cancelled.

[3] It would be possible to assume that *vālikā-* is due to a change of suffix. But that *-l-* has a palatal colouring is proved by the fact that clusters containing *-l-* are split up by *-i-*. This *svarabhakti* vowel is used, as a rule, only when palatals are involved (see § 7.13).

[4] (Μενάνδρος >) **Melanda* > *Milinda* seems to be influenced by *inda-* < indra- (see TRENCKNER 1908: 104).

[5] On this term see BECHERT (1958: 314-315 n. 1) and SAKAMOTO-GOTO (1988: 88). For *samprasāraṇa* in Pāli see GEIGER § 25 (cf. ibid. § 19.1) and VON HINÜBER § 129-133. For Prakrit see PISCHEL § 151-155.

[6] See SAKAMOTO-GOTO (1988: 88).

[7] *majjhima-* was grouped with the 'quasi-ordinals' *antima-* 'final, lowest' and *pacchim(ak)a-* 'last; western' (cf. *abbhantarima-* 'interior', Ja V 38,12, *uparima-* 'high[est]', D III 180,16, *orima-* 'near', A II 50,26, *bāhirima-* 'outer', Ja V 38,14, Vin III 149,29, *heṭṭhima-* 'lower, lowest', S V 452,13 [cf. AiGr. II,2 § 226aβ]). On

etymologies: *abbhihāsi* 'offered' (abhyahārṣīt), *kāhiti* 'will make' (~ kariṣyati, see § 49), *nigrodha-* '*banyan* tree' (nyagrodha-), *majjhima-* 'middle' (madhyama-)[1], *sakkhi-* 'friendship' (sakhya-). This vowel functions as (**13**) a *svarabhakti* sound (see § 21) between two consonants (**a**) one of which has a palatal colouring – (**b**) unconditioned *-i-* is an eastern feature[2] – and also (**14**) as a prothetic vowel[3]: (**13a**) *aggini-* 'fire' (agni-, [see § 21]), *agghiya-* 'respectful oblation to a guest' (arghya-), *kiloma-* 'bile' (kloman-)[4], *kilanta-* 'tired' (klānta-), *gilāna-* 'sick' (glāna-), *pilakkha-* 'fruit of the *plakṣa* tree' (plakṣa-)[5], *mariyādā-* 'boundary' (maryādā-), *rājinā* 'by the king' (rājñā), *siliṭṭha-* 'adhering' (śliṣṭa-), (**13b**) *tasiṇā-* 'thirst' (tṛṣṇā-), (**14**) *itthī-* 'woman' (strī- [> *thī-*, Sn 769, Ja I 295,8*, V 81,16*]).

rem. (**a**) Pāli disposed with *vṛddhi* in derivations from three-syllabic words

---

carima- and *parima-* see 8b, above.

1 See BERGER (1955: 32) and SAKOMOTO-GOTO (1988: 106). For Prakrit see PISCHEL § 101.

2 See VON HINÜBER § 153.

3 See GEIGER § 29-30. For Prakrit see PISCHEL § 133-137.

4 *kilomassa*, Ja III 49,23*, scans - -⏑ (i.e. *$k_i$lomassa*). On this passage see KERN, *Verspreide Geschriften* II.2 ('s-Gravenhage 1913), p. 236-237.

5 See OBERLIES (1995: 129).

whose first syllable is closed (see § 9 rem. b)[1]: *sindhava-* 'belonging to Sindh' (*sindhava- [≠ saindhava-])[2]; (**b**) The Caland suffixation is responsible for *candimā-* 'moon' (**candimas-* vs. Vedic *candrámas-*)[3]; (**c**) Sometimes a word-final *i* corresponds to an (OIA) *(i)ya/ika* (*Isi[patana]-* ~ Ṛṣya- [see § 1], *āveṇi-* ~ *āveṇiya-* 'specific, particular'[4], *ceti-* ~ *cetiya-* 'sepulchral monument', *pāni-* ~ *pānĭya-* 'water'[5], *pācitti-* ~ *pācittiya-* '[requiring] expiation', *anvādhi-* ~ *anvādhika-* 'extra supplying')[6]; (**d**) On *dvinnaṃ* 'of

---

1 See BLOCH (1965: 42), BERGER (1955: 63) and VON HINÜBER § 117 (cf. GEIGER § 15.2). Occasionally abstracts are formed also from disyllabic words without *vṛddhi*: *sūriya-*, Ja I 282,17* (~ *sūra-* 'heroism', S V 227,17, 228,3). Words whose first syllable is open form abstracts after the rule '*vṛddhi* of the first syllable and doubling of the final consonant' (see NORMAN 1991: 237-238 n. 4): *pāmujja-* 'joy', *vekalla-* 'deficieny', *vepakka-* 'ripening'. On suffixless derivations (e.g. *[app]ossuka-* 'careless, unconcerned', Ja V 8,16*, Thī 457 [so read], *[a]pesuṇa-* '[freedom from] slander', Ja V 397,8*, VI 295,22*, Sn 362, 928 [see ALSDORF 1968: 17], *sāmaṇa-* 'holy life', M I 386,7* [see ALSDORF 1968: 19], S I 7,13* [so read], *sūra-*, see above; cf. *cora-* [~ *caurya-*] 'being a thief', Arthaśāstra IV 8,7) see NORMAN (1991: 237-238 n.4), VON HINÜBER, *Indological and Buddhist Studies. Volume in Honour of Professor J.W. de Jong*. Canberra 1982, 243, and CPD s.v. apesuṇa, on words 'with double vṛddhi' – e.g. *poroseyya-* 'urbane', *sāmāyika-* 'timely' – see TRENCKNER (1908: 128).

2 One of the few exceptions to this rule is *nekkhamma-* 'suppression of desire' ([*]naiṣkāmya- [see BAPAT, *B.C. Law Volume. Part II*. Poona 1946, 260-266]).

3 See Sadd V 1372 (s.v.), CAILLAT, *Mélanges Linguistiques offerts à Émile Benveniste*. Paris 1975, 65-74, ea. (1970: 10-11) and ea. (1980: 50 with n. 25).

4 See also § 14.2.

5 On *pāni-* see OBERLIES (1996: 149).

6 See SMITH, *BSL* 34 (1933) 116, id., *JAs* 1950, 192-193, id., *Orientalia Suecana* 2 (1953) 126, CPD s.v. *anvādhika-* (see also ibid. p. 558b) and CAILLAT, *JAs* 1968, 179-180 (cf. BHAYANI 1997: 140-141). If SMITH's explanation of *uddalomī-* / °*mikā-*

two' (:: *tiṇṇaṃ*) see § 43.2 (*pace* GEIGER § 15.1); **(e)** *pasibbaka-* 'bag' is a remodelling of (OIA) *prasevaka-* after *sibbati* 'sews' (sīvyati)[1]; **(f)** *ubbilla-* 'elation, excitement does not belong to √*vell* (*pace* GEIGER § 15) but to *udbila-* 'out of the hole > beside oneself' (see Sadd V 1277 and CPD s.v.); **(g)** *hemantagimhisu* 'in summer and winter' (: °*hesu*)[2], Dhp 286, seems to be influenced by *hemantiko/aṃ ...gimhiko/aṃ* (Vin I 15,3, D II 21,8); **(h)** *iriyati* 'leads his life', Sn 1097, scans -‿x, i.e. *ir̥yati*, a remodelling of OIA *īrte* under the influence of the noun *iriyā-* (see BHSD s.v. iryati); on the passive *[sam]īrati* see § 3.2b; **(i)** *ingālakuyā* 'from the charcoal pit' (Thī 386 [so read]) goes back to 'eastern' (abl.) **ingālakuvā* and finally to *aṅgārakūpāt*[3].

§ 8. *ī* continues OIA **(1)** *ī*, followed normally **(1)** by one, but sometimes **(2)** by two consonants (see § 3.2b):

(1) *īdisa-* 'of such a kind' (īdr̥ś[a]-), *pīti-* 'joy' (prīti-), *pokkharaṇī* 'lotus ponds' (puṣkariṇīḥ [see § 36.1])

(2) [1]*kīrati* 'is scattered' (kīryate).

(**3a**) At the seam of compounds/stem-suffix/preverb-root (see § 3.4 and

as 'hair of an otter' (see Sadd V 1264) is right these words belong here (°*ī-* ~ °*ikā-*).

[1] See OBERLIES (1996: 93 n. 13) *pace* GEIGER § 15.1.

[2] Cf. GEIGER § 32.2. Sadd V 1359 (s.v. gimha), however, derives °*gimhisu* from **gimhasu* (< *grīṣman-), regarding it (most probably) as an *i_i* < *i_a*-assimilation.

[3] See HAEBLER, *MSS* 16 (1964) 21-31, CPD s.v., and VON HINÜBER § 214. For *a(ṅg)-* > *i(ṅg)-* see WACKERNAGEL, *Kleine Schriften* p. 370. On Prakrit *iṅgāla-* see PISCHEL § 102.

below 3e)[1] or due to (**3b**) *pluti*[2], (**3c**) analogical, (**3d**) rhythmical ([‿|i|‿x]) or (**3e**) compensatory lengthening (see § 3.4) it corresponds to (primary/secondary) *i*:

(**3a**) *diṭṭhī+gata-* 'come into the field of vision' (dṛṣṭigata-), Sn 836 (so read)[3], *appaṭisandhīko* 'irreparable', Ja II 230,16* (so read)[4], *jutī+ma(nt)-* 'brilliant' (dyutimant-), Ja V 405,13*, Sn 508 (~ *jutima[nt]-*, Sn 539), *dhitī+ma(nt)-* 'possessed of firmness', Sn 462 (~ *dhitima[nt]-*, Sn 542)[5], *maṇī+maya-* 'made of gems', Ja IV 60,20* = 85,15*[6]

(**3b**) *uṭṭhehi tvaṃ dhātī* 'get up, nurse!' (dhātri), Ja V 184,3* (so read [Ee *dhāti*][7])

(**3c**) *aggīhi, aggīsu* 'with / in the fires' (:: *aggīnaṃ*, see § 32.7)[8]

(**3d**) *anītiha-* 'not received through tradition' (*anitiha-), *irīyasi* 'you lead your life' (~ *iriyasi*), Ja III 498,27*, *karīyati* 'is made' (~

---

1 See GEIGER § 32.1 and 33.

2 For Prakrit see PISCHEL § 71.

3 On *jātī+maraṇa-* 'birth and death' (jāti-), Ja V 31,20*, see SMITH (1950: 8).

4 On the lengthening of *°i-* before the suffix *°ka-* see § 1-2. This lengthening which is also seen (e.g.) in *asucīka(missitā)* '(mixed up with) impure things', Sn 243, *upassutīkā* 'eaves-dropper', Ja V 81,24* = VI 389,1* (so read [see OBERLIES 1995/96: 272 n. 5]), *kosīkaṃ* 'owl', Ja V 120,15* (so read), and *brāhmaṇajātīko* 'by birth a brahmin', Ja II 84,2* (so read [see OBERLIES 1993/94: 159 n. 54]), may be due to the interchangeability of *°īya-* and *°iya-* (for which see § 14.2).

5 See SMITH (1950: 9).

6 Cf. *no saṅghassa pariṇataṃ* (‿-‿-), Vin V 218,37* (see Sadd V 1566 s.v. pariṇata).

7 See ALSDORF (1968: 33).

8 See GEIGER § 10.1.

kariyati < kriyate x ka[roti]), *harīyati* 'is brought' (~ *hariyati* < hriyate x ha[rati])[1]

(**3e**) *sīha-* 'lion' (siṃha-), *hīyo* 'yesterday' (~ *hiyyo*[2] < hyaḥ), Ja IV 270,16, Sum. I 311,10, *nīhata-* 'removed' (nirhṛta-), Ja III 471,23*[3], *nīyanti* 'they leave' (niryānti), Dhp 175 (= *niyyanti*, S V 6,16*)[4].

It goes back (**4**) to the *-e* of the middle endings *-se/-te* (see p. 218)[5]: *icchasī* 'you seek, wish' (icchase), Ja III 109,14*, V 477,2*, *jāyatī* 'is born' (jāyate), Dhp 193, 212-216, *vattatī* 'exists' (vartate), Th 574[6]. In a number of words *ī* corresponds to (**5**) OIA *e*, due to (**a**) assimilation to a neighbouring *i* or *l*[7], (**b**) re-composition or (**c**) analogy[8]:

(**a**) *abhijīhanā-* 'striving after' (: √jeh), *anīlaka-* 'pure' (: *ela-*)

---

1 See Bloch (1965: 225) and CPD s.v. *abhikīrati*.

2 On this word see Bloch (1965: 94).

3 See Oberlies (1995a: 143).

4 Conversely *siriṃsapa-* 'serpent' < sarīsṛpa- (see § 3.5 and 7.9).

5 See Manu Leumann, *Asiatische Studien* 6 (1952) 151, and von Hinüber § 416 (for Prakrit see Pischel § 73). Th 10 apparently has *vihari* 'may destroy' (⏑⏑- [!]) from (OIA) *viharet* (see Norman 1969: 121).

6 Cf. *ādiyatī* ([*]ādiyate), Ja V 221,2*, *nadatī*, Th 832 (cf. Geiger § 32), *āpajjatī*, Ja III 323,24* = V 304,15*, Dhp 309, *cavatī*, Ja II 124,21* (see Oberlies 1993/94: 161), *bajjhatī*, Sn 508, *ramatī*, Ja VI 23,10*, Th 580, 992, Dhp 116, *ruccatī*, Th 835, *vassatī*, Ja II 124,20*, *vijjatī*, Dhp 127, *sahatī*, Th 400-401 (cf. Norman 1969: LIV-LVII).

7 See Trenckner (1908: 132).

8 See von Hinüber § 119.

(**b**) *itarītara-* 'each other; whatsoever' (itara+itara, cf. *añña-m-aññam* [for the sandhi see § 23 (p. 118)])
(**c**) *gīveyyaka-* 'piece of jewellery' (*geveyyaka- [< graiveyaka-] :: gīva-)[1], *dīpa-* 'car covered with the skin of a leopard', Ja V 259,8* ≠ VI 48,10* (x : dvīpin- = sindhava- : sindhu-, see § 7 rem. a [instead of *depa- < dvaipa-])[2].

Due to metathesis (see § 22.3) and contraction *-ī(r)-* resulted from (**6**) *-(r)iy-*: [2]*kīrati* 'is made' (*kiyirati < kiriyate < kriyate), *(°)hīrati* 'is brought' (*hiyirati < hiriyate < hriyate)[3]. As to the contraction *-ī-* < **-iyi-* cf. *vīti-* **vi-y-iti-* < v_iy*-ati-* and *kittaka-* 'how much?'< **kiyittaka-* < *kiyattaka-[4]. *(a)saṃhīra-* '(im)movable' (°hārya-) and *([s]ap)pāṭihīra-* 'with(out) arguments' (°hārya-) beside *°hera-* (see § 11.5) are formed in analogy to these passives. It cannot, however, be ruled out that the 'diphthong' *-a(y)i-* was involved in these formations and left its traces in a changing vocalism (see § 3.1)[5].

rem. (**a**) There is no *saṃprasāraṇa -ī- : -yă-* (*pace* GEIGER § 25.1): *dvīha-* '(a period of) two days' and *tīha-* '(a period of) three days' are the regular

---

[1] On this word see OBERLIES (1997: 21).

[2] See VON HINÜBER § 118.

[3] *mīyati ~ miyyati* 'dies' (mriyate) is analogical to [2]*jīyati* 'grows old' < jīryate (cf. TEDESCO, *Language* 20 [1944] 220-221) as can be seen from a passage like M III 168,9: *santi, bhikkhave, tiracchānagatā pāṇā andhakāre jāyanti andhakāre jīyanti andhakāre mīyanti* (cf. Aśvaghoṣa, Buddhacarita XII 22: *jāyate jīryate caiva ... mriyate ca ...*).

[4] See TRENCKNER (1908: 134), GEIGER § 27.6-7 and VON HINÜBER § 130.

[5] For details see VON HINÜBER § 148 (cf. TRENCKNER 1908: 132-134).

sandhi forms of */dvi|ti + aha-/* conditioned by *ekāha-* '(a period of) one day' (see also § 10 rem. a)[1], *jīna-* 'loss' and *thīna(-middha)-* 'stupefaction' continue **jīna-* and **stīna-* (and not *jyāna-* and *styāna-*)[2], and *visīveti* (/*visibbeti*) 'warms himself' (Mil 47,2) goes back to **viśīpayate*, a transformation of *(*)viśyāpayate* under the influence of *śīta-* "frozen" (SAKAMOTO-GOTO 1991: 15; diff. BERGER 1955: 78: < **visīvati* < **viśīyate*); (**b**) *vījanī-* 'fan, whisk' instead of **vijanī-* (cf. Skt. *vyajana-*) has its *-ī-* from the present *vījati* 'fans'.

§ 9. *u* continues OIA (**1**) *u* and (**2**) *ū*, followed by (**a**) one (see § 3.3) or more than one consonant (see § 3.2) or (**b**) at the seam of a compound or of a stem and a suffix, (**3**) *r* in the neighbourhood of a labial (incl. *ŭ*), but if preceded by a consonant in word-initial position only after ≠*p-*[3], (**4**) *l*[4], (**5**) *o*, (**6**) *ava-*, (**7**) *au* before more than one consonant (in the cases 5-7 this substitution is regular only before a primary/secondary palatal and a cerebral; here *u* stands for *ŏ*[5]):

(**1**) *ugga-* 'fierce' (ugra-), *puratthaṃ* 'before' (purastāt)

(**2a**) *udukkhala-* 'mortar' (ulūkhala-)[6], *kubbara-* 'board of a car' (kūbara-), *uddhaṃ* 'above, upwards' (ūrdhvam)

---

[1] See VON HINÜBER § 131.

[2] See OBERLIES (1995a: 136) and SAKAMOTO-GOTO (1991: 14-15). On *middha-* see p. 124 n. 4.

[3] See BERGER (1955: 51-60), GEIGER § 12 and VON HINÜBER § 122. For Prakrit see PISCHEL § 51-53/55/57.

[4] See GEIGER § 14 and VON HINÜBER § 127. For Prakrit see PISCHEL § 59 and JACOBI § 5.

[5] See BERGER (1955: 33).

[6] On the *l__l*-dissimilation see § 14.14b.

(**2b**) *sassu+deva-* 'mother- and brother-in-law' (śvaśrū+devṛ-)[1]
(**3**) *utu-* 'weather' (ṛtu-), *pucchati* 'asks' (pṛcchati)[2]
(**4**) *(issara)kutta-* 'work (of a creator)' ([°]kḷpta-)
(**5**) *puñchati* 'wipes off' (proñchati), *(a)manuñña-* '(dis)agreeable, (un)pleasant' ([a]manojña-), *avasucchati* 'will become dry' (avaśokṣyati)[3], *sussaṃ* 'I shall hear' (śroṣy[āmi])[4]
(**6**) *uññā-* 'contempt' (avajñā-), *ujjhāyati* 'becomes indignant, complains' (avadhyāyati)[5], *ussāva-* 'dew' (avaśyāya-)[6], *ukkāra-* 'excrements' (: *avakkāra-* [← avaskara-]), *uggharati* 'oozes' (ava-√ghṛ), *uttarati* 'descends' (: *otarati* [avatarati])
(**7**) *muñja-* 'made of *muñja* grass' (mauñja-), *muṇḍiya-* 'baldness' (mauṇḍya-).

Due to analogy/blending it corresponds to (**8**) *ū*, (**9**) *o* and (**10**) *au*:

---

1 See OBERLIES (1995a: 139).

2 Here would belong *bhukuṭi-* 'frown', Ja V 296,1* (so read: OBERLIES 1993/94: 168) if actually < *bhṛkuṭi-*. On *apāruta-* 'open' (apāvṛta-) and *rukkha-* 'tree' (~ *mālāvaccha-* [cf. Aś RE II G *rvachā* ~ *vrachā*]) < vṛkṣa- see GEIGER § 13, BERGER (1955: 73-74) and VON HINÜBER § 125 (cf. CPD s.vv. apāruta- / araññaja). *rakkha-*, Ja III 144,15*, seems to be a wrong reading of Ee (FRANKE, *Literarisches Zentralblatt* 1917, p. 1040, PED s.v. rakkhā [*note*], BERGER l.c. 74 and VON HINÜBER l.c.; diff. NORMAN 1992a: 265-266).

3 On *-cch-* < -kṣy- see § 17 and 18.2.

4 Pāli has *(a)kutūhala-* '(free from) superstitious regards' beside *kotūhala-* as has Skt. *kutūhala-* beside *kautūhala-*.

5 See DHADPHALE, *Synonymic Collocations in the Tipiṭaka: A Study*. Poona 1980, 47, and SAKAMOTO-GOTO (1987/88: 359 n. 4).

6 See GEIGER § 15.4 and BERGER (1955: 33/54); cf. Sadd V 1281 (s.v. *ussāva-*).

(**8**) *luta-* 'cut off' (*lūta / lūna :: lunāti)[1]

(**9**) *tutta-* 'goad' (tottra- :: tudati)[2]

(**10**) *aggihutta-* 'oblation to the fire' (agnihotra- :: huta-), *juṇhā-* 'moonlight, the bright fortnight of the month' (**joṇhā-* [jyotsnā-] :: *juti-* [dyuti-]), *paputta-* 'grandson' (prapautra- :: putra-)[3].

It may go back (by ass/dissimilation) to (**11**) *a*, (**12**) *āCC* or (**13**) *i*, preceded or followed by a labial (incl. *ŭ*)[4]:

(**11**) *uḷuṅka-* 'spoon' (udaṅka- [see p. 88]), *navuti-* 'ninety' (navati-), *brahmuno* 'of the brahmin' (brahmaṇaḥ), *(saṃ)muti-* '(general) opinion' ([saṃ]mati-)[5], *nimugga-* 'plunged, fallen into' (nimagna-), *anusuyyaka-* 'not envious' (anasūyaka-), *puthujjana-* 'ordinary person' (*puthajjana- < pṛthagjana-)[6], *paṇṇuvīsati-*

---

[1] See OBERLIES (1995: 156 [s.v. luta-]).

[2] *a(saṃ)kuppa-* 'immovable' does not go back to *°kopya-* (*pace* GEIGER § 15.3) but to *°kupya-* (see BERGER 1955: 63).

[3] See BERGER (1955: 64-65). *khudda-* 'honey' is not a continuation of *kṣaudra-* (*pace* GEIGER § 15.4) but of *kṣudra-* (see FALK, *Comparative-Historical Linguistics: Indo-European and Finno-Ugric*. Edited by B. BROGYANYI and R. LIPP. Amsterdam 1993, 215-216 n. 20, and NORMAN, *JPTS* 20 [1994] 220-221).

[4] See GEIGER § 16a/b, 17a, 18.1, 19.2, TRENCKNER (1908: 128-129) and BERGER (1955: 52 / 60). For Prakrit see PISCHEL § 104 / 117 / 177 and BHAYANI (1997: 33-34).

[5] See BERGER (1955: 60). Diff. TRENCKNER (1908: 107) who derives *(saṃ)muti-* from *smṛti-* (cf., however, OLDENBERG, *Kleine Schriften* p. 1174).

[6] See EDGERTON, *JAOS* 73 (1953) 115-116 n. 1. It is, however, possible that *puthu°* is a blending of *pṛthak°* and *prthu°* (see Sadd V 1616 and BERGER 1955: 53 n. 101). For Prakrit see PISCHEL § 78.

'twenty-five' (pañcaviṃśati-)[1]

(**12**) *ummujjati* 'understands' ([ep.] unmārjati)

(**13**) *ucchu-* 'sugar-cane' (ikṣu-), *kukku-* 'particular measure of length' (kiṣku-), *susu-* 'child' (śiśu-).

Due to *saṃprasāraṇa* it results from (**14**) (< (CC)u < *(C)vu <) (*C*)*va* and (*C*)*ma(__n)* (see § 16.6)[2]: *addhuno* 'of the way' (adhvanaḥ), *°khattuṃ* '-times' (: °kṛtvaḥ, see § 4.5), *turita-* 'quick' (tvarita-), *supina-* 'dream' (*svupina- < svapna-), *susāna-* 'burning-ground' (*śvaśāna- < śmaśāna-)[3]. It figures (**15**) as a split vowel (see § 21) between two syllables of which (at least) one contains a labial[4]: *usumā-* 'heat' (ūṣman-), *kurūra-* 'bloody, raw' (krūra-), *sakkuṇāti* 'is able' (śaknoti), *(app)ātuma-* '(with a small) self, personality' (ātman-), *chadumaṭṭha-* 'veiled' (chadmastha-), Ja V 142,22* (so read[5]), *sukhuma-* 'subtle' (sūkṣma-), *sumarati* 'remembers'

---

[1] Surely, the analogy of *catuvīsati* (Sn 457) played a role in the development *-a-* > *-u-*.

[2] See BERGER (1955: 61), VON HINÜBER § 134 and SAKAMOTO-GOTO (1988: 105).

[3] The particle *su* which is often univerbated with other words (*tayas-su* [> *assu* (see CPD s.v. [5]assu)], *tadā̆-ssu*) seems to be based likewise on OIA *sma* and *svid*. Such a mingling would account for the fact that beside *(s)sa* the derivatives *(s)su* and [3]*so* of OIA *sma* are met with in Pāli (see NORMAN 1969: 168 [ad Th 225]) and that the interrogative particle *sū̆* (svid) occurs also in the form *(s)sa* (see NORMAN 1969: 130 [ad Th 37], 1991: 175/181 and 1992 [ad Sn 168]). By the way: OIA *svid* never develops to *si*. In the sole example the PED cites (following GEIGER § 22 / 111), Dhp-a I 91,18 (*kaṃ si tvaṃ āvuso uddissa pabbajito*), *si* is the 2nd person of *atthi* (see FRANKE, *Literarisches Zentralblatt* 1917, p. 1063). This phrase is also to be found at Vin I 40,1-2 = 14-15 = 41,11-12, and OLDENBERG prints *kaṃ 'si*! On *sudaṃ* (**svudaṃ* < **smadaṃ* < ** sma taṃ* < sma tad) see VON HINÜBER § 134.

[4] See GEIGER § 31.2, VON HINÜBER § 154-155 and id. (1994: 162-172).

[5] See LÜDERS (1954: 111-112) and OBERLIES (1995: 120-121).

(smarati), *duvija*- 'tooth' (dvija-)[1], *suvāna*- 'dog' ([ep.] śvāna-).

rem. (**a**) *u* is not used as a prothetic vowel. GEIGER'S sole example, *umhayati* 'smiles at' (§ 29), goes back to *ut-smayati*[2]; (**b**) Pāli disposed with *vṛddhi* in derivations from three-syllabic words whose first syllable is closed (see also § 7 rem. a): *ussukka*- 'endeavour, zeal' (*utsukya- [≠ autsukya-])[3]; (**c**) *kudācanaṃ* 'at any time' (≠ kadācana) is a new formation based on the stem *ku*-; (**d**) *Pajjunna* as the name of the god of rain seems to be a confusion of **Pajjanna*/°*ñña* (< Parjanya) and **Pajjunna* (< Pradyumna)[4]; (**e**) (°)*hetu* 'because of, for the sake of' often scans -- and probably stands for **hetū* < hetoḥ[5] as *asu* 'that one' stands for *aso* < asau (cf., however, *kissa hetu* with AMg. *kassa heuṃ*, i.e. *hetu* ~ *hetuṃ* [?]); (**f**) *sajju* 'on the same day', Dhp 71[6], is remodelled from **sajjo* (sadyaḥ) after *aparajju* (aparedyuḥ) which itself is influenced by *ajja* 'today' (adya)[7]; (**g**) *udāhu* 'or' (utāho) has its final due to the influence of interrogatives like *ādu*, *kim-u*, *kiṃ nu* or *kiṃ su* (cf. D I 157,15-16: *kiṃ nu kho ... udāhu*)[8]; (**h**) *sāluka*-

---

1 On this word see OBERLIES (1995a: 138).

2 See Sadd V 1279 (s.v.) and VON HINÜBER § 243.

3 *Pace* GEIGER § 15.4.

4 See Sadd V 1527 (s.v.) and cf. BHSD s.v. Pradyumna.

5 See GEIGER § 83.2 and NORMAN (1971: 177).

6 On this stanza see LÜDERS, *Philologica Indica* p. 184 with n. 3.

7 *aparajju* 'on the next day' has influenced *ajjuṇho* 'this day' (~ *ajjaṇho* [so Be Vin I 25,19*, III 220,29] < *adyāhnaḥ) and *tadahū̆* 'on this day' (**tadaho* < tadahaḥ); see BLOCH, *Recueil d'Articles* p. 541.

8 (**e**) - (**g**) *pace* GEIGER § 22.

'the edible root of the water-lily', Vin I 246,16[1], shows a normalisation of the 'suffix' *°ūka-* (Skt. *śālūka-*)[2]; **(i)** *āhuneyya-* 'sacrificial, venerable' < **āhonīya-* < āhavanīya- has its *-u-* from forms like *āhuti-* (SAKAMOTO-GOTO 1987/88: 357 and VON HINÜBER 1994: 130)[3].

§ 10. *ū* goes back to OIA *ū*, followed by **(1)** one, sometimes by **(2)** two consonants (see § 3.2b):

(1) *mūla-* 'root' (mūla-), *ūkā-* 'louse' (yūkā-)[4], *ahū* 'it was' (abhūt), *Sayambhū* (Svayaṃbhūḥ)

(2) *ūmī-* 'wave' (ūrmi-), *(deva)tūra-* 'heavenly music' (tūrya-), *pūrati* 'is filled' (pūryate), *lūkha-* 'rough' (rūkṣa-).

Due to **(3a)** *pluti*[5], **(3b)** analogical, **(3c)** rhythmical ([˘|u|˘x])[6] or **(3d)** compensatory lengthening (see § 3.4) it corresponds to OIA *u* (in case of **3d** to primary and secondary *-u[CC]-*):

---

1 The reading is confirmed by Sp 1102,14.

2 Cf. AMg. *uluga-* 'owl' < ulūka- (PISCHEL § 78). On the different suffix of *geruka-* 'red chalk' as compared with Skt. *gairika-* see PISCHEL § 118 and VON HINÜBER § 159.

3 The derivation of *pek(k)huṇa-* 'tail-feather' (Ja I 207,22*, VI 218,5* [*-kh-*], 497,16*) from *preṅkhaṇa-* alone (GEIGER § 19.2 following PISCHEL § 89) is hard to accept. Could it result from a crossing of this word (or of *pakṣman-* > *pakhuma-* 'hair; eyelashes'?) with *sakuṇa-* 'bird'?

4 On this word – which shows ø- < *y-* – see OBERLIES (1996: 106). For Prakrit see PISCHEL § 335 and ALSDORF, *Kleine Schriften* p. 826.

5 For Prakrit see PISCHEL § 71.

6 See CPD, *Epilegomena* 31* (s.v. *rhythm. length.*).

(**3a**) *hanassū* 'kill!', Ja VI 152,7* (Āryā)[1], *etū* 'he should come', Ja V 197,5* (so read), *dīyatū* 'it is to be given', Cp 29
(**3b**) *bhikkhūhi*, *bhikkhūsu* 'by / with the monks' (:: *bhikkhūnaṃ*, see § 32.7), *abbūḷha-* 'pulled out' (*°buḍha- [< °vṝḍha-][2] :: *rūḷha-*)
(**3c**) *anūdaka-* 'without water', *anūpadhīka-* 'free from attachment', *anūpama-* 'incomparable', Ap 68,21 (so read *m.c.*), *anūpalitta-* 'not clinging to' (anu°), *nirūdaka-* 'without water', Ja I 282,3 (niru°), *nirūpadhi-* 'without substratum' (niru°)[3]
(**3d**) *cūḷa-* 'small' (kṣudra-)[4], *jūhato* 'of one who sacrifices' (juhvataḥ), *(a)dūbha-* '(not) doing harm' (*[a]dubbha-* [← druhyati x dabhnoti]), *brūheti* 'promotes' (bṛṃhayati)[5].

Due to (**4**) analogical levelling it answers to *o*: *(°)rūhati* 'grows' ([rohati][6]

---

1 See ALSDORF (1968: 48).

2 See BARTHOLOMAE, *ZDMG* 50 (1896) 684-685, BERGER (1955: 56) and OBERLIES (1999: 43). It cannot, however, be ruled out that Pāli has preserved a trace of the original *-ṝ- (see AiGr. I p. XXIII n. 3, § 28 [p. 32] and WACKERNAGEL, *Kleine Schriften* p. 416 [*pace* PISCHEL § 126]). But this is certainly *not* the case (*pace* PISCHEL § 58) in the gen. pl. *-ūnaṃ* of the *r*-stems (see EDGERTON, *JAOS* 73 [1953] 118).

3 Cf. *tadūpika-* 'suitable to that' (Ja II 160,11*) < *tadupiya-* (D II 198,17). On this word see TRENCKNER (1908: 131-132) and LÜDERS (1954: 78 n. 3).

4 On this word see § 3.4.

5 On this word (with *br[ū]-* < *bṛ-*) see BERGER (1955: 69) *pace* GEIGER § 13 (on GEIGER's second example for *-ra-* < *-ṛ-*, viz. *braha[nt]-*, see p. 103).

6 Tradition has secondarily restored *-u-*: *durāruho* 'difficult to be climbed', Ja I 272,1* (cad. of *pada a* where ⏑-⏑- is not allowed). See OBERLIES (1993/94: 161 with n. 63)

: *rūḷha-* = *gūhati* : *gūḷha-*)[1]. As a preverb it goes back to (**5**) *ud-*(*h* °)[2] and (**6**) *upa-*[3]:

(**5**) *ūhasati* 'bursts out laughing' (/ud-hasati/), *(sam)ūhacca* 'having drawn out' (/[sam]ud-hṛtya/), (**6**) *ūsaḍhi-* (*upasṛṣṭi- [see § 16.9]), *ūhanati* ' soils' (← upa-hanti [x *ūhadati* (~ *ohadati*)])[4].

(7) The words (**a**) *addhagū-* 'traveller', *antagū-* 'having gone to the end of', *chandagū-* 'complying with one's desires', Sn 913, *dhammagū-* 'knower of the *dhamma*', Ja VI 261,11*, *paddhagū-* 'follower'[5], *pāragū-*

---

and id. (1996: 109). But see the next foot-note.

[1] See CPD s.v. abhirūhati, BERGER (1955: 47) and SAKAMOTO-GOTO (1987/88: 356). Beside *rūhati* (and *rohati*) *ruhati* is used (sometimes concealed by the *ū*-form: *abhi-rūha*, Thī 378, scans ⏑⏑⏑⏑ [see CPD s.v.]), and that not only in compounds (*pace* GEIGER § 133.3): Ap 26,33. It is formed in analogy to aor. *(°)ruh-* and absol. *°ruyha*. Cf. *gūhati* ~ *guhati* (see OBERLIES 1995a: 145 [s.v. paṭigūhati]). It is, however, possible that we have to do with *two* verbs ('grows' and 'climbs') which were confused.

[2] The exact nature of the phonological process (*ū-h°* < **u-hh°* < */ud-h°/* [see § 3.4 and 20] or *ū-h°* < **uṣ-h°* [this theory of SMITH, Sadd V 1282, postulates a form of the preverb *ud* unknown to Vedic Sanskrit]) is a point of some controversy (see the literature cited in the following foot-note).

[3] See GEIGER § 28, Sadd V 1282 (s.v. ū), LÜDERS (1954: 95-97), ALSDORF, *Kleine Schriften* p. 769-775, SAKAMOTO-GOTO (1987/88; 1988: 89; 1991: 21 n. 7) and VON HINÜBER § 282.

[4] See SAKAMOTO-GOTO (1987/88: 361 / 377-379), for Prakrit see PISCHEL § 327^{a}. *ummihati* 'urinates' goes back to *ud-√mih* and not to *upa-√mih* (SAKAMOTO-GOTO 1987/88 381 n. 25 *pace* LÜDERS 1954: 95 n. 1).

[5] On this word see JOHNSTON, *JRAS* 1931, 586-587.

'well-versed in', *vedagū-* 'who has knowledge'[1], (**b**) *attaññū-* 'knowing one's self', *(a)kataññū-* '(un)grateful', *apakataññū-* 'not knowing the matter in question'[2], *dirasaññū-* '(with a split tongue =) snake'[3], *viññū-* 'wise', *sabbaññū-* 'omniscient' (etc.[4]), (**c**) *gotrabhū-* 'destroyer of the lineage'[5], *vatrabhū-* 'killer of the demon Vṛtra', *bh/brūnahū-* 'abortionist' (see § 14.7) and (**d**) *pāṇabhū-* 'living creature' (whose nom. sg. ends in *-ū*) are transformations of compounds ending in (**a**) *°ga-*, (**b**) *°ñña-* (< °jña-), (**c**) *°han-* and (**d**) *°bhṛt-* under the influence of those in *°bhū-* (and [**b**] of *vidū-*)[6]. The words in *°ññū-* turned (OIA) *(a)vadānya-* into *(a)vadaññū-* '(un)kind' (see CPD s.v. avadaññū̆).

rem.: (**a**) *catūha-* and *catuha-* 'period of four days' (as well as *dvīha-* and *tīha-*)[7] are *sandhi* forms of */catu+aha-/* (resp. of */dvi+|ti+aha-/*)[8]; (**b**) *vūpa-*

[1] On this word see SAKSENA, *IHQ* 20 (1944) 290-292, and NORMAN (1992: 208 [ad Sn 322]).

[2] On this word see ANDERSEN, *Indian Studies in Honor of Charles Rockwell Lanman*, Cambridge (Mass.) 1929, 33.

[3] On this *kenning* see ALSDORF, *Kleine Schriften* p. 798.

[4] See PED s.v. *°ñū*. For Prakrit see PISCHEL § 105.

[5] On this word see WIJESEKERA, *Studies in Pali and Buddhism – A Memorial Volume in Honor of Bhikkhu Jagdish Kashyap*. Delhi 1979, 381-382, and VON HINÜBER (1994: 91-100).

[6] See CAILLAT (1970: 11-15). On *aggañña-* (← acc. *agrȧṇyam* [?]) 'principal, primeval' see CPD s.v.

[7] For references see CPD s.v. aha(n), aha(r) and OBERLIES (1995a: 137 [s.v. tīhaṃ]).

[8] Cf. *sabbahaṃ* 'every day', Ja VI 51,10* (so read with metre and C-mss.). Analogy of *ekāha-* played also surely a role (see § 8 rem. a and cf. VON HINÜBER § 131).

is a contracted form of **vu-y-upa-* < *v$_i$y-upa-* (cf. *vīti-* < *viyiti- < v$_i$yati-, see § 8.6)[1]; (**c**) [(1)]*dūhana-* 'giving milk' is a new formation (with *-ū-* as 'full grade vowel'[2]) based on *duhati*; [(2)]*(pantha)dūhana-* 'way-laying' from **dūbhana-* (see 3d, above) is patterned after it as a kind of folk-etymology.

§ 11. *e* – as well as its allophone *ĕ* which is (as a rule[3]) restricted to the position before a double consonant (for final *ĕ* see below, rem. a) – continues OIA (**1**) *e(C≠)*, (**2**) *ai(ḥ≠)*[4], (**3**) *ī̆* followed by a cerebral that closes the syllable[5], (**4**) *-aya-* (over **-a<y>i-*)[6], (**5**) *-ayi-* / **-ayi[r]-* (< *-)r$_i$y-* [as to the metathesis see § 22.3]) and (**6**) *-avi-* (over *-aï̆-*)[7]:

(**1**) *eti* 'goes', *ise* 'wise one!' (ṛṣe [see § 32.3]), *ce* 'if' (ced)

---

[1] See von Hinüber § 130.

[2] In a number of words *o* as the *full grade* of *u* was replaced by *ū*. In that way *ū* and *o* gained a certain interchangeability in open syllables (see Sakamoto-Goto 1987/88: 355-358).

[3] Only rarely does *-ĕ-* occur in an open syllable (see Warder 1967: 28-29): *jigucchati kammehi* (-⏑⏑) *pāpakehi*, Sn 215, *natthi etaṃ mamaṃ gehe* (⏑-⏑-), Pv 449 (Ee unmetr. *mama gehe*). For Prakrit cf. Pischel § 85.

[4] See Geiger § 15 and von Hinüber § 116. For Prakrit see Pischel § 60 and Jacobi § 6.

[5] See Berger (1955: 62); cf. Geiger § 10.2 and von Hinüber § 114. For Prakrit see Pischel § 119.

[6] See Geiger § 26.1 and von Hinüber § 138. *-aya-* is not always contracted: *pantañ ca sayanāsanaṃ*, Dhp 185 = Sn 338 (see Geiger § 26.1 and von Hinüber § 140).

[7] See Geiger § 27.5 and von Hinüber § 146-147. For Prakrit see Pischel § 176 and Jacobi § 15.2.

(**2**) *pettika-* 'paternal' ([*]paitrika-[1]), *pesuñña-* 'slander' (paiśun-ya-), *mettī-* 'benevolence' (maitrī-), *ucce* 'high' (uccaiḥ) (**3**) *nekkha-* 'golden ornament ' (niṣka-), *Vāseṭṭhī* (Vāsiṣṭhī), *Veṇhu* (Viṣṇu; cf. *Andhakaveṇhu*)[2], *seṭṭhi-* 'dregs' (*śiṣṭi-)[3], *heṭṭhā* 'below' (*[a]dhiṣṭāt [adhastāt :: upariṣṭāt])[4], *bhesma-* 'awful' (bhīṣma-)[5] (**4**) *ajjhena-* 'learning' (adhyayana-), *neti* 'leads' (nayati), *bhāveti* 'develops' (bhāvayati), *appesakkha-* 'unrespected' (*alpayaśaska-) (**5**) *acceka-* 'extraordinary' (ātyayika-)[6], *acchera-* 'marvellous'

---

[1] See Sadd V 1624 (s.v.) and TURNER (1975: 423 [*pace* GEIGER § 6.2]). This word seems to have developed – over the intermediate stage **pettiya-* – to *petti-* (see § 7 rem. c) which then was crossed with *piti-* 'father' (pitṛ-) yielding *petti-* 'father' (cf. *pettika-sambhava-*, Ja VI 485,20*, ~ *matti-sambhava-*, Sn 620): *pettighāti(n)-* 'murderer of the father', Ja V 268,23* (cf. *pitighāta-*, Ja IV 45,25 [B[d] *pitu°*], *pitughātaka-*, Vin I 88,24), *pettivisaya-* 'realm of the deceased (fore-fathers)', D III 234,8, *pettirāja(n)-* 'king of the deceased (fathers)', Kv 597,1 (cf. *[a]petteyya-* '(not) loving one's father' < pitrīya-, Mahābhāṣya II 340,2). In the same way *mattika-* (Ja VI 485,20*) was blended with *māti-* (mātṛ-) to *matti(gha)-* 'mother', Ja V 269,10* (diff. NORMAN 1993: 77-78, who derives *matti-* from *mātṛ-* through **māti-* [as the PED before him]). Or was it a simple confusion of simplex (*pitṛ-*) and its *vṛddhi* derivation (**paitrika-*) which gave rise to the word *petti(ka)-* (see *bhātika-/bhātuka-* 'brother' p. 136)?

[2] See SMITH, *MSL* 23 (1935) 273. On *Veṭha°* (< Viṣṇu°) see § 18.5.

[3] See NORMAN (1994: 98).

[4] See OBERLIES (1993: 167 [s.v. *heṭṭhā*]).

[5] This process is carried further in Prakrit (i.e. it occurs when the cerebral is the initial of the following syllable): *kheḍḍā-* 'play, sport' < *khiḍḍā-* < krīḍā-, *neḍḍa-* 'nest' < *niḍḍa-* < nīḍa- (see PISCHEL § 122 / 194).

[6] See CPD s.v. (diff. GEIGER § 27.6 who derives it – as well as *accāyika-* – from *atyāyika-). On *accāyika-* see, however, p. 120.

(āścarya-), *ācera-* 'teacher' (ācārya-), *issera-* '(royal) power, kingship' (aiśvarya-), *peyyāla-* 'repetition' (**peyāra-* < *payirāya- < par$_i$yāya- [see p. 15]), *macchera-* 'selfishness' (mātsarya-), *sundera-* 'beauty' (saundarya-)[1]

(**6**) *thera-* 'elder' (sthavira-)[2], *hessati* 'will be' (bhaviṣyati).

In (**7**) word final position it corresponds (often due to *u/v__o*-dissimilation) to *-o* < *-aḥ* (see § 4.2), in (**8**) medial position due to *o__u*-dissimilation to *-o*[3]. And it goes back to (**9**) *a*, followed by a geminate (consonant one of which is a) palatal (incl. *l* and *y*)[4] or to (**10**) *ī̆* before *-j-* / *-y-* (secondary *-yy-*) and (MIA) *-l-*. Due to (**11**) analogy or (**12**) blending it corresponds to *i*[5]:

(**7**) *pure* 'formerly' (puraḥ), *suve* 'tomorrow' (śvaḥ), *jīve* 'living being' (jīvaḥ), *bhikkhave* 'o monks!' (bhikṣavaḥ)

(**8**) *ahesuṃ* 'they were' (: *ahosi* 'he was').

(**9**) *pheggu-* 'wood that is not part of a tree's core' (phalgu-), *akkheyya-* 'undecaying' (akṣayya-)[6], *seyyā-* 'bed' (śayyā-)[7]

---

[1] Beside these words we find *acchariya-*, *ācariya-* and *macchariya-*.

[2] Pv 345 is to be read *paccānayitvā(na) *thavirin sudubbalaṃ* (Ee *theriṃ*).

[3] See TRENCKNER (1908: 133-134).

[4] See PISANI (1952: 279); cf. GEIGER § 9 and VON HINÜBER § 157 (for Prakrit see JACOBI § 15.1).

[5] *metteyya-* (~ *matteyya-*) 'mother-loving' (*mātreya-) has its *-e-* from *petteyya-* (see CDIAL 10024). By the way: *petteyya-* does not only mean 'father-loving' (so PED), but also 'father's brother' (see e.g. A III 348,4, Ja V 35,15, Mhv LXIV 36, LXVI 8).

[6] On this word see KATRE, *Calcutta Oriental Journal* 1 (1934) 172-173.

[7] *seyyā-* < śayyā- was certainly also influenced by *seti* 'lies'.

(**10**) *adejjha-* 'strung (said of a bow)' (adhijya-), *apeyyamāna-* 'not being drunk' (apīyamāna-)[1], *atīraṇeyya-* 'impracticable' (°anīya-)[2], *pesuṇeyya-* 'slander' (~ *pesuṇiya-*)[3], *veyyatta-/veyyatti-* 'accomplished / cleverness' (**viyyatta-* / **viyyatti-* < vyakta- / vyakti-), *nela(ṅga)-* 'inner sitting-place (of a chariot)' (nīḍa-), Ud 76,26* (so read)[4].

(**11**) *janettī-* 'mother' (janitrī- :: *janeti*)

(**12**) *pareta-* 'overcome by' (parīta- x upeta-)[5], *mahesī-* 'chief queen' (mahiṣī- x *mahesi-* 'great sage' < /mahā-ṛṣi-/[6] [see p. 15]).

In non-Aryan words *e* may alternate (**13**) with *ī*[7]: *kaṇavera-* 'oleander' (~

---

[1] It might be influenced by *apeyya-* (see CPD I, 559 s.v.).

[2] See also *akammaneyya-* 'not fit for any work' (akarmaṇya-), *anaddhaneyya-* 'not lasting', *apacineyya-* 'to whom honour is due', *apāraṇeyya-* 'that which cannot be carried to the goal', *alabbhaneyya-* 'unattainable', *asakkuṇeyya-* 'impossible'. The suffix *°teyya-* of the *participium necessitatis* (see § 55) is a blending of *°aneyya-* (< °anīya-) and *°tabba-* (< °tavya-).

The absol. *oceyya* 'having collected', Ja IV 440,16*, goes back to **ocīya* (cf. *samuccīya*, Mahābhārata 2,54.25, *vicīya*, ibid. 5,15.28). On the suffix see § 58 (p. 267 / 268).

[3] On *ādhipateyya-* 'authority' see VON HINÜBER § 213.

[4] See Sadd 439 n. 1 (cf. DHADPHALE, *ABORI* 58/59 [1977/78] 595-597, and OBERLIES 1995a: 143).

[5] See LÜDERS (1954: 56 n. 3) and CPD, *Epilegomena* 22* (s.v. *blend.*).

[6] *mahesi-* 'great sage' is re-composed out of *mahā+isi-* (cf. *mahā-ise*, Ja V 321,16*). As to the *sandhi* see p. 119

[7] See BERGER (1955: 61) and VON HINÜBER § 119.

kaṇavīra-), *bella-* '(fruit of the) Bilva tree' (~ *billa-* [~ *mella-*][1]). In (**14**) derivations *e* is the *vṛddhi* of (secondary [< *ṛ/u* and as a split-vowel]) *i*[2]: *(pali)gedha-* 'greed' (x : *giddha-* [< gṛddha-] = *nisedha-* : *nisiddha-*, *bodha-* : *buddha-*)[3], *jeguccha-* 'contemptible' (← *jigucchati* [jugupsate]), *gelañña-* 'sickness' (← *gilāna-* [< glāna-])[4], *veyyāvacca-* 'occupation, duty' (← **viyyāvata-* [< vᵢyāpṛta-]).

rem. (**a**) At the end of a word *-e* can be shortened, repeatedly in hiatus (originally according to the rule *vocalis ante vocalem corripitur*[5]): *api bhīrukĕ api*, Ja IV 286,11* (Āryā), *tĕ ayirā*, Ja IV 288,9* (Āryā)[6], *desentĕ ajānantā*, Thī 453[7], *upadhi-saṃkhayĕ vimutte*, Vin I 42,34*[8], *bhaddĕ sattavo*, Ja V 95,26*, *mā Candĕ rucci maraṇaṃ*, Ja VI 152,17* (Āryā)[9]; (**b**) *e*-

---

1 Ja III 77,24*, VI 578,18* (*bella-*), III 319,15* (*mella* [*bellaṃ ti vā-pāṭho*, ct.]), VI 563,5* (*[paṇḍ]ubeluvaṃ* ⏑-⏑-).

Here seems to belong *āveḷa-* 'garland' ~ (Skt.) *āpīḍa-* (see BERGER, *Donum Indogermanicum. Festgabe für Anton Scherer*. Heidelberg 1971, 67; diff. TEDESCO, *Archaeologica Orientalia in Memoriam Ernst Herzfeld*. New York 1952, 225, who derives the words from *ā-vṛtta-* resp. **ā-pṛṣṭa-*). Cf. *Uruvelā* ~ (BHS) *Uruvilvā* (see, however, WACKERNAGEL, *Kleine Schriften* p. 310 n., and GEIGER § 10.2).

2 See GEIGER § 3 and LÜDERS (1954: 84), for Prakrit see PISCHEL § 78.

3 See BHSG § 3.68 (*pace* GEIGER § 10.2 and PISCHEL § 119).

4 See CPD, *Epilegomena* 21* (s.v. *anal.*). For the Prakrits see PISCHEL § 78.

5 See BECHERT, *'Alte Veḍhas' im Pāli-Kanon*. NAWG 1988.4, p. 11 n. 44.

6 See ALSDORF (1968: 30 n.).

7 See NORMAN (1971: § 72).

8 See ALSDORF (1968: 69).

9 See also OBERLIES (1995/96: 279 n. 32).

for *a*- and *ĭ̄*- in pronouns (*ettaka*-, *ettha*, *edisa*-[1]) is due to the influence of the stem *eta(d)*-[2]; (**c**) *paleti* 'goes away', Dhp 49, Sn 1074, does not continue *palāyati* (*pace* GEIGER § 26 rem. 2 and 139.1) but *paraiti* (parā-√i)[3], and *bhemi* 'I am afraid of', S I 111,2*, is not a contraction of *bhāyāmi* (*pace* GEIGER § 26 rem. 2 and 139.1) but a 'root present' (ə: <*bi*>*bhemi*; see § 45); (**d**) °*vedhati* 'trembles' does not continue **vīthate* (*pace* GEIGER § 25.1 and 38.4) but is based on the verbal adjective *vidhita*-, which was formed within Pāli by blending *viddha*- (√vyadh) and **vithita*- (vyathita- [√vyath])[4]; (**e**) *vegha*- 'noose, knot' does not continue *vighna*- but (**vekha*- <) *v[l]eṣká*-[5] (see § 16.9); (**f**) *ke([ca] chave sigāle ke [pana] sīhanāde)*, D III 25,3(*)-4(*), is the 'eastern' nom. sg. of the interrogative pronoun (~ kaḥ) whose double employment serves to denote a wide discrepancy between two things, viz. 'the wretched jackal and the roaring of the lion' (LÜDERS 1954: 15 [diff., but not convincing BERGER 1956: 98]).

§ 12. *o* – as well as its allophone *ŏ*, which is (as a rule) restricted to the position preceding a double consonant (for final -*ŏ* see below, rem. a)[6] – continues OIA (**1**) *o(≠)*, (**2**) *au(≠)*[7], (**3**) *u* followed by a cerebral that

---

1 BLOCH (1965: 81) sees in this word a haplological shortening of **e(dā)disa*- < *etādṛśa*-.

2 See SCHWARZSCHILD (1991: 34-35 [*pace* GEIGER § 11 and 27.7 and PISCHEL § 107/121]).

3 See LÜDERS (1954: 55-56, 139).

4 See OBERLIES (1996: 95-97); cf. CPD s.v. [1]asoka (on *paccavyathā*, Vin I 40,34*).

5 See Sadd V 1365 (s.v. *gh*); diff. SAKAMOTO-GOTO (1993: 301-302 n. 21).

6 Cf. PISCHEL § 85.

7 See GEIGER § 15 and VON HINÜBER § 116. For Prakrit see PISCHEL § 61a and JACOBI § 6.

closes the syllable[1], (**4**) *(-)ava-* (over **-a<v>u-*)[2] and (**5**) *-ayū-*:

(**1**) *ogha-* 'flood' (ogha-), [1]*oṭṭha-* 'lip' (oṣṭha-), *Sutano* (see § 32.3)

(**2**) *orasa-* 'own; legitimate son' (aurasa-), *ubho* 'both' (ubhau), *ratto* 'at night' (rātrau)

(**3**) [2]*oṭṭha-* 'camel' (uṣṭra-)[3], *koṭṭima-* 'artificial floor' (~ *kuṭṭima-* < kṛtrima-)[4], *pokkharaṇī-* 'lotus pond' (puṣkariṇī-, see 12 below)[5]

(**4**) *oma-* 'inferior' (avama-), *ora-* 'this bank, shore' (avara-), *olambati* 'hangs down' (avalambate), *koja-* 'mail' (~ *kavaca-*), *nonīta-* 'cream which rises to the top as one begins to churn milk' (~ *navanīta-*), *hoti* 'is' (bhavati), *uposatha-* 'day for the recitation of the Pātimokkha' (upavasatha-), *poṇa-* 'sloping' (pravaṇa-)[6]

(**5**) *mora-* 'peacock' (mayūra-)[7].

---

[1] See BERGER (1955: 62); cf. GEIGER § 10.2 and VON HINÜBER § 114.

[2] See GEIGER § 26.2 and VON HINÜBER § 138. *-ava-* is not always contracted: *sabbā va tā upabhogā bhavanti*, Ja VI 361,20* (see VON HINÜBER § 140).

[3] Is *okkā-* 'firebrand', Ja V 161,7*, beside (regular) *ukkā-* < *ulkā-* a wrong reading?

[4] On these words see GEIGER, *Cūlavaṃsa, being the more recent part of the Mahāvaṃsa* (PTS Text Series Nos. 20, 21), p. 640-641. As to Prakrit see PISCHEL § 125.

[5] See BERGER (1955: 38).

[6] On *ud(d)osita-* 'store-house' (udavasita-) see OBERLIES, *ZDMG* 147 (1997) 534-535. Does *soṇṇa-* 'golden', Ja V 169,10* (read *soṇṇa-mayaṃ*), VI 203,8*, go back to **savarṇa-* < *suvarṇa-*? Or is it a somewhat irregular outcome of *sauvarṇa-* which is normally continued by *sovaṇṇa-*?

[7] **-ayū-* is retained in *mayūkha-* 'ray of light' (see GEIGER § 27 n. 8 and VON HINÜBER § 145).

In word-final position, it corresponds (also) to (**6**) *-aḥ*: *asso* 'horse' (aśvaḥ), *ceto*(+) 'mind' (cetaḥ[+]), *mano*(+) 'mind' (manaḥ[+]), *no* 'our' (naḥ), *ito* 'from here' (itaḥ), *bhikkhavo* 'monks' (bhikṣavaḥ), *rattiyo* 'nights' (rātr$_{i}$yaḥ), *kudho* 'you were angry' ([a]krudhaḥ), *mā pamādo* 'do not be indolent' (prāmadaḥ, see § 2)[1]. As a preverb it goes back to (*ava-* [see **4**]), (7) *apa-* and (**8**) *ut-C°*[2]:

(7) *ottapate* 'shrinks from' (apatrapate), *ovaṭa-* 'closed' (apavṛta-)[3]
(**8**) *otappati* 'is heated' (uttapyate), *opunāti* 'winnows' (utpunāti)[4].

It derives by *saṃprasāraṇa* from (**9**) *(C)va* in closed syllables[5]: *sotthi-* 'well-being' (svasti-), *sobbha-* 'hole' (śvabhra-). Due to metrical reinterpretation, it corresponds to *ŭ̄*, (**10**) primary or (**11**) rhythmically lengthened[6]:

---

[1] See GEIGER § 66.2 and VON HINÜBER § 169 (for Prakrit see PISCHEL § 342-347). On *labhetho* 'you would obtain', Sn 833, see VON HINÜBER § 443, and on *kappayavho* 'make!', Sn 283, see p. 222 with n. 2.

[2] See CPD s.v. [4]o.

[3] See GEIGER § 28.2 and VON HINÜBER § 139.

[4] See BROUGH (1962: 259).

[5] See GEIGER § 25.2, VON HINÜBER § 134 and BERGER (1955: 61-62). Other than *l.c.* 61 BERGER (1956: 98) sees in [2]*ko* 'where' – which is not only to be found S I 199,16* and Vin I 36,24 (GEIGER § 25.2) but also Ja IV 433,19*, V 258,4*, VI 155,18*, 179,28*, 515,8*, Cp 185 (*koci-koci*), M II 52,9, III 155,11 – not the *saṃprasāraṇa* form of (OIA) *kva* (cf. GEIGER § 25.2, SAKAMOTO-GOTO 1991: 20 n. 3), but a hyper-Pālism for *ke* ([allegedly (see p. 64, *rem.* f.)] ~ kasmin).

[6] Long *ū* can by no means become *o* in an open syllable only due to a phonological process. The examples GEIGER (§ 11) adduces are non-Aryan loan-words (see BERGER, *Donum Indogermanicum. Festgabe für Anton Scherer*. Heidelberg 1971,

(10) *porisa-* 'man' (pūruṣa-)[1]

(11) *accodara-* 'too much of a belly' (atyudara-), *anodaka-* 'waterless' (*anūdaka-* ← anudaka-), *anopama-* 'incomparable' (~ *anūpama-* ← anupama-)[2].

(12) If preceded in word-initial position by a labial, it may go back to (primary or secondary) *u*[3]: *pokkhara-* 'lotus' (puṣkara-), *potthaka-* 'book' (pustaka-), *poso* 'the man's' (puṃsaḥ [see p. 172])[4], *bhogga-* 'bent' (bhugna-), *bondī̆-* 'body' (*bundī̆- < vṛndī-)[5]. By **(13)** assimilation and **(14)** analogy it answers to *e* and *ā̆* respectively:

(13) *oṇojana-* 'dedication as a gift' (avanejana-), *oṇojeti* 'dedicates by pouring water' (avanejayati)[6]

67-69): *gaḷocī-* 'name of a shrub' (guḍūcī-), *jambonada-* 'special sort of gold' (jāmbūnada-). And the same seems to hold good for Prakrit (*pace* PISCHEL § 127).

1 See BERGER, *WZKSO* 1 (1957) 76-80 (cf. CAILLAT 1970: 9, BECHERT, *'Alte Veḍhas' im Pāli-Kanon. NAWG* 1988.4, p. 11 / 13, and OBERLIES, 1995/96: 274 n. 11).

2 See SMITH (1950: 10) and SAKAMOTO-GOTO (1987/88: 357). On *anokkamma* 'having followed' (anukramya), Ja VI 571,21*, see ALSDORF, *Kleine Schriften* p. 317 n. 56. On *upocita-* see VON HINÜBER § 160.

3 See BHAYANI (1997: 15-16) and cf. PISCHEL § 125.

4 See also Sadd V 1628 (s.v. posa). Cf. *poṅkh(ânupoṅkhaṃ)* ~ *puṅkha-* 'arrow' (see PED s.vv.).

5 See LÜDERS, *Philologica Indica* p. 566-569, and EDGERTON, *JAOS* 69 (1949) 229.

6 Does *ponobhavika-* 'leading to rebirth' (< *pona[b]bhavika- < paunarbhavika-) belong here? Or is it a derivation from **puno-bhava-* (see PED s.v. [where, however, an entry *puno* is missing and the statement [s.v. puna] that "the form *puno* is doubtful" is simply wrong; this form is attested Thī 397 and ten times in the Apadāna]).

(**14**) *āmo* 'yes' (āma :: [voc.] *bho, āvuso*)[1], *dhovati* 'washes' (dhāvati :: *dhota-* [< dhauta-])[2].

We have (**15**) *o* for *u* by wrong resolution of compounds: *odaka-* 'water' (*[sīt]odaka-*). In (**16**) derivations *o* is the *vṛddhi* of *u* (also secondary [< *ṛ*, due to *saṃprasāraṇa* and as a split-vowel])[3]: *opadhika-* 'pertaining to material objects' (← upadhi-), *phoṭṭhabba-* 'tangible' (← *phusati* [spṛśati]), *pothujjanika-* 'common, ordinary' (← *puthujjana-*, see § 9.11), *mosa+* 'false' (← *musā+* < mṛṣā+)[4], *dohaḷa-* 'the longing of a pregnant woman' (← **duhaḷa-* [see § 13]), *sosānika-* 'one who lives near a burning-ground' (← *susāna-*, see § 9.14)[5], *dovārika-* 'gate-keeper' (← d$_u$vāra-), *sovaggika-* 'heavenly' (← s$_u$varga-), *sovatthika-* 'safe' (← s$_u$vasti-).

rem.: (**a**) Also *-o ≠* is liable to be shortened[6], especially in hiatus (see also § 11 *rem.* a): *ādiccŏ va* (--˘), Sn 1097, *ajjuṇhŏ aggisālamhi*, Vin I 25,19*

---

1 See CAILLAT, *IF* 71 (1966) 308.

2 See GEIGER § 34 (as to ibid. § 27.3 *atidhoṇa*[*cāri*(*n*)]- see VON HINÜBER § 145). On *adosaka-* 'innocent', Ja VI 579,4* (< *adūsaka-* x *dosa-* [on this see GEIGER § 25.3]) see SAKAMOTO-GOTO (1987/88: 356).

3 See GEIGER § 3.

4 For Prakrit see PISCHEL § 78. According to CPD *(a)sammosa-* '(non-)bewilderment' belongs to √*muṣ* 'to steal' while PED (s.v.) and BHSD (s.v. asaṃmoṣa) connect it with √*mṛṣ*. In that case it would belong here (see also BERGER 1955: 60 and VON HINÜBER § 122).

5 On *sopāka-* 'outcast' as a *vṛddhi*-derivative of **supāka-* (< śvapāka-) see BERGER (1955: 62); for AMg. see PISCHEL § 78.

6 Only very sporadically such an *ŏ* is represented by *u* in the manuscripts (see NORMAN 1994: 42 who points to *piya-vadu*, D III 154,3*, standing for *piya-vadŏ*).

(Āryā)[1], *adhicetasŏ appamajjato*, Ud 43,20* = Th 68 (Vait.), *anapekkhŏ ahaṃ*, Ja V 183,2*[2], *apaṇḍarŏ aṇḍa °*, Th 599, *Asitŏ isi addasa divāvihāre*, Sn 679 (Tri.), *uñchātŏ ehiti*, Ja VI 543,15*[3], *udakatŏ ubbhataṃ*, Thī 379, *gāmatŏ ārakā*, Ja I 272,1*, *guṇehi etehi upetŏ khattiya*, Ja III 443,18*, *dāmatŏ kuñjaro* (˘-˘-), Ja IV 93,27*, *anumajjhatŏ majjhakaṃ* (˘-˘-), Ja V 387,19*, *bhariyāyŏ haññamānāyo*, Ja VI 155,18* (Āryā)[4], *mūlaphalātŏ etu*, Ja V 200,22* (Ee *°phalato*), *yonisŏ anuvicinantī*, Thī 472 (so read [see Ee App. II p. 246]); (**b**) On *kho* (khalu) see § 14.11; cf. *cuddasa-* 'fourteen' < [*]coddasa- < ca<t>urdaśa- (see § 14.3); (**c**) The abnormal contraction of *-oya-* in *koṭṭha(ka)-* (koyaṣṭi[ka]-) 'woodpecker' (Ja VI 539,9*, *rukkhakoṭṭha[ka]-*, Ja II 163,8, III 25,29 [v.l. *koṭa[ka]-* in both places!]) is due to the influence of *koṭṭeti* 'beats' (*pace* GEIGER § 27.8); (**d**) [2]*oka-* 'water' (*okapuṇṇehi cīvarehi*, Vin I 253,14)[5] seems to be a contracted form of *odaka-* (see above, 15); (**e**) *ojā-* 'strength' is formed out of *oja(s)-* after the pattern *ūrjā- : ūrjas-* (*pace* GEIGER § 10); (**f**) [(2)]*vo* 'indeed' (Sn 560, 760, Khp VI, Ja I 256,7*, III 131,11*) as a hyper-translation is equivalent to *ve* < vai forming a group with other *o*-particles (but cf. the Vedic particle *vaḥ*, on which see FRANKE, *BB* 23 [1897] 168 and AiGr. III § 236d [p. 478])[6].

---

[1] See ALSDORF (1968: 59).

[2] See BECHERT (1961: 19), diff. ALSDORF (1968: 32).

[3] See OBERLIES (1993/94: 159 n. 52).

[4] See ALSDORF (1968: 50).

[5] Note the '*pi-pāṭha*' ***ogha****(puṇṇehi)*, Sp 1106,11-14 (see CPD s.v. [2]oka).
oka-m-okata, Dhp 34; may belong to [1]*oka-* (< okas-) 'from whatever home' (see FRANKE, *Ostasiatische Zeitschrift* 6 [1917/18] 294 and CPD s.v. [1]oka and [2]oka *rem.*).

[6] See also CPD I,531b (s.v. [δ] *no*). Cf. [2]*so* (Th 9 [so read against Ee *sv-*]) ~ *se* ← *taṃ* (see NORMAN 1969: 120). See also p. 185 n. 1.

2.3. The consonants

§ 13. Apart from *ḍ(h)*, *ś* and *ṣ* simple initial and intervocalic consonants of OIA are generally preserved in Pāli[1], and thus it has by and large the same *consonant* system as OIA[2]; only *ṅ* is lost as a phoneme[3], whereas *ñ* has acquired phonemic status (see also § 15.1)[4]: *ñante* 'nearby' (nyante)[5], *ñāya-* 'right conduct' (nyāya-), *ñāṇa-* 'knowledge' (jñāna-). OIA *ś* and *ṣ* are continued by *s*[6], intervocalic *ḍ(h)* by *ḷ(h)*[7] (see *rem.* **a-f** below): *sisira-* 'cold season' (śiśira-), *osadhī-* 'herb' (oṣadhī-)[8], *upakūḷita-* 'scorched'

---

[1] Only very rarely consonants of different classes correspond: *(an)aṅgaṇa-* '(free from) dirt' / *saṅgaṇa-* 'blemished' (M I 24,18, Sn 279) < (an)añjana- / sāñjana- (see CPD s.v. [2]aṅgana [pointing to PISCHEL § 234 where forms of *abbhaṅgei* are listed]), *udaṅgaṇa-* 'drawing up (the bucket)' (ud-√a[ñ]c [see OBERLIES 1997: 19-20]).

[2] See GEIGER § 2.2.

[3] See BERGER (1955: 53 n. 103) and VON HINÜBER § 161 / 202.

[4] See VON HINÜBER § 161, ELIZARENKOWA, *Pratidānam ... presented to Franciscus Bernardus Jacobus Kuiper* ... Den Haag – Paris 1968, 302, and CAILLAT, *BEI* 4 (1986) 9*. Single *ñ* occurs only initially (see VON HINÜBER § 202).

[5] On this word see ANDERSEN, *Indian Studies in Honor of Ch. R. Lanman*. Cambridge 1929, 31.

[6] See GEIGER § 35 and VON HINÜBER § 219. For Prakrit see JACOBI § 20.2b and PISCHEL § 227-229.

[7] See GEIGER § 2.3 / 35, LÜDERS, *Philologica Indica* p. 547, KATRE, *B.C. Law Volume. Part II*. Poona 1946, 22-34, WITZEL, in: *Dialectes dans les littératures indo-aryennes* (édité par COLETTE CAILLAT). Paris 1989, 211-212, and VON HINÜBER § 198. For Prakrit see PISCHEL § 226 / 240-242 / 244.

[8] On *osadhī-* 'morning star' see OBERLIES, *WZKS* 34 (1990) 81-82 with n. 9.

([*]°k(r)ūḍita-[1]), *tāḷeti* 'beats' (tāḍayati), *aḷāra-* 'curved' (arāḍa-)[2], *biḷāra-* ~ *biḷāla-* 'cat' (biḍāla-)[3], *Āsāḷha* (Āṣāḍha), *mūḷha-* 'confused' (mūḍha-)[4]. In word-initial position[5], however, ≠*ṣ-* and ≠*ś(v)-* are sometimes represented by *ch-*[6]: *cha(t)-* 'six' (ṣaṣ-)[7], *chakaṇa-* 'dung of animals' (: śakan-), *chava(ka)-* 'corpse' (śava[ka]-), *chap/vaka-* 'out-caste' (śvapaka-)[8], *chāpa-* 'the young of an animal' (śāva-). This seems to point to a rather 'slurred' pronunciation of these sounds. A(n 'OIA') *-ḍ(h)-* > P. *-ḷ(h)-* may be secondary due to a dissimilation of *ḍ(h)* against a neighbouring *d(h)* (*dohaḷa-* 'the longing of a pregnant woman' ← *duhaḷa- < *duhaḍa- < *duhada- <

---

1 On √*krūḍ* see KUIPER. *Aryans in the Rigveda*. Amsterdam 1991, 75-76.

2 On this word see LÜDERS, *Philologica Indica* p. 560 (ibid. p. 558 on *dāḷima-* 'pomgranate' < **dāḍima-* ← daṃṣṭra-)

3 See GEIGER § 45.

4 How is *līḷhā-* 'facility, skill, grace' (used in the phrase *Buddha-līḷhāya dhammaṃ deseti*) to be explained? Is it actually the same word as *līlā-* 'play'? COHEN, in: *Vidyopāsanā*. Studies in Honour of Harivallabh C. Bhayani. Mumbai – Ahmedabad 1999, 37-60, regards both (*līlā-* < **līḷā-* < *līḷhā-*) as "abstract nouns phonologically equivalent to **līḍhā*" (l.c. 55) which is connected with the root *lih* 'to lick'.

5 For the treatment of initial consonants in Prakrit see PISCHEL § 184-185.

6 See GEIGER § 40 and VON HINÜBER § 167. For Prakrit see JACOBI § 8 and PISCHEL § 211.

ḍāka- 'vegetable', Thī 1 (for further references see PED s.v.), must be different from *śāka-* (cf., however, Skt. *ḍākinī-* ~ *śākinī-*).

7 TURNER (1975: 361) postulates a basic form **kṣakṣ-* (cf. Av. *xšuuaš*) whose initial *k* is abnormally dissimilated (see also AiGr. III § 182d and VON HINÜBER § 399).

8 See ALSDORF, *Kleine Schriften* p. 767 n. 2.

*dvihṛda- [see § 12.16])[1], *adveḷhaka-* 'not ambiguous' < *advaiḍhaka- < advaidha[ka]-[2]) or against a *-r-*[3] (*koviḷāra-* ~ *kuviḷāra-* 'a tree in *devaloka*' < kovidāra-)[4] or due to a contamination (*āḷāhana-* 'place of cremation', *pariḷāha-* 'fever' < ādahana- / paridāha- x *ḍāha-/ḍahati* [see also *rem.* **c**]). Words which have *-ḷ-* < -ṭ- (GEIGER § 38.6) like *Āḷavī* (Āṭavī), *paḷaccari(n)-* 'beggar', Ja VI 227,23* (cf. paṭaccara-)[5] and *phaḷikā̆-* 'crystal' (sphaṭikā̆-) presuppose intermediate (eastern) *-ḍ-* (see § 14.2)[6].

rem. (**a**) Intervocalic *-ḍ-* is only very rarely retained: *Vidūḍabha*,

---

[1] BURROW, *BSOAS* 49 (1986) 593, however, derives *dohaḷa-* from *durhṛd-* pointing to Jaiminīya-Brāhmaṇa II 23: *tasmād u strī durhṛdinī vīva glāyati* (v.l. *duhṛdinī*).

[2] See THIEME, *Kleine Schriften* p. 976-977 (cf. GEIGER § 42.4); diff. CPD s.v., SMITH, *BSL* 1929, XVIII, and VON HINÜBER § 10 who derive the word from **advaiḍhā* ← **dvīḍhā* < **dvizḍhā* (as against OIA *dvidhā* [cf. EWAia s.v. dvídhā]).

[3] Is the *-ḷ-* of *daḷidda-* 'poor' (daridra-) and of *dāḷiddiya-* 'poverty' (*dāridrya-) due to a *ḷ__d* < *r__d*-dissimilation (see also p. 87)? LÜDERS, *Philologica Indica* p. 548, however, regards *daḷidda-* as a wrong form. But *-ḷ-* seems to be the result if *-r-* is dissimilated: *kaḷīra-* 'sprout' < karīra-. As to the 'dental' nature of *r* see § 14.14 *rem.*

[4] *cūḷa-* 'small' seems to presuppose an intermediate form (**cūḍa-* <) *kṣuḍra- < kṣudra- (cf. PISCHEL § 294). On *culla-* see § 16.7. Most difficult is the explanation of *cūḷāsīti-* (~ *cullāsīti-*) 'eighty-four'. Is it a kind of folk-etymological transformation of **corāsīti-* < (*)*caurāsīti-* < (*)caturāśīti- (cf. Pkt. *corāsīi-* / *caurāsīi-*)?

[5] See OBERLIES (1995a: 148).

[6] For Prakrit see PISCHEL § 238 / 244.

On Pāli *unnaḷa-* (allegedly < *unnata-* [KERN, Toev. II,101, PED s.v.]) see BROUGH (1962: 279-281).

kuḍumal(ak)a- 'bud'[1]; (**b**) Sometimes *-ḷ-* (from older *-ḍ-*) develops to *-l-*[2]. Moreover, the Pāli manuscripts very often write *-l-* where we expect *-ḷ-* (see LÜDERS, *Philologica Indica* p. 548, and VON HINÜBER § 198)[3]; (**c**) The word-initial *ḍ-* of the (new) 'root' √*ḍah* 'burns' (see § 14.6) is only once changed to *-ḷ-* between vowels in a verbal form (a means to keep the root intact): *viḷayhase* 'you are burnt', Ja II 220,12*; (**d**) *uḷāra-* 'excellent' (udāra-) has an 'emphatic' cerebral[4]; (**e**) *veḷu-* 'bamboo' is reshaped from *veṇu-* after *naḷa-*[5]; (**f**) *mālā+guḷa-* 'garland' has its *-ḷ-* by assimilation from *guṇa-*; (**g**) Pāli keeps *b* and *v* – as a rule[6] – apart: *buḍḍha-* 'old' is not < vṛddha- but < *bṛḍḍha- ← *bṛḍha-[7], and Epic *kavala-* 'mouthful' is a Sans-

---

1 *sahoḍha-* 'together with the stolen goods', Mhv XXIII 11, XXXV 11 (and a lot of [sub]commentaries), however, is not *saha* + *ūḍha-* (*pace* GEIGER § 35 and PED s.v. saha[1]) but *sa* + *hoḍha-* the latter being (probably) an Iranian loanword which is also attested in the Dharmaśāstra (see BURROW, *Ural-Altaische Jahrbücher* 47 [1975] 30-34). Burmese manuscripts (of the [sub]commentaries) regularly change the word to *sahoḍḍha-* (cf. Sadd 71,13 n. a, 781,6 and VON HINÜBER § 198).

2 Cf. *Koliya*, D II 167,7, ~ *Kraudya*, MPS (Ed. Waldschmidt) 51,13, *nāla-* 'stalk', Vin I 306,8, ~ *nāḷī-* (< nāḍī-).

3 And *vice versa* (see LÜDERS 1954: 52).

4 See BERGER (1955: 73 n. 144).

5 See VON HINÜBER § 207 (*pace* GEIGER § 43.3). For the Prakrit word see PISCHEL § 243.

6 Cf. *vusīma(nt)-* 'having a seat of grass' (bṛsīmant-) – on this word see CAILLAT, *Panels of the VIIth World Sanskrit Conference: Vol. VI.* Leiden 1991, 90-91 – and *Saṃvara* (Śambara), Ja V 452,31*, *savara-* (śabara-), Vin I 168. And also *-hv-* results in *-bbh-* (see § 18.6). As to geminated *-v-* > *-bb-* see § 14.9. For *b* ~ *v* in Prakrit see PISCHEL § 201.

7 See BERGER (1955: 55) and CDIAL 9271 (*pace* GEIGER § 46.1 and LÜDERS, *Philologica Indica* p. 568).

kritisation of (MIA/Pāli) *kabal/ḷa-* < *kabaḍa-[1]; (**h**) Onomatopoetic words (cf. MORRIS, *JPTS* 1884, 106-107, 1889, 209, MALLIK, *Indian Culture* 15 [1948/49] 159-161, and EMENEAU, *Language* 45 [1969] 274-299) and words of uncertain etymology are not taken into account in the following *conspectus* of the evolution of consonants from OIA to Pāli.

§ 14. There are, however, a number of exceptions to this general rule (§ 13). – **1.** Word-initial *≠k- ≠t-*, *≠p-* and *≠b-*[2] are often aspirated due to the presence of a following *-S-* or *-r / -l- / -ḷ-*[3]: *khuṃseti* 'scolds' (kutsayati)[4], *khīla- / khīḷa-* 'peg' (kīla-)[5], *khiḍḍā-* 'play, amusement' (**khīḷa-* < *kīḷā-* < krīḍā-)[6], *thusa-* 'husk of grain' (tuṣa-), *pharasu-* 'hatchet, axe' (pa-

---

[1] See LÜDERS, *Philologica Indica* p. 559. On *jalābu-* 'womb, placenta' (jarāyu-) see LÜDERS (1954: 53-54) and BERGER (1956: 103).

[2] *ghara-* 'house' is (most probably) not cognate to OIA *gṛha-* and (consequently) does not belong here (see TURNER 1975: 188-190).

[3] See GEIGER § 40.1a / 62.1 and VON HINÜBER § 185 (cf. TEDESCO, *Language* 22 [1946] 187-188, MALLIK, *Journal of the Andhra Historical Research Society* 34 [1974/75] 60-62, and – for New Indo-Aryan – TURNER 1975: 118 and BLOCH, *La formation de la langue marathe* § 84). For Prakrit see JACOBI § 21, PISCHEL § 206-209 and BHAYANI (1997: 27-28).

[4] On this word see OBERLIES (1995: 119).

On *khanti-* 'preference', Sn 897, see DHADPHALE, *Synonymic Collocations in the Tipiṭaka: A Study*. Poona 1980, 48, and NORMAN (1992: 335).

[5] See CPD s.v. indakhīla (on which see also RAU, *Jñānamuktāvalī: Commemoration Volume in Honour of Johannes Nobel*. New Delhi 1959, 72) and OBERLIES (1995a: 132).

SMITH, Sadd V 1346, explains *khujja-* 'humpbacked' as a crossing of *kujja-* (kubja-) and *khañja-* 'lame' (/ *khoṇḍa-* 'lame').

[6] See also § 3.3.

raśu-), *pharusa-* 'rough' (paruṣa-)[1], *phalita-* 'grey' (palita-), Ja V 178,7*, *phalu-* 'knot of a reed' (parus-), *phāsukā-* 'rib' ([*]pārśva[kā]-), *anuphusīyati* 'is poured' / *phusāyati* 'drizzles' / *paripphoseti* 'sprinkles' (√pruṣ), *phussa-* 'name of a month' (pauṣya-), *phulaka-* 'a kind of gem' (pulaka-)[2], *bhisa-* 'lotus fibres' (bisa-), *bhisī-* 'bolster, roll' (bṛsī-), *bhusa-* 'chaff' (busa-).

rem. (**a**) *phāsuka-* 'comfortable' is not connected with Vedic *prāśu-* (*pace* GEIGER § 62.1) but is a continuation of **spārśuka-* (see TURNER 1975: 431)[3]; (**b**) Emphatic *h-* is prefixed to a number of words[4]: *hambho* 'look here!', *halaṃ* 'enough!', *hare* 'hey!', *hetaṃ* 'this one', *hevaṃ* 'thus' (see also § 25)[5]; (**c**) *katta(r)-*, Ja VI 268,6*, is a mere distortion of *khatta(r)-* 'eminent attendant of a king' (kṣattṛ-)[6]; (**d**) *bhamukha-* 'eyebrow' (~ *bhamu[ka]-* id.) shows the influence of *mukha-* 'face'[7].

---

1 On *p(h)alasata-* / *pālāsata-* '(of a) rhinoceros' (parasvant- / pārasvata-) see LÜDERS, *Kleine Schriften* p. 520-521, OBERLIES (1993/94: 161) and id. (1995a: 150 [s.v. pālāsata-]). For the *-l-* see § 14.10.

2 On *phuliṅga-* 'spark' see OBERLIES (1995a: 151).

3 On this word see CAILLAT, *JAs* 1960, 41-55.

4 See BLOCH (1965: 70, 95) and VON HINÜBER § 166. For Prakrit see PISCHEL § 338 and BHAYANI (1997: 32).

5 On *halaṃ* see PIND, *Bauddhavidyāsudhākaraḥ. Studies in Honour of Heinz Bechert on the Occasion of His 65th Birthday*. Swisttal-Odendorf 1997, 529. According to the PED also *hindagu-* 'man' belongs here (*h-inda-gu-* 'sprung [!] from Indra').

Such forms with initial *h-* (cf. *hida, hedisa-, hevaṃ*) are frequent in the eastern versions of the Aśoka inscriptions (MICHELSON, *IF* 23 [1908/09] 128 n. 5, and NORMAN 1994: 79).

6 See LÜDERS, *Kleine Schriften* p. 48, and ALSDORF, *Kleine Schriften* p. 289.

7 As to Prakrit see PISCHEL § 124.

– **2.** In some words belonging to the 'eastern' stratum of Pāli intervocalic tenues are voiced (cf. Aś Bairāṭ *adhigicya* < adhikṛtya)[1]: *paṭigacca* 'previously' (*pratikṛtya)[2], *jalogi-* 'leech' (← jalaukas-)[3], *koja-* 'armour' (kavaca-), *ekodi-* 'concentrated' (eka+ūti-)[4], *(niy)yādeti* 'cedes something to a person' (yātayati), *abhiruda-* 'cry of an animal' (°ruta- [x rudati]), *medhaga-* 'quarrel' (methaka-)[5], *thevati* 'drips' (√stip)[6]. Quite often the *-k-*

[1] See GEIGER § 38 (see also § 61), LÜDERS (1954: 77-85) and VON HINÜBER § 177 (cf. CPD. s.vv. anupadati, anussada, abhido). For Prakrit see JACOBI § 20.2a and PISCHEL § 202-204.

[2] Cf. *paṭikacca*, A III 103,13, S I 57,19 (on the etymology of *paṭigacca* see TRENCKNER, Ee of Mil, p. 421-422). See also OBERLIES (1995a: 145 [s.v. paṭigacchati]).

[3] See OBERLIES (1995: 121).

[4] On this word see LÜDERS (1954: 81 n. 1).

[5] The same softening is – most probably – seen in *udāhu* 'or' (uta), *kaliṅgara-* 'log, piece of wood' (kaḍaṅkara-), *(aggi)parijita-* 'damaged' (°paricita-), *pasada-* 'spotted' (pṛṣata-), *vidatthi-* 'span' (vitasti-), *vedana-* 'wages', Ja III 349,19* (vetana-) and *saṅghādisesa-* 'entailing suspension from the *saṅgha*' (see BLOCH 1965: 80, LÜDERS 1954: 81 n. 1 and GEIGER § 38.3). On *Māgandiya* (Māk°) see DEVAPRASAD GUHA, *Indian Culture* 10 (1944) 167-170. On *laguḷa-* 'club' (< lakuṭa- ~ laguḍa-) see CDIAL 10875. *gadhita-* 'greedy' (Ud 75,10, Mil 401,29), however, owes its *-dh-* (< grathita-) to the influence of *giddha-* with which it is used in the formula *giddhā gadhitā mucchitā ajjhopannā* (see OBERLIES 1996: 103 [*pace* GEIGER § 38.4]). On *pavedhati* see p. 64 (*rem.* d). On *gandha-* ~ *gantha-* 'tie' see NORMAN (1969: 235 [ad Th 768] and 297 [ad Th 1268]).

[6] One of the most difficult problems of Pāli phonology is the sporadic representation of OIA / Skt. *-p-* by *-v-* (on *p_v* / *v_p* > *p_p* / *v_v*-assimilations see § 14.14; on *b* ~ *v* see § 13 *rem.* g). What follows is not more than a random sample (cf. GEIGER § 38.5, VON HINÜBER § 181, Sadd V 1516 [s.v. p]): *avaṅga-* 'a line drawn at the outer corner of the eye' (apāṅga-), *avaruddha-* 'banished' (aparuddha- [see LÜDERS,

of the suffix *°ika-* is (palatalised and subsequently) dropped, a development due to terminational weakness that was favoured by the interchangeability of (*°iya-* <) *°ika-* and *°(i)ya-*[1]: *adūsiyā-* 'innocent' (~ *adūsikā-*), *anacchariya-* 'unarticulated before' (*anakṣarika-)[2], *āveṇiya-* 'specific' (~ *āveṇika-*), *etādisiya-*[3] 'such' (~ *etādisika-*), *odariya-* 'gluttonous' (~ *odarika-*), *kāsiya-* 'belonging to Benares' (~ *kāsika-*)[4], *kosiya-* 'owl' (~ *kosika-)*, *titthiya-* 'heretic' (ə: **titthika-*), *lokiya-* 'worldly' (ə: *lokika-*), *supāsiya-* '(a needle) of good eye' (ə: **supāsika-*)[5]. After *u* the

---

Philologica Indica p. 68 n. 1; diff. CPD s.v.]), *kaviṭṭha-* 'wood-apple tree' (~ *kapiṭṭha-*), *āveti* ~ *āpeti* (see p. 224 n. 4). As to *-v-* ~ *-p-* cf. *Isipatana* (*Ṛśyavṛjana- [see p. 4 with n. 4]) and *niddhāpeti* 'chases out' (nirdhāvayati). See also p. 79 n. 4. On *avaharati* 'takes away' (ava° x apa°) see SAKAMOTO-GOTO (1987/88: 369 n. 17). For Prakrit see PISCHEL § 199.

1 See VON HINÜBER § 178 (cf. GEIGER § 36, LÜDERS 1954: 78-79, BLOCH 1965: 81, NORMAN 1969: 136 [ad Th 57] and FALK, *Asiatische Studien* 45 [1991] 262-263). Diff. BERGER (1956: 104). For Prakrit see JACOBI § 20.3 and PISCHEL § 186-187.

If the *-t-* of *°ita-* was ever elided is questionable (on *pasāṭiya-* '[broken], a sort of rice' < praśāṭita- see OBERLIES 1995a: 149). But cf. NORMAN (1971: 70 [ad Thī 43] and 141 [ad Thī 382]) and id. (1992: 250 [ad Sn 531]).

2 See VON HINÜBER (1994: 17-24) and § 233 (cf. OBERLIES, *ZDMG* 147 [1997] 534).

3 Ja VI 318,14* (Ee against the mss. *°disīya-*).

4 This word – as well as *kosiya-* and *lokiya-* – may show a *k__k*-dissimilation. It is, however, possible that *kāsiya-* goes back to *kāśya-* (see BERGER, *MSS* ²4 [1954] 31 n. 4).

5 See also CPD s.vv. agārika, agghika, atthika, anucchavika/iya, PED s.vv. gamika, paccanīka, piṭṭhimaṃsika, pessiya, posāvanika, bhātika, mahatthiya (s.v. mahant → mah°), mahikā, sobhiya, sovaṇṇaya, KERN, Toev. I/19 (*veyyañjanika- / °niya-* 'soothsayer') and VON HINÜBER, *Der Beginn der Schrift und frühe Schriftlichkeit in Indien*. AWLM 1989.11, p. 48 (*Pātaligāmika- / °iya-*); on *pessika-*, Ja VI 552,5*, see Sadd

hiatus was bridged by *v*[1]: *suva-* 'parrot' (śuka-)[2].

rem. (**a**) See, however, p. 5 as to the flaws of pronunciation in the Mahāvihāra tradition; (**b**) *kālagata-* 'dead' (~ *kāla[ṃ]kata-*) is a kind of 'folk-etymology'[3].

– **3.** Sometimes intervocalic mediae are lost[4]: *sārāṇīya-* 'friendly word' (saṃrāganīya-, see § 6.3d)[5], *niya-* 'one's own' (nija-), *khāyita-* 'eaten' (khādita-), *sampāyati* 'replies' (see § 6.8). It is only in the numeral

---

452 n. c. The same alternation is probably seen in *vanamūlaphalabhāriyā*, Ja VI 563,3*, vs. *vanamūlaphalahārikā*, ibid. 578,19* (see Sadd V 1655 and cf. LÜDERS 1954: 78 n.3 [*āhariya-* < āharika-]). Here belongs also *bhariyaṃ* 'very', Ja V 387,10, if it goes back to **bharikam*.

On the abstract suffix *°ikā-* / *°itā-* (as a possible hyper-correction for *°iyā-*) see CAILLAT, *IF* 78 (1973) 248.

[1] For this (so-called) '*va-śruti*' in Prakrit see PISCHEL § 230-231, CHANDRA, *Sambodhi* 4 (1975/76) 34, and UPADHYE, *Līlavaī. A Romantic Kāvya in Māhārāṣṭrī Prākrit of Koūhala*. Bombay 1966 (Singhi Jain Series XXXI), p. 74.

[2] That means that *°ka-* was treated as a suffix. Cf. *māluvā-* < *mālukā- and *roruva-* < *ruruka- (see LÜDERS 1954: 80). On the 'hyper-Pālism' *ālupa-* , for *ālupa-* 'plant with edible tubers' (**āluva-* < *āluka-*) see LÜDERS, op. cit. 115, and NORMAN (1990: 44).

[3] See CPD s.v. anabhava.

[4] See GEIGER § 36 and VON HINÜBER § 177 (diff. BERGER 1956: 102); cf. VON HINÜBER, *Untersuchungen zur Mündlichkeit früher mittelindischer Texte der Buddhisten*. AWLM 1994.5, p. 13-14. This loss is at least as old as Pāṇini (6th century BC), as *maireya-* (< *madirá-*) shows (see p. 32 n. 8). For Prakrit see JACOBI § 20.3 and PISCHEL § 187.

[5] See LÜDERS (1954: 85-87). Diff. BAPAT, *Vāk* 2 (1952) 158-162, and BHSD s.v. sārāyaṇīya (see also VON HINÜBER § 283).

cuddasa- 'fourteen' < caturdaśa- (cf. Aś Nigalisagar *codasa-*) that a tenuis is dropped, favoured by the dissimilation of *t__d* (cf. Aś PE V *cāvudasa-* '14th day'[1] [as to *-v-* see above 2. end]). As usual, this development appears earlier in numerals than in other words.

– **4.** 'Hyper-translations' (see § 1) are responsible for the occasional representation of original mediae by tenues[2]: *ajakara-* 'Python' (ajagara-), *chakala-* 'he-goat' (chagala-), *bhiṅkāra-* 'water jar' (bhṛṅgāra-), *vilāka-* 'slender' (*vilāga- < vilagna-), *Chandoka* (Chandoga), D I 237,11,[3] *palikha-* 'bar' (parigha-), *pāceti* 'drives' (prājati), *opapātika-* 'spontaneously produced' (upa-√pad), *(a)kusīta-* '(not) lazy' ([a]kusīda-), *katana-* 'harm, injury' (kadana-), *jannutaggha-* 'reaching up to the knees' (jānudaghna-), *patara-* 'split, cleft' (pradara-), *(a)pithīyati* 'is covered' (api-√dhā), *chāpa-* 'young of an animal' (śāva-)[4]. And a genuine *°(i)ya-* may be rendered as

---

[1] See BLOCH (1965: 39 / 81) and CDIAL 4606.

[2] See LÜDERS (1954: 102-115) and VON HINÜBER § 179 (cf. GEIGER § 39 / 61 and TRENCKNER 1908: 112-114 with n. 16-19).

[3] *akilāsu-* 'untiring' is surely < aglāsnu- (as maintained by LÜDERS 1954: 102-103) and does not belong to √*klam* (so CPD I,540 [s.v.] and Sadd V 1322, s.v. kilāsu).

[4] On *(indriya)paropariya-* 'higher and lower state (of the sense faculties)' (*°paro-'varya-, see § 1) and *supicchita-* 'much desired' (*su-v-icchita-) see CPD s.v. resp. BERGER (1956: 102 n. 18) and OBERLIES (1995a: 163). On *pāpuraṇa- / pārupana-* 'dress', *pārupati* 'dresses' and *pāruta-* 'dressed' as hyper-forms of *pāvuraṇa-*, M I 359,13, / **pāruv°* (prā-√vṛ) see GEIGER § 19.2 and NORMAN (1992a: 262). See also p. 76-77 n. 6.

majjhantika- 'noon' (≠ madhyandina-) seems to remodelled after *aparanta-* and *pubbanta-* (see TRENCKNER 1908: 128). For *akalu- ~ agaru- / agalu-* 'aloes' see HIERSCHE, *Serta Indogermanica. Festschrift für Günter Neumann*. Innsbruck 1982, 121-128 (cf. PISCHEL § 123), for *Makhādeva* Sadd V 1667.

°*ika*- (cf. above 2): *rathikā*- 'street' (~ *rathiyā*- < rath$_i$yā-)[1].

rem. (**a**) Folk-etymologies are *pajāpatī*- 'wife' (prajāvatī- :: Prajāpati), *lāpa*- 'lapwing' (lāba- :: lapati)[2] and *supāna*- 'dog' (*suvāna- :: pāna-)[3]; (**b**) *hupeyya* 'might be', Vin I 8,30 (= *huveyya*, M I 171,16 *qu.* Sadd 454,24), corresponding to OIA *bhave(yya)*, characterises the rustic slang of an Ājīvika ascetic; (**c**) *khipati* 'sneezes' seems to be a remodelling of **khuvati*[4] (*kṣuvati ← [3pl.] kṣuvanti) after *khipati* 'throws'; (**d**) *hāpeti* (~ hāvayati) replaces original *jhapeti* < kṣapayati 'lights a fire'[5].

– **5.** OIA *-t(h)-* which follows a(n original) *-ṛ-* or a *-r-* is cerebralised (see § 16.5)[6], possibly an 'eastern' feature of Pāli (see p. 2): *uddhaṭa*- 'lifted; removed' (uddhṛta-), *kaṭa*- 'made' (kṛta-), *paṭi*+ (prati+), *paṭhavī*- 'earth' (pṛthivī-), *paṭhama*- 'first' (prathama-)[7].

---

1 See LÜDERS (1954: 107-108) and BERGER (1956: 104). Cf. also CPD s.v. appaṭisandhiya.

2 Cf. *alāpu*- 'bottle-gourd' (alābu), Dhp 149.

3 See OBERLIES (1996: 103-104).

It is not more than a conjecture that *dhopana*-, which signifies D I 6,13 *not* (*pace* PED s.v. and FRANKE, *Dīghanikāya*, Göttingen 1913, 9 n. 2) the 'ceremonial washing of the bones of the dead' but the 'rite of the fanning of the urn' (dhuvana-), was influenced by (OIA) *dhūpana*- 'fumigating'.

4 It is possible that the base form should be **khivati* whose *-i-* stems from the verbal adjective **khivita*- < *kṣuvita- (this explanation I found in TRENCKNER's *Radices Linguae Pālicae*).

5 See OBERLIES (1996: 103-105).

6 See GEIGER § 42.1-2 / 64 and VON HINÜBER § 195 (cf. BLOCH 1965: 58). For Prakrit see JACOBI § 21.4 and PISCHEL § 218-220.

7 See also *ambāṭaka*- 'wild mango' (ā̆mrātaka-).

rem. In some words like *āsāṭikā-* 'egg of an insect' (āśātika-), *paṭaṅga-* 'moth' (pata[ṅ]ga-), *vaṭaṃsa(ka)-* 'ear-ornament' (avataṃsa[ka]-) (and *pheṇ[ak]a-* 'foam') the reason for the cerebralisation is unclear (hence called 'spontaneous cerebralisation'[1]).

– **6.** In *ḍasati* 'bites' and *ḍahati* 'burns' the cerebral is transferred from the verbal adjectives **ḍatta-* (< **ḍaṭṭ[h]a-* < daṣṭa-) and **ḍaddha-* (a dissimilation from **daddha-* < dagdha-)[2]; see p. 87.

– **7.** OIA *-n-* is sometimes cerebralised after *ū̆*, *o*, *v* or a palatal[3]: *abbhuṇṇata-* 'raised, elevated' (abhyunnata-), *oṇata-* 'bent down' (avanata-), *oṇamati* 'bends down' (avanamati), *oṇīta-* 'taken out, removed' (avanīta-), *oṇojeti* 'pours water' (avanejayati), *goṇī-* 'cow' (*gonī-)[4], *jaṇṇu(ka)-* 'knee' (jānu[ka]-)[5], *chakaṇa-* 'dung of animals' (śakan[a]-), *(viñ)ñāṇa-* 'knowledge' ([vi]jñāna-), *pāpuṇāti* 'reaches, attains' (prāpnoti)[6], *dantapoṇa-* 'a piece of wood used for cleaning the teeth' (°pavana-), *lasuṇa-* 'garlic' (laśuna-), *vaṇi-* 'wish' (vani-), *sakuṇa-* 'bird' (śakuna-),

---

1 See VON HINÜBER § 196. For Prakrit see JACOBI § 21.4 and PISCHEL § 218 / 333.

2 See SMITH *apud* BLOCH (1965: 61) and THIEME, *Kleine Schriften* p. 979-980 (cf. GEIGER § 42.3 and TIEKEN, *Hāla's Sattasaī*, Leiden 1983, 263). For Prakrit see JACOBI § 21.4 and PISCHEL § 222.

3 See CHARPENTIER, *Indian Linguistics* 2 (1932) 56, and NORMAN (1992: 169-170 [ad Sn 100]). NORMAN, however, restricts this cerebralisation to *-n-* after a palatal consonant; for *[-]uṇ- / [-]oṇ-* he gives a different explanation (see 1992: 188 [ad Sn 206]). Cf. also GEIGER § 42.5 and VON HINÜBER § 203-206.

4 On *goṇaka-* 'blanket' see LÜDERS, *Kleine Schriften* p. 447 n. 3.

5 GEIGER's proposal (§ 64.3) to emend to *jannuka-* is certainly wrong.

6 The *-ṇ-* of Pāli is not more original than the *-n-* of OIA *prāpnoti* which is analogical (cf. AiGr. I § 168).

sakkuṇoti 'is able' (śaknoti), *saṇa-* 'hemp' (śana-), *saṇiṃ* 'gradually' (śanaiḥ), *sobhaṇa-* 'adorning' (śobhana-), *sūṇā-* 'chopping block' (sūnā-)[1]. Conversely, *-ṇ-* is analogically decerebralised[2]: *dhammena* 'by the doctrine' (dharmeṇa), *sahassāni* 'thousands' (sahasrāṇi), *savana-* 'hearing' (śravaṇa-), *kubbāna-* 'doing' (kurvāṇa-). The change *-n-* < *-ṇ-* may also occur in 'eastern' words (cf. Aś G *kāraṇa-* vs. Kh *kālana-*)[3]: *bhūnahū-* 'abortionist' (bhrūṇahan-)[4].

rem. The cerebral in *saṇati* 'rustles, roars' (~ *sanati* < svanati) is (most probably) onomatopoetic[5].

– **8.** *y* is (**a**) dissimilated to *v* in the vicinity of a palatal sound[6] and (**b**) assimilated to a neighbouring *ŭ̄*: (**a**) *ussāva-* 'dew' (avaśyāya-), *kulāva(ka)-* 'nest' (kulāya-), *Tāvatiṃsa* (*Trāyastriṃśat), *paṭiviṃsa-* 'share, part' (**paṭiyiṃsa-* [see § 7.11] < prat$_i$yaṃśa-), *migavā-* 'hunt' (*migayā- < mṛgayā-)[7], *(iddhi)visavitā-* 'mastery (of magic powers)' (°*viṣayitā-), cf.

---

1 On this word see OBERLIES (1995a: 163 [s.v. sūnā-]).

2 See MICHELSON, *IF* 27 (1910) 296 n. 2, and OBERLIES (1996: 93 n. 13).

3 Cf. VON HINÜBER § 205.

4 See SAKSENA, *BSOS* 8 (1936) 713-714, and ALSDORF, *Les Études Jaina*. Paris 1965, 46-47 (cf. NORMAN 1992: 270 [ad Sn 664]).

5 Cf. HOFFMANN, *Aufsätze zur Indoiranistik* I,131-132.

6 See GEIGER § 46, BERGER (1955: 54) and VON HINÜBER § 214 (cf. LÜDERS 1954: 54 with n. 4 and NORMAN 1992: 169 [ad Sn 100]). Cf. Aś RE XIII K °*viśava-* (°viṣaya-), PE VII Kh/Dh *vasevŭ̄* (vaseyuḥ). For Prakrit see PISCHEL § 254.

7 On *māgavika-* 'hunter' (← **magaviya-* 'hunt') see WACKERNAGEL, *Kleine Schriften* p. 338.

vanibbaka- ~ *vaṇibbaka-* 'mendicant' (*vanīvaka- < vanīyaka-)[1], (**b**) *āvudha-* 'weapon' (āyudha-), *āvuso* 'friend(s)!' (← *āyuṣvaḥ)[2], *kaṇḍūvati* 'itches' (kaṇḍūyati), *dīghāvu-* 'long-lived' (dīrghāyus-), cf. *nibbujjhati* 'wrestles' (**nivudhyati* < niyudhyate)[3], *pubba-* 'rotten matter' (*pūva- < pūya-)[4]. Conversely, *v* is dissimilated to *y* in the vicinity of *v*: *lāyitvā* 'having cut off' (*lāvitvā)[5].

rem. The articulation of the cerebral causes *v* < *y* in *kasāva-* 'astringent; yellow', *kāsāva-* 'yellow robe of a monk' (kāṣāya-).

– **9.** *-y-* has a propensity for being geminated after *ī* and *e*[6]: *dutiyyatā-* 'friendship' (*dutīyatā- < *dvatīyatā-), *bhiyyo* ~ *bhīyo* 'more' (bhūyaḥ)[7], *miyyati* 'dies' (mriyate), *veyy+* (v_iy+; on *i* > *e* see § 11.14), *hiyyo* 'yester-

---

1 On *pavecchati* 'gives' (prayacchati) see VON HINÜBER § 214 (pointing to Sadd V 1583 and BERGER 1955: 54) and OBERLIES (1995: 128-129).

GEIGER § 46 / 111.5 and BLOCH (1965: 23) see in *kīva(ṃ)* 'how many?' (≠ kiyant-) a continuation of Vedic *kī́vant-* whereas SMITH, Sadd V 1324, explains it as due to the proportion *x* : *kīdṛś-* = *tāvat-* : *tādṛś-*.

2 On this word see TEDESCO, *Gedenkschrift Paul Kretschmer*. Wien 1957, 186.

3 See VON HINÜBER § 214 / 216 (cf. KERN, *Toev.* I/171).

4 This sound change led to hyperforms like *parissaya-* 'onrush of the flood, danger' < (Eastern) *palissava-* (see SCHMITHAUSEN, in: *The Dating of the Historical Buddha*. Part 2. Göttingen 1992, 117 n. 47; the other way round BHSD s.v. parisrava).

5 See BERGER (1955: 54). On *(iṅgāla)kuyā* 'from the (charcoal) pit', Thī 386 (so read), see HAEBLER, *MSS* 16 (1964) 21-31 (cf. VON HINÜBER § 214). On *dāya-* 'forest, grove' ~ (Skt.) *dāva-* (and *dāva-* 'fire') see OBERLIES (1996: 95 n. 21).

6 See VON HINÜBER § 213. For Prakrit see PISCHEL § 91 / 252.

7 But also *yebhuyyena* 'mostly, as a rule' (see LÜDERS 1954: 13-14).

day' (h$_i$yaḥ)[1], *(a)peyya-* '(un)drinkable' ([a]peya-), *ātitheyya-* 'gift of hospitality' (āthiteya-), *koleyyaka-* 'of good breed' (kauleyaka-)[2], *theyya-* 'theft' (steya-), *dhoreyya-* 'beast of burden' (dhaureya-)[3], *bhaveyya* 'it might be' (← **bhaveyyaṃ* < [1sg.] bhaveyam)[4], *rāhaseyyaka-* 'living in seclusion' (*rāhaseyaka-)[5]. Only rarely is also *-v-* geminated[6]: *yobbana-* 'youth' (yauvana-); see § 3.3 and 14.8 (on *pubba-*).

– **10.** In eastern Aś every *-r-* developed into *-l-*, while western Aś has retained old *-r-*, and Pāli has both old *r/l* and new (eastern) *l*, sometimes side by side[7]: *antalikkha-* 'sky' (antarikṣa-), *ārabhati* 'sacrifices, kills' (ā-√labh < √rabh), *kira* 'so they say' (kila < kira), *dāleti* 'tears, cuts' (dārayati), *p(h)alasata-* / *pālăsata-* '(of a) rhinoceros' (parasvant- / pārasvata-), *māluta-* 'wind' (māruta-), *uggilati* ~ *uggirati* 'vomits', *(Isi)gili* ~ *°giri*, *pali+/pari+* (pari+). And sometimes *r* corresponds to an old *l* due to hyper-translations: *virāgita-* 'slender' (*vilāgita- ~ vilagna-), *suruddha-* 'very greedy' (sulubdha-)[8].

– **11.** Due to its enclitic nature *khalu* 'surely' lost the (feebly pronounced)

---

[1] On this word see BLOCH (1965: 93-94).

[2] On this word see OBERLIES (1997: 20-21).

[3] See VON HINÜBER § 149, id. (1999: 153-156) and NORMAN, *JPTS* 20 (1994) 225-227.

[4] On the optative suffix *-eyya-* see § 46.3 (for Prakrit see PISCHEL § 91).

[5] On this word see SMITH, *Orientalia Suecana* 4 (1955) 112.

[6] See VON HINÜBER § 216.

[7] See GEIGER § 44-45, LÜDERS (1954: 31-76), BERGER (1956: 99), NORMAN (1992: 142 [ad Sn 29]) and VON HINÜBER § 217-218. For Prakrit see PISCHEL § 256-259.

[8] See LÜDERS (1954: 36).

-*l*-, and subsequently *a* and *u* were contracted to *(kh)o*[1]. Further weakening led to *khŏ* (Ja IV 285,10*, VI 135,29*, Vin I 25,20*[2]) and *khu* (Thī 509)[3]. – **12.** The sporadic correspondence between P. *l* and OIA *y*[4] (*laṭṭhi*- 'stick, staff' < yaṣṭi-) points to a *l mouillé*[5]; the (alleged) equivalence of P. *y* and OIA *r* is due to analogy (*sakhāraṃ*, see § 33) or a difference in suffix (*vedhavera*- 'son of a widow' ~ vaidhaveya-, *sāmaṇera*- 'novice' ~ śrāmaṇeya-)[6]. As to *nhāru*- 'sinew' (≠ snā́van-) see § 1(p. 7)[7].

rem. As to *v*/*m* see § 14.14b.1 (below p. 87).

– **13.** Single consonants may arise (out of clusters) by (**a**) compensatory lengthening (see § 3.4), (**b**) shortening (of a geminate consonant) when preceded by an originally long vowel (see § 3.2b) or (**c**) analogy (*dukha*- 'pain' < *dukkha*- [< duḥkha-] after *sukha*- 'happiness')[8].

---

1 See PISANI (1952: 281), OBERLIES (1996: 107 n. 99) and id. (1997: 14) *pace* GEIGER § 20.

2 See ALSDORF (1968: 29, 39, 59).

3 Cf. *no* ~ *nu* (see SMITH 1950: 13).

4 For Prakrit see PISCHEL § 255.

5 See OBERLIES (1996: 106); cf. GEIGER § 46.3.

6 See GEIGER § 46.3. On the different meanings of the suffix *°era*- see SMITH *apud* NORMAN (1992a: 89); cf. MORRIS, *JPTS* 1891/93, 7.

7 *bāhira*- 'external' is not a direct continuation of *bāhya*- (as is suggested by PED) but a remodelling of this word under the influence of *bahir[-]* (see OBERLIES 1995: 130).

8 See SMITH (1950: 13), BECHERT (1958: 310) and OBERLIES (1993/94: 163 n. 84, 1995: 124, 1995/96: 272). The word is not recorded by PED though it is rather frequently attested: Ja I 139,10*, II 223,12*, 236,29*, 317,16*, III 204,28*, IV 118,16*, V 4,8*, 9,29*, 28,18*, 117,8*, 146,23*, 266,18*, 268,21*, 269,10*, VI

rem. On futures with *-s-* < *-sy-* see § 49.

– **14.** A number of sound sequences were prone to (**a**) assimilation (mainly *p___p* < *p___v* and *vice versa*[1]) and (**b**) dissimilation[2]: (**a**) *apilapati* 'floats (before one's mind)' (āplavate), *opilāpeti* 'immerses' (caus. of *opilavati* < avaplavate), *(abbha)sampilāpa-* 'heaping together (of clouds)' (*samplāva-), *(a)palāpa-* '(free from) chaff' (palāva-), *apāpurati* 'opens (a door)' (apā-√vṛ), *pāpuraṇa-* 'dress, cloak' (prāvaraṇa-), *pettāpiya-* 'paternal uncle' (*paitrā̆vya-)[3], *vivina-* 'forest', Ja V 70,2* (~ *vipina-*, D I 248,18)[4], *(a)v[y]āvaṭa-* '(not) occupied' ([a]vyāpṛta-)[5], *pipati* 'drinks' (*pivati*, see below)[6]; (**b**) 1. one of two identical sounds is dissimilated (often *l___n* < *n___n*, *n___l* < *l___l*[7], *v___m* < *m___m*, *l___r* < *r___r*[8] and *p___v* < *p___p*): *kipillikā-* 'ant' (pipīlikā-), *deṇḍima-* 'kettle-drum' (~ *ḍiṇḍima-*)[9],

237,11* (see also GEIGER § 32.2). For Prakrit see PISCHEL § 329.

[1] See CPD s.v. apilapati (cf. s.v. [1]avyāpajja), VON HINÜBER § 182, SMITH, *Orientalia Suecana* 2 (1953) 120 n. 2, and OBERLIES (1996: 92 n. 6).

[2] See GEIGER § 47 (on some of the words discussed above see GEIGER § 39.6). On assimilation and dissimilation see *AiGr., Nachträge zu Band I*, p. 156-159, and HOCK, *Principles of Historical Linguistics*. Berlin 1986, 61-66, 107-108.

[3] See Sadd V 1624 (cf. TRENCKNER 1908: 112 n. 16 / 128).

[4] See CDIAL 11797 (cf. VON HINÜBER § 181).

[5] For the Prakrit word see PISCHEL § 218.

[6] Most probably *pivati* (see GEIGER § 132) was also influenced by *pipāsā- / pipāsita- / pipāsi(n)-*. On *(an)eḷagala-* (*[an]elagada-) see OBERLIES, *HS* 108 (1995) 190-191.

[7] For *ṇ- / n-* < *l-* in Prakrit see PISCHEL § 260.

[8] See BERGER (1956: 100).

[9] Cf. also *dindima-* and *tindima-*, (both) Ja VI 580,30*.

takkola- 'Bdellium' (kakkola-)[1], *kaṭhita-* 'boiling' (kvathita-)[2], (**ḍaddha-* [see § 14.6] <) *ḍaḍḍha-* 'burnt' (*daddha- < dagdha-), *naṅgala-* 'plough' (lāṅgala-), *naṅgula-* 'tail' (lāṅgūla-)[3], *nalāṭa-* 'forehead' (lalāṭa-), *pilandhati* 'adorns' (~ [a]pinandhati [see p. 91]), *nisadā-* 'grindstone' (*disadā- < dṛṣad-), *vīmaṃsā-* 'consideration' (mīmāṃsā-)[4], *pabbaja-* 'reed' (balbaja-), *Nerañjarā* (Nairañjanā), *Milinda* ([gr.] Μενάνδρος)[5], *dalidda-* 'poor; beggar' (daridra-), *ludda-* 'hunter' (r[a]udra-)[6], *palissuta-* 'flowing over' (parisruta-), *(sajju)lasa-* 'resin' ([sarju]rasa-), *haliddā-* 'turmeric' (haridrā-)[7], *pavajjati* 'arrives' (prapadyate)[8], *pūva-* 'cake' (pūpa-), *posā-*

---

1 See GEIGER § 47.1 (on the Pāli word cf. LÉVI, *Études asiatiques, publiées à l'occasion du 25e anniversaire de l'École française d'Extrême-Orient*, 1925, 7-16).

2 On the verb *kaṭhati* and its transmission in the Pāli canon see VON HINÜBER (1994: 107-115). For Prakrit *paḍai* < patati see PISCHEL § 218 and OBERLIES (1993: 105 [s.v.]).

3 This word is blended with *aṅguṭṭha-* yielding *naṅguṭṭha-* (see SAKSENA, *P.K. Gode Commemoration Volume*, Poona 1960, 335).

4 See VON HINÜBER § 210. As to *m/v*-alternations see ibid. § 209 (VON HINÜBER regards *sāmi-* 'porcupine', Ja V 489,32' [< śvāvidh-] – on which LÜDERS, *Philologica Indica* p. 177, should be compared – as a 'Sinhalesism'; but even in this word a *v_v*-dissimilation may have worked). Cf. also *Upavāṇa*, D II 138,25, ~ *Upamāno*, MPS (Ed. Waldschmidt) 35,1. For this phenomenon in Prakrit see PISCHEL § 261. A *m_n* < *m_m*-dissimilation is to be found in *Mahā-Neru* (Mahā-Meru), Th 1203.

5 See GEIGER § 43.2.

6 LÜDERS, *Philologica Indica* p. 43-44 (diff. LÜDERS [1954: 68] who holds that *ludda-* is remodelled out of *lubdha-* under the influence of *raudra-*).

7 See BLOCH (1965: 77) and BERGER (1956: 100).

8 See OBERLIES (1995a: 149).

vita- ‘brought up’ (*poṣāpita-); 2. one of two similar sounds is dissimilated (often [**a**] *ṇ__t* < *n__t*, [**b**] *ḷ/l__n/m* < *d__ṅ/n/m*[1], [**c**] *dh__p/bh/m* < *bh__p/bh/m*[2], [**d**] *t__r* < *t__d* and ss__n < *sv__n < sm__n [see § 16.6]): (**a**) *khaṇati* ‘digs’ (khanati), (**b**) *uḷuṅka-* ‘ladle, spoon’ (udaṅka-)[3], *ālāna-* ‘tethering post’ (ādāna-)[4], *ālimpeti* ‘kindles’ (*ādimpeti < ādīpayati [see § 3.4]), *kalamba-* ‘name of a tree’ (kadamba-)[5], (**c**) *adhipanna-* ‘come into the power of’ (abhipanna-), *adhippāya-* ‘intention’ (abhiprāya-), *adhibhūta-* ‘overpowered’ (abhibhūta-), *adhimāna-* ‘pride’ (abhimāna-), (**d**) *tārisa-* ‘such’ (tādṛśa-)[6], *sattarasa-* ‘seventeen’ (saptadaśa-)[7]; *tikicchā-* ‘the art of healing’ (cikitsā-)[8], *digucchā-* ‘disgust’ (jugupsā-), *dighacchā-* ‘hunger’ (~ *jighacchā-* < jighatsā-), *dighañña-* ‘inferior, low’ (~ *jighañña-* <

---

[1] See OBERLIES (1995b: 191).

[2] On this dissimilatory change see HENDRIKSEN, *Acta Orientalia* 27 (1963) 71, NORMAN (1992: 273 [ad Sn 671]) and THIEME, *Kleine Schriften* p. 970-971.

[3] On *u__u* < *u__a* see § 9.11.

[4] See OBERLIES (1995b: 191).

[5] For the Prakrit word see PISCHEL § 244.

[6] See BERGER (1955: 42-43), BLOCH (1965: 81), BROUGH (1962: 255-256) and CAILLAT, *Hinduismus und Buddhismus – Festschrift für Ulrich Schneider*. Freiburg 1987, 91. The ‘suffix’ *°risa-* spread to other words (cf. CAILLAT, *Indianisme et Bouddhisme: Mélanges offerts à Mgr Étienne Lamotte*. Louvain 1980, 33-40): *kīrisa-* ‘of what kind?’ (~ *kīdisa-*), *sārisa-* ‘such, similar’ (~ *sādisa-*). On *edisa-* see p. 63-64 (*rem.* b). For Prakrit see PISCHEL § 245.

[7] For Prakrit see PISCHEL § 245.

[8] Cf. also *uttiṭṭha-* ‘left over, leavings’ < ucchiṣṭa- (see CPD s.v.).

jaghanya)[1], *pivati* 'drinks' (pibati)[2], *kumina-* 'fish net' (**kuvina-* < *kupina-[3]), *°pasmani* 'at the side of', Ja V 396,5* (*pārśvani)[4].

rem. The dissimilation of *d* to *r* is explained by the fact that *r* was pronounced as a dental flap[5].

– **15.** Folk-etymologies[6] and crossings[7] cause unetymological aspiration in medial syllables (*pace* GEIGER § 40.1b, 62.1[8]): *kakudha-* 'bull's hump'

---

1 On the dissimilation of palatals see GEIGER § 41.2 and NORMAN (1992: 356 [ad Sn 968]). LÜDERS (1954: 100-102) regards the depalatalisation of (≠)ji- > *(≠)di-* as a feature of the 'eastern' language (see also NORMAN, l.c.). For Prakrit see PISCHEL § 215 and SCHWARZSCHILD (1991: 168).

2 The next stage is the loss of such a *-v-* as we find it in Prakrit *piai* (*pivati* < pibati) and *paisai* (praviśati). A (kind of) *b_p* > *b_v*-dissimilation would be *ubbilāvita-* 'elated, happy, arrogant' if < **ubbilāpita-* (see p. 46).

3 See MORRIS, *JPTS* 1891/93, 45, and OBERLIES (1995a: 130). For *-m-* < *-p-* in Prakrit see PISCHEL § 248.

4 See CPD I,523b (discussing this form in the context of its treatment of *asmase*, Ja IV 56,23*-24*, 57,2* < [*]āśvaset). In the same way is *niddhamana-* 'outlet, drain' (Vin II 120,37, Ja VI 390,7-8) formed: *niddhamana-* < **nirdhavaṇa-* (see KERN, *Toev.* I,30 [s.v. udakāyatika] and OBERLIES 1989/90: 179 n. 65).

5 See BERGER (1956: 100) and BROUGH (1962: 255-256). NORMAN (1992: 160 [ad Sn 81]) gives a number of examples of '*d/r*-alternation'. Some of them – it seems – are due to *r_t* < *d_t*-dissimilation.

6 See TRENCKNER (1908: 108 n. 6), VON HINÜBER § 185 and OBERLIES (1996: 105).

7 See OBERLIES (1996: 105).

8 GEIGER's example *acchi-* (arcis-) is only a different spelling found in Burmese mss. (see CPD s.v.).

(kakuda- x kakubha-), *sunakha-* 'dog' ([*]śunaka- :: nakha-)[1], *sukhumāla-* 'graceful' (*sukumāla-* [°kumāra] x *sukhuma-* [sūkṣma-]); cf. *aññattha* 'elsewhere' (anyatra x itthā)[2], *pipphalī-* 'pepper' (pippalī- :: *phala-*), *sakkharā-* 'gravel' (**sakkarā-* [śarkarā-] :: *khara-*), *sotthiya-* 'learned man, brahmin' (**sottiya-* [śrotriya-] :: *sotthi-* [svasti-])[3].

rem. (**a**) *°khattuṃ* 'x-times' (-kṛtvaḥ, see § 4.5) owes its aspiration to the generalisation of *(ti/catuk)khattuṃ* 'twice / three times' < [*]triṣ/catuṣ-kṛtvaḥ[4]; (**b**) *Pace* GEIGER § 37[5], an aspirate lost its occlusion[6] only due to (**I**) dissimilation, (**II**) blending[7] or (**III**) phonetical weakness of sounds at the end of a word which are often subject to changes which do not take place elsewhere and (**IV**) in words which are used very frequently ('wear and tear' effect): (**I**) *lahuka-* 'light, triffling' (laghuka-), *dahati* 'puts' (*dadhati < dadhāti), *niṭṭhuhati* / *nuṭṭhuhati* 'spits out' (**niṭṭhu-*

---

1 For Prakrit see PISCHEL § 206.

2 See MEILLET, *BSL* 30 (1930) 74 (cf. BLOCH 1965: 94 and SCHWARZSCHILD 1991: 28-36).

3 See SCHWARZSCHILD (1991: 31). On *kaccha-* ~ *kaca-* see ALSDORF, *Kleine Schriften* p. 289. If *paṭisambhidā-* belongs to √*vid* it also suffered a folk-etymological remodelling.

4 See PRINTZ, *ZII* 5 (1927) 96, SMITH, *BSL* 1929, XVIII, OBERLIES (1996: 105 n. 85) and AiGr. III § 214 gβ (*pace* GEIGER § 33, 40.1a).

5 On *suhatā-* 'friendliness' (*suha-* [< suhṛd-] + *°tā-*; cf. Skt. suhṛttā-, Mahābhārata 8,29.40) and *samīhati* 'strives after' (sam-√īh) see OBERLIES (1989/90: 171) and id. (1996: 100-101). Cf. also Pāli *Rāhul(ovāda)* vs. Aś Bairāṭ *Lāghul(ovāda)*.

6 For Prakrit see PISCHEL § 188.

7 Blendings are rather often to be met with in Pāli. Thus *santike* 'before' is a blending of *samīpe* and *antike* (SAKSENA, *P.K. Gode Commemoration Volume*. Poona 1960, 335).

bhati [√stubh])[1], *pahu-* 'able' (prabhū-)[2], *heṭṭhā* 'below' (*[a]dhiṣṭhāt, see § 11.3, 27)[3], (**II**) *pahaṃsati* 'strikes, sharpens' (*°ghaṃsati* [√ghṛṣ] x °harati), *ruhira-* 'blood' (rudhira- x lohita-)[4], (**III**) *°ehi* (°ebhiḥ)[5], (**IV**) *sāhu* 'well!' (sādhu), *hoti* 'is' (bhavati)[6]; (**c**) An aspirate loses its aspiration also due to dissimilation against another aspirate (see § 19a)[7]: *khudā-* 'hunger' (kṣudh[ā]-), *dhaṅka-* 'crow' (dhvāṅkṣa-), *pihā-* 'desire' (spṛhā-)[8]; (**d**) The correspondence of OIA *-h-* and a Pāli aspirate is (apart from *idha* 'here', see § 1 [p. 6-7]) only due to blending: *pilandhati* 'adorns' ([api]nandhati < °nahyati x °bandhati, see p. 87 above), *saṃgharati* 'collects, accumulates' (saṃharati x saṃgṛhṇāti)[9].

– **16.** The initial consonant of the second member of a 'compound' (in the

---

1 See OBERLIES (1996: 98) and PISCHEL § 120.

2 Cf. also *bahūta-* 'much' < *pahūta-* (prabhūta-) x *bahu-* (see OBERLIES 1995: 130)..

3 See OBERLIES (1996: 97-98).

4 See OBERLIES (1996: 99-100). On *momūha-* 'bewildered' (momuha- [x mūḍha-]) – allegedly from *momugha-* (GEIGER § 37) – see ibid. 100 with n. 53.

5 See TURNER (1975: 293) and BERGER, *MSS* 11 (1957) 112 n. 5.

6 See OBERLIES (1996: 100).

7 See LEUMANN, *Kleine Schriften* p. 496 n. 1 (on Pkt. *abbhuttaṇa-* < **abbhutthana-*), BERGER (1956: 108), NORMAN (1992: 151) and OBERLIES (1996: 98-99 / 105-106 [*pace* GEIGER § 37 / 40.2]). *katikā-* 'agreement' is not < *kathikā- (*pace* GEIGER § 40.2) but < **kṛtikā-* (see OBERLIES 1996: 106).

8 On *kapoṇi-* 'ellbow' (allegedly < *kaphoṇi-* [see GEIGER § 40.2b]) see OBERLIES (1996: 106 n. 89).

9 See OBERLIES (1996: 101-102). On this phenomenon in Pkt. see PISCHEL § 266-267.

broad sense) is liable to be doubled[1] (in analogy with an etymological geminate[2]): *suggati-* 'happy destiny' (~ *sugati-* [:: *duggati-*]), Dhp 18, Vv 801, *subbaca-* 'of mild speech' (~ *suvaca-* [:: *dubbaca-* < durvacas- 'of harsh words']), A III 180,1, *saparijjana-* 'together with the attendants', Pv 672, Bv X 14, *bahujjana-* 'many people'[3] (bahujana- [:: *puthujjana-*]), Ja VI 329,2*, 358,23*[4], Ap 24,7, Pv 678, *kummagga-* 'wrong path' (kumārga- [:: *(d)ummagga-*]), Ja VI 234,35*, *oggata-* 'descended' (avagata- [:: *uggata-* 'risen']), *niggilati* 'swallows down' (nigirati [:: *uggilati* 'spits out'])[5], *(ap)paṭikkūla-* '(not) disgusting'[6] (pratikūla- [: *paṭikk(ama)-*]), *rasati-bbayo* 'youth fades away', Ja III 95,18* (cf. *hrasate vayaḥ*, Mahābhārata 12,224.24)[7]. This is one of the metrical licences of the poetic language: *addiṭṭham abbhatītaṃ* (|--|◡-◡|--|) 'invisible, what has been passed', Vin I 40,34*[8], *addasa padumassare* (◡-◡-) 'he saw (me) in a lotus-

---

[1] Conversely, geminates can be simplified in this position (see also § 20): *tejasi(n)-* 'having strength' (Bv VIII 1) ~ *tejassi(n)-* (Ja V 172,14*). Such degemination – also within words – is an analogical process: *pabbajiṃ isipabbajaṃ* 'he went forth like a *ṛṣi*', Bv XVIII 9 = Ap 23,28 (Ee unmetr. *°pabbajjaṃ*).

[2] See GEIGER § 33.1, EDGERTON, *JAOS* 41 (1921) 462-465, BLOCH (1965: 93) and VON HINÜBER § 281.

[3] ~ *bahūjana-*, Ja II 208,18*.

[4] See OBERLIES (1995/96: 271).

[5] See also *anujavaṃ* (◡-◡-), Ja VI 452,6* (cf. CPD s.v. anujavati). On the other hand, the tradition secondarily introduced geminates at the seam of preverb and verb (see § 20).

[6] Beside we have *appaṭikūlaṃ*, Vv 882, which scans -◡◡--.

[7] See OBERLIES (1996: 121).

[8] See CPD s.v. [1]adiṭṭha and ALSDORF (1968: 67).

pond', Cp 152[1].

§ 15. 1. In *word-initial* position only single consonants are allowed[2] (*nh-* and *mh-* [< sn-/sm-][3] are most probably unitary phonemes – viz. 'aspirated nasals' (/N^h/)[4] – and hence can occur initially[5]: *nhāru-* 'sinew', *nhusā-* 'daughter-in-law'[6], *mhita-* 'smile')[7]. Clusters are assimilated according to § 16-18 (unless they are split up by a vowel [see § 21] – the first a western, the latter an eastern feature of Pāli) but only the second sound is retained (*khāyati* 'appears like' < khyāyate, *ñante* 'near' < nyante, *ñāṇa-* 'knowledge' < jñāna-, *vajati* 'walks' < vrajati, *thana-* 'breast' < stana-, *ṭhāna-* 'place' < sthāna-). *≠C-* as a rule corresponds to OIA *≠C(r/l/v)-*: *kamati* 'walks' (kramate), *kaṭhita-* 'boiling' (kvathita- [see p. 87]), *gāma-* 'village' (grāma-), *saṇha-* 'smooth, gentle' (ślakṣṇa-), *semha-* 'phlegm'

---

1 Gemination has also emphatic force (see CPD, *Epilegomena* 24* s.v. *doubling*, BLOCH 1965: 94): *abbhu(ṃ)* ~ *abhu* 'interj. expressive of terror', *aha-(d)dhi* 'pooh!' (see CPD s.vv. and Sadd 889 n. 8). On *ujju-* see OBERLIES (1993: 38 n. 40).

2 See GEIGER § 51.2 and VON HINÜBER § 162. Only in enclisis are two consonants allowed in word-initial position (see VON HINÜBER l.c.): *na-ppajjahe*, Ja III 14,6* (so read [see OBERLIES 1995/96: 271]). See also p.122.

3 As to 'inorganic' *-h-* after nasals see p. 225 n. 1.

4 On the phonematical status of *nh* and *mh* see VON HINÜBER § 239-242. VON HINÜBER postulates also the existence of aspirated semi-vowels, viz. y^h and v^h, and of r^h (1999: 154-155).

5 For Prakrit see PISCHEL § 268.

6 On this word see Sadd 198 n. e (cf. VON HINÜBER § 239 and OBERLIES 1996: 122).

7 See also FRANKE, *ZDMG* 50 (1896) 597. For Prakrit see PISCHEL § 210 who speaks of the "aspiration of nasals and semi-vowels".

(śleṣman-), *sita-* 'smile' (smita-)[1]. *hr-* and *hn-*, however, result in *r-* (*rassa-* 'short' < hrasva-) and (see § 22.3) *r(a)h-* (*r[a]hada-* 'pond, lake' < hradas-) and *n-* respectively (*nāvati* 'rejects' < *hnāvati)[2]. Initial palatals can *also* result from a dental followed by *-y-* (secondary from ≠*Cv__j*): *cavati* 'passes from one existence to another' (cyavate), *cāga-* 'liberality' (tyāga-), *jāni-* 'deprivation' (jyāni-), *jotati* 'shines' (dyotate), *jhāna-* '(state of) meditation' (dhyāna-), *jhaya-* '(three-cornered) pennon' (*dhyaja- < dhvaja-)[3], *ñāya-* 'right manner' (nyāya-). Only very rarely was this group split up as was ≠*Cl-* regularly (if *C* ≠ *S* [cf. *semha-*, see above]) and others sporadically: *jhiyāyati* 'meditates' (see § 21), *kilesa-* 'defilement' (kleśa-), *gilāna-* 'sick' (glāna-), *pilava-* 'a kind of duck', Vv 649 (plava-), *siliṭṭha-* 'adhering' (śliṣṭa-), *milāta-* 'withered' (: mlāna- [see § 56]), *silesuma-* 'phlegm', Pv 118 (śleṣman-), *sumarati* 'remembers' (smarati), *suve* 'tomorrow' (śvaḥ). An aspirate may go back to *SC(h)* or *CS* (for *ch-* and *jh-* see § 18.2): *khandha-* 'shoulder' (skandha-), *khalati* 'stumbles' (skhalati)[4], *khīyati* 'is exhausted' (kṣīyate), *khudda-* 'small' (kṣudra-), *chāta(ka)-* 'hungry' (psāta- 'chewed' [!]).

– **2.** Initial *sth-* of √*sthā* 'stands' and at the seam of 'compounds' develops

---

[1] On this word see VON HINÜBER § 240 / 243.

[2] See GEIGER § 49.2 and VON HINÜBER § 246. On *nāvati* see OBERLIES (1996: 120).

[3] Cf. *jhayālu-* 'adorned with pennons' (see OBERLIES 1995a: 136) ~ *dhajālu-*, Th 164. Note the development *y* < *j* in this word (due to *jh_j*-dissimilation [?]); cf. Pkt. *jhaya-* < dhvaja- (PISCHEL § 299). The suffix *°ālu-* is a common one in Pāli: *apihālu-*, Sn 852, Th 1219, *abhijjhālu-*, D III 82,10, *taṇhāluka-*, Ja II 278,22*, *piṇḍālu-*, Ja IV 46,11'. It has the characteristic *-l-* of many suffixes (see BLOCH 1965: 96 / 164 and JOHNSTON, *JRAS* 1931, 582): *mahallaka-*, Sn 313, 603, *sukhallika-*, Vin I 10,12, *aṭṭhilla-*, Vin II 266,22, *hasula-*, Ja VI 503,15* (see KERN, *Toev.* I,134), *duṭṭhulla-*, Th 114, *apāsāṇasakkharilla-*, A IV 237,28. For Prakrit see PISCHEL § 595.

[4] See OBERLIES (1995: 132).

to *(t)ṭh-* (in analogy with *[ti]ṭṭhati* < tiṣṭhati and [e.g.] *adhiṭṭhāna-* < adhiṣṭhāna-)[1]: *ṭhita-* 'standing' (sthita-), *saṇṭhāna-* 'shape, form' (saṃsthāna-), *kūṭaṭṭha-* 'immovable' (kūṭastha-).

– **3.** The sibilant of word-initial *śm-* was dropped by dissimilation against a following *ś*: *massu-* 'beard' (śmaśru-)[2]. If, however, a nasal follows the *m* was dissimilated to *v* (see § 14.14b.2, 16.6) and *sva- suffered *samprasāraṇa* (see § 9.14): *susāna-* 'burning-ground' (śmaśāna-)[3].

– **4.** On the treatment of word-initial *≠ṣ-* and *≠ś(v)-* see § 13, on that of *≠kṣ-* and *≠sk-* see § 18.2.

rem. (**a**) *dūta-* 'gambling' beside *jūta-* (dyūta-) – see Ja VI 256,28 (C^{ks}) – is a Sinhalesism[4], and *dosinā-* 'moonlit night' instead of **josinā-* (< jyotsnā-) is influenced by *dosā-* 'night' (doṣā-)[5]; (**b**) The initial *ts-* of *tsaru-* is metathesised to *st-* resulting in *th(aru)-* '(handle of a) sword' (CDIAL 6088, cf. GEIGER § 57 and PISCHEL § 327).

§ 16. **1.** Internally, two-consonant-clusters can occur. These are, however,

---

[1] See GEIGER § 64.2 and VON HINÜBER § 229. For Prakrit see PISCHEL § 309.

[2] See GEIGER § 50.2. It is, however, possible that *massu-* stands for **m^hassu-* (see § 15.1).

[3] See VON HINÜBER § 244.

[4] See M. / W. GEIGER, *Die zweite Dekade der Rasavāhinī*. München 1918, p. 74 (ad 10,2), Sadd V 1452, s.v. [1]dūta, and VON HINÜBER § 248 (on sinhal. *d* < *j* see CPD s.v. addhā-bhavati and SMITH, *JAs* 1950, 186-187 [§ 9.1] / 189 [§ 12]).

[5] See BERGER, *MSS* 14 (1959) 53-54, and VON HINÜBER § 167 (diff. NORMAN 1992: 356 [ad Sn 968]). For the Prakrit word see PISCHEL § 215.

only of the following three types[1]: (**a**) The second consonant is the same as the first one, (**b**) the first consonant is the homorganic nasal of the second (including the combination of [non-vocalic] resonants[2] plus *h* and *anusvāra* plus *s*)[3], and (**c**) the second consonant is the corresponding aspirate of the first one (e.g. *-kk-*, *-kkh-*, *-ṅk-*, *-ñh-*, *-yh-*, *-ṃs-*).

OIA consonants of different classes are treated according to the rule that the consonant of lesser power of resistance is assimilated to that of greater resisting power[4]. The general principle is that the occlusive is dominant in all positions (*sappa-* 'snake' < sarpa-, *kibbisa-* 'fault' < kilbiṣa-, *°mugga-* 'sunk down' < magna-); but the articulation of a dental (and of *ṇ*[5]) is adapted to that of a following *y*[6]: *sacca-* 'truth' (satya-), *paccamati* 're

---

[1] See ELIZARENKOVA, *Phonologie der Gegenwart*. Vorträge und Diskussionen anläßlich der Internationalen Phonologie-Tagung in Wien .... (ed. by J. Hamm). Graz – Wien – Köln 1967, 93, and VON HINÜBER § 225. For Prakrit see PISCHEL § 269.

[2] (*Non-vocalic*) *resonants* are the semi-vowels (*v*, *y*), the liquids (*r*, *l*) and the nasals.

[3] For Prakrit see PISCHEL § 272.

[4] See GEIGER § 51-54 and VON HINÜBER § 226. For Prakrit see PISCHEL § 270 / 272 / 276 / 277 / 287-288 / 296-297 and JACOBI § 27-30.

[5] Other cerebrals are not palatalised: *pāṭekkaṃ* 'for every single one', Vin IV 15,3 (< **paṭṭekkaṃ* [on the quantitative metathesis see § 3.3 / or *pā°* < *pa°* according to § 6.4] < pratyekam). On *pāṭiyekka-* (*-tyV-* > *-ṭi+ V-*) see p. 120 n. 3. A hyper-Pālism for (eastern MIA) *patteyabuddha-* (< *prāpteyabuddha- [see Sadd V 1548 s.v. patteyya (*pace* NORMAN 1991: 241)]) is *paccekabuddha-* (see also VON HINÜBER § 248). Other wrong backformations are BHS *pratyayabuddha-* and Jaina-Skt. *pratyekabuddha-*. GEIGER's (§ 55) explanation of *vekurañjā-*, M II 153,33 – allegedly from **vaikuraṇḍya-* (with palatalisation of *[ṇ]ḍ*) – is highly problematic (on this word see also DHADPHALE, *ABORI* 51 [1970] 226-228).

[6] See GEIGER § 55 and VON HINÜBER § 247, for Prakrit see PISCHEL § 280-282. If VON HINÜBER's explanation of *je* < **ajje* < *ayye* < **ā̆rye* used for addressing (female)

turns' (pratyamati)[1], *(a)taccha-* '(un)true' ([a]tathya-)[2], *kacchamāna-* 'being narrated' (kathyamāna-), *ajja* 'today' (adya), *vijjhati* 'pierces' (vidhyati), *añña-* '(an)other' (anya-), *(a)puñña-* '(de)merit' ([a]puṇya-). In some words (most probably of the eastern stratum of Pāli) this palatalisation does not take place (cf. p. 96 n. 5): *pattiya-* 'trust' (pratyaya-), *pattiyāyati* 'believes' ([*]pratyayāyati), *vyattaya-* 'reversal' (vyatyaya-)[3]. For the treatment of the groups *-tm-*, *-dm-* and *-sm-* see 6., below.

rem. In newly formed 'compounds' *-cch-* may be simplified (as a metrical licence): *achambhī* 'fearless', Sn 42, *citra-chadā* '(birds) with variegated wings', Th 1108, *abbha-chāditā* 'covered with clouds', Th 1068, *kāma-(c)chandānaṃ* (-˘---) 'of sensual pleasures', Sn 1106, *nava-chandake* 'new donation', Ja III 288,13* (B[d] *°channake*)[4], *kaṅkha(c)chidaṃ* (-˘˘-) 'cutter-off of doubts', Sn 87, *taṇha(c)chidaṃ* (-˘˘x) 'cutter-off of craving', Sn 1101[5] (cf. *ūpacchinde* [-˘--] 'he should cut off', Sn 972,

servants (see *Untersuchungen zur Mündlichkeit früher mittelindischer Texte der Buddhisten*. AWLM 1994.5, p. 8-9) is correct we have here a first trace of the development of internal *-y(y)-* to *-j(j)-* (for Prakrit see PISCHEL § 284). See also above p. 4 with n. 2.

1 See OBERLIES (1995a: 144).

2 On Pkt. *tacca-* 'truth' (**taccha-* x *sacca-* < tathya- x satya-) see SAKSENA, *P.K. Gode Commemoration Volume*. Poona 1960, 335-336 (*pace* PISCHEL § 281)

3 See NORMAN (1991: 237-244) and id. (1992: 356 [ad Sn 968]). As pointed out by NORMAN *udāvatta* 'having turned around' (udāvṛtya) can be explained as an analogical formation (*udāvatta* ~ *upagamma* [etc.]). Note *-tti-* vs. *-tta-* in the words cited!

4 See LÜDERS (1954: 17).

5 See Sadd V 1382 (s.v. ch) and SMITH, *Analecta rhythmica* (Studia Orientalia XIX:7, Helsinki 1954), p. 12 with n. 2 (cf. CPD s.v. abhi-[c]channa). For *acchādana-*, D III 160,11*, read *chādana-* with metre.

păricchatta- 'coral tree' [-⏑-x], Ja V 393,15* [cf. Sn 64][1]).

– **2.** A sibilant causes the aspiration of the assimilated cluster[2]: *acchera-* 'marvellous' (āścarya-), *sukkha-* 'dry, dried up' (śuṣka-), *pakkha-* 'fortnight' (pakṣa-), *aṭṭha-* 'eight' (aṣṭa[n]-).

– **3.** The groups *ñc* (over **ñj*) and *jñ* result in *ññ*, the latter initially in *ñ*[3] (see § 15.1): *paññavīsati-* 'twenty-five' (pañcaviṃśati-), *aññā-* 'liberating insight' (ājñā-). In the east both these groups (also if secondary [*ññ* < ny]) ended in *-ṇṇ-* (*paṇṇuvīsa-* 'twenty-five'[4], cf. *āṇā-* [see § 3.4 and 8., below]) or in *-nn-* (*pannarasa-* 'fifteen' < pañcadaśa-, *saṃmannanti* 'they decide together' < °manyante, *[u]dadhi-sannaṃ*, Ja VI 203,12*, < °saṃjñam)[5].

– **4.** If two occlusives or two nasals are in contact the first one is assimilated to the second as the stronger articulated[6]: *satthi-* 'thigh' (sakthi-), *ninna-* 'low land' (nimna-). Among the non-occlusives, sibilants and nasals dominate over liquids/semi-vowels[7] (*assa-* 'horse' < aśva-, *kassaka-* 'ploughman, peasant' < karṣaka-, *kammāsa-* 'mottled; stain, blemish' < kalmāṣa-, *mamma-* 'vulnerable point, joint' < marman-). And within the

---

1 This tree is called *pārijāta-* in the Epics (see Sadd V 1601-1602).

2 See GEIGER § 51.1 and VON HINÜBER § 228. For Prakrit see PISCHEL § 301-311.

3 See BLOCH (1965: 57) and cf. above p. 2 n. 3. For Prakrit see PISCHEL § 273.

4 On the different forms of this numeral see LEUMANN, *Maitreya-samiti*. Straßburg 1919, p. 220. Cf. *paṇṇatti- ~ paññatti-* 'designation, notion' (see PED s.v. paññatti and SMITH 1950: 39).

5 See LÜDERS (1954: 127-128) and VON HINÜBER § 250-251 (cf. GEIGER § 48 / 63.2).

6 See GEIGER § 52 and VON HINÜBER § 226. For Prakrit see PISCHEL § 270 / 278.

7 For Prakrit see PISCHEL § 279 / 315.

liquids/semi-vowels the power of resistance diminishes in the order *l*, *v*, *y*, *r*[1]: *ayya-* 'noble' (ăr̥ya-)[2], [2]*kapalla-* 'lamp-black' (*kapālya-), *pallaṅka-* 'squatting position' (*palyaṅka- < paryaṅka-), *pallate* 'is protected', Ja V 242,19* (pālyate)[3]. Resulting *-vv-* (< -vy-, -vr-, -rv-) is medially represented by *-bb-*, initially by *v-* (often written *vy-*[4]): *°tabba-* (°tavya-), *paribbaya-* 'expense, cost' (parivyaya-), *subbata-* 'strict in observing religious vows, virtuous' (suvrata-), *kubbanti* 'they make' (kurvanti), *sabba-* 'all' (sarva-), *vāḷa-* 'beast of prey' (vyāḍa-), *vyaggha-* 'tiger' (vyāghra-), *vata-* 'vow, observance' (vrata-).

Hence, the hierarchy of the Pāli consonants is as follows (see GEIGER § 51 and VON HINÜBER § 226): (**1**) (Non-palatal) occlusives, (**2**) nasals, (3) palatals, (4) sibilants, (5) *l* → *v* → *y* → *r*.

rem. (**a**) *tippa-* 'sharp, acute' (tīvra-) has got its (emphatic) *-pp-* due to its formulaic association with *dukkha-*: *dukkhā tippā kaṭukā vedanā*, M I 92,29 = 241,10 = 246,22, *vedanāhi dukkhāhi tippāhi kharāhi kaṭukāhi*, A II 116,13 ~ 143,30, cf. *vedanā dukkhā tibbā kharā kaṭukā*, S I 27,17 =110,17-18 (see TRENCKNER, Ee of Mil, p. 425 [*ad* 148,16])[5]; (**b**) On *-m/ṃr(/s/h)-* and *-m/ṃl-* see § 3.4.

---

1 For Prakrit see PISCHEL § 285-286.

2 Cf. *ayira- / ariya- < ăr̥ya-*.

3 See OBERLIES (1995a: 148).

4 See SMITH, Sadd p. X, and VON HINÜBER § 255 (cf. OBERLIES 1989/90: 174). The reason for this representation which is also used for initial *ve-/vi-* (*vyamha-* 'palace' < veśman-) is not known.

5 If FALK's conjecture that *suppa-*, Ja VI 590,28* (as *pāṭha* of the *pāḷi*), belongs to *śulba-* 'cord' (*BIS* 8 [1995] 74-75) is correct this word can be compared.

– **5.** An *r* may cerebralise a following dental (see § 14.5)[1]: [1]*aṭṭa-* 'hurt, tormented' (ārta-), *aḍḍha-* 'a half' (ardha-)[2].

– **6.** The groups *-tm-*, *-dm-* and *-Sm-* are – as a rule – split up (and *-sm-* > *-mh-*). If, however, a nasal follows, *-m-* is dissimilated to **-v-*[3] which is subsequently assimilated to its neighbouring consonant according to the above rules (see § 15.3)[4]: *atta(n)-* 'self' (*atvan- < ātman-), *assamuṭṭhika-* '[with a stone in his fist =] a particular ascetic' (aśmamuṣṭika-), *chadda(n)-* 'veil' (chadman-), *bhassanta-* 'ashes' (bhasmānta-), [1]*vissa-* 'palace' (veśman- [see § 7.4]).

– **7.** These rules are violated only in some colloquial words: *culla-* 'small'[5]

---

[1] See GEIGER § 64.1 and VON HINÜBER § 256. For Prakrit see PISCHEL § 289-291 / 333 and JACOBI § 33.

[2] See GEIGER § 64.1 and VON HINÜBER § 256.

[3] On the other hand, *-v-* if preceded by *-n-* develops to *-m-* to which the *-n-* is subsequently assimilated: *(daḷha)dhamma-/°dhammi(n)-* 'of firm bow' < (dṛḍha)dhanvan- (see OLDENBERG, *Kleine Schriften* p. 1097 n. 1, BOLLÉE, *JOIB* 33 [1983] 114 and OBERLIES 1989/90: 166-167), *Dhammantari*, Ja IV 496,7* (Dhanvantari), *dhammani* 'on dry land', S I 103,20* ([Ee *dhammaniṃ*, v.l. °*ni*] dhanvani [see TANIGAWA, *The Mikkyo Bunka* 158 (1987) 142-130]). Cf. also VON HINÜBER § 254.

[4] See SMITH, *MSL* 23 (1935) 270-271, and VON HINÜBER § 244. For Prakrit see PISCHEL § 277.

[5] Beside *khudda-* and *cūḷa-* (< *kṣudra- [see p. 21 and 72 n. 4]). Note also the initial *c-* instead of expected *ch-* (see BERGER 1955: 73).

(*kṣudla-[1] < kṣudra-)[2]; cf. *alla-* 'wet' (*ā[r]dla- < ārdra-)[3].
– **8.** The possibility of multiple development (due to 'eastern' vs. 'western' features) was also a means of differentiating meaning (see also p. 33-34)[4]: *āṇā-* 'order, command'[5], *aññā-* 'liberating insight' (ājñā-)[6], *vattati* 'exists', *vaṭṭati* 'is fit / proper (for)' (vartate)[7], *ubbattati* 'rises, swells', *ubbaṭṭeti* 'shampoos' (udvartate)[8].
– **9.** Change of the mode of articulation occurs as a rule only if the proto-canonical eastern language is involved (unless it is due to ass/dissimilations, see § 14.14; as to the depalatalisation of *≠j[i]-* see p. 89 n. 1)[9]: *ūsaḍhi-* 'sorrow, grief' (**uvasa[ṭ]ṭhi-* < *upasṛṣṭi-), Ja IV 284,11* (so read)[10], *sagghati* 'will be able', Sn 834 (śakṣyati), *bhejjati* 'will break'

---

1 Cf. *kṣullaká-*, AVŚ II 32,5, V 23,12.

2 See PISCHEL § 325, EMENEAU, *IT* 14 (1987/88) 198 n. 10, BHAYANI (1997: 5), SMITH, *JAs* 1950, 196, and CDIAL 4877 (cf. GEIGER § 62 [end]).

3 For Prakrit see PISCHEL § 111 / 294.

4 See GEIGER § 64, FRANKE, *Kleine Schriften* p. 269, and VON HINÜBER § 251 / 256.

5 Characteristic for the word in this meaning is the preservation of the preverb *ā-* (see also PISCHEL § 88).

6 See GEIGER § 63.2, CPD s.vv. and OBERLIES (1993: 30 [s.v. āṇā-]).

7 See FRANKE, *Kleine Schriften* p. 269.

8 On this word see FRANKE, *Ostasiatische Zeitschrift* 6 (1917/18) 295.

9 See VON HINÜBER § 167.

10 On this word which shows lenition *and* degemination of the consonant cluster *-ṭṭh-* < *-ṣṭ-* see OBERLIES (1989/90: 174-179). For this phenomenon in Prakrit see PISCHEL § 67.

(bhetsyati)[1], *leḍḍu-* 'clod of earth' (leṣṭu-), *aḍḍhuḍḍha-* 'three and a half' (ardha[ca]turtha-), *saṃmannanti* 'they decide together' (saṃmanyante)[2]. 'Hyper-Pālisms' are a consequence of such sound changes: *vihañña-* 'faeces' (vihanna-), *manta(bhāṇi[n])-* '[speaking] softly' (*manda- < mand[r]a-)[3].

rem. (**a**) Sometimes clusters with (**1**) sibilants and (**2**) liquids/semi-vowels are (seemingly) not assimilated[4]: (**1**) *asnāti* 'eats', *asmase* 'he should put confidence in'[5], *bhasma-* 'ashes' (Ja IV 354,2*), *(vaṅka)ghasta-* 'having swallowed the hook', *bhasta-* 'bag' (Th 1151)[6], (**2**) *-ky-* (*vākya-* 'speech', *Sakyakule* 'in the Sakya clan', Th 911), *-gy-* (*agyāgāra-* 'hut for the ritual fire[s]', *bhāgya-* 'fortune'), *-my-* (*°kamya[tā]-* 'wishing, desiring', *vinamyate* 'is bent down', Th 416), *-ly-* (*kalyāṇa-* 'good deed', *[a]tulya-* '[un]equal[led]', *balya-* 'stupidity', *dussīlya-* 'evil conduct', Dhp 162), *(-)vy-* (*apasavya-* 'situated to the left', *[a]vyatta-* 'unskilled', *avyāseka-* 'not mixing [with things impure]', *vyappatha-* 'speech' [˘-x], D III 175,25*,

---

[1] As to the dissimilation of aspirates (< **bhejjhati*) see p. 91 and § 19(a).

[2] Cf. Aś PE IV *caghati* (śakṣyati), VII *aḍha-* (aṣṭa-), *niṃsiḍhi-* (*niśliṣṭi-), *aṃbāvaḍikyā* (*āmravārtikāḥ). For Prakrit see PISCHEL § 304.

[3] See LÜDERS (1954: 126-129) and ALSDORF, *Kleine Schriften* p. 206 (cf. PISCHEL, *ZvS* 42 [1909] 167 [on *handa* < hanta]).

[4] See GEIGER § 50.2/4/6, 53.2-3, 54.5 and VON HINÜBER § 225, 242, 252-254, 258 (cf. MALLIK, *Vishveshvaranand Indological Journal* 8 [1970] 103-108).

[5] Cf. CPD s.v. assasati. On *asmiye*, Ja V 397,29*, see CPD s.v. asnāti and LÜDERS (1954: 132).

[6] See Sadd V 1652 (s.v. 1/2bhasta). On Ja IV 301,14*-15* (*bhastā mātā* ...) see LÜDERS, *Philologica Indica* p. 353-356, and SMITH, *Orientalia Suecana* 2 (1953) 125.

vyamha- 'palace'[1], *vyādhi-* 'illness', *pathavyā* 'on earth' [⏑--], Ja IV 340,8*, *Koravyo*, Ja IV 364,6*), *-tr-* (*[t]atra* '[t]here', *utrasta-* 'frightened', *gotrabhū-* 'destroying the lineage'[2]), *-dr-* (*adrūbha-* 'not doing harm', Ja V 222,14*[3], *udraya-* 'result', *gadrabha-* 'donkey' [-⏑x], Ja II 110,12*, V 453,26*, *ludraṃ* 'cruel', Ja VI 306,26*)[4], *br-* (*braha[nt]-* 'high'[5], *brahmacāri[n]-* 'living a holy life', *brāhmaṇa-* 'brahmin', *brūmi* 'I say'), *-kl-* (*uklāpa-* 'dirty', *niklesa-* 'without defilement'[6]), *-pl-* (*suplavatthaṃ*, Ja V 408,24* [cf. PED s.v.]), *(-)dv-* (*dvāra-* 'door', *[a]vidvā* '[not] wise', *dvi-/dve-* 'two'), *-nv-* (*anvāgameti* 'wishes something back'[7]), *sv-* (*svākāra-* 'of good disposition', *svāgataṃ* 'welcome!', *sve* 'tomorrow'), *-vh-* (*Sīhasavhayo* [-]⏑-⏑-, Dīp IX 3). These conjuncts are merely orthographical (as they are in Aś Bairāṭ [*prasāde*]) as most of them do not make position[8] (as even

---

1 On this word see CHARPENTIER, *IL* 2 (1932) 68-70, and OBERLIES (1989/90: 172-174).

2 On this word see WIJESEKERA, *Studies in Pali and Buddhism. A Memorial Volume in Honor of Bhikkhu Jagdish Kashyap*. Delhi 1979, 381-382, and VON HINÜBER (1994: 91-100).

3 See CPD s.v. [1]adūbha and VON HINÜBER § 258.

4 On *udra(b)hati* 'eats', M I 306,12/15, which puzzled GEIGER (§ 53 n. 3 [= p. 96 n. 3 in GHOSH's English translation]), as an outcome of OIA *ud-aśnāti* see § 6.3d (and cf. VON HINÜBER 1999: 153).

5 According to BERGER (1955: 21) this word is a remodelling after *mahant-*. This accounts for the development of *ṛ* into *a* but *not* for *br-* < bṛ-. What we expect is **bahant-*.

6 See BECHERT (1958: 309).

7 See also CPD s.v. anv°.

8 See WARDER (1967: 39-42), NORMAN (1969: LXI-LXII), id. (1971: LXXXIX-XC) and OBERLIES (1993/94: 155-156).

in Epic Sanskrit: *martyānāṃ ye tu vyādhayaḥ* [⏑-⏑-], Mahābhārata 11,7.7, *dināni trīṇi* [-⏑--], ibid. 5,183.27, *paralokaṃ sma draṣṭum* [-⏑--], ibid. 5,32.22, *sānukrośaś ca tvaṃ sadā* [⏑-⏑-], ibid. 3,67.14). This points to their very feeble articulation, a fact that favoured their restoration in Pāli [1]. Only sporadically do *tv*- and *dv*- scan as *tuv*- and *duv*-: *dakkhiṇamhi duvāramhi* 'at the southern door', Ap 240,14[2]; (**b**) In *ārammaṇa*- 'sense-object' < ālambana- (x ārambhana-) the occlusive is assimilated to the nasal, this perhaps being an 'eastern' feature[3] (cf. *paṇṇuvīsa*- ← pañcaviṃśati-, see above, and Aś Rum *Luṃmini-gāme* < Lumbinī°)[4]; (**c**) *aparaṇṇa*- 'primary food [rice, barley etc.]' and *pubbaṇṇa*- 'secondary food [sesame seed, beans etc.]' have preserved the historical *-ṇṇ-* as against Skt. *(°)anna*-[5].

§ 17. Clusters of three consonants are assimilated[6] according to § 16[7], except that the last consonant is not taken into account unless it is a sibilant or a *-y-* which follows a dental[8]: *abhiṇhaṃ* 'repeatedly' (abhīkṣ-

---

1 See VON HINÜBER, *WZKS* 31 (1987) 201-202.

2 See Sadd 806 n. 9 and BECHERT (1958: 309).

3 See LÜDERS (1954: 36-37 with n. 2).

4 On *ummāra*- (< umbara-) – a doubtful derivation – see LÜDERS (1954: 36 n. 2).

5 See BLOCH (1965: 58) and VON HINÜBER § 205 (cf. BAPAT, *University of Ceylon Review* 10 [1952] 67-71, BLOCH, *BSL* 36 [1935] 31 [comptes rendus] and SCHMITHAUSEN, *The Problem of the Sentience of Plants in Earliest Buddhism*. Tokyo 1991, 41 n. 231).

6 With the exceptions of clusters containing *-r-* (e.g. *indriya*-) the sequence of three consonants is – as a rule – avoided in Pāli.

7 Unless they are split by a *svarabhakti*-vowel: *dakkhiya*- 'skill' (dākṣya-), Ja I 282,17*.

8 See GEIGER § 58-59 and VON HINÜBER § 260-261. For Prakrit see PISCHEL § 334.

ṇam[1]), *aggha-* 'respectful reception of a guest' (arghya-), *atandita-* 'unwearied' (atandrita-), *kaṅkhā-* 'uncertainty' (kāṅkṣā-), *ānañca-* 'infinity' (ānantya-)[2]. The groups *-kṣn/m-* and *-tsn-*, however, were assimilated as **-ṣṇ-/-sn-/-sm-*: *tiṇha-* 'sharp' (tīkṣṇa-), *saṇha-* 'smooth' (ślakṣṇa-), *pamha-* 'eye-lash' (pakṣman-), *juṇhā-* 'moonlit night' (jyotsnā-)[3]. In the 'east' these clusters developed differently (cf. Aś Dh SE I *sakhina-* < ślakṣṇa-): *tikhiṇa-* 'sharp' (*tikhṇa- < tīkṣṇa-), *pakhuma-* 'eyelash' (*pakhma- < pakṣman-), *sukhuma-* 'minute, subtle' (*sukhma- < sūkṣma-), *kasiṇa-* 'entire, whole' (*kaṣṇa- < kṛtsna-), *dosinā-* 'moonlit night' (*josnā- < jyotsnā-)[4]. The various results are perhaps due to different syllabification (*/tīkṣ-ṇa-/* vs. */tīk-ṣṇa-/*)[5].

rem. *dāṭhā-* 'fang; row of teeth' (daṃṣṭrā-) shows compensatory lengthening (see § 3.4)[6].

§ 18. 1. The groups *-ts(y)-* and *-ps(y)-* result in *-cch-*[7]: *vaccha-* 'calf'

---

[1] This is *not* a late hyper-Sanskritism of (MIA) *abhikkhaṇaṃ* as maintained by LEUMANN, *Asiatische Studien* 18/19 (1965) 210: It is attested as early as the Jaiminīya-Brāhmaṇa and the Śrautasūtras. Pāli *abhikkhaṇaṃ* – other than Aś Bairāṭ *abhikhiṇaṃ* – seems to be re-composed out of *abhi* and *khaṇa-* < kṣaṇa- (cf. CPD s.v. and PISCHEL § 132).

[2] On *alla-* see § 16.7.

[3] On the *-ṇ-* see § 14.7.

[4] See BERGER (1955: 76-77) and p. 95 (§ 15.4 *rem.* a).

[5] See VON HINÜBER § 261 (diff. SAKAMOTO-GOTO 1988: 102); cf. TURNER, *Some Problems of Sound Change in Indo-Aryan*. Poona 1960, 16.

[6] See LÜDERS, *Philologica Indica* p. 558.

[7] See GEIGER § 57 and VON HINÜBER § 237-238. For Prakrit see PISCHEL § 327-328.

(vatsa-), *vacchati* 'will dwell' (vatsyati), *maccha-* 'fish' (matsya-)[1], *accharā-* 'female divinity' (apsaras-), *lacchāmi* 'I shall get' (lapsyāmi). As to *-ñch-* < -nts(y)- see 4. below.

– **2.** *ks* shows a twofold development. In the west it develops (over dissimilated **ṭṣ*[2]) to *cch* (/ ≠*ch-*), and in the east to *kkh* (/ ≠*kh-*)[3]; this cluster, however, results in the neighbourhood of a dissimilating *k* also in *cch*[4]: *dakkhiṇa-* 'right, southern' (dakṣiṇa-), *bhikkhu-* 'monk' (bhikṣu-), *rukkha-* 'tree' (vṛkṣa-)[5], *chamā(yaṃ)* 'on the earth', Sn 401 (kṣamā)[6], *chuddha-* 'trembling' (kṣubdha-)[7], *akkocchi* 'he abused' (ākrukṣ[at]), *chārikā-* 'ashes' (: *khāra-*), *churikā-* 'knife' (kṣurikā-). The different development is used to differentiate meaning (see § 5 *rem.* a/b): *khaṇa-* (kṣaṇa-) 'moment', *chaṇa-* 'festival'[8]. Also initial *sk-* shows this twofold representation (see §

---

[1] *kacchapa-* 'tortoise' is a remodelling of **kassapa-* (kaśyapa-) after *maccha-* (see OBERLIES, *OLZ* 93 [1998] 103).

[2] See VON HINÜBER § 235 (cf. HOFFMANN, *Aufsätze zur Indoiranistik* III,828).

[3] See OBERLIES (1996: 92 with n. 9).

[4] See BERGER (1955: 65-87), TEDESCO, *Language* 32 (1956) 501-504, GEIGER § 56 and VON HINÜBER § 232-234 (cf. KATRE, *The Journal of the Bihar and Orissa Research Society* 23 [1937] 82-96). For Prakrit see PISCHEL § 318-324.

[5] See also p. 51 n. 2.

[6] See Sadd V 1385 and VON HINÜBER § 143 (cf. TEDESCO, *Language* 32 [1956] 502-503 *pace* BERGER 1955: 73).

[7] On *nicchubhamāna-* 'throwing out', Cp 89 (~ *saṃcukṣubhe*, Jāt-m 54,2*), see OBERLIES (1995: 125).

[8] See VON HINÜBER § 234 (for Prakrit see PISCHEL § 322). Do here belong also *lakkha-* ~ *lañch°* / *nillacch°* / *nilañch°*? The word group *nil(l)añch°* which denotes 'castrating' (etc.) seems to be due to a blending (or confusion) of *nir-lakṣ(a)y°* and *nir-√akṣ* (cf.

15.1 [p. 94]): *khandha-* 'shoulder' (skandha-), *khambha-* 'prop' (skambha-), *chambhita-* 'paralysed with fear' (ska[m]bhita-). The correspondance of (voiced) ≠*jh-* to Skt. (voiceless) ≠*kṣ-* ([1]*jhāyati* 'burns, is on fire' < kṣāyati, *jhāma-* 'on fire' < kṣāma-)[1] and that of *-ggh-* to *-kṣ-* (*paggharati* 'oozes' < prakṣarati) is due to a difference in the Vedic dialects on which both languages are based (see § 1 [p. 6])[2].

rem. seḷeti (~ *usseḷ[h]eti*) 'whistles' is a continuation of *kṣveḍ(ay)ati*; this word shows yet another rendition of initial *kṣ(v)-*[3].

– **3.** Clusters of *h* and nasals or *y/v* are metathesised[4]: *pubbaṇha-* 'forenoon' (pūrvāhṇa-), *paṇhe* 'early in the morning' (prāhṇe), Ja V 24,14* / 27*[5], *(a)jimha-* '(not) crooked' ([a]jihma-), *sayha-* 'possible' (sahya-), *avhayati* 'invites' (āhvayati), *jivhā-* 'tongue' (jihvā-), *bavhābādha-* 'very ill' (bahvābādha-). Resulting *-uvh-* (< -uhv-) develops into *-ūh-* (see § 3.4). As to *-hv-* > *-bbh-* see 6. below.

rem. brāhmaṇa- 'brahmin' is a Sanskritism and hence does not comply with any Pāli sound law. Its 'etymologies' (e.g. *bāhitapāpo ti brāhmaṇo*,

---

TRENCKNER 1908: 104 and BERGER 1955: 77).

[1] Do also *jalla-* 'dirt', Ja VI 578,25*, Sn 249, and *jallikā-* 'dirt', Sn 198, (~ [Pkt.] *jhalla-*) < kṣā̆lya- ('what is to be washed off' [cf. PISCHEL § 206 and OBERLIES 1993: 79]) belong here (cf. GEIGER § 40.2)?

[2] See KATRE, *Calcutta Oriental Journal* 2 (1935) 97-105, and VON HINÜBER § 236. For Prakrit see PISCHEL § 326.

[3] Diff. KERN, *Toev.* II,78, who derives *seḷeti* from **sveḷayati*, a postulated by-form of *kṣveḍayati*.

[4] See GEIGER § 49.1 and VON HINÜBER 245. For Prakrit see PISCHEL § 330-332.

[5] See OBERLIES (1995a: 146).

Dhp 388[1]) show that it was pronounced as *b*(r)*āhaṇa-*.

– **4.** When in contact with nasals *s* develops to *h*, which is metathesised[2]; an original *ś* palatalises a following *n*: *pañha-* 'question' (praśna-), *amhanā* 'with a stone' (aśmanā), *uṇha-* 'hot' (uṣṇa-), *kaṇha-* 'black' (kṛṣṇa-), *semha-* 'phlegm' (śleṣman-), *nhāyati* 'bathes' (snāyati), *vimhita-* 'astonished' (vismita-).

– **5.** Between *-ns-* and *-ṣṇ-* a *-t-* can be inserted (a process called *abhinidhāna*)[3]: *āgañchuṃ* 'they came' (āgan$_t$suṃ)[4], *gañchāmi* 'I shall go' (*gan$_t$syāmi < *gaṃsyāmi), *hañchāmi* 'I shall beat' (*han$_t$syāmi)[5], *Kaṭṭhaka* (*Kṛṣ$_t$ṇaka)[6], *Veṭha(dīpako)*, D II 165,21 (~ Viṣṇu[dvipīyaka], MPS [Ed. Waldschmidt] 51,12). Between *-m-* and *-r-* or *-l-* a *-b-* is inserted[7] and only then is the cluster assimilated or split up[8]: *amba-* '(the fruit of the)

---

1 See Saksena, *Jhā Commemoration Volume. Essays on Oriental Subjects.* Poona 1937, 317.

2 See Geiger § 50 and von Hinüber § 239-244. For Prakrit see Pischel § 312-314.

3 On this phenomenon see Smith *apud* Bloch (1965: 91), Smith (1952: 180) and von Hinüber § 285 (cf. Manu Leumann, *Kleine Schriften* p. 333, Jacobi, *Kleine Schriften* p. 106-110, and Pisani, *IF* 48 [1930] 226-227).

4 On this form see Norman (1992: 175 [ad Sn 132]).

5 See von Hinüber § 474.

6 On this word see Katre, *Calcutta Oriental Journal* 2 (1934) 57-59, and Bloch (1965: 91).

7 Cf. Greek ἀνδρός < *ἀνρός (~ ἀνήρ).

8 See Geiger § 51.5 and von Hinüber § 284. For Prakrit see Pischel § 295 and Bhayani (1997: 11-14). Also some words of Pischel's § 267 belong here (*-ṃgh-* < -ṃh-, *-mbh-* < -mh-, *-ndh-* < *-*nh-* < -hn-).

mango tree' (*ambra- < āmra-), *tamba-* 'copper' (*tambra- < tāmra), *gumba-* 'thicket' (*gumbla- < *gumla- [see § 22.3] < gulma-), *ambila-* 'sour' (*ambla- < amla-). The *anusvāra* of the prefix *saṃ+* is elided before *-r-*, sibilants and *-h-* (see § 3.4 and 6.3d), while it is assimilated to a following *l*[1]: *sallapati* 'talks (with)' (saṃlapati), *sallitta-* 'smeared (with)' (saṃlipta-), *(a)sallīna-* '(not) disheartened' ([a]saṃlīna-).

– **6.** *v* is able to labialise a preceding occlusive[2]: *ubbha-* 'high, upwards' (ūrdhva-)[3], *bārasa-* 'twelve' (dvādaśa-). Aś Girnār *dbādasa-* shows that *v* developed into a fricative *β, which was assimilated. The cluster *-hv-* resulted in (also [see § 18.3, above]) *-bbh-*[4]: *abbheti* 'rehabilitates a monk who has been temporarily expelled' (āhvayati), *(a)pabbhāra-* '(not) steep' ([*]prahvāra-)[5], *gabbhara-* 'slope' (gahvara-).

– **7.** Under strong metrical pressure, geminate *-ss-* of terminations was simplified[6] (see § 49): *parirakkhis<s>āmi* (-˘--) 'I shall protect', Ja IV 480,11*, *passis<s>āmi* (-˘--) 'I shall see', Pv 528, *musāvādaṃ abhā-*

---

1 See VON HINÜBER § 283.

2 See GEIGER § 53.3 / 54.6 / 59.3 and VON HINÜBER § 252-255. For Prakrit see PISCHEL § 300.

3 Beside *uddha-*.

4 See VON HINÜBER § 245 and (for Prakrit) PISCHEL § 332.
The fact that *-hv-* resulted in *-bbh-* seems to show that */-vh-/* stands for */-vvh-/*. The same might hold good for */Nh/* and */yh/* (i.e. these clusters would represent */NNh/* and */yyh/*).

5 See AiGr., *Introduction générale* p. 105 n. 455, and OBERLIES, *OLZ* 93 (1998) 107 (s.v. pabbhārā-); cf. OBERLIES (1993/94: 168).

6 See OBERLIES (1996: 115-116). Cf. *tasa* 'his', Thī 406 (so read *m.c.*) < *tassa* < tasya (see VON HINÜBER § 222), *tahiṃ*, Cp 29, < *tasmin* (see ALSDORF, *Apabhraṃśa-Studien*. Leipzig 1937, 33-34) and *kāmehi* , Ja V 295,15*, < *kāmesi* (see p. 217 n. 3).

sis<s>aṃ (⏑-⏑-) 'I spoke (the oath) falsely', Pv 33 (as read by Pv-a). And this *-s-* is liable to be further weakened to *-h-* (see § 49): *kāhinti* (~ kariṣyanti) 'they will do'[1]

§ 19. Due to (**a**) dissimilation of aspirates (see p. 91 [rem. c]), (**b**) folk-etymologies and (**c**) expressive articulation in affective usage *CCh*-clusters may be deaspirated[2]: (**a**) *ugghaṭṭa-* 'rubbed, made sore' (udghṛṣṭa-), *abhivaṭṭa-* 'rained upon' (abhivṛṣṭa-), *bhejjati* 'will break' (bhetsyati [see § 16.9]), *majjhatta-* 'impartial, indifferent' (madhyastha-), *dhaṅka-* 'crow' (dhvāṅkṣa-), [1]*puṭṭha-* 'touched' (spṛṣṭa-)[3], *pihā-* 'desire' (spṛhā-), *piheti* 'longs for' (spṛhayati-); (**b**) *catukka-* 'a place where four roads meet' (*catukkha- [catuṣka-] x tika-), *takkara-* 'thief' (*takkhara- [taskara-] x °kara-[4]), *saṃtatta-* 'frightened' (**°tattha-* [°trasta-] x *tatta-* [tapta-]); (**c**) *ikka-* 'bear' (ṛkṣa-), *babbu-* 'cat' (babhru-)[5]. On the aspiration of occlusives see § 14.15.

---

[1] For the development of a sibilant into *-h-* in Prakrit see PISCHEL § 262-264 (cf. BHAYANI, *Baburam Saksena Felicitation Volume*, Poona 1965, 71-74, id. 1997: 3-4, and TURNER, *BSOS* 8 [1935/37] 210-211 *pace* BLOCH 1965: 196).

[2] See BERGER (1955: 35-37) and OBERLIES (1996: 98-99) *pace* GEIGER § 40.2, 60.2, 62.2 (cf. MALLIK, *Journal of the Ganganatha Jha Kendriya Sanskrit Vidyapeetha* 32 [1976] 50-52, and VON HINÜBER § 186). For Prakrit see PISCHEL § 213-214 / 302.
These phenomena do not explain all words which show deaspiration (see GEIGER § 62.2), e.g. *kuḍḍa-* (kṣudra- [see OBERLIES 1995a: 130]), *kukku-* (kiṣku- [see OBERLIES 1995: 117]), *leḍḍu-* (see § 16.9) or *lodda-* (rodhra-).

[3] Cf. Pkt. *puṭṭha-* (see PISCHEL § 311).

[4] Cf. *takkara-* 'one who is doing that', Dhp 19.

[5] Names of animals often show abnormal phonetics (see MEILLET, *Introduction à l'étude comparative des langues indo-européennes*. Paris [8]1937, 132, and BLOCH 1965: 95).

rem. (**a**) [2]*aṭṭa-* (artha-) 'law-suit' shows Dravidian influence[1]; (**b**) In *muccati* 'curdles, coagulates', Dhp 71 (Ee conjectures *mucchati*), the roots √*mūrch* and √*muc* are mingled[2].

§ 20. The rules of § 16-18 are partly annulled at the seam of compounds in order not to obscure the initial sound of the posterior member especially if a verb(al derivative)[3]: *ussāha-* 'effort' (utsāha-), *samussaya-* 'accumulation; body' (/sam-ut+śraya-/), *uyyāna-* 'park' (udyāna-), *tabbiparīta-* 'different from this' (tadviparīta-), *ūhasati* 'bursts out laughing' (/ud-hasati/)[4], *dovacassa-* 'ill-conduct' (daurvacasya-)[5], *duccarita-* 'misbehaviour' (duścarita-)[6], *nippesika-* 'one who uses pressure to get alms' ([*]naiṣpeṣika-)[7], *duttara-* 'difficult to be passed' (duṣṭara-)[8], *vanap-*

---

1 See D'ONZA CHIODO / PANATTONI, *IT* 5 (1977) 69-84 (cf. VON HINÜBER § 72).

2 See LÜDERS, *Philologica Indica* p. 184.

3 See GEIGER § 55 / 57 / 62.2, SAKAMOTO-GOTO (1988: 88-90) and VON HINÜBER § 237 / 249 / 280. For Prakrit see PISCHEL § 196 / 302 / 327[a].

4 See § 10.5.

5 See VON HINÜBER § 216 (cf. also PED s.v.).

6 On *niḍḍāyati* 'cuts out' (< *niṣ ḍā°) see TURNER, *Some Problems of Sound Change in Indo-Aryan*. Poona 1960, 19. On the form of the preverb cf. p. 57 n. 2.

7 On this word see RAMERS, *Die 'Drei Kapitel über die Sittlichkeit' im Śrāmaṇyaphala-Sūtra*. Bonn 1996, 278-279 (unpublished diss.); cf. OBERLIES (1995: 126) and WOGIHARA, *Asanga's Bodhisattvabhūmi. Ein dogmatischer Text der Nordbuddhisten nach dem Unikum von Cambridge im allgemeinen und lexikalisch untersucht*. Leipzig 1908, 27.

8 On *nettiṃsa-* 'sword' (~ niṣtriṃśa-) see OBERLIES (1989/90: 167 with n. 33).

pati- 'tree' (vanaspati-), *govata-* 'mode of cows' (govrata-)[1]. One of the few exceptions is *saññ°* from *saṃ-y°* in some words like *saññata-* 'self-controlled' (saṃyata-) or *saññojana-* 'bond, fetter' (saṃyojana-). The tradition, however, secondarily introduced the 'regular' geminates: *akkhobhiyā* (⏑-⏑-), Ap 19,8, *yathā haritvā nikkhipeyya* (⏑⏑-x), It 13,9* (see Sadd V 1485), *asantaṃ yo pagganhāti* (⏑--x), Ja I 511,1*[2]. As to doubling of the initial consonant of the second member of a 'compound' see § 14.16.

rem. (**a**) *adhuvaṃ* 'not permanent' (adhruvam), Ja III 63,9*, lost its geminate consonant due to the immediately following *dhuvena*; (**b**) *abbhidā* 'he split', Ja I 247,29*, II 163,25*, is a blending of *acch(indi)* and *abhidā̆* (D II 107,5* [⏑⏑-])[3]; a similar blending is *pammussati* 'forgets': *pamussati x sammussati* (pra-√mṛṣ x saṃ-√smṛ)[4].

§ 21. Conjuncts of a sonant and a stop or another sonant can be split up by a vowel (see § 5.9, 7.13, 9.15). Sometimes, however, the consonant group is assimilated *and* split up by a *svarabhakti* vowel[5] – judged by Aś

---

[1] Most probably *nittaddana-* 'paralysing', D I 11,19, belongs here (instead of **nittaddhana-* [?] < *ni-stambhana- x ni-stabdha-).

[2] Cf. *parikkhitta-* (⏑⏑-x), Anāg 115 c (see Sadd V 1564).

[3] See OBERLIES (1996: 96 n. 29).

[4] See CPD s.v. apamuṭṭha. Cf. Pkt. *pamhusai* for which see OBERLIES (1993: 109 [s.v. pamhaṭṭha-]).

[5] As a matter of fact, Indian grammarians (cf. Pāṇ 8,4.46-52) and authors of Prātiśākhyas teach that (e.g.) *-rC-* is to be pronounced as *-rCC-*. The outcome of splitting up such a cluster by an anaptyctic vowel is a *-rVCC*-syllable (see JACOBI, *Kleine Schriften* p. 58-59).

The development of *aggini-* (< agni-) – assimilation and *svarabhakti* – is comparable to *ācariya-* (< ācārya-) – shortening of a long vowel <u>and</u> *svarabhakti* (see p. 19). As to this sound change see BERGER (1955: 31), OBERLIES (1996: 108-109) and

Bairāṭ *adhigicya* (adhikṛtya)[1] and AMg. *ciyatta-* (tyakta-) an eastern feature: *aggini-* 'fire' (~ *aggi-* < agni-) – also *gini-* may go back to <*ag*>*gini-* (see § 27) –, *āroggiya-* 'good health' (ārogya-), *ekacciya-* 'single' (~ *ekacca-* < *ekatya-)[2], *Kampilliya* (Kāmpilya), Ja VI 433,15*, 464,8*, *dessiya-* 'disagreeable' (~ *dessa-* < dveṣya-), Cp 66, 119, 263, 305, *paṇḍicciya-* 'wisdom' (~ *paṇḍicca-* < pāṇḍitya-)[3], *pessiya-* 'messenger' (~ *pessa-* < preṣya-), *sakkuṇāti* 'is able' (śaknoti), *soracciya-* 'gentleness' (~ *soracca-* < sauratya-), Ja III 453,4*[4], *jhiyāyati*[5] 'meditates' (~ ^{2}*jhāyati* < dhyāyati), Th 414, 466.[6] This combined sound change occurs – as it seems – also at the seam of verbal compounds: *upakkiliṭṭha-* 'obstructed', *upakkilesa-* 'imperfection' (upa-√kliś)[7].

SMITH, *JAs* 1950, 181 (cf. CPD s.vv. *alabbiya* and [Add. and corr.] *akuppiya*, TEDESCO, *JAOS* 65 [1945] 91 n. 62, id., *JAOS* 85 [1965] 382-383, and VON HINÜBER § 156). For Prakrit see PISCHEL § 195.

[1] On this absolutive see BLOCH, *Recueil d'Articles* p. 404-408.

[2] On this word see WACKERNAGEL, *Kleine Schriften* p. 337 (*ekacca- / ekacciya-* < **ekatya- / ekatiya-* [Th 1009] < *eka-* x *dut[i]ya-*). See also Sadd 791 n. a and VON HINÜBER § 132.

[3] Cf. Sadd 624 n. 8.

[4] The metre requires °*soraciya-* or °*soracca-*.

[5] Such a 'semi-assimilation' of ≠*dy-* shows also OIA √*jyut* (see EWAia s.v. JYOT).

[6] In younger commentaries we met *kālussiya-* 'dirtiness' (kāluṣya-) which belongs here. Cf. also *Uddiyāna* < *Audyāna (see LÜDERS, *Philologica Indica* p. 496, and Sadd V 1264).

[7] It is, however, possible to see in all these words *contaminations* of the word with assimilated consonant cluster and the one with *svarabhakti* vowel: *aggini-* < *aggi-* x **agini-* .... *upakkiliṭṭha-* < **upakkiṭṭha-* x **upakiliṭṭha-* (cf. GEIGER § 33 n. 3 [= p. 79

§ 22. Beside assimilation/dissimilation (see § 14.14) Pāli knows other irregular sound changes. **1.** A special type of dissimilation is when a whole syllable is lost before or after a phonetically similar or identical syllable (*haplology*)[1]: *accu<pa>patī* 'flew up towards' (aorist of *acc-upapatati*), *aḍḍh<at>atiya-* 'two and a half' (ardhatṛtīya-), *ana<va>vajja-* 'blameless' (*anavavadya-), *anuvi<ci>cca* 'having searched thoroughly' (anuvicitya), *appaṭiss<av>a-* 'disobedient' (< * *{[s]agāravo}-[s]appaṭissa<vo>*), *avara<ra>tta-* 'the later half of the night' (apararātra-), *ā<sa>samāna-* 'hoping' (*āsasamāna-), *e<va>m-evâhaṃ ... gacchissaṃ* 'so ....', Bv II 23 (so read m.c.; cf. Ja II 40,1*, 223,15*, III 173,9*, V 504,8*, Sn 1146 [m.c.])[2], *Kara<ka>ṇḍu* (Karakaṇḍu)[3], *cira<ra>ttaṃ* 'for a long time' (cirarātram), A IV 228,4*[4], *tāvad-e<va>* 'straightway', Pv 694[5], *paccā<sā>santo* 'longing' (*paccāsāsa*nt-* < pratyā-√śaṃs), Pv 742, *paccū<sa>samaye* 'in the morning', Ja V 289,17, *pā<ya>cittiya-* 'requi-

n. 4 in GHOSH's English translation] and § 148 n. 1 [= p. 182 n. 1 in GHOSH's English translation], EDGERTON, *JAOS* 41 [1921] 464 and VON HINÜBER § 132).

[1] See CPD, *Epilegomena* 25* (s.v. *hapl(ol).*) – cf. ibid. *Additional Abbreviations (1933)* p. XXVI (s.v. *hapl.*) –, GEIGER § 65.2 and CAILLAT, *IF* 88 (1983) 313. For Prakrit see PISCHEL § 149.

[2] See MICHELSON, *IF* 23 (1908/09) 128-129, SMITH, *Orientalia Suecana* 2 (1953) 123, Sadd 632 n. f, CPD, *Epilegomena* 25* (s.v. hapl(ol).), and OBERLIES (1993: 44 [s.v. em-eva]).

[3] See CHARPENTIER, *IF* 28 (1911) 172. On *gacchisi*, Th 356, see p. 248 with n. 2.

[4] Cf. CPD s.v. anutapati.

[5] See OBERLIES (1995a: 137).

ring expiation' (*prāyaścittika-)[1], *bhuso* 'exceedingly' (*bhṛ<śa>śaḥ), Ja V 218,17*[2], *sampajān<ān>a-* 'mindful'[3]. Haplology accounts also for 'shortened' case-endings (see § 28.7, 30.8, 31.1). – **2.** (Only) in words which are subject to abnormal shortenings – such as terms of address ('allegro-vocatives') – does vowel / syllable loss occur in a medial syllable (*syncope*)[4]: *bhante* 'your honour' < *bhad(d)ante*[5] < *bhaddaṃ te*, Ja III 77,10* (cf. *bhaddaṃ vo*, Th 402)[6].

rem. It is after the model of *(pa)mutta-* ~ *(pa)mucita-* (etc.) that *patita-* loses its *-i-*: [2]*patta-* 'fallen'[7].

– **3.** Transpositions of phonemes or syllables[8] (*metathesis*) occur especially with sonants (see also § 18.3-4)[9]: *kuyirā* 'might do' (~ *kuriyā* < kuryāt),

---

[1] See Sadd V 1591. It cannot be ruled out that we have to do with a contraction of *-āya-*.

[2] See Sadd V 1661.

[3] See SMITH, *Orientalia Suecana* 3 (1954) 32 n. 3, and BERGER (1956: 110). On *upañña<pa>yissaṃ* and *upajjh<āy>ācariyā* see CAILLAT, *IF* 88 (1983) 313-314.

[4] See OBERLIES (1996: 107 n. 98) and id. (1997: 13-15) *pace* GEIGER § 20 and PISCHEL § 148.

[5] See AiGr. III § 235e (*pace* GEIGER § 98.3) and NORMAN (1969: L / 205 [ad Th 527]).

[6] On this word see LÜDERS (1954: 30), BROUGH (1962: 264) and BHAYANI, *Anusaṃdhān* 9 (1997) 104-105 (= BHAYANI 1998: 206-208).

On *pitucchā-* and *mātucchā-* see BERGER (1955: 81-82); diff. Sadd V 1608 (s.v. pitar).

[7] See GEIGER, *ZvS* 33 (1895) 576, and KERN, *ZvS* 34 (1896) 160 (cf. OBERLIES 1995: 128 [s.v. pattakaṇṇaka]).

[8] On this kind of *metathesis* see THIEME, *Kleine Schriften* p. 967-969.

[9] See GEIGER § 47.2, 49 and 65.1. For Prakrit see PISCHEL § 176 / 354.

payirupāsanti 'they honour'[1] (par$_{i}$yupāsate), *palibodha-* 'hindrance, impediment' (*pravirodha-)[2], *acchera-* 'marvellous' (*acchayira- < āścarya- [see § 11.5]), *mayhaṃ* 'me' (mahyam), *duyhati* 'is milked' (duhyate), *gadrabha-* 'ass' (gardabha-), *aḷāra-* 'curved' (arāla-), *āḷārika-* 'cook' (ārālika-)[3], *upāhanā̆-* 'sandal' (upānah-)[4], *kasaṭa-* 'dregs' (*sakaṭa- ← śakṛt-)[5], *cimilikā- ~ cilimikā-* 'kind of cloth', *makasa-* 'mosquito' (maśaka-), *vehāsaya-* 'open air' (~ *vehāyasa-* [see § 28.2l])[6], *suṇisā-* 'daughter-in-law' (*sinusā- < snuṣā- [> *suṣṇā- > suṇhā-])[7].

2.4. *Sandhi*

§ 23. External *sandhi*[8] in Pāli differs fundamentally from that in Sanskrit. It is always optional and applies only to words which are syntactically closely connected. It permits all kinds of hiatus (e.g. *so ahaṃ*, Sn 192)

---

1 On the metrical value (-‿--x) see Sadd V 1560.

2 See Thieme, *Kleine Schriften* p. 970.

3 On these two words see Lüders, *Philologica Indica* p. 560 (cf. id., *Kleine Schriften* p. 95).

See Oberlies (1995: 114).

5 On this word see Trenckner, *The Milindapañho* (PTS edition) p. 423, and Franke, *Ostasiatische Zeitschrift* 6 (1917/18) 294-295 (cf. Oberlies 1995: 116).

6 Norman (1992: 139) gives other examples of this phenomenon.

7 See Berger (1955: 82-83), Turner (1978: 378) and Oberlies (1995: 141). Diff. Norman (1992: 170): *snuṣā- > *suṇṣā- > suṇisā- / suṇhā-*.

8 See CPD, *Epilegomena* 32* (s.v. sandhi), Geiger § 66-74, Warder (1967: 43-52), Norman (1992a: 219-224), id. (1994: 169-179) and von Hinüber § 262-268 (cf. Oberlies 1993/94: 157). For Prakrit see Pischel § 156-175.

and elides and contracts initial as well as final vowels (including 'nasal' ones). Therefore it is not always obvious what vowels suffered *sandhi* change, the more so as the law of *mora* can obscure vocalic length. This is one of the reasons why the scribes secondarily restored long vowels even before geminates[1]. A historical outline of *sandhi* operations is extremely difficult, particularly as our texts show a great number of Sanskritic *sandhis* which were introduced as a result of the application of the rules of the Pāli grammarians. For practical reasons the following account is purely descriptive.

Vocalic *sandhi* is basically of two kinds, (**1**) elision and (**2**) contraction – both characterised by the replacement of two syllables by one. Each of these types exhibits several varieties. – **1.** Other than in Sanskrit, *all* vowels (*incl.* 'nasal' vowels) of *both* (**a**) the final of the previous word *and* (**b**) the initial of the following one may be elided (for the elision of a vowel before/after a similar vowel see **2.b**): (**a**) *sīharāja v' asambhīto* (va a°)[2], *ten' upasaṃkami* (tena upa°), *iv' ossajanti* (iva o°), *manas' icchasi* (°sā icch°), *Mahiy' eka°* (Mahiyā eka°), *yath'-odhikāni* (yathā-o°), *sā kath' ajja anuccaṅgī* (kathaṃ ajja), *man' amhi ... mārāpito* (manaṃ amhi)[3], *anagāriy' upetassa* (anagāriyaṃ upe°), *kath' eko ramasī araññe* (kathaṃ eko), *h' apeti* (hi ap°), *sayaneh' āvasathehi* (°hi āvas°), *p' etāni* (pi etāni), *paripucch' ahaṃ* (°pucchiṃ ahaṃ), *sādh' āvuso* (sādhu āvuso), *t' atthi* (te atthi), *tamanud' āsīno* (°nudo āsīno), *mokkh' ito* (mokkho ito), *vāyas' etto* (vāyaso etto), *jan' ocināyatu*, Ja VI 4,19* (*jano oci°*, thus Ee [unmetr.]); (**b**) *iti 'haṃ* (iti ahaṃ), *kati-haṃ* 'a few days', S I 7,15* (*kati-ahaṃ),

---

1 See SCHELLER (1967: 44).

2 See CPD s.v. asambhīta and BECHERT (1958: 309) *pace* GEIGER § 69.1.

3 See SCHELLER (1967: 12 n. 4).

karonti 'pāyaso (karonti upā°), *añjali 'ssa* (°liṃ assa), *samatimaññi 'haṃ* (°iṃ ahaṃ), *te 'bhirattā* (te abhi°), *me 'daṃ* (me idaṃ), *°khīro 'haṃ* (°khīro ahaṃ), *yo 'dha* (yo idha). If two identical vowels come together one is elided (this could be regarded as a peculiar contraction): *kec' ime* (keci ime), *m' etaṃ* (me etaṃ). In both cases (**c**) the remaining (short) vowel can be lengthened by compensation[1], even if a double consonant follows the elided vowel of the second word (in the case of *-' ā- < -e/o a-* an intermediate stage **-a a-* can be assumed[2]): (**I**) *ken' īdha* (kena idha), *saddh' īdha* (saddhā idha), *c' ūpatapeti* (ca upa°), *id' āhaṃ* (idaṃ ahaṃ)[3], *yes' īdha* (yesaṃ idha), *kukkucciy' ūpacchinde* (°iyaṃ upa°), *kassac' āhaṃ* (°ci ahaṃ), *ās' ūpasaṃpadā* (āsi upa°), *k' āhaṃ* (kiṃ ahaṃ), *sādh' āhaṃ* (sādhu ahaṃ), *s' īdha* (su idha), *am' āhaṃ* (amuṃ ahaṃ), *y' ābhivadanti* (ye abhi°), *rat' āhaṃ* (rato ahaṃ), (**II**) *Cundā ti* (Cunda iti), *bhuñjāmī ti* (°mi iti), *sū 'dha* (su idha). Repeatedly the elided vowel, especially that of a monosyllabic word (see GEIGER § 71c), was secondarily restored in form of the corresponding half vowel[4]: *ty-atthu* (t' atthu < te atthu), *ty-ābhivadī* (*t' ābhivadī < [i]ti abhi°), *ky-āssa* (*k' assa < ke assa), *ky-āhaṃ* (*k' āhaṃ < kiṃ ahaṃ)[5], *pātv-ākāsi* (*pāt' ākāsi < pātu akāsi), *khv-āssa* (kh' assa < kho assa), *sv-ājja* (s' ajja < so ajja). If *-i* and *-u* are elided before a long vowel or before a short one without its lengthening, 'Sans-

---

[1] See MICHELSON, *IF* 23 (1908/09) 269 n. 1, and SMITH *apud* BECHERT (1958: 308-309).

[2] See VON HINÜBER § 265.

[3] See OLDENBERG, *Kleine Schriften* p. 1173.

[4] See SMITH (1950: 12) and VON HINÜBER § 267.

[5] See GEIGER § 71.2, NORMAN (1971: 77) and VON HINÜBER § 268.

kritic' *sandhis* result[1]: *kāmesv-ādīnavaṃ* (°esu ādīn°), *bhavesv-ahaṃ* (bhavesu ahaṃ), Ap 516,14. Sometimes, however, this restoration went wrong: *itv-eva*, Th 869 = M II 100,5*, instead of +*ity-eva* < *it-eva < iti eva[2], *pamuty-atthi* (*pamutt' atthi < pamutti atthi). A special kind of 'elision' involves the assimilation of a final *-i* to a preceding consonant: *app ekacce*, Vin I 6,27, *app eva*, Sn 460, *app ekadā*, M I 238,30, *icc abravī*, Sn 355, *icc āha*, Ja IV 177,20*, *kacci-ss-amajjapo* (kacci si ama°), Ja VI 23,7*[3]. – **2.** Taking into account type **1.c.**, it might be said that – other than in Skt. – *all* vowels (*incl.* nasal vowels) can be contracted (and, indeed, some editors write *kenīdha* or *kenîdha* [cf. Sn 793], etc.). But if we regard this *sandhi* as an elision with (compensatory) lengthening, we have in principle the same contractions as in OIA: (**a**) Vowels, which differ in quantity only, coalesce to the corresponding long vowel (i.e. basically a *sandhi* of type **1.c**): *yassānusayā* (yassa anu°), *panāyasmā* (pana ā°), *yathābhirantaṃ* (yathā abhi°), *gavaṃpatīdha* (°pati idha). If a double consonant follows, this vowel is generally shortened (i.e. basically a *sandhi* of type **1.a**), only rarely is the long vowel restored: *yassatthāya* (yassa a°), *uṇṇassa* (uṇṇā assa), *yaṃ picchaṃ na labhati* (pi icchaṃ); *nāccasārī* (na acc°), *sāssa* (sā assa). In the same way *-aṃ*, *-iṃ* and *-uṃ* are contracted: *vācābhikaṃkhāmi* (vācaṃ abhi°), *munīdha* (muniṃ idha); (**b**) Like OIA Pāli allows the contraction of final *-a* and *-ā* with a following dissimilar vowel into *-e-* and *-o-*[4]: *nigrodhasseva* (°assa iva), *atho* (atha u), *nopa-*

---

[1] See NORMAN (1992a: 223).

[2] See TRENCKNER, Ee of Mil p. 423,19-26, and VON HINÜBER § 267. The neighbouring sounds (*i[t]v_ev* < *i[t]y_ev*) certainly favoured this 'wrong restoration' (cf. BERGER 1955: 54).

[3] See SCHELLER (1967: 20 n.), NORMAN (1994: 176-177) and PISCHEL § 174.

[4] See GEIGER § 70.

lippati (na upa°). On *kho* see § 14.11.

rem. A peculiar *sandhi* (and only very rarely attested) is *-aṃ 'C-* < *-aṃ VCC-* (*evaṃ 'sa te āsavā* [< *evaṃ assa*], M I 9,28, *pupphaṃ 'sā uppajji* [< *pupphaṃ assā*], Vin III 18,16)[1].

These *sandhi*s occur also (**a**) at the seam of (newly formed) compounds[2] and (**b**) within words (of usually more than three syllables): (**a**) *mahodadhi-* 'ocean', *mahesi-* 'great sage' (mahā+isi- [< ṛṣi-]), *att'ukkaṃsanā-* 'self-praise' (atta+ukk°), *sati'paṭṭhāna-* 'application of mindfulness' (sati+upa°), *udadh'ūpama-* 'comparable to the ocean' (°dhi+upa°); (**b**) *accāyika-* 'urgent, pressing' (āt$_i$yayika-), *accāsana-* 'eating too much' (at$_i$yaśana-), *accāhita-* 'very unfriendly' (at$_i$yahita-), *anvādhika-* 'extra supplying' ([ə: *annādhika- <] an$_u$vadhika-), *paccāmitta-* 'enemy' (prat$_i$y-amitra-), *paccūsa-* 'dawn of day' (*prat$_i$y-uṣa[ṣ]-)[3]. As to *vūpa°* (< **v$_i$y-upa°*) see § 10 rem. b (p. 58-59).

§ 24. If we disregard the preservation/restoration of (historically final) consonants as hiatus bridgers (see § 25), only *-ṃ* can suffer consonantal *sandhi* within a sentence[4]. Apart from its (frequent) replacement by

---

[1] See VON HINÜBER § 268.

[2] See GEIGER § 67.

[3] See CPD, *Epilegomena* 32* (s.v. sandhi [→ 'sandhi-*lengthening*']), and VON HINÜBER § 266.

Pāli knows a different vocalisation at the seam of preverb and noun (cf. PISCHEL § 163 and OBERLIES 1993: 21 n. 16): *pāṇā duppaṭi-ānayā* 'his vital spirits are difficult to be brought back', Ja IV 43,4* (*matassa ... pāṇaṃ paṭi-ānetuṃ na sakkā*, ct.), *paṭi-oloketha* 'look back', Ja II 406,15 (prat$_i$yavalokayati), *pāṭi-ekka-* ~ *pāṭi-y-ekka-* 'several' (prat$_i$yeka- [on *pāṭi-* see p. 96 n. 5 and cf. VON HINÜBER § 270]).

[4] See GEIGER § 66.2 / 74.3. For Prakrit see PISCHEL § 348.

-*ñ* before palatals (*karissañ ca*, Ja III 437,25*, *bheriñ carāpetvā*, Ja III 410,11), it is only affected before enclitics (incl. vocatives) which form a whole with the preceding word, thus entailing a peculiar *sandhi*[1]: *evañ-hi*, Vin I 112,8, *kathañ-hi*, *yañ-hi* ... *tañ-hi*, Th 226, *cittañ-hi*, It 13,8*, *evan-te*, *kin ti*[2], *han ti*, *man tāta*, Thī 274, *evam-eva*, *evam-me*, *evam-pi*, *yam-pi* ... *tam-pi*. If followed by *y(eva)* it is assimilated to this (see § 16.1): *tañ ñeva* (taṃ yeva)[3].

rem. The (alleged) "retrograde mutation of Anusvāra into *m*" (GEIGER § 71.2b; cf. PISCHEL § 349) is a (historical) *sandhi* (°-*Vm*-*V*°) that provides a *short* final syllable (see p. 17-18 n. 6)[4]: *yathā bandhitum icchati* (⏑-⏑-), Thī 299, *devānam issaro* (⏑-⏑-), Cp 53.

Consonants at the seam of compounds (on which see *rem.* below) and of prefix and 'root', and at the junction of a word and a following enclitic (*pace* GEIGER § 72) are assimilated, though in part according to special rules (see § 20)[5]: *jaraggava*- 'an old cow' (jarad+g°), *(a)bahiggata*° '(not) directed outside', Vv 835, *puthujjana*- (see p. 52 n.6), *gaddūhana*- (*gāṃ-dohana-)[6], *punabbhava*- (punar+bhava-)[7], *tappaccayā* (tad+pratyayāt), Cp

---

[1] See GEIGER § 74.3 and SCHELLER (1967: 11 / 19-21).

[2] See NORMAN (1994: 71-74).

[3] Cf. VON HINÜBER § 269.

[4] There are certainly cases which may be attributed to the scribes, who thus avoided writing difficult initial vowel-letters.

[5] For Prakrit see PISCHEL § 340.

[6] See OBERLIES (1995: 119).

[7] But cf. *ponobhavika*- (see p. 67 n. 6). On the *sandhi* of /-*ar*/ in Pkt. see PISCHEL § 343.

8, *tammaya-* (tad+maya-)[1], *tabbiparīta-* (tad+vi°), *accuggamma* (atyudgamya), *pituc-ca* (pituḥ+ca), Ja V 28,8*, *mātuc-ca*, Ja VI 511,2*[2], *kaccin-nu* (kacci[d]-nu)[3], *tayas-su* (trayaḥ+su), Sn 231, *lūkhas-sudaṃ homi*, M I 77,25. This gemination of consonants is, however, often analogical (see § 14.16).

Words which stand in close syntactical juncture are sometimes treated like members of a compound[4]: *na-ccaje*, Ja V 340,5*, *na-ppajahanti*, M I 14,15, *tatra-ssu,* M I 77,28. Such cases served as pattern for other units: *muni-ppakāsayi*, Sn 251.

rem. Pāli knows some peculiar types of compounds[5]: (loose cpd.) *asati-amanasikāro tasmiṃ puggale āpajjitabbo*, A III 186,1, (echo-cpd.) *akkula-pakkulikaṃ akāsi*, Ud 5,5 (CPD, s.v., reads *°bakk°*), (quasi-cpd.) *bahu[-]duccaritāni*, Sn 665 (see Ee p. 128 n. 13), (split-cpd.) *aggihuttaṃ saraṇaṃ*, Ja VI 211,25*, *ajakaraṃ medaṃ*, Ja III 484,16*, +*maraṇe kāle*, Ja III 212,5* (m.c.), *Nandane vane*, Ja V 153,29*, *amataṃ bheriṃ*,

---

1 Mind the 'tmesis' in *kāc'amha-ca-mayā khurā*, Ja VI 268,17* (so read: Sadd 202 n. e).

2 See SCHELLER (1967: 19 n. 1). According to VON HINÜBER § 344 *mātuc-ca* conceals an accusative. But it is a genitive construed (ellipitically) with *vandati*.

3 See NORMAN (1992: 369 [ad Sn 1045]).

4 See p. 93 n.2.

5 See CPD, *Epilegomena* 23* (s.v. *cpd.* → *loose cpd.*), 24* (s.v. *echo-cpd.*), 31* (s.v. *quasi-cpd.*), 32* (s.v. *split-cpd.*, cf. Additional abbreviations [1933] XXVI and SMITH, *BSL* 33 [1932] 172 n. 1), 33* (s.v. *tautol. cpd.*, cf. Additional abbreviations [1933] XXVI), 33* (s.v. *tmesis*, cf. Additional abbreviations [1933] XXVI), OBERLIES (1989/90: 157-172), id. (1996: 118-120), BECHERT (1958: 310), NORMAN (1992: 177-178) and CPD s.v. [1]amara.

Ap 5,25, 49,26, *timiraṃ pupphaṃ*, Ap 289,2, *paṭhamaṃ akāsiṃ kiriyaṃ aggaṃ saccaṃ var'uttamaṃ*, Cp 341, *gimhāne paṭhame māse*, Dīp XV 1, (tautol. cpd.) *atīta-gata-satthuno*, Th 1035, (tmesis) *mahā me bhayaṃ āgataṃ*, Ja III 210,4* (ə: *mahābhayaṃ*), *yo dhammaṃ ca vibhāgaññū* (ə: *dhammavibhāgaññū*), Ja V 121,11*, *aṭṭhārasañ ca vasso 'haṃ*, Ap 58,26 (cf. ibid. 92,23 [see CPD s.v. aṭṭhārasa-kkhattuṃ]), *ussīs'-amhi-karo*, Ap 31,6 (see Sadd 481 n. 12). Rather common are compounds with (**a**) an inversion of the expected word-order (see OBERLIES 1989/90: 159-160 n. 7), (**b**) (so-called) 'syntactical compounds' (see NORMAN 1992: 157 [ad Sn 72]) and (**c**) compounds of the type *phalāphala* (see CPD s.v. ⁴ā, SPEYER *ZDMG* 65 [1911] 316-318 and HOFFMANN, *Aufs.* I,118): (**a**) *ambapakka(ṃ)* 'ripe mango fruit', Ja III 54,14*, *akkhac-chinno* 'whose axle is broken', S I 57,22*, *hatthacchinno* 'whose hands are cut', Ja II 120,11*, *aṅgulicchinnaṃ* 'whose finger has been cut off', Vin I 91,10, *veṇikatā* 'having braided hair', Ja V 425,13** (ct. *kata-veṇiyo*), *veṇikato*, II 185,10*, *vaṅkaghastā* 'having swallowed the hook', Ja VI 113,6* (*gilitabalisā*, ct.); (**b**) *viceyyadānaṃ* 'a gift given with forethought', Ja IV 361,9; (**c**) *maggāmaggassa kovidaṃ* 'knowing every path', Sn 627. Cases as *kuttavālehi vaḷavārathehi* 'with cars (drawn by) mares whose manes were braided', D I 105,9, rather belong to the domain of syntax. On univerbated phrases see LANMAN, *JAOS* 40 (1920) 194-198, and EDGERTON, *JAOS* 79 (1959) 43.[1]

Also in compounds the sequence of three short syllables is avoided (see p. 35 n. 2): *añjanāvana-*, Ja III 274,11*, *sarabhāmigā*, Ja VI 537,31* (cf. ct.), *sāmāmigī-* 'black hind', Ja II 44,20 (Bⁱ *sāmaṃ nāma migī*), *agha-m-miga-* 'wild dangerous beast', Ja VI 247,26*, 507,5* (see CPD, *Epilegomena* 31* [s.v. *rhythm. length.*], I,549 [s.v. ajā-migga] and OBERLIES 1989/90: 160-161; cf. VON HINÜBER § 160 and NORMAN 1992: 184 [ad Sn 181-182]).

---

[1] On the abbreviation of compounds see p. 137 n. (cf. also CPD, *Epilegomena* 22* [s.v. *brachyl.*]).

§ 25. A *hiatus*, though generally permitted (including in compounds[1]), can be bridged by (**a**) a glide[2] or (**b**) a (so-called) *sandhi* consonant, which may be a relic from OIA or analogically inserted[3]. (**a**) Glides close the hiatus inside words (including compounds[4]): *aggi-m-āsīna-* 'sitting near a fire', M I 79,30*, *añña-m-añña-* 'each other, various, different'[5], *puppha-m-āsane* 'on a seat of flowers', Dhp-a I 108,20*/21*[6] (~ *pupphāsanaṃ*, ibid. 18*), *di-y-aḍḍha-* ~ *du-v-aḍḍha-* 'one and a half'[7], *piṇḍi-y-ālopa-* 'morsel of food', *vi-y-ūhati* 'removes'[8], *du-v-aṅgula-* 'two finger-breadths', *anu-v-āsati* 'sits down after' (anu-√ās)[9], *su-b-āḷhika-* 'very rich', Ja V 214,8*, *su-p-icchita-* 'much desired' (*su-v-icchita-), Ja

---

1 Cf. *hiri-ottappa°*, Ja I 129,21*, *porāṇa-isayo*, Ja VI 100,6*.

2 See GEIGER § 72.2 and VON HINÜBER § 270. For Prakrit see PISCHEL § 353.

3 See WINDISCH, *Berichte der Königlichen Sächsischen Gesellschaft der Wissenschaften* 1893, 228-246, GEIGER § 72-73 and VON HINÜBER § 271-277 (cf. id., *MSS* 44 [1985] 93-103). For Prakrit see PISCHEL § 353.

4 (Historically false) resolution of compounds creates new words (see also § 6.5 and 12.15): *middha-* 'torpor' ← *thīna-m-iddha-* < styāna+ṛddhi- 'increase of stupefaction' (see EDGERTON, *NIA* 2 [1939] 607-610; diff. SAKAMOTO-GOTO [1993: 302 n. 22] who derives *middha-* from Vedic *mṛddhá-*).

5 On these meanings see EDGERTON, *JAOS* 79 (1959) 43.

6 A parallel, viz. Ap 69,12, has *kusamāsana-* (!).

7 See CPD s.v. [1]aḍḍha.

8 In analogy *ā-y-ūhati* 'strives' is formed (see Sadd V 1243 and CPD apa-viyūhati; diff. KERN, *IF* 25 [1909] 234-239).

9 GEIGER (§ 72.2) cites *ādicco-v-udayaṃ*, It 85,4*. But this is, of course, *ādicco v' udayaṃ* 'like the rising sun'. Likewise *ubhaya-v-okiṇṇa-* is to be segmented into *ubhaya-vokiṇṇa-* (see CPD s.v.).

V 197,18*, *sa-h-Indakā* 'including Indra'[1], Pv 153, Vv 153, 292, 803, *su-h-uṭṭhitaṃ* 'well arisen', Sn 178, Vv 613; (**b**) The retention of final consonants before enclitics or in fossilised formulas (*pag-eva, sabbhir-eva, chaḷ-eva, etad-avoca, pātur-ahosi*)[2] is generalised and different (voiced) consonants (*-d-*, *-m-*, *-y-*, *-r-*, *-v-*, *-h-*)[3] are inserted to bridge *hiatus* between two words: *anva-d-eva* 'afterwards' (anvak + eva), *samma-d-aññāya* 'having understood [it] properly', *giri-m-iva* 'like a mountain', *mā rocaya-m-abhisaṅgaṃ* 'do not find delight in attachment', Ja V 6,8*, *mā pādaṃ khaṇi-y-asmani* 'do not dig in the stone', Ja III 433,11*, *dhi-r-atthu* 'woe upon ...', *°dhammena-v-onatā* 'cast down by (anything) having the characteristic of ...', Th 662, *°piyaka-h-asana°* '*piyaka*- and *asana*- trees', Ja V 420,2**. Often historical sandhis (*aggir-iva, dharaṇīr-iva*) furnish the pattern for new formations (*rājā-r-iva*), sometimes due to rhyme (*kata-r-asmāsu ... bhatti-r-asmāsu* 'done towards us ... devotion towards us' [kṛtam asmāsu ... bhaktir asmāsu], Ja V 352,10*-11*, ... *bhavanti-r-assa / ... narassa*, Ja VI 206,5*-6*)[4]. A *-y-* is inserted especially between the components of the 'umlaut' *-ai-* (see § 3.1): *na-y-idaṃ*, Thī 166, *cha-y-ime*, M I 51,16 (as to the shortening of a long vowel before a sandhi consonant, see below). In a number of words these consonants have become fixed (*yiṭṭha-* 'sacrificed' < iṣṭa-, *vutta-* 'said' < ukta-, *vuppati* 'is sown' < upyate) – a process creating doublets (*[y]eva ~ eva*, *[v]ubho*, Ja VI

[1] This word could, however, equally well be analysed as *saha* + *Indaka-*.

[2] For Prakrit see PISCHEL § 341.

[3] On these *sandhi* consonants see SMITH, *Orientalia Suecana* 2 (1953) 121, and NORMAN (1992: 142 [ad Sn 29], 163 [ad Sn p. 16,1], 174-175 [ad Sn 132], 213-214 [ad Sn 352]).

[4] See SMITH, *Orientalia Suecana* 2 (1953) 121, and CPD I,532b.

509,24*, ~ *ubho*)[1].

rem. (1) As only voiced consonants function as hiatus-bridgers, the cases where apparently *-t-* is used as such must be differently explained (*ajjatagge-* < /ajjato + agge/ [?])[2]; (2) The preverb *vo°* can continue OIA *vyapa-/vyava-*[3] as well as *(v)ava°* (*vokkamati* 'deviates from' < vyapa-/vyavakrāmati, *vohāra-* 'trade, business dealing' < vyavahāra[4], *vokkanti-* 'descent [into the womb]' < avakrānti-)[5].

Before *sandhi* consonants[6] a long vowel can be shortened (*-e* and *-o* to *-a*), and a nasal vowel may lose its nasality[7]: *(... bhariyā ... / samugga-pakkhitta) nikiṇṇa-m-antare* '(his wife) .... is put inside', Ja III 529,10*-11* (= *nikiṇṇā*, ct.), *hitva-m-aññam* 'having left the other behind', Sn 1071, *sobhañjanā lodda-m-atho pi padmakā* '*sobhañjana-*, *lodda-* and *padmaka*-trees', Ja V 405,19*, *yatha-r-iva* 'like', D I 90,17, *sarada-r-iv'* 'like ... in autumn', Sn 687, *hamsa-r-iv' ajjhapatto* 'I have arrived ... like a goose ... ', Sn 1134, *rūpañ ca-h-idaṃ bhikkhave attā abhavissa* 'If (*ce*)

---

[1] See GEIGER § 66.2. For Prakrit see PISCHEL § 336-337.

[2] See VON HINÜBER, *MSS* 44 (1985) 98-99. Note, hoewever, *su-p-icchita-* (p. 124).

[3] On Prakrit *vo-* see SCHWARZSCHILD (1991: 141-145).

[4] On this word see ANDERSEN, *Indian Studies in Honor of Charles Rockwell Lanman*, Cambridge (Mass.) 1929, 32.

[5] See GEIGER § 66.1. On *vossa-kamma-* 'making a man an eunuch', D I 12,5, see MORRIS, *JPTS* 1889, 208.

[6] In *oka-m-okata ubbhato*, Dhp 34, the *-o* of **okato* is shortened without a *sandhi* consonant being inserted (BECHERT 1955: 10).

[7] See BECHERT (1955) and VON HINÜBER § 276.

the body here were the self, o monks, ...', Vin I 13,19[1], *tassa dajjaṃ imaṃ selaṃ jalanta-r-iva tejasā* '... this stone blazing with splendour', Ja VI 181,6*. This contributed to the variety of renderings of the 'umlaut' *-ai-* (see above): *yatha-y-idaṃ* (⏑--), Sn 1092.

§ 26. Final *-aṃ* can be lengthened before an enclitic, either to *-ām-* or to *-am-m-*[2]: *bako kakkaṭām-iva* 'like the heron the crab', Ja I 223,27*, *n' etaṃ ajjatanām-iva* (m.c. for *eva*[3]) 'this does not hold true for today only', Dhp 227, *supaṇṇo uragam-m-iva* 'like an eagle ... a snake', Ja III 334,3*[4], *mam-m-iva* 'like me ... ', Ja IV 71,23*, *ghora-visam-m-iva* 'like the terrible poison', Ja V 18,4* (C^s [see also p. 18]), *sīla-paññā-sutām-iva* 'virtue, knowledge and learning', Ja III 357,18*. This *sandhi* – according to Aś Pkt. an 'eastern' feature (see p. 3)[5] – seems to be analogical to the genuine *sandhi -ām-iva*[6] (*asso ... kasām-iva* 'like the horse ... the whip', Dhp 143, *mām-iva* 'like me ...', Ja III 468,4*, *paññavatām-iva* 'like .... of

---

[1] It is, however, possible that we have to do here with *ca* 'if' (on which see p. 11).

[2] See CPD s.v. iva, OBERLIES (1993/94: 156-157 n. 39; 1995: 142; 1996: 93 with n. 10) and VON HINÜBER § 269. For Prakrit see PISCHEL § 68 / 349.

[3] On *iva* ~ *eva* see CPD s.v. iva, NORMAN (1991: 177-178) and OBERLIES (1997: 16-17).

[4] This is also to avoid the sequence of four short syllables (see CAILLAT, *BSL* 68 [1973] 113). See also p. 35 n. 2.

[5] See LÜDERS, *Philologica Indica* p. 573, and MICHELSON, *IF* 23 (1908/09) 129 n. For Prakrit see PISCHEL § 68 (Amg. *evām eva, kisām avi*).

[6] Cf. GEIGER § 71.2b.

the wise', Ja V 378,20*[1], *arahatām-iva* 'like ... of the Arhats', D II 265,19, *āloko passatām-iva* 'for those who see [it is] ... like a light', Sn 763).

§ 27. In *sandhi* any initial vowel could be dropped (see § 23), and such *sandhi* forms were sometimes generalised[2]: *(ag)gini-* 'fire' (see above § 21), *(a)re* 'hey!'[3], *tuma-* 'oneself' (ātman-)[4], *(a)neka-* 'many'[5], *(a)vaṭaṃsa(ka)-* 'a kind of ornament', *ratani-* 'cubit' (aratni-), *heṭṭhā* 'below' (adhastāt), *(i)dāni(m)* 'now' (see § 4.1)[6], *(u)daka-* 'water', *(u)posatha-* 'Uposatha' (upavasatha-), *pāna(d)-* 'sandal' (upānah-)[7], *(u)lūka-* 'owl'[8]. It is a striking fact that most of these words have a parallel

---

[1] On *bhusām-iva*, Ja II 420,18* (*bhusam eva* [!], ct.), see Sadd 636 n. 14 (pointing to Ap 547,20 for which see also BECHERT 1958: 309).

[2] On *aphaeresis* in Pāli see GEIGER § 66.1, VON HINÜBER § 278, and MALLIK, *Vishveshvaranand Indological Journal* 5 (1967) 196-197.

[3] On this word see CPD s.v. are and VON HINÜBER, *Untersuchungen zur Mündlichkeit früher mittelindischer Texte der Buddhisten*. AWLM 1994.5, p. 9.

[4] See Sadd V 1424 (s.v. tuma) where RV *tmán-* is compared (cf. OLDENBERG, *Kleine Schriften* p. 1167). The initial *ā-* of *ātman-* was also later liable to being elided in *sandhi*: *vinindan sa dvijo 'tmānam*, Mahābhārata 3,197.44 = 198.1, *dhārayeta mano 'tmani*, 12,294.13, *sarasīvāmale 'tmānam*, 1,68.64.

[5] See BECHERT (1958: 309); cf. CPD s.v. anek'-atthapada-nissita.

[6] Ja V 183,13* has to be read +*dānī* (cf. ALSDORF 1968: 33).

[7] On this word see OBERLIES (1995a: 149). Cf. *pānahā-*, Cp. 31.

[8] On *valañjeti* 'spends (money)' see GEIGER § 66.1, on *(u)raṇi-* 'ewe' see Sadd V 1279 (s.v. uraṇa), on *bhujissa-* 'free person, not a slave' (abhujiṣya-) and *sithila-* 'firm', Dhp 346 (< aśithila-), see DHADPHALE, *ABORI* 51 (1970) 228-229, on *lakāra-* 'sail', allegedly < *alaṅkāra-* (but in fact < Sinhalese **layara-* from Javanese *layar*), see

in AMg. (see PISCHEL § 141-145 and OBERLIES 1996: 107 n. 97)[1]. With 'enclitics' *aphaeresis* is particularly frequent (see GEIGER § 66.1 and VON HINÜBER § 278; for Prakrit see PISCHEL 143 and JACOBI § 14.3): *pi* (api)[2], *ti* (it'), [2/3]*va* (iva[3] / eva[4]), *mhi* (asmi), *si* (asi).

HAEBLER, *ZvS* 79 (1965) 112-122 (cf. VON HINÜBER § 113).

[1] As to the loss of initial consonants – in Pāli only in *ūkā-* 'louse' (see § 10.1) – in Prakrit see PISCHEL § 335.

[2] Cf. also *pi-thīyati* ~ *api-thīyati*, *pi-dahati* ~ *api-dheti*, *pi-landhana-* ~ *api-landhana-* (see p. 87).

[3] Synonymous with *yathā* 'like', *(i)va* received a long final: *nāgo vā ekako carati*, Ja V 190,22* (so read m.c. against Ee *va* [see ALSDORF 1968: 36]).

[4] *va* = eva, Dhp 136, Sn 38, 67, 831, *va* = iva, Dhp 28, Sn 1142.

3. Morphology

3.1. The noun

§ 28. **1.** Like OIA, Pāli distinguishes three (grammatical) genders, masculine, feminine and neuter (see GEIGER § 76 and BLOCH 1965: 149)[1]. Neuter nouns are inflected like masculines except for the nom./acc. sg. and pl., which are always identical. Pāli has lost the dual (a process partly due to the development *au* > *o* [see § 12.2][2]) which is replaced by the plural: *dve pi cakkhūni* 'both eyes', Ja IV 137,16[3], *candimasuriyānaṃ* 'of sun and moon', D I 10,14. Only a few dual forms have survived[4]: *Kakusandha-*

---

[1] The nominal system of Pāli formally distinguishes nouns and adjectives on the one hand and pronouns on the other. In addition, Pāli has – like OIA/Sanskrit – indeclinable terms (*ca, ce* [on which see OLDENBERG, *Kl. Sch.* p. 939 n. and OBERLIES 1997: 17-18], *āmo* [cf. CAILLAT, *IF* 71 (1966) 308], *no, tarahi, yadā*) including pre- and postpositions (*nadiṃ Nerañjaram pati*, Sn 425 = Thī 306 = 309 ≠ 317 = 319, *pitu gharaṃ paṭi | nayiṃsu*, Thī 419, *saddo tiro janapadaṃ suto*, Ja VI 423,26*) and preverbs, which – as a rule – occur immediately preceding the verb or another preverb. Sometimes, however, they can be separated from a verb by one or more words (see CPD, *Epilegomena* 33*-34* [s.v. *tmesis*], *Additional Abbreviations* [1933] p. XXVI, and s.vv. ajjha, antaradhāyati, anto, apagacchati, api [290a], Sadd 481 n. 12, and cf. NORMAN 1992: 273 [ad Sn 672]): *ajjha so vasi*, Bv V 22 ≠ II 207 = III 26, *antarā-pi-dhāyati*, Vin IV 54,24 (cf. *saha vā seyyaṃ kappeyya*, Vin IV 139,34**, *sacchi vā karissati*, M II 201,4-5). On adverbs see GEIGER § 102.

[2] See GEIGER § 77.1 and BLOCH (1965: 129). For Prakrit see PISCHEL § 360 and JACOBI § 38.

[3] But the nom.-acc. *akkhī* 'the eyes' (Ja II 357,6*) may well continue the old dual *akṣī́* (see AiGr. III § 158b).

[4] See CPD, *Epilegomena* 24* (s.v. *dual*), VON HINÜBER § 288, NORMAN (1991: 115-117) and OBERLIES (1995: 142).

On the elliptical dual *Vāseṭṭhā*, D III 81,1 v.l. (*tumhe khv attha* + *Vāseṭṭhā* [Ee °*ṭha*] *brāhmaṇa-jaccā brāhmaṇakulīnā brāhmanakulā agarasmā anagāriyaṃ*

Koṇāgamano, Th 490, *(ubho daṇḍaparāyanā ...) kaṭaggaho* 'both [of us] will throw the winning die', Th 462, *jaraggavāsā* 'two old oxen', Ja II 420,18* (*ubho goṇā ... mantayiṃsu*, 420,14-15)[1], *(paggayha) bhujo (kandati)* 'having stretched out his arms ...', Ja VI 113,31* (cf. *paggayha bhujāni kandati*, Ja V 28,19* [~*pragṛhya ...bhujau*, Rāmāyaṇa 3,59.2]; on the acc.pl. m. in *-āni* see § 30.6[2]), *mātāpitaro* 'mother and father', D III 66,3, Sn 404 (mātāpitarau), *vaṃ* 'you two', Ja V 375,11* (vām), *Yuvañjaya-Yudhiṭṭhilo*, Ja IV 123,15*[3]. Though the words for 'two'and 'both' (see § 43.2) are continuations of old forms, they do not represent a dual any longer (*pace* GEIGER § 77.1)[4]. – **2.** In accordance with the tendency towards simplification of the morphological system of OIA, Pāli changed consonant into vowel stems[5]: (**a**) Starting from the nominative in *-a/-āni*, *-i*, *-u* and *-ā* (< -iḥ/-uḥ/-āḥ, see § 4.2) the neuter *an-*, *is-*[6] and *us*-stems and

---

pabbajitā), see OBERLIES (1989/90: 172) – such a dual is also *Sāriputtā*, Vin II 12,29-30 = III 182,34-35 (... *Sāriputta-Moggallāne āmantesi: gacchatha tumhe Sāriputtā*). See also p. 144 n. 5.

[1] See Sadd V 1233 (s.v. *ā*); but cf. VON HINÜBER § 288 (reads *jaraggavā* with C[e]B[e]).

[2] A word like *bhuja-* may have suffered a change of gender. But *bhujo* < bhujau is no doubt masculine (cf. B[d] [ad Ja VI 113,31*] *bhuje*).

[3] So read (see Sadd 634 n. 19 and OBERLIES 1993/94: 159 n. 52).
On *Jāli-Kaṇhājine*, Cp 112 v.l. (Ee °*jinā*; cf. *Jāli-Kaṇhājinā vubho*, Ja VI 509,24*), see CPD s.v. Kaṇhājinā, on *Nārada-Pabbatā*, Sn 543, see NORMAN (1992: 253 [ad loc.]) and on *devo* (< devau), Th 245, see NORMAN (1969: 171).

[4] But a sentence like *yathā payo ca saṅkho ca ubho samānavaṇṇino* (ubhau °varṇinau), Ja VI 572,3* (ct. *samānavaṇṇā*), may attest a feeling for the correct use of the dual.

[5] See GEIGER § 75, BLOCH (1965: 129-130) and BHSG § 15.1.

[6] On *acci-* (fem.) 'flame' (arcis- [ntr.]) see GEIGER § 101 (and cf. CPD s.v. ²aṭṭhi [I 68b lines 44-45]). At Sn 1074, however, it is a masculine.

the fem. *an*- and *as*-stems became vocalic ones[1] (*kamma*- 'work', *thāma*- 'strength', *nāma*- 'name', *pabba*- 'joint, section', *mamma*- 'vulnerable point', *sappi*- 'ghee', *āyu*- 'duration of life'[2], *sīmā*- 'boundary', *accharā*- 'female divinity'[3]); (**b**) Due to the elision of final consonants in MIA (see § 4.1), the nominative of the old consonant stems ended in a vowel, becoming the source of new stems (*maru*- '[wind] god', *vijju*- 'lightning') which normally retained their original gender (*āpā*- 'misfortune' [< āpad-][4], *upanisā*- 'cause, condition' [< upaniṣad-], *parisā*- 'assembly' [< pariṣad-])[5]; (**c**) The starting-point for the transformation of the neuter *as*-stems was the nom. in *-o*, the base of an acc. in *-aṃ* which itself gave rise sometimes to a (masc.!) nom. in *-o*[6]: (*ayo* >) acc. *ayaṃ* 'iron', D II 351,7, (*uro* >) acc. *uraṃ* 'chest' (> nom. *uro*, Vin I 77,22 [cf. also Sp 867,4-6]), (*tapo*, *tamo* >) acc. *tapaṃ* 'religious austerity', D I 161,10, acc. *tamaṃ* 'darkness', Ja VI 98,6*, 447,4*, Sn 248, 278, 956 (> nom. *tamaṃ*, Ja VI 247,4*, *tapena*, *tamā*), (*mano* >) acc. *manaṃ* 'mind', Ja VI 299,28*, Sn 659 (> nom. *manaṃ*, *manena*, *manato*, *manassa*, *manasmiṃ*, *mane*), (*yaso* >) acc. *yasaṃ* 'fame', Ja I 445,29*, (*rajo* >) acc. *rajaṃ* 'dust, pollution',

---

1 See BLOCH (1965: 138). For Prakrit see PISCHEL § 358 / 404 / 411.

2 *āyu*- has become a masculine (nom. *āyu*, acc. *āyuṃ*).

3 See GEIGER § 100.4 and 101. For Prakrit see PISCHEL § 410.

4 See CPD s.v. āpadā. Beside (loc. pl.) *āpāsu* Pāli knows (loc. sg.) *āpade* and *āpadiyā* / *āpadiyaṃ* (with the ending of the *ī*-stems).

5 For Prakrit see PISCHEL § 395.

6 Cf. *setataro siro*, Ja V 69,5* (v.l. *setataraṃ*). See GEIGER § 99 and VON HINÜBER § 290-291, 343 (cf. FRANKE, *Kleine Schriften* p. 274). For Prakrit see PISCHEL § 356 / 407.

Sn 275 (> nom. sg. m. *rajo*, Sn 662)[1], (*siro* >) acc. *siraṃ* 'head', A I 141,13, Ja VI 226,15* (> nom. *siraṃ*, Thī 255, loc. *sirasmiṃ*, *sire*)[2]; (d) Often, however, *-ā̆* is added[3], sometimes effecting a change of gender[4] (*āpadā-* 'misfortune', *ojavanta-* 'invigorating', *khudā-* 'hunger', *girā-* 'speech', *disā-* 'quarter', *dhura-* 'yoke', *padā-* 'footprint'[5], *pāvusa-* 'rainy season' [prāvṛṣ- f.], *barihisa-* 'sacrificial grass', *vācā-* 'speech', *vijjutā-* 'lightning', *santa-* 'good, true', *saṃpadā-* 'accomplishment', *sarada-* 'autumn' [śarad- f.], *saritā-* 'river', *sirasa-* 'head', *sumedhasa-* 'wise', *°disa-/°risa-* 'like ...'[6]) – a process that started from the acc. sg.[7] (cf. *addhāna-* 'road'[8] [adhvānam], *gāmaṇīya-* [grāmaṇiyaṃ] 'headman', Ja V

---

[1] Cf. also (*vayo* >) nom.-acc. *vayaṃ* (though not attested) 'lifetime' > nom. sg. masc. *(paripakko) vayo*, Dhp 260.

[2] The principle not to obscure the initial sound of the posterior member of a 'compound' (see § 20) promoted the transfer of consonant into vocalic stems: *oja+va(nt)-* 'full of strength' (ojas-), *pesa+kāra-* 'weaver' (peṣas-).

[3] See FRANKE, *Kleine Schriften* p. 270-290 (for Prakrit see JACOBI § 37 and PISCHEL § 355).

[4] On (the change of) gender see GEIGER § 76 and VON HINÜBER § 291-292 (cf. JACOBI § 37).

[5] See OBERLIES (1995a: 146).

[6] See GEIGER § 112.3. On *upāhanā̆-* 'sandal' (~ *pānad[hī]-*) < *(u)pānadhā- (= vāc- : *vācā-*) see SMITH, *JAs* 1950, 193, Sadd V 1597-98 (s.v. pānadhī) and CPD s.v. apiḷayhati (cf. VON HINÜBER § 186).

[7] See VON HINÜBER § 289.

[8] On *attāna-* see VON HINÜBER (1968: 41-42). For Prakrit see PISCHEL § 401-402.

258,28*, VI 579,29*[1], *nāvā-* 'boat' [nāvam], *suvāna-* 'dog' [śvānam][2]; for the *°in[a]*-stems see § 34); **(e)** *gimhāna-* 'summer' and *vassāna-* 'rainy season' are, however, abstracted from the gen. pl.[3] while *tiracchāna-* 'animal' goes back to **tiraścāyana-*[4]; **(f)** The nom. pl. *āpo* 'water' (< āpaḥ)[5] was understood as nom sg. (*āpo ca paṭhavī ca*, Sn 307; see § 38), the base of the masculine stem *āpa-*; **(g)** The stem *yuva-* 'youth' is based on the OIA nominative *yuvā* which looked in Pāli like a nom. pl.: *yuva-* ← *yuvo* ← *yuvā*[6]. OIA *puṃs-* 'man' seems to have undergone similiar re-analysis[7], while *śreyas-* 'better' was transformed into an *a*-stem due to its

---

[1] The *-ī-* – we expect **gāmaṇiya-* – can be accounted for by metrical exigencies as *gāmaṇīya-* invariably forms the last word of an odd *śloka-pāda* (mostly *ārūḷhā gāmaṇīyehi*) which must not end in ⏑⏑-- (see OBERLIES 1993/94: 166-167). Of the old *gāmaṇī-* only the nom. *gāmaṇī* is preserved; otherwise it inflects as a normal *i*-stem: (nom.) *gāmaṇi*, (acc.) *gāmaṇiṃ* (cf. also § 35).

[2] See GEIGER § 93.1. On *nāvā́-*, RV 1.97.8, see TEDESCO, *Language* 21 (1943) 138.

[3] See LÜDERS, *Philologica Indica* 283 n. 3, Sadd V 1359 (s.v. gimha), SMITH, *BSL* 33 (1932) 171 n. 2, and CAILLAT, *ABORI* 68 (1987) 551.

[4] See LÜDERS, *Philologica Indica* 284 n. 3 (diff. Sadd V 1421 [s.v. tiraccha]). On Ja V 453,29* (*tira[c]chāna-yoniyaṃ*) see OBERLIES (1995/96: 288). Cf. *tiraccha-yoniṃ*, Ja V 186,22* (see SMITH apud BECHERT 1961: 23).

TSUCHIDA (*StII* 13/14 [1987] 301 n. 4) opines that the Dīpavaṃsa employs even *therānaṃ* (XII 83-84) and *°dīpānaṃ* (XV 2) as accusatives.

[5] On *āpo-* as stem used in nominal compounds see p. 166 n. 1.

[6] Cf. (nom. sg.) *bhātā* 'brother' → *bhāta-* (Dīp VI 21-22).

[7] *puma-*, Ja VI 239,2* (*pumadevo*), *pumo*, D II 273,18*, Ap 42,11, Cp 289, *pumaṃ*, Ja V 154,10*, *pumā*, Ja III 459,13*, *(itthi)pumā*, D III 85,8, Ap 599,25, *°ānaṃ*, Ja IV 76,5*. For Prakrit see PISCHEL § 412.

neuter *seyyo* (see § 38)[1]; (**h**) The stem *patha-* 'road' is abstracted from OIA compounds (like *catuṣpathá-*, *supátha-*)[2]; (**i**) The apparent equivalence of genitive syntagmas (with possible *sandhi* loss of the ending [*raññ' ovādo*]) and compounds gave rise to stems like *rañña-* 'king' and *suṇa-* 'dog'[3]; (**j**) Only rarely is -*ī̆* added: *vacī°* 'speech', Thī 277, Sn 408, *vyappathi-* 'way of speech' (← [loc.] pathi)[4]; (**k**) Only very occasionally are *ī̆*-stems (directly) converted into *ă*-stems[5] (*ratte* 'at night', Ja VI 80,14*, influenced by *aḍḍharatte* 'at midnight'; *aḍḍharattāyaṃ* 'at midnight' [fem. like *ratti-*], Vv 1179, under the influence of *cirarattāya* 'for a long time'[6]; loc. *ise* 'towards the wise man', Ap 588,5[7], *°gire* 'at the mountain', Ja III 157,25, *raṃsaṃ* 'ray of light', Ap 518,5, *raṃsena*, Ap 42,9, Bv X 28, *raṃse*, Ap 130,5)[8]; **(l)** Another means of transferring stems to the *a*-inflexion was

---

1 See GEIGER § 100.3.

2 See also GEIGER § 93.4. *pantha-* (on which see GEIGER l.c.) seems to be based on the old nom. sg. *panthāḥ*. Was it interpreted as nom. pl., giving rise to corresponding *pantho* (cf. *yuvā* → *yuvo*)? For Prakrit see PISCHEL § 403.

3 For *rañña-* see § 39, for *suṇa-* see GEIGER § 93.1 who cites *suṇena*, Ja VI 353,29*, 354,12* (cf. *soṇa-*, Sn 675).

4 See SMITH, *Analecta rhythmica* (Studia Orientalia XIX:7, Helsinki 1954), p. 8 n. 4, and *Orientalia Suecana* 4 (1955) 112 n. 2 (cf. BLOCH, *Recueil d'Articles* p. 551 and – for Prakrit – JACOBI § 37).

5 What about *pilakkha-* ~ *pilakkhu-* '*plakṣa* tree' and *milakkha-* ~ *milakkhu-* 'foreigner (*mleccha*)', doublets also in Prakrit (see PISCHEL § 105)?

6 See GEIGER § 86.5.

7 See CPD II,312b l. 5-9.

8 See Ee of Ap, vol. II p. IX.

Was (acc.) *bāhuṃ* 'arm' patterned after *hatthaṃ* 'hand' and *pādaṃ* 'foot'

substitution of the simplex by a °*ka*-, °*tā*- or a *vṛddhi*-derivation or a (pleonastical) compound[1]: *gāmaṇika*- 'headman', *bhātika*- / *bhātuka*- 'brother' (: bhrātṛ-), *bhisakka*- 'physician' (: bhiṣaj-[2]), *tāvataka*- / *yāvataka*- 'just so / how much' (: tāvant- / yāvant-)[3], *vehāyasa*- 'air' ([vaihāyasa-[4] ←] : vihāyas-), *Kapilavatthava* (: °vatthu), Ap 42,19, 507,9[5], *pokkharañña*- 'lotus pond' (: puṣkariṇī-), Ja IV 409,2*, VI 173,27*, *Vetarañña* (: Vetaranī), Ja VI 250,19*, *mānasa*- 'mind' (: mana[s]-), *bandhava*- 'kinsman, relative' (: bandhu-), *suhajja*- 'friend' (: suhṛd-)[6], *suhaj+jana*- 'friends' (suhṛjjana-), Ja VI 290,24.[7] – **3.** Seven of the eight OIA cases survived[8],

---

yielding *bāhaṃ* 'arm', the base of *bāhā*-? Or is *bāhā*- due to a false segmentation of compounds like *bāhālaṃkāra*- (bāhu+alaṃkāra-)? BERGER (1955: 16) regards *bāhā*- as a 'Magadhism'. Note that "in several Indo-European languages the *u*-stem (scil. of the word 'arm') was transferred to other stem classes" (EWAia II 224).

1 See FRANKE, *Kleine Schriften* p. 274-275, and BLOCH (1965: 154). Cf. OBERLIES (1989/90: 171 n. 44).

2 Cf. BHS *bhiṣatka*- (see BHSD s.v.).

3 See GEIGER § 112.3.

4 *vaihāyasa*- 'air' is attested Mahābhārata 7,114.54 v.l. (CE [acc.] *vihāyasam*).

5 See BECHERT (1958: 310).

6 See OBERLIES (1989/90: 171 n. 44).

7 On such plural merkers see BLOCH (1965: 154). — In historical forms consonantal stems *can* retain their final at the end of compounds (cf. GEIGER § 94). But a lot of compounds which were 'thematicised' in OIA by adding a *samāsānta* suffix are transferred to the consonantal inflexion in Pāli (see OBERLIES 1989/90: 158-169 n. 35): *rāja*- vs. *mahāraja(n)*- (OIA *mahārāja*-). For Prakrit see PISCHEL § 400.

8 Young texts such as the Buddhavaṃsa and the Dīpavaṃsa use the bare stem instead of case-forms (see OLDENBERG, *Kleine Schriften* p. 1166, DE VREESE, *JAOS* 79

while the dative disappeared in favour of the genitive (cf. also 5.). It is only preserved in the singular of the *a*-flexion as *dativus 'finalis'* (*samaṇo Gotamo assāsāya dhammaṃ deseti* '... to comfort [mankind]', A IV 182,29, *saggāya gacchati* ' ... goes to heaven', Dhp 174) and *dativus temporis* (*ajjatanāya* 'for today', *cirarattāya* 'for a long time', Ja V 267,23*, VI 80,15*, Pv 57, *yāvajīvāya* 'life-long', Ja V 343,17*, *svātanāya* 'for the following day', D I 125,9, Vin I 27,36)[1]. As in Sanskrit, the nominative is used as vocative if a proper vocative is missing from the paradigm (as is generally the case with the pronouns)[2]; see 6 below. – **4.** The suffix *-to* is added to any stem to form an ablative; sometimes the stem final is lengthened (see § 30.4), sometimes it is shortened (see § 5.2c, 7.2b)[3]. – **5.** The instr. and the abl. pl. have merged. – **6.** Traces of case syncretism are rare: (nom.) *kahaṃ ... Nāgita ... so bhavaṃ Gotama viharati* 'How is ... the venerable Gotama, o Nāgita?', D I 150,27-28, (voc.) ... *āvuso bho Gotamo* ... ' ... venerable Gotama!', D I 157,15, (*etha Lakkhaṇa) Sītā (ca)* 'Come, Lakkhaṇa and Sītā!', Ja IV 126,6* (reminding of

---

[1959] 13, TSUCHIDA, *StII* 13/14 [1987] 305-307; for Prakrit see PISCHEL § 364, EDGERTON, *JAOS* 59 [1939] 369-371, BHSG § 8.3-11 [*et passim*], CAILLAT, *Sanskrit and World Culture*, Berlin 1986, 371-373, CHANDRA, *Sambodhi* 4 [1975/76] 34-35 and BHAYANI 1998: 18). TSUCHIDA (l.c. 307) points out that some cases are due to an abbreviation of compounds: *dīpāgamanaṃ buddhassa dhātu ca bodhiyāgamaṃ* (ə: *dhātu-āgamaṃ*), Dīp I 1. On this class of compounds see also VON HINÜBER, *Ṛtam* 16-18 (1984-86) 155-159 = *JBORS* 63/64 (1977/78) 817-821, and cf. p. 123 n. 1.

1 See GEIGER § 77.2 and VON HINÜBER (1968: 179-198). The same holds true for the Prakrit dative in *-ā(y)a* and *-āe* < -āya (see PISCHEL § 364, id. *BB* 1 [1877] 119, JACOBI § 38, ALSDORF, *Kleine Schriften* p. 65, and VON HINÜBER § 299).

2 Cf. PISCHEL § 366ᵇ.

3 See GEIGER § 77.2.

vā́yav índraś ca, RV 1.2.5)[1], (acc. pl.) *rājāno* 'kings', Dhp-a II 15,6[2] (see also § 32.2, 37, 38a, 40). – **7.** Haplology (see § 22.1) accounts for 'shortened' case-endings[3]: *anussāvane<na> salākena*, Vin V 203,8*, *na kāme<na> haññate kvaci*, Ja II 178,21*, Mil 52,24, *bhikkhu<ni> nisinne*, Vin III 189,6, *acchā<ni> ... ambūni*, Ja VI 278,2*, *aññā<ni> koṭisatāni*, Sn 677, *ubho<hi> hattehi*, Ja V 365,29*, Ap 58,8 = 87,21 = Bv XVIII 11[4], *mantā ime brāhmaṇā<na(ṃ)>*, Ja VI 212,17* (*brāhmaṇānaṃ*, 215,30'), *pāṇesu tasathāvare<su>*, Sn 704, *appakesu vanibbake<su>*, Pv 296, *mahāsālesu aḍḍhake<su>*, Ap 75,10 = 77,6 = 439,4, *ubho<su> kūlesu nadiyā*, Ap 15,15 (Ee *kulesu*, see Sadd 286 n. 7), *saṃkhāresu sati<su>*[5], S II 6,34, *taṇhāya kho sati<yā>*, D II 31,25, *mamaṃ rodantiyā sati<yā>*, Ja VI 188,2*[6], *jātiyā asati<yā>*, Mil 52,24, *bhariyā<ya> yo padassati*, Ja III 279,15*[7], *senāya caturaṅginī* (ə: *°aṅginiyā*[8], ct. [= D II 190,1, III 63,3, Pv

---

[1] For the voc. sg. fem. in *-ā* in Prakrit see PISCHEL § 375.

[2] See GEIGER § 92.

[3] See BECHERT (1955: 13 n. 25), id. (1958: 311 n. 1), DE VREESE, *JAOS* 79 (1959) 12-13, Sadd 286 n. 7-8, CAILLAT (1980: 59-60) and VON HINÜBER § 327 / 490.

[4] See VON HINÜBER (1968: 175 n. 3).

[5] On the loc. pl. *-isu* (with short *-i-*) see § 32.9.

[6] See CPD I,113a (s.v. sa(t) / santa) and 530b and CPD II,99a (s.v. āpadā). Note, however, that *(a)sati* is used as a kind of *indeclinabile* (see CPD s.v. [7]asati).

Cf. *paññ<ay>ā viriyena diṭṭhiyā*, A IV 98,4*, *anāgatapajappāya atītassānusocan<ay>ā*, S I 5,8* = Ja VI 25,8* (see CPD s.v. anusocana), *rathiyā<ya>* 'on the road', Ja VI 165,18* (ct. *rathikāya*) = 166,4*, Cp 258, Dīp VI 34 (see p. 149 n. 3).

[7] See ANDERSEN, *A Pāli Reader*, Copenhagen 1935, 123, and Sadd V 1552.

[8] This haplology points – to be exact – to *caturaṅginīyā* (see § 36.3).

660]), Ja V 319,19* = 322,18* (see § 30.8, 31.1)[1].

rem. (**a**) The three gender distinction persists throughout Pāli in nouns and non-personal pronouns. The plural, however, (particularly that of *a*-stems) already at an early date shows evidence of confusion between masculine and neuter (*sabbe kaṭṭhamayā vanā*, Ja I 289,29* [~ nom. *vanaṃ*], *ete ... lakkhaṇā*, Ja V 434,25*/29* [~ nom. *lakkhaṇaṃ*])[2]; especially the use of *-āni* for the acc. pl. m. points to the incipient break-down of the gender system, which seems to have begun in the east (see SCHWARZSCHILD 1991: 188)[3]. And the simplification of the complicated OIA inflexion sometimes entailed a change of gender (on the frequent transference of neuter *as*- to masc. *a*-stems see. 2.c [above])[4]. This was used as a (kind of) metrical licence (especially) in younger texts: *balākayonimhi* 'in the womb of a heron' (⏑---), Ap 42,11 (*qu.* Sadd 205,10-11); (**b**) Some apparent instances, however, are due to gender attraction[5]: *pubbe kira so vanasaṇḍo arañño ahosi*, Ja I 170,11 (see CPD s.v. arañña), *dānaṃ sīlaṃ ... akkodhaṃ*, Ja III 274,2* (see CPD s.v. akkodha), *pabbatāni vanāni ca*, Dhp 188 (~ *pabbato*), *Kusāvatimhi nagare*, Cp 28; (**c**) The negative prefix *a*- (before vowels *an*- for which sometimes *n*- may be substituted [*neka*- 'several', Sn 308 (see § 27), *nāgamo* 'non-arrival', Ja VI

---

1 Cf. *(kūṭāgāra-sahassāni ...) jalanti sakatejena disā sabbā pabhāsayan<ti>*, Ap 34,4.

2 See GEIGER § 76. For Prakrit see PISCHEL § 357.

3 See PISCHEL § 358, CAILLAT (1997: 22) and ea., *Sanskrit and World Culture*, Berlin 1986, 370 n. 32.

4 See BLOCH (1965: 149-152).

5 On this phenomenon see CPD, *Epilegomena* 25* (s.v. *gender attr.*), BECHERT (1958: 315), VON HINÜBER § 292 and id. (1994: 69-70).

82,29*][1]) is doubled in a few words such as *ana-bhāva-* 'non-existence'[2].

§ 29. Nouns are organised mainly into five paradigms, all of which are inherited types. The case terminations of these declensions are as follows (as a rule, only the endings of the *i*-stems are listed, as *u*-stems take corresponding ones)[3]:

---

1 See also CPD s.v. asippa. For Prakrit see PISCHEL § 171.

2 See CPD s.vv. ^{3}a- (8./9.) and ^{1}an-a- (cf. BURLINGAME, *American Journal of Philology* 39 [1918] 303-304 and 41 [1920] 69-75, NORMAN 1969: 271 [ad Th 1089], and [diff.] SASAKI, *Buddhist Studies in Honour of Hammalava Saddhātissa*, Nugegoda 1984, 236-237).

3 The following chart is inserted as a folder after page 281.

	a-stems (see § 30)	*ā*-stems (see § 31)	*i/u*-stems (see § 32)	*ī/ū*-stems (see § 36)	cons. stems (see § 38)
nom.sg.	*devo* (*-e*)	*kaññā*	*aggi* (*-ī*)	*devī*, *jāti*	-ø
nom/acc.sg. ntr.	*rūpaṃ* (nom. *-e*)	—	*akkhi(ṃ)*	—	-ø
acc.	*devaṃ*	*kaññaṃ*	*aggiṃ*	*deviṃ* (*-iyaṃ*)	*-aṃ*
instr.	*devena* (*-asā*)	*kaññāya* (instr. *-ā*, abl. *-ǎ̄to*)	*agginā*	*deviyā* (*-īyā*, *-CCā*), *dhenuyā* (*-ūyā*)	*-ā*
(*dat. fin.*)	*arthāya*		—		—
abl.	*devā*, *devasmā*, *devamhā*, *devǎ̄to* (*-āhi*, *-aṃ*)		*aggismā*, *aggimhā*, *agginā*, *aggito*		= instr.
gen.	*devassa*		*aggissa*, *aggino*		*-o*
loc.	*deve*, *devasmi(ṃ)*, *devamhi*	*kaññāya(ṃ)* (*-āye*)	*aggismiṃ*, *aggimhi* (ntr. *ambuni*)	*deviyā*, *deviyaṃ* (*-CCaṃ*), *-uyā*, *-uyaṃ*	*-i*
voc.m./ntr.	*deva* (*-ā*, *-aṃ*; ntr. *citta*)	*kaññe*	*aggi* (*ise*, *Sutano*)	*devi*	= nom.
nom/voc.pl.	*devā* (*-āso*, *-āse*)	*kaññā*, *kaññāyo*	*aggayo*, *aggī bhikkhavo*, *bhikkhū* (*-iyo*, *-uyo*; voc. *-ave*)	*deviyo* (*-ī*, *-īyo*), *dhenuyo* (*-ū*)	*-o*
acc.	*deve* (*-āni*)				
nom./acc.pl.ntr.	*rūpāni* (*-ā*, acc. *-e*)	—	*akkhīni*, *akkhī*	—	–
instr./abl.	*devehǐ* (*-ebhi*, *-e*)	*kaññāhi*	*aggīhi* (*-ibhi*, *-ihi*)	*devīhi*	*-(b)hi*
gen.	*devāna(ṃ)*	*kaññānaṃ*	*aggīnaṃ* (*-inaṃ*)	*devīnaṃ* (*-inaṃ*)	*-aṃ*
loc.	*devesu*	*kaññāsu*	*aggīsu* (*-isu*)	*devīsu* (*-isu*)	*-su*

§ 30. 1. The nom. sg. of the masc. *a*-inflexion[1] in °*o* is characteristic for the western language, that in °*e* for the (proto-canonical) eastern language (see § 1)[2]; some such forms, however, have been adopted in Ceylon from the local vernacular (which had an *e*-nominative) to characterise uncultivated language, e. g. of heretics[3] (see also § 4.2)[4]. – **2.** It is only in *pādā* 'with the foot', which is formed in analogy with (petrified) *padā*, that the instr. sg. ends in *-ā*[5](*pace* GEIGER § 78.1). The instr. in *-asā* is taken over from the *as*-stems[6]. – **3.** The alleged[7] dat. sg. in °*ā* (*esanā* 'in

[1] See GEIGER § 78-80 and VON HINÜBER 296-324. For Prakrit see PISCHEL § 363-372 and JACOBI § 39.

[2] See LÜDERS (1954: 14-27), CPD s.vv. *attakāra* and ²*avitakka* and VON HINÜBER § 296 (cf. GEIGER § 80.1a, ALSDORF, *Kleine Schriften* p. 328 / 386, NORMAN 1990: 238-246, 1991: 59-70, 1992: 193 [ad Sn 233], 226 [ad Sn 427], 228 [ad Sn 431], 232 [ad Sn 453]). This form is not attested in the Vinayapiṭaka (see VON HINÜBER 1968: 40-41). For Prakrit see PISCHEL § 17 / 345 and BALBIR, in: *Dialectes dans les littératures indo-aryennes* (édité par COLETTE CAILLAT). Paris 1989, 505-506.

[3] See BECHERT, *WZKSO* 1 (1957) 71-75; cf. SMITH, *JAs* 1950, 184, CPD s.v. ²avitakka, rem., and BLOCH, *Recueil d'Articles* p. 191.

[4] The nom. *kitavā* 'gambler', Ja VI 228,19*, Dhp 252, is based on *kitavo* which is remodelled under the influence of the *vant*-stems (see LÜDERS, *Philologica Indica* p. 786).

[5] See VON HINÜBER (1968: 168-173). NORMAN (1992: 172 [ad Sn. 119]), however, argues with such an *ā*-instrumental (the alleged instrumental *abbatā*, Sn 839 [NORMAN 1992: 319], is however a simple ablative; see CPD s.v. abbata).

[6] See GEIGER § 79.1, VON HINÜBER § 298 and id. (1968: 175). Add to the examples given there: *oghasā*, Ja V 5,29*, *kāmasā*, Ja VI 182,14* (on *akāmasā*, Ja V 121,4*, see CPD s.v.), *kodhasā*, Ja V 117,6*, *talasā*, Ja II 223,13*, *thāmasā*, Ja III 334,2*, Th 1165, D II 282,27, M I 257,4, *pemasā*, Ap 555,22 (cf. BECHERT 1958: 310),

order to search', Ja II 34,16) is due to the alternation of *°ā* and *°aṃ* (i.e. the ending of the acc. sg.) in word-final position (see § 4.6). – **4.** The suffixes of the abl. (*°asmā, °amhā*) and loc. sg. (*°asmi[ṃ]*[1], *°amhi*, see § 1) are taken over from the pronominal flexion (for *-mh-* < *-sm-* see § 18.4, for *-sm-* p. 102). The ablative in *-āto*[2] is a blending of *-ā* (-āt) and *-to* (-taḥ); the texts usually write (often against the metre) *-ato*[3] (*cāpāto*, Dhp 320, *°bandhanāto*, Sn 367, *mūla-phalāto*, Ja V 200,22* [Ee *°phalato*], *Sāketāto*, Thī 406 [Ee *Sāketato*])[4]. The rare ablative in *-āhi* (*kāmāhi* 'out of love', Ja VI 138,28*) seems to be an 'eastern' feature[5]. The same holds

balasā, Ja II 60,9*, Th 1141, *mukhasā*, Pv 6, *rasasā*, Ja III 328,15*, Vv 1037, *vāhasā*, Th 218, 1127, Ap 77,15, 462,22, *vegasā*, Ja III 185,2*, V 117,4* (cf. Sadd 663,6-13). For Prakrit see PISCHEL § 364 and BALBIR, in: *Dialectes dans les littératures indo-aryennes* (édité par COLETTE CAILLAT). Paris 1989, 507.

7 See AiGr. III § 42 (p. 94) and NORMAN (1992: 157 [ad Sn 75], 341 [ad Sn 916]).

1 The locative in *°asmi* (e.g. *tidivasmi*, Th 534, *lokasmi*, Th 986, Sn 598 [m.c.], *andhabhūtasmi*, Vin I 8,26*, *appasmi*, S I 20,14* [cf. Ja II 136,5* (see OBERLIES 1993/94: 160); on Dhp 224 see VON HINÜBER § 308 *pace* CPD s.v.], *paṭhasmi*, Sn 233 [m.c.], *vipulasmi*, Ja V 96,19*) is not registered in GEIGER's grammar (for Prakrit see PISCHEL § 366[a] and ALSDORF, *Kleine Schriften* p. 65 / 825-826).

2 See GEIGER § 77.2, for Prakrit see PISCHEL § 365.

3 *-ato* (e.g *anussāvanato*, Vin V 220,5) is the stem vowel *a* with added suffix *-to*. For Prakrit see PISCHEL § 99 and 365.

4 See BLOCH (1965: 131), CAILLAT (1970: 22), NORMAN (1992: 187 [ad Sn 198]) and VON HINÜBER § 302 (cf. CAILLAT, *IF* 75 [1970] 301 and PISCHEL § 69).

5 See OBERLIES (1996: 110-111) *pace* INSLER, *ABORI* 72/73 (1993) 15-21 (cf. LÜDERS, *Philologica Indica* p. 222, and VON HINÜBER § 303). SMITH, *MSL* 23 (1929) 271-272, and BLOCH (1965: 131) – following PISCHEL § 365 – see in *-āhi* a continuation of the "ancient adverbial suffix expressing direction (not origin): Skt.

good for that in *-aṃ* (... *bhamaro pupphaṃ* ... *paleti* '... the bee flies away from the flower ...', Dhp 49, ~ ... *puṣpād* ..., Udānavarga XVIII,8) which may directly derive from *-āt* (see § 4.6a)[1]; the few genuine forms are increased by instances due to syntactic innovations (e.g. √*bhī* + acc.) or scribal idiosyncrasies (as, e.g., the Ceylonese tradition tends to write nasalised [short] vowels instead of long ones, and vice versa [cf. Ee Cūlavaṃsa p. XXX])[2]. – **5.** The ending of the voc. sg. may be lengthened by *pluti* (which as a rule is not marked[3]): *tasmāhaṃ Upakā*, Vin I 8,29* *sace te Kassapā agaru*, Vin I 25,19*, *Gotamā*, S I 200,1* (*vait.*), *devā*, Ja VI 384,23* (*aup.*), *Sutasomā*, Ja V 179,19*[4], *Nāgadattaṃ*, S I 201,7* (with *-aṃ* ~ *-ā*, see § 4.6[b])[5]. The vocatives in *-e* – like *Godhe*, S V 372,1,

---

uttarāhi from the direction of the North ... hence Pa. *kāmāhi* by desire, Pkt. *chettāhi* from the field" (BLOCH l.c.; cf. ibid. 140). On the Prakrit form (°*āhi[ṃto]*) see PISCHEL l.c.

[1] See also A.N. UPADHYE, *Dhūrtākhyāna of Haribhadra Sūri*. Bombay 1944, 51 = *Papers*. Mysore 1983, 151 (cf. VON HINÜBER 1994: 224).

[2] See LÜDERS (1954: 138-143), ALSDORF, *Kleine Schriften* p. 67-68, DE VREESE, *BSOAS* 17 (1955) 369-371, BROUGH (1962: 79, 266-267), NORMAN (1992: 200 [ad Sn 48,8,9]) and VON HINÜBER § 304; cf. ALSDORF, *Kleine Schriften* p. 388 (*dīgharattaṃ* ~ dīrgharātrāt, Ja VI 265,8*) and SAKAMOTO-GOTO, *WZKS* 28 (1984) 51 n. 30, 52 n. 32 (*nekāyatanaṃ* ~ °āyatanāt, Ja IV 110,6*, *paralokaṃ* ~ paralokāt, ibid. 8*). On +*asajjanaṃ*, Ja V 208,20* (< a-saj-janāt [cf. CPD s.v. āsajjanaṃ]), see OBERLIES (1996: 137 n. 30).

[3] See BHSG § 8.27 (*pace* GEIGER § 79.2) and VON HINÜBER § 311 (for Prakrit see PISCHEL § 366[b]).

[4] These examples are emendations of ALSDORF (1968).

[5] *Anuruddhā*, M I 206,9, is an elliptical vocative pl.: 'You, Anuruddha, and the others' (cf. Sadd 19,9, 737,8). See p. 130-131 n. 4.

Takkāriye, Ja IV 247,24*, *Bhesike*, D I 225,7, 226,9, *Medakathālike*, S V 168,22 – (allegedly *Magadhisms*[1]) are feminine forms used as nick-names (see CPD s.v. ²avitakka, rem.)[2]. *khattiye* 'prince!', Ja III 109,12*, however, shows the 'productive' *e*-suffix (see p. 170). – **6.** The nom. pl. in *°āso* (*samuppilavāso* 'jumping up and down', Sn 670) is a continuation of Vedic *°āsaḥ* (see § 1), with *°āse* as the corresponding 'eastern' form (*ariyāse* 'good ones', Ja IV 222,21*, *paṇḍitāse* 'wise men', Sn 875, *samaṇa-brāhmaṇāse* 'ascetics and brahmins', Sn 1079-1082, *saṃkhāta-dhammāse* 'for who the doctrine is well-taught', S II 47,13*)[3]. The same holds true for the acc. pl. in *°āni* (*puttāni āmantaya tambanette* 'summon the ... boys!', Ja VI 290,9*) as Aśoka proves (*pulisāni*, PE IV)[4]. This ending is used sporadically for the nominative: *tālataruṇāni* 'young shoots of the palmyra tree', Vin I 189,11 (acc. *°taruṇe*, ibid. 10)[5]. – **7.** The acc. pl.

---

[1] See GEIGER § 80.2 (cf. LÜDERS, *Bhārhut und die buddhistische Literatur*. Leipzig 1941, 97). An altogether different explanation of *Takkāriye*, Ja IV 247,24*, was given by MEHENDALE, *Proceedings of the Seminar in Prakrit Studies*. Poona 1970, 125-129.

[2] A vocative nt. is *citta*, Th 1108-1109, 1123.

[3] See OLDENBERG, *Kleine Schriften* p. 1163, GEIGER § 79.4 and VON HINÜBER § 312 (cf. NORMAN 1992: 134 [ad Sn 7], 218 [ad Sn 376], CAILLAT 1994: 46-48 and 1997: 18-21). For Prakrit see PISCHEL § 367.

[4] See LÜDERS, *Philologica Indica* p. 288-290, BECHERT (1958: 310), NORMAN (1971: 59 [ad Thī 13] and 1992: 149 [ad Sn 45]) and VON HINÜBER § 315. Add to LÜDERS' list: *puttāni*, Ja IV 294,7*, VI 290,14*, 563,10* (see LÜDERS, *Kleine Schriften* p. 42 n. 2 and ALSDORF, *Kleine Schriften* p. 323), Thī 312, Ap 452,3, 577,10. See also PERNIOLA (1997: 229 [§ 185]).

[5] See LÜDERS, *Philologica Indica* p. 290-291.

ends in °*e*[1]. This ending, which is called for by the instr. in °*ehi* and the loc. in °*esu* (due to the analogy with *kaññā* - *kaññāhi* - *kaññāsu* or *aggī/bhikkhū* - *aggīhi/bhikkhūhi* - *aggīsu/bhikkhūsu*), is taken over from the pronominal flexion (see § 42.2). For the acc. in °*āni* see *6*. The employment of *-e* and *-āni* avoids the homonymity of the acc. sg. and the acc. pl. (**-aṃ* < *-ān*). – **8.** The ending of the instr. and abl. pl. *-ehī*[2] developed out of Vedic °*ebhiḥ*[3] (see p. 91), an ending which is only very rarely preserved: *ariyebhi* 'by the noble ones', Ud 61,2*, Vin IV 204,11*[4]. The rare instr. pl. in °*e* continues OIA °*aiḥ* (*citraggale-[r-ugghusite]* '[(in the home of the king of the Sivis) noisy] with jewelled doorbolts', Ja VI 483,5*, *sañātake* 'with our own kinsmen', Ja IV 296,22*, *dhīre* 'with wise men', Dhp 207 [*coni.*], *musale* 'with clubs', Ja V 267,13*)[5]. Some instances,

---

[1] See von Hinüber § 314 (for Prakrit see Pischel § 367[a]). There is no acc. pl. in *-ān* (*pace* Geiger § 79.5) or *-aṃ* (*pace* Lüders 1954: 143-150) in Pāli (see Bechert 1955: 18-25 and von Hinüber § 313).

[2] On °*ehī* see Oberlies (1995/96: 273) and id. (1996: 112). For Prakrit see Pischel § 368- 369.

[3] Though OIA °*ebhyaḥ* would have given *°*ebbho* (cf. Bloch 1965: 132), it cannot be ruled out that this ending has suffered (irregular) *saṃprasāraṇa* resulting also in °*ehi* (cf. von Hinüber § 317). And also the pronominal declension (instr. pl. *tebhiḥ*, etc.) may have contributed to its formation (see Berger 1955: 83 n. 166, and Witzel, in: *Dialectes dans les littératures indo-aryennes* [édité par Colette Caillat]. Paris 1989, 213-214).

[4] See Oldenberg, *Kleine Schriften* p. 1164-1165, and Geiger § 79.9. The readings, however, might be corrupt (cf. *ariyehi*, Sn 761).

[5] See Geiger § 79.6 and von Hinüber § 316 (cf. von Hinüber 1968: 174-175, Alsdorf, *Kleine Schriften* p. 286, CPD s.v. aggaḷa and Norman 1969: 146 [ad Th 102], 253 [ad Th 922], 266 [ad Th 1031], 271 [ad Th 1087], and 1992: 253 [ad Sn 547], 262 [ad Sn 609]). On Dhp 207 see Lesny, *JPTS* 1924-1927, 235-236.

however, are due to a haplology of the endings: *raṭṭhe<hi> janapadehi vā*, Ja VI 294,27*, *vasanehi 'nūpame<hi>*, Thī 374, *kusale<hi> dasah' upāgato*, Cp 20, Bv II 31[1], *viha-vihābhinadite<hi> sippikābhirutehi ca*, Th 49. The same holds true for the instr. sg. and loc. pl. in *-e* (see § 28.7). – **9.** The gen. pl. sometimes lost (perhaps under the influence of the corresponding ending of the sg. in *°assa*) its final *-ṃ* (see § 4.1)[2]: *Aṅgāna*, Th 484, *ariyāna*, Ja II 354,18*, *ariyasaccāna*, Sn 267, Vv 133, *(dibba)kāmāna*, Ja V 468,19*, *khattāna*, Ja VI 208,11*, *(purāṇa)corāna*, Ja I 188,9*, *dipadāna*, Ja IV 97,11*, *devāna*, Th 1266, Ja IV 109,15*, 356,20*, *domanassāna*, Sn 1106, *dhammāna*, Th 1253, Sn 167, *nāgāna*, Ja VI 21,20*, *puttāna*, S I 6,23*, *bālāna*, Ja VI 213,25*, *buddhāna*, Thī 161, Dhp 183, *maccāna*, Ja IV 113,1*, Dhp 182, *santāna*, Ja III 247,22*[3]. Only in some words with pronominal meaning does the gen. end in *°esaṃ* (*sesesaṃ* 'to the other [servants]', Ja I 468,18). – **10.** The nom. sg. ntr. in *-e* (*dullabhe ... dassane* 'difficult to obtain is the sight of', Ja VI 263,13* = 264,9*, *dāne* 'a gift', Ja III 288,13* [C^{ks}], *Bhogavatī nāma mandire* 'the palace called Bhogavatī', Ja VI 269,3*[4], *nagare ni[m]mite kañcanāmaye*[5] 'the [well-]planned golden town', Ja VI 269,5*[6], *°saṃyojane se bhinne* 'that

---

1 Diff. VON HINÜBER (1968: 175 with n. 3).

2 See GEIGER § 32.2 (Ee often has unmetrical *-ānaṃ*). For Prakrit see PISCHEL § 370.

3 See BECHERT (1961: 16 n. 1), OBERLIES (1993/94: 154 n. 24), id. (1996: 112), id. *WZKS* 34 (1990) 98 n. 86, and SAKAMOTO-GOTO, *WZKS* 28 (1984) 51 n. 28 (cf. BLOCH 1965: 44).

4 See ALSDORF, *Kleine Schriften* p. 388.

5 So read (*pace* ALSDORF, *Kleine Schriften* p. 391 [*nagare nimmite kañcane*]).

6 See LÜDERS (1954: 21) and ALSDORF, *Kleine Schriften* p. 388 n. 24 (*ad loc.*). But this form may well be a locative (*Bhogavatī nāma mandire ... nagare ni[m]mite*

fetter is rent', M II 255,6/17[1]) is a feature of the eastern language, where it stood beside an acc. in *-aṃ* (cf. Aś Delhi nom. *maṃgale*, acc. *maṃgalaṃ*)[2]. The nom/acc. ntr. pl. ends also in *-ā* (see § 1)[3]: *gaganā v' abbhachāditā* 'like the (lit.) skies covered with clouds', Th 1068, *gharā* 'houses', Dhp 241, 302, *dumā* 'trees', Th 527 (cf. *dumāni*, ibid. 528), *bhassarā ... nettā* 'my eyes (were) shining', Thī 257, *phalā* 'fruits', Ja IV 203,22*, *rūpā (saddā gandhā ...)* 'forms', Vin I 21,19*, *tīṇ' assa lakkhaṇā gatte* 'there are three marks on his body', Sn 1019[4], *jīno ... maṇikuṇḍalā* 'deprived of his jewelled earrings',Ja III 153,12* (*maṇikuṇḍalāni jīno ... maṇikuṇḍale ti pi-pāṭho*, ct.). The (apparent) merger of masc. and ntr. gave rise to an acc. pl. ntr. in *-e*[5]: *ambare* 'clothes', Ja VI 230,29*, *chidde* 'holes', S I 43,20* (*cha ... chiddāni ... te chidde ... vivajjaye*), *nagare* 'towns', Ja VI 59,1*, *rūpe* 'forms', Ud 30,23, M I 61,15, III 281,8, S IV 18,4 (see p. 139)[6].

---

kañcanāmaye ... niṭṭhitaṃ 'the palace ... is situated in the town built of gold').

[1] See LÜDERS (1954: 15).

[2] See GEIGER § 80.1b, LÜDERS (1954: 22-23), VON HINÜBER § 323 and CAILLAT, *Sanskrit and World Culture*. Berlin 1986, 370 n. 34. For Prakrit see BALBIR, in: *Dialectes dans les littératures indo-aryennes* [édité par COLETTE CAILLAT]. Paris 1989, 506.

[3] See GEIGER § 78.6 and VON HINÜBER § 324 (for Prakrit where *-ā* stood beside *-āṇi* and *-āiṃ* see PISCHEL § 367 and SCHWARZSCHILD 1991: 185-190).

[4] But see § 28.7 (on this haplological loss of *°ā<ni>* see also CAILLAT 1994: 40-46 and ea. 1997: 21-23).

[5] See BECHERT (1955: 15 n. 34).

[6] See GEIGER § 78.7 and VON HINÜBER § 324 (cf. NORMAN 1969: 273 [ad Th 1099], 274 [ad Th 1101], 1992: 294 [ad Sn 755]).

rem. There is no ('eastern') loc. pl. in *-ehi*. The alleged instances are due to syntactic innovations, i.e. *-ehi* is used as a generalized oblique case ending (*ajinamhi haññate dīpī, nāgo dantehi haññati* 'the leopard is killed for his skin, the elephant for his tusks', Ja VI 61,4*)[1].

§ 31. **1.** The instr. *-āya* (instead of the expected **-ayā*) of the *ā*-stems (see § 29)[2] reflects generalisation of a single oblique form (as does the loc. in *-āya*[3] < -āyām); for this form (*-āya* < -āyāḥ) see § 4.4.[4] The instr. in *°ā* (*appaṭipucchā* 'without inquiry', Vin I 325,33[5], *avijjā* 'with ignorance', Th 572[6]) is originally due to haplological contraction of *-cch/jj/ññ/yā<ya>* (see § 6.8)[7], but was also generalised[8]: *amattā paribhuñjati* 'enjoys immo-

---

[1] See CAILLAT (1997: 23-26), OBERLIES (1997: 2-9) and SCHMITHAUSEN, *Maitrī and Magic: Aspects of the Buddhist Attitude toward the Dangerous in Nature*. Wien 1997, 37 with n. 77 (*pace* LÜDERS 1954: 152-157); cf. VON HINÜBER § 321.

[2] See GEIGER § 81 and VON HINÜBER § 333-336. For Prakrit see PISCHEL § 374-376, JACOBI § 41 and SCHWARZSCHILD (1991: 42-46).

[3] *rathiyā* 'on the road' stands for *rathiyāya* (*pace* GEIGER § 81.1); see p. 138 n. 6.

[4] As in Skt. *amma* 'dear!' (Ja V 182,20*, Th 44, Thī 33) is the voc. sg. of *ammā* (see CPD s.v. and GEIGER § 81.2).

[5] Cf. *paṭipucchā*, A I 72,22, S III 104,1 (see STEDE, *JRAS* 1927, 886).

[6] See CPD I,468b. *anāpucchā* and *āpucchā* are possibly also such instrumentals (see CPD s.vv.).

[7] See also BECHERT (1958: 311 n. 1). Cf. Vedic (instr.) *vacasyā́* ~ *vacasyáyā* 'with eloquence' (see AiGr. III § 59aβ [p. 116-117]).

[8] See VON HINÜBER § 143 (cf. NORMAN 1992: 171 [ad Sn 110], 185 [ad Sn 186]).

derately', Ja II 432,17* (Ee *amatto*[1]), *saddhā* 'with faith', S I 198,9* (so read m.c. [Ee *saddhāya*]), *asīlatā* 'by absence of virtuous conduct', Sn 839-840[2]. – **2.** The stem-final can be shortened before the suffix *-to* (*jivhato*, S IV 175,1, *parisato*, Vin V 221,12, *sīmato*, Vin V 221,5); see § 5.2c[3]. – **3.** The rare loc. in *-āye* (*sabhāye* 'in the assembly', Vin III 200,19, *puṇṇamāye* 'on the full moon day', Cp 81, Bv II 184 [as quoted Sadd 243,26-29, 675,9-10]) is a contamination of (fem.) *-āya* and (masc.) *-e*[4]. – **4.** The nom./acc./voc.[5] pl. *kaññāyo* 'girls' is formed analogical to the *ī*-stems (proving their ending *-īyo*, see § 36.6) to differentiate it from the sg. (both OIA *kanyā* and *kanyāḥ* > *kaññā*)[6]. This form is used above all in collocations with an adj. in *-ā* (*imā anacchariyā gāthāyo* 'these stanzas unarticulated before', Vin I 5,6)[7] to end a phrase ('colon') with a long word: *chinnikā dhuttikā ahirīkāyo* 'deceitful, wicked, shameless (women)' (Vin III 128,1), *adhuttī athenī asoṇḍī avināsikāyo* 'not depraved, not thieves, not addicted to drink, not aquandering (women)' (A III 38,7-8)[8].

---

[1] See CPD s.v. amattā.

[2] See CPD s.v. (cf. NORMAN 1992: 319).

[3] Or is this *-ato* analogical to masc. *-ato* which consists of stem and suffix (see § 30.4)?

[4] See BLOCH (1965: 140) and VON HINÜBER § 334.

[5] *vadhuke*, M II 63,12, is used as a voc. pl.: *etha tumhe vadhuke yena alaṃkarena alaṃkatā pubbe Raṭṭhapālassa kulaputtassa piyā hotha manāpā*. On *ayye* as voc. pl. see CPD s.v. ayyā (cf. VON HINÜBER § 335).

[6] For Prakrit see PISCHEL § 376.

[7] See OLDENBERG, *Kleine Schriften* p. 1165.

[8] See OLDENBERG, *Kleine Schriften* p. 1165, SMITH, *JAs* 1952, 170, and CPD s.v. asoṇḍa. The use of *-ā* ~ *-āni* in the neuter is determined by similar conditions: "The

rem. The opposition of (OIA) masc. °*a*- and fem. °*ī*-stems is partly replaced/supplemented by masc. °*a*- *vs.* fem. °*ā*-[1]. This possibility of forming feminines either with -*ā* or with -*ī* was used for semantic differentiation: *mettī*- 'friendship', *mettā*- 'sympathy' (see FRANKE, *Kleine Schriften* p. 267-268).

§ 32. 1. The paradigm of the *i/u*-stems[2] (see § 29) is composed of forms continuing the old *i/u*-flexion (*aggi*, *aggiṃ*, *agginā*, ntr. *akkhi*, *akkhīni*[3]; *bhikkhu* ... ntr. *assu*[4]), and of forms built analogical to the *a*- (*aggismā*, *aggimhā*, *aggissa*, *aggismiṃ*, *aggimhi*, ntr. *akkhiṃ*[5], *akkhī*[6]), the fem. *ī*- (*aggī* :: *jātī*)[7] and the ntr. *i*-/*u*-stems (*aggino*, *bhikkhuno*). – **2.** The nom. and voc. sg. masc. end also in -*ī*/-*ū* (*nidhī*, Ja III 24,28*, *bhūtapatī*, V

-*ā* ~ -*āni* nt. endings generally occur in close clusters" (CAILLAT 1997: 21-22).

1 See FRANKE, *ZDMG* 50 (1896) 591.

2 See GEIGER § 82-85 and VON HINÜBER § 325-332. For Prakrit see PISCHEL § 377-382 and JACOBI § 40.

3 Prakrit has – beside °*īṇi* and °*ūṇi* – °*īiṃ* and °*ūiṃ* (see PISCHEL § 381).

4 Thī 220, M I 187,6 = 422,6.

5 The analogy of *(phal)aṃ (mūl)aṃ* served to differentiate the neuters – nom.-acc. sg. *(akkh)iṃ*, Ja VI 294,10*, *(suc)iṃ*, Ja VI 534,11*, *(ass)uṃ*, Ja III 163,25, *(bah)uṃ*, A II 183,31, Vv 171, *(madh)uṃ*, Ap 13,30 – from the masculines (see BLOCH 1965: 133; cf. GEIGER § 85.1-2 and PISCHEL § 377-379).

6 It is, however, possible that the nom.-acc. pl. of the neuters in -*ī* and -*ū* (e.g. *aṭṭhī*, Ja I 483,29* [see CPD s.v. ²aṭṭhi], *madhū*, Ja VI 537,20* [see GEIGER § 85.3]) is carried on from the Vedic dual (see BLOCH 1965: 134 and cf. p. 130 n. 3).

7 See VON HINÜBER § 313 (diff. BLOCH 1965: 134).

139,16*, *bandhū*, Ja II 29,16*, *mudū*, Ja IV 192,16* [m.c.], *munī*, Sn 220; voc. *munī*, Sn 1075)[1], the abl. in *-i/uto*[2]. – **3.** The old endings of the voc. sg. are only rarely attested: *ise* 'seer!', Ja IV 320,1*, 325,5*, Sn 1025, *mune* 'wise man!', Ap 157,11[3], *Sutano*, Ja III 329,8*[4]. – **4.** *n*-endings (outside the oblique cases / the ntr. [cf. loc. *ambuni* 'in the water', Ja V 6,5*, *paṃsuni* 'in the dust', Ja II 437,16*]) occur in the nom./acc. sg. ntr. (*pabhaṅguṇaṃ*, Dhp 139, 148), the acc. sg. m. (*ādiccabandhunaṃ*, D II 287,21*, III 197,14*, S I 192,6* = Th 1237, *bhikkhunaṃ*, Sn 87/88[5], 513) and the nom. (*aggino*, Saddh 584, *sāramatino*, Dhp 11 [on which see below], *dummatino / mittadduno*, Mhv IV 3, *akilāsuno*, Vin III 9,2, *pabhaṅguno*, Ja I 393,3, cf. *°viduno*, § 35) and acc. pl. (*kapikacchuno*, Pv 143)[6]. They are due to the analogy of *n*-cases of the masc. and ntr. *i/u*-inflexion and, though only indirectly[7], to the influence of the *in*-stems (cf. *asāre sāramatino sāre cāsāradassino*, Dhp 11, *avajje vajjamatino vajje cāvajjadassino*, Dhp 318). – **5.** Due to the forms of the nominative and the accusative plural being confused the nom. pl. ends in *-ī -ū* and the acc. pl. (though very

---

1 See OBERLIES (1993/94: 166 n. 108 / 167) and id. (1996: 113). For Prakrit (*muṇī* < mune) see PISCHEL § 379.

2 See GEIGER § 77.2.

3 See BECHERT (1958: 311).

4 GEIGER erroneously states that the ct. 'treats it as nom.' (§ 83.4).

5 Unless *bhikkhunaṃ* in these stanzas is a gen. pl. (on which see **9.** below). The same holds true for *muninaṃ*, Sn 208.

6 See GEIGER § 85, VON HINÜBER § 330 and Sadd 235 n. 2. A form like *pabhaṅgune*, Thī-a 95,1 (cf. Sadd l.c.) shows thematisation (see BLOCH 1965: 134). On *ariyavuttine* see p. 158.

7 See BHSG § 12.2.

seldom [see SMITH *apud* CPD II,312b]) in *-ayo -avo* (*isayo*, S I 226,18, *sattavo*, Ja V 95,26*)[1]. – **6.** The nom. pl. *Kāsiyo*, Ja V 377,6*, *sāliyo* 'rice', Ja I 325,5, V 405,28*[2], *Andhakaveṇhuyo*, Ja V 267,12*, *Kuruyo*, Ja II 214,9*, 215,3*, and the acc. pl. *Kuruyo*, Ja VI 278,16* (cf. *dhātuyo* 'elements' [see p. 154]), seemingly have endings of the (fem.!) *ī/ū*-inflexion (see § 34), while the acc. pl. *ise* 'wise men', Ja V 92,24*, takes its ending from *samaṇe brāhmaṇe* of the same line. – **7.** Instr. and loc. pl. in *°ī/ūhi* and *°ī/ūsu* are analogical to the gen. *(agg)īnaṃ (bhikkh)ūnaṃ*[3]; cf. 9 below. – **8.** After a short vowel *-bhi* sometimes persists late in Pāli[4]: *isibhi*, Ja III 29,10*, Th 1065, Thī 206 (Ee unmetr. *isībhi*[5]), *ñātibhi*, Ja III 186,20* (Ee misprints *°hi*) = 329,19* = 495,23*, Ap 538,6, Cp 122, *taracchibhi*, Ja VI 562,17* (L^k)[6] (cf. *vaggubhi*, Ap 333,21 v.l. [Ee *vagguhi*]). – **9.** The plural forms with short stem-vowels (*°i/uhi*, *°i/unaṃ*, *°i/usu*) have the vocalism of the singular[7] (apparently) preserving – as far as the instr. and the loc. are concerned – the old vowel length[8]: *akkhihi*, Sn 608, *kimihi*, Th 315,

---

[1] For Prakrit see PISCHEL § 380-381 and CHANDRA, *Proceedings of the Seminar on Prakrit Studies (1973)*. Ahmedabad 1978, 132.

[2] Cf. *kimiyo*, Mp-ṭ II 341,19 (see CPD s.v. kaṭukīṭaka).

[3] See BLOCH (1965: 134). For Prakrit see PISCHEL § 381.

[4] SMITH *apud* BLOCH (1965: 67).

[5] There should be a break after the fourth syllable in the *ra-vipulā*.

[6] See Sadd V 1414.

[7] See CAILLAT (1970: 19).

[8] For Prakrit see PISCHEL § 99 / 381.

bhikkhuhi, S I 202,29* (so read), *sādhuhi*, Dīp IV 6[1], *ñātinaṃ*, Th 240, Pv 416, Khp VII 4, *(appa)buddhinaṃ*, Th 667 (beside *appabuddhīnaṃ* in the same stanza), *sivinaṃ*, Ja IV 405,24*[2], *bandhunaṃ*, Th 240, *abandhunaṃ*, Ap 323,22 (Ee *abandhanaṃ*), *bhikkhunaṃ*, D II 123,9*, Th 1231, S I 190,15, *sādhunaṃ*, Mhv XXXVII 232, *asisu*, M I 86,31, 87,1, *samādhisu*, Ap 379,9[3], *ususu*, M I 86,30, *bhikkhusu*, Th 241, 1207, Dhp 73, M I 338,29*. – **10.** The voc. pl. *bhikkhave* 'monks!' showing *-e* < -aḥ (by *v__o*-dissimilation, see § 4.2[4]) is the 'eastern' form corresponding to 'western' *bhikkhavo* (Vin I 19,30 = 20,28)[5].

rem. (**ad 6.**) *dhātuyo* 'elements', Thī 14, *dhātuyā* 'in a [world] element / sphere', A I 28,2, D II 109,1[6], and *(sukatāya) massuyā* 'with a [well-trimmed] beard', Ja III 315,22*, show confusion of gender (← *dhātu*- masc. / *massu*- ntr. [see GEIGER § 76 and BLOCH 1965: 151]).

---

[1] As final member of a *bahuvrīhi*-compound *pāṇi*- 'hand' may inflect as an *°in*-stem (*°pāṇihi*, Ja VI 579,29*), as it does in Epic Sanskrit (cf. *śūlapāṇinam*, Mbh 10,6.34).

[2] *sālinam*, Ja VI 510,2*, seems to be a printing error of Ee for *sālīnam* (Ja III 144,24*, Th 842, Vin IV 204,10*, Mil 16,28 [cf. ALSDORF, *Kleine Schriften* p. 767 n. 4]). If not, it should probably be corrected to *sālīnam* (*odanaṃ*) as the syllables 2-4 of the odd *pāda* should not scan ⏑⏑- (but cf. Ja VI 516,3*: *suddhaṃ sālinam odanaṃ*). It is one of the many mistakes of the PED to regard *sālīna*- as a stem.

[3] See BECHERT (1958: 311).

[4] See OBERLIES (1996: 108).

[5] See GEIGER § 82.5 and VON HINÜBER § 332.

[6] Cf. also *dasasahassimhi lokadhātuyā*, Mil 96,20 – a solecism like *imamhā tiracchānayoniyā*, Ja II 398,13.

§ 33. The stems *sakha-*, *sakha(r)-* (abstracted from the nom. *sakhā* after the pattern *pitā : pita[r]-*) and *sakhāra-* (formed according to the proportion *x : sakhā = satthāraṃ : satthā*) supplement the paradigm of *sakhi-* 'friend' which inflects as an *i*-stem[1]: nom./voc. sg. *sakhā* (Ja II 29,16*, V 509,20*, Sn 253, S I 36,2*; voc., Ja III 295,20*), *sakho* (Th 648), acc. *sakhaṃ* (Ja II 299,13*[2]), *sakhāraṃ* (Ja II 348,20*), instr. *sakhinā* (Ja IV 41,29*), abl. *sakhārasmā* (Ja III 534,2*), gen. *sakhino* (Ja IV 426,23*, VI 478,1*), nom. pl. *sakhā* (Ja III 323,10*), *sakhāro* (Ja III 492,14*, IV 292,27*), acc. pl. *sakhino* (D III 160,18, 161,20*), gen. pl. *sakhīnaṃ* (Ja III 492,14*, IV 42,8*), *sakhinaṃ* (Ja IV 292,27*, VI 498,27*), *sakhānaṃ* (Ja II 228,20*, Sn 123).

	singular	plural
nom.	*sakhā, sakho*	*sakhā, sakhāro*
acc.	*sakhaṃ, sakhāraṃ*	*sakhino*
instr.	*sakhinā*	–
abl.	*sakhārasmā*	–
gen.	*sakhino*	*sakhī̆naṃ, sakhānaṃ*
loc.	–	–
voc.	*sakhā*	–

[1] See GEIGER § 84. For Prakrit see PISCHEL § 379.

[2] See, however, GEIGER's note (§ 84 note 2 [= p. 124 n. 1 of GHOSH's English translation]).

§ 34. The old endings of the *mi(n)*-, *vi(n)*- and *i(n)*-stems[1] are preserved throughout (sg. m. *°ī*, ntr. *°i*[2], *°inaṃ*, *°inā*, *°ino*,[3] pl. *°ino*, *°i[b]hi*, *°inaṃ*, *°isu*[4]; fem. *°inī*-); the abl. is also formed with the suffix *°to* (*hatthito* 'from the elephant', Ja IV 257,20). Besides, the *in*-stems inflect in analogy to the *i*-stems[5], since some cases (instr. sg./pl. and loc. pl.) were homophone: (nom. sg.) *kalyāṇakāri*, Ja II 202,6* = III 158,28* (so read m.c.), *tirīṭi*, Ja V 9,25* (so read m.c.), *visesi*, Th 370-374, Sn 799, 905,[6] (acc. sg.) *(evam)akkhāyiṃ*, D III 34,11 = M I 140,7[7], *antevāsiṃ*, S V 168,21, Vin III 143,21, *jhāyiṃ*, Sn 1105, *°dassiṃ*, Sn 57, 176, 219, *(gāma)vāsiṃ*, Ja III 10,11, *°sāmiṃ*, Sn 83, (gen. sg.) *°anupassissa*, Dhp 253, *seṭṭhissa*, S I 90,1, Vin I 16,29, *hatthissa*, Vin II 195,26, (loc. sg.) *antevāsimhi*, Mil 90,4, *seṭṭhimhi*, Vin I 17,33, (nom. pl.) *paripanthayo*, Ja

---

1 See GEIGER § 95 and VON HINÜBER § 354-358. For Prakrit see PISCHEL § 405.

2 E.g. *upekkhāsukhānusāri viññāṇaṃ*, M III 226,26 (Ee *°sārī*, cf. CPD s.v.).

3 A loc. sg. in *°ini* is not attested in the canonical texts as Sadd 188,3 rightly remarks: *daṇḍinī ti bhumm'ekavacanañ ca nāgataṃ*.

4 *°dassibhi*, Th 4, *°dhāribhi*, Ja II 77,23*, *jhāyibhi* (-⏑x), It 71,8*, *pāṇihi* (prāṇibhiḥ), Ap 65,26 (BECHERT 1958: 311), Vv 28, *tapassihi*, Ap 19,23, *tādihi*, Ap 21,26, *atthadassinaṃ* (⏑-⏑-), Ja III 323,25*, *vajjadassinaṃ*, Dhp 76, *pakkhinaṃ* (-⏑-), A III 43,5*, *pāṇinaṃ* (⏑-⏑-), Ap 20,29, Ja VI 594,19(*), Dhp 135, Sn 307, *asayhasāhinaṃ* (-⏑-⏑-), Ja III 6,25*, *anomadassisu* (⏑-⏑-⏑x [Vait.]), Ja III 408,17* (cf. GEIGER § 95.3 and VON HINÜBER § 356).

5 See GEIGER § 95.1.

6 Sn 855 has the 'regular' nominative *visesī*.

7 See MICHELSON, *IF* 19 (1906) 210 n. 2.

VI 57,11*, *pāṇayo*, Sn 201, S V 370,5[1], *anupanāhī*, M I 42,37, *gihī*, D III 124,5, M I 490,34, *jhāyī*, Sn 1009, *dhaṃsī* 'the brave ones', M I 236,1, *hatthī*, S I 211,14*, Vin I 218,38, (acc. pl.) *brahmacārayo*, D II 88,29* (= Ud 89,21* = Vin I 229,36*[2]), A IV 245,6*, Vv 625 v.l. (*qu*. Sadd 192,16), *antevāsī*, M III 1,18, *pakkhī*, Sn 606, *hatthī*, Dhp-a II 45,25, (instr. pl.) *jhāyībhi jhānasīlībhi*, M III 13,25[3], (gen. pl.) *jhāyīnaṃ*, A I 24,11, 25,23, Sn 719, (loc. pl.) *(a)rūpīsu*, D III 111,11. The forms of the nom. pl. masc. *oṭṭhagīviyo* (Ja VI 29,7*), *°dīpiyo* (Ja V 408,29*, VI 538,4*), *pakkhiyo* (Ja V 408,30*) and *hatthiyo* (Ja II 144,2* [see n. 1 below], VI 537,30*) are analogical to the fem. (!) *ī*-stems (cf. § 32.6).

	singular	plural
nom.	*hatthī*, *°i* (ntr. *°i*)	*hatthino*, *°ī*, *°ayo*, *°iyo*
acc.	*hatthinaṃ*, *°iṃ*	*hatthino*, *°ī*, *°ayo*
instr.	*hatthinā*	*hatthi(b)hi*, *°ī(b)hi*
abl.	*hatthinā*, *hatthito*	
gen.	*hatthino*, *°issa*	*hatthinaṃ*, *°īnaṃ*
loc.	*seṭṭhimhi*	*hatthisu*, *°īsu*
voc.	*hatthi*	*hatthino*, *°ī*

[1] See Sadd 192 n. 4. Here belongs *hatthayo*, Ja II 144,2* = S II 279,28* (Ee *hatthiyo*) as quoted Sadd 196,14.

[2] So read (see VON HINÜBER § 355).

[3] As *°bhi* – as a rule – persists only after a short vowel (see § 32.8), I suspect we have to read *jhāyīhi jhānasīlīhi*.

Starting from the acc. sg. in *-inaṃ* the *in*-stems were thematicised[1]: (nom. sg. masc.) *katavedino*, Ras II 6:5[2], (acc. sg. ntr.) *ohāriṇaṃ*, Dhp 346[3], (loc. sg.) *ariyavuttine*, Ja IV 42,13*, *yasassine*, Ja IV 389,27* = V 267,10*, (nom. pl.) *verinā*, Dhp-a II 37,1, (acc. pl.) *gamine*, Sn 587, *tādine*, Th 1173, *°dassāvine*, M I 169,22, *palokine*, Thī 101, *pāṇine*, S I 102,21* (ms. B), Sn 220, 587, *°mānine*, Sn 282, *māladhārine*, Ja VI 543,17*, *°vāsine*, D II 272,25*, Sn 682, (loc. pl.) *verinesu*, Dhp 197[4]. The corresponding feminine ends in *°inā-*[5]: (acc.) *gabbhadhārinaṃ mātaraṃ* '[your] mother who carried [you as] a foetus', Ja VI 470,23*, *bhikkham ādāya sūpinaṃ* 'with your seasoned food', Ja III 328,5*, (voc.) *khīṇa-kulīne* 'you whose family is annihilated', Thī 220 (*-ī-* m.c. [*āryā*])[6].

---

1 For Prakrit see PISCHEL § 406.

2 In the introduction of M. / W. GEIGER, *Die zweite Dekade der Rasavāhinī*. München 1918, p. 7, it is pointed out that *katavedino* might be a wrong reading for *katavediko* which is attested at Ras II 8:1.

3 On this stanza see LÜDERS (1954: 70).

4 See GEIGER § 95.2. On comparable *n*-forms of *i*- and *u*-stems see § 32.4.

5 See VON HINÜBER § 358.

6 The voc. *uppalamāladhārine āveḷine*, Vv 293 = 314 = 804, which GEIGER (§ 95.2) records, is a wrong reading for *°ini* (see CPD s. vv. āveḷi(n), appalamālā) resp. *°inī* (so Ee).

§ 35. Apart from the historical form of the nom. sg. (in *-ū*, see § 10.7) the masc. *ū*-stems – all *nomina verbalia*[1] – are inflected as *u*-stems[2]: (nom. sg.) *abhibhū*, It 122,7, D I 18,7, S I 121,16*, *(a)vadaññū*, Sn 663, Pv 548, *pāragū*, D I 88,5, *rattaññū*, D I 48,2, *viññū*, Sn 39, 403, *pāragu*, Th 66, *vedagu*, Sn 322, 1060, *matañña*, S IV 175,29, (acc.) *abhibhuṃ*, Dhp 418, Sn 534, 642, *vadaññuṃ*, Sn 487, (instr.) *sayambhunā*, Mil 214,29, (gen.) *abhibhussa*, S I 157,10, *akataññussa*, Ja I 322,10*, *aviññussa*, Vin III 28,4 (*amattaññūno*, S IV 103,27, seems to have its *-ū-* from the nom.), (loc.) *abhibhusmiṃ*, M I 2,28, (nom.-acc. pl.) *addhagū*, Thī 55, *amattaññū*, Ja II 293,16*, *rattaññū*, Sn 92,22, *vadaññū*, Ja IV 34,15*, S I 34,21*, (instr.) *amattaññūhi*, S II 218,19, *viññūhi*, D II 93,33, S I 9,14, (gen.) *viññūnaṃ*, Th 667, S IV 93,22, *rattaññūnaṃ*, A I 25,18, (loc.) *viññūsu*, A III 153,24. The nom.-acc. pl. in *-uno* is analogical to the *in*-stems (see § 32.4): °*abhibhuno*, It 5,3*[3], *amattaññuno*, M I 32,10, *gotrabhuno*, M III 256,7, *kataññuno*, Vin I 56,1, *vedaguno*, Ud 14,17*, *mattaññūno*, S IV 105,8 (with the *-ū-* of the above-mentioned plural forms). In the same way *(a)vidū-* '(not) intelligent' (< vidu[ṣ]-) and *(a)viddasū-* '(not) knowing'[4] are inflected[5]: (nom. sg.) *(°)vidū*, D II 93,29, Sn 996, (acc.) *viduṃ*, Vv 302, (nom. pl.) °*viduno*, Vin II 241,7, *vidūhi*, Mil 277,21 (*vidūhi*, Sn 677, scans ⏑⏑–, i.e. *viduhī* [~ *viduhi*, D III 178,4*]), (gen.) *vidūna(ṃ)*, Vv 641, Mil 276,7, (nom. sg.) *aviddasu*, Th 342, Dhp 268, (gen.) *(a)viddasuno*, M I 65,5, (nom. pl.) *aviddasū*, Th 518 = 1112, Sn 762, *aviddasuno*, M I 65,26.

---

[1] See HAEBLER, *MSS* 16 (1964) 29 n. 7.

[2] See GEIGER § 87.2. For Prakrit see PISCHEL § 383.

[3] See CPD s.v. [1]abhibhū.

[4] This is a blend of *vidu[ṣ]-* and *vidvāṃs-* (see CPD s.v.).

[5] See GEIGER § 100.2. For Prakrit see PISCHEL § 411.

§ 36. 1. The OIA fem. *i-/u-* and *ī-/ū*-inflexions[1] have merged in one *ī-/ū*-class (only the nom. sg. has *-i/u* or *-ī/ū*[2]) which has only one oblique form in the singular (see § 29): (nom.) *jāti*, *devī*, (acc.) *deviṃ*[3], (instr./abl./gen./loc.) *deviyā*[4], (voc.) *devi*, *vadhu*, Vin III 16,25, (loc.) *deviyaṃ*, (nom./voc. pl.) *deviyo*[5], (acc.) *devī*, (instr.) *devīhi*, (gen.) *devīnaṃ*, (loc.) *devīsu*. The *ū*-stems take over the glide consonant *-y-* from the *ī*-stems[6]: (obl. sg.) *dhenuyā/aṃ*, (nom./voc. pl.) *dhenuyo*. Under the influence of the *ā*-inflexion the nom. pl. in *-iyo* (/ *-īyo*) and *-uyo* was used also as acc. and *vice versa* the acc. in *-ī/ū* as nom.[7]: (nom.) *pokkharaṇī*, Vv 1168 (if not a sg.), *puthū*, Th 1190, (acc.) *pokkharaṇiyo*, D II 178,23 (so read? Ee *-īyo*, for which see 6. below), *dhenuyo*, Vv 1157. – **2.** The regularity of the paradigm is disturbed by historical forms[8]: (acc. sg.) *ajiyaṃ*, Ja V 241,24*[9], *dahariyaṃ*, Ja VI 521,28*, *nadiyaṃ*, D II 135,3*,

---

1 See GEIGER § 86 / 87.1 and VON HINÜBER § 337-341. For Prakrit see PISCHEL § 384-388 and JACOBI § 41.

2 See BLOCH (1965: 135).

3 Sn 462 must be read (m.c.) *jāti(m)*.

4 The dat. fin. *santaye* '[conductive] to peace', Thī 342, seems to be a sanskritism (< *śāntaye*).

5 Prakrit has *-io* / *-uo* as well as *-īo* / *-ūo* (see 6., below).

6 See BLOCH (1965: 135) and VON HINÜBER § 338.

7 See GEIGER § 86.4.

8 See GEIGER § 86.2.

9 Cf. *Aciravatiyaṃ*, Mp I 248,5.

(jina)bodhiyaṃ, Ap 108,9, Bv II 183, *Rohiṇiyaṃ*, Th 529[1], (instr.) *anusāsaññā*, Ja III 231,20*-21*[2], *jaccā*, Ja III 395,6*, Dhp 393, Sn 136, *sammuccā*, Sn 648[3], (gen.) *najjā*, D II 112,22, Vin I 1,6, *pokkharaññā*, Pv 355, (loc.) *Naliññaṃ*, Ja VI 313,9*,[4] *Bārāṇassaṃ*, Ja II 435,14*, V 68,28* (*qu.* Sadd 644,7 as *Bārāṇasiṃ* [!]), (nom. pl.) *dasso*, Ja IV 53,29*, *najjo*, S III 202,6, 221,11, *pokkharañño*, S I 233,1*, Pv 113, 440, Vv 734[5]. The unassimilated *-y-* of some case-endings (*tithyā*, Sn 891, *nikatyā*, Ja III 88,14*, *bhumyā*, Ja III 389,18*, *ratyā*, Ja VI 26,16*, 491,21* = Th 517 = 628, *rudatyā*, Ja V 183,24*[6], *nābhyo*, Vv 1012[7], *ratyo*, Ja VI 26,16*[8]) is due to the influence of Sanskrit[9]. – **3.** The oblique case ends also in *-īyā* and *-ūyā* (with the long vowel of [the nom. sg. and] the oblique forms of the plural)[10]: *asanīyā*, Ap 105,24 ≠ 421,6, *°kuttīyā*, Ja III 314,28*, *kumārī*

---

[1] See Sadd 201 n. 5, 203 n. 12, CPD s.vv. ajī (see also *Additions and corrections*, I,549a) and Aciravatī (I,547b), BECHERT (1958: 311) and VON HINÜBER § 339.

[2] See CPD s.v. anusāsanī.

[3] *uppaccā*, S I 209,6*, however, is an absolutive (VON HINÜBER § 338 *pace* GEIGER § 86.2).

[4] It was not possible to trace the loc. *pokkharaññā*, Vin II 123. which the PED (s.v. pokkharaṇī) records.

[5] See also BECHERT (1958: 311).

[6] See GEIGER § 86.2.

[7] On this form see VON HINÜBER, *IT* 10 (1982) 138.

[8] So read against Ee *ratyā* (see OBERLIES 1995/96: 300).

[9] See VON HINÜBER § 338 (cf. INSLER 1994: 71).

[10] As ALSDORF pointed out (*Kleine Schriften* p. 66) final *-ya* (after a long vowel) developed in MIA to *-e*. As *mayā* 'by me' and *tvayā* 'by you' > *mae* / *tae* show, *-yā*

yā, Ja VI 65,11*, *°chāpīyā*, Ja VI 193,20*, *jātīyā*, Ja III 192,15*, *°dhāranī-yā*, Ja IV 223,18*, *purāṇīyā*, Ja II 114,23*, *brāhmaṇīyā*, Ja VI 524,15*, *bhūmīyā*, Ja VI 19,29*/31*, *mandīyā*, Ja III 38,4*, *varākīyā*, Ja IV 285,10* = 288,9*, Vv 189, *vijānīyā*, Ap 334,18[1], *vilapantīyā*, Ja III 481,22*, V 179,5*/9*[2], Ap 404,15, 529,23, *sarantīyā*, Ja II 425,27*, *kāsūyā*, Ja VI 12,20* (Ee throughout metrically faulty *-i/uyā*)[3]. – **4.** The abl. has also a form in *-to* (see § 7.2b)[4]. – **5.** The loc. in *-o* (< *-au*) is preserved only in a formula like *divā ca ratto ca* 'day and night', Ud 15,3*, Thī 312, Sn 223[5].

---

developed in the same way. So we can assume that the oblique endings *-īyā* and *-ūyā* (see above) resulted in *-īe* and *-ūe*. And precisely these endings are the common ones in Prakrit (see PISCHEL § 385). This purely phonetical explanation would dispense with the derivation of Pkt *-āe*, *-īe* and (analogical) *-ūe* from (Br+) dat.-gen. *-āyai* and *-(i)yai* (*pace* PISCHEL § 6 / 375, BLOCH 1965: 135, VON HINÜBER § 334 and WITZEL, in: *Dialectes dans les littératures indo-aryennes* [édité par C. Caillat]. Paris 1989, 214). For *-āe* such an explanation (Pkt. *mālāe* < [Pāli] *mālāya*) was suggested already by ALSDORF, l.c. (cf. SCHWARZSCHILD 1991: 44-46).

1 See BECHERT (1958: 311).

2 See BECHERT (1961: 16) and OBERLIES (1993/94: 168).

3 See Sadd 448 n. c, CPD I,531a (s.v. [γ] me), BECHERT (1958: 311), CAILLAT (1970: 23-24), VON HINÜBER § 341 and OBERLIES (1993/94: 160 with n. 56). These forms offend against 'Insler's law' (see § 4.4). Therefore we have to assume that they were created when this law had ceased to operate, i.e. we have to do with *young* forms.

4 See GEIGER § 76 and VON HINÜBER § 340. For Prakrit see PISCHEL § 386 and CHANDRA, *Proceedings of the Seminar on Prakrit Studies*. Ahmedabad 1987, 133.

5 See SCHULZE, *Kleine Schriften* p. 788, and GEIGER § 86.5. *bhuvi*, Ap 539,31, is most probably a pure Sanskritism (cf. GEIGER § 86.5).

– **6.** The nom./acc. pl. may also end in *-īyo*, a forerunner of Pkt. *-īo*[1]: *āveḷinīyo*, Vv 1023 (so read), *ūmīyo*, Ap 23,11, 323,16[2], *jātīyo*, Thī 511, *nārīyo*, Ja V 449,5*/7*, VI 249,20*[3], *pāṭalīyo*, Ja VI 530,1*, *pātīyo*, Ja I 269,30*[4], *pokkharaṇīyo*, A I 145,10, *bhāginīyo*, Thī 408 (so read), *bhūmīyo*, Ja VI 277,14*[5], *saṃgītīyo*, Ja VI 528,30*, *sallakīyo*, Ja VI 535,19* (Ee except A I 145,7 [unmetr.] *°iyo*)[6]. – **7.** The vocalism of the plural may conform to that of the singular[7]: (gen.) *anudiṭṭhīnaṃ* (⏑⏑-⏑-), Th 754, *nārinaṃ*, Ja IV 494,26*[8], *mātinaṃ*, Ja VI 263,1* (see § 40), (loc.) *jātisu*, Th 346, *nārisu*, Ja V 448,17*, Dhp 284. – **8.** The nom. pl. *najjāyo* 'rivers', Ja VI 278,1*, based on **najjā-* (abstracted from obl. *najjā*), anticipates the following *supatiṭṭhāyo*[9].

---

1 See CAILLAT (1970: 23-24) and VON HINÜBER § 341. For Prakrit see PISCHEL § 387 (on *-io* and *-uo* see ibid. § 99 and 387).

2 See BECHERT (1958: 311).

3 See ALSDORF (1968: 37) and OBERLIES (1993/94: 168).

4 See OBERLIES (1993/94: 167).

5 See OBERLIES (1993/94: 168).

6 *(vikkand)antiyo*, Ja V 180,2* (C[s] B[d] [Ee *pi kandantiyo*]) – see ALSDORF (1968: 32) –, *(har)antiyo*, Pv 510, and *(āy)antiyo*, Pv 513, scan -- (i.e. *-antyo*).

7 See GEIGER § 86.3. For Prakrit see PISCHEL § 99 / 387.

8 See Sadd 1481 (s.v. nārī) and OBERLIES (1995a: 141 [s.v. nārī-]). GEIGER § 86.3 gives also Cp I 6,2 (= 41) as reference. But the new edition of JAYAWICKRAMA reads *°narādinaṃ*.

9 Somewhat differently VON HINÜBER § 341 (see also GEIGER § 86.2 and NORMAN 1991: 176).

rem. *itthī-* 'woman' (strī-) and other originally mono-syllabic nouns are inflected as regular *ī*-stems[1]. Thus the nom. sg. *may* end in *-i* (*itthi*, A III 68,23, Th 151, D II 273,18*, Vin I 269,5[2], ~ *itthī*, Ja I 307,14*, *thī*, Sn 769, *siri*, Ja V 182,7, VI 373,2* (so read), S I 44,12*, ~ *sirī*, Ja VI 357,21*, 360,10*[3], *hiri*, It 36,6, A I 51,17, IV 11,22, ~ *hirī*, S I 33,11*).

§ 37. 1. Of the *diphthong-stems* of OIA only *go-* 'cow' (and *div-* 'heaven; day') survived, and this only in some historical forms[4]: *go*, Ja V 15,27*, S I 221,34*, Sn 580[5], (nom. pl.) *gāvo*, A II 43,18, D I 141,26, M I 225,10, Sn 20, ([due to the confusion of nom. and acc.] acc. pl.) Ja VI 549,6*, Dhp 19, 135, M I 225,9, S IV 181,12, Sn 295, *gohi*, S I 6,9*, Sn 33/34, *gavaṃ(pati)*, Ja III 111,17*, IV 97,26*, 172,11*, 422,6*, S V 436,27, Sn 26-27, *gonaṃ* (< Ved. *gónām* [?]), Dīp I 76, *gunnaṃ* (< id.[6]), A I 229,13, II 75,33* = 76,2* M I 388,36, S II 188,9; *divaṃ*, Ja IV 134,3*, V 123,27*, Sn 507 (*rattiṃ-divaṃ*), (adv.) *divā*, Ja VI 293,7*, Dhp 296, Sn

---

[1] See GEIGER § 87.1. For Prakrit see PISCHEL § 147.

[2] On *itthi*, Th 151, see NORMAN (1969: 155). It is used as acc. (< *itthi[m]*, cf. § 4.1) at Ja V 448,16*. Also Prakrit knows (nom. sg.) *itthi* (e.g. Vasudevahiṇḍi 10.21) beside *itthī* (see CHANDRA, *Sambodhi* 4 [1975/76] 35).

[3] See OBERLIES (1995/96: 272).

[4] See GEIGER § 88 and VON HINÜBER § 342. For Prakrit see PISCHEL § 393-394 (on nom. pl. *gāo* and *gāvo* – the latter not recorded by PISCHEL § 393 – see ALSDORF, *Kleine Schriften* p. 69).

[5] The accusative *gaṃ* (gām) seems to be attested in *gaddūhana-* 'unit of time measurement' (see OBERLIES 1995: 119).

[6] See BERGER (1955: 64).

223, *divi*, D II 206,8[1]. – **2.** The new stem *gava-* 'cow' is based on the instr. *gavā*, which evidently was understood as an abl. (acc. *gavaṃ*, Ja IV 308,16*, 481,12*, abl. *gavā*, D I 201,25, *gavassa*, M I 429,32, *gave*, Sn 310, nom. pl. *gavā*, M I 226,16). The corresponding feminine is *gāvī-* which got its *-ā-* from the old nom./acc. plural *gāvo*[2]. – **3.** Another stem, *goṇa-* 'cow', was extracted from the (newly created) feminine *goṇī-* (*goṇo*, S IV 195,32, Vin IV 7,16, *goṇaṃ*, M I 10,36, nom. pl. *goṇā*, M III 167,24, *goṇe*, Dhp-a III 302,18[3], *goṇānaṃ*, Dhp-a III 239,22)[4].

rem. The acc. *gāvuṃ*, Vin I 150,9, seems to be a transformation of *gavaṃ* caused by preceding *vatthuṃ* and following *gāviṃ* (cf. Sadd V 1358).

§ 38. 1. Only traces of (**a**) the root nouns[5] and (**b**) the consonant stems without vowel alternation – mainly neuter nouns in *-as*, *-is* and *-us*, and very few masc./fem. *as*-nouns – have survived (see § 28.2)[6]: (**a**) (acc. sg.) *diso-disaṃ*, Ja III 459,22*, (instr.) *padā* (see § 30.2), *vācā*, Sn 130, 232, (loc.) *parisati* (and °*tiṃ*, see § 4.5 [with analogical *-t-*]), Ja V 61,24*,

---

1 See OBERLIES (1995: 124).

2 On *suggavāsu*, Ja IV 53,23*, see PED s.v. su+ggava.

3 Cf. *gone*, Aś PE V.

4 See CAILLAT, *JAs* 1960, 55-60.

5 For Prakrit see PISCHEL § 413.

6 See GEIGER § 89 / 99-101 and VON HINÜBER § 343. For Prakrit see PISCHEL § 408 / 411 / 413.

M I 68,8, *saṃsati*, Ja III 493,1* = 495,15*, (nom. pl.) *āpo*[1], Sn 307, (acc. [< nom.], Ja IV 302,5*), *pāvuso*, Ja V 5,31*[2], (acc.) *pānado*, Ja VI 251,23* (Ee *pādukā*[3]), (gen.) *dvipadaṃ* ... *catuppadaṃ*, S I 6,22*/24*, (**b**) (nom./acc.) *ayo*, Ja IV 102,10* (acc. S I 127,15*), *tapo*, Dhp 184, *payo*, Ja VI 572,3*, *mano*, Ja III 66,6* (acc. Ja IV 405,9*), *yaso*, Sn 438 (acc. Ja III 87,25*), *vaco* (acc. Sn 1147, Ap 153,19), *siro* (acc. Ja VI 527,21*, Sn 768), (instr.) *ayasā*, Dhp 240[4], *āyusā*, Sn 149[5], *jarasā*, Sn 804, 1123[6], (gen.) *cetaso*, M III 196,27, Vin I 4,33, *chandaso*, Sn 568, *jagato*, It 120,14, *manaso*, Dhp 390, (loc.) *urasi*, Ja III 148,13*, *sarasi*, Ja VI 534,14*, (acc. pl.) *sarado sataṃ*, Ja II 16,15*, VI 239,6*, (gen.) *saritaṃ*, Ja II 442,8*; (nom. sg.) *candimā*, Th 871-873, Dhp 172, 382, (acc.) *vyāsattamanasaṃ*, Dhp 47, (gen.) *ananvāhatacetaso*, Dhp 39[7], (gen. pl.) *accharasaṃ*, Ja IV 450,11* (so read). – **2.** The nom. in *°o* was a favourable

---

[1] *āpo* is also used as prior member in compounds (see CPD s.v.) forming a series with *tejo+* and *vāyo+* (!). See also PISCHEL § 355.

[2] See CPD s.v. abhisandati and OBERLIES (1995: 129).

[3] See CPD s.v. apiḷayhati. This word is also attested as the prior member of the compound *pānadūpama-*, Ja II 223,18*.

[4] Here the 'instr.' is used as an ablative: *ayasā va malaṃ samuṭṭhitaṃ*. Or is *ayasā* the genuine ablative of a stem *ayasa-*?

[5] On the gender of *āyu(s)-* see CAILLAT, *IF* 74 (1969) 224.

[6] See also *urasā* (Ap 505,24, Ja VI 508,2*, Th 27, 233), *cetasā* (Vin I 4,17), *chandasā* (Ja II 326,15* = V 451,5*), *tapasā, tamasā, tejasā* (Ja V 322,2*, VI 23,1*), *manasā, yasasā* (Ja IV 406,2*), *vacasā* (A II 185,10, Sn 365, 663), *vayasā* (Ja V 343,12*, D II 151,25), *sirasā* (Ja I 65,8*, M II 120,1, Vin I 4,23).

[7] See GEIGER § 100.1.

basis for transferring the neuter *as-* into *a*-stems (see § 28.2c)[1], and the compounds with *as*-stems as posterior members followed this development[2]: (nom. sg. masc.) *attamano*, Dhp 328, M I 432,3, Sn 45, *dummano*, Vin I 21,22, (nom. pl.) *sumanā*, Sn 222, (acc.) *muditamane*, Sn 680[3]. The (historical) acc. in *°saṃ* gave rise to *a*-enlargements[4]: (nom. sg.) *avyāpannacetaso*, S V 74,9, (nom. pl.) *adhimanasā*, Sn 692. And new *°(as)a*-stems were evidently abstracted from such compounds: *sirasaṃ (muñcati)* 'she loosens (lit.) her head (= her hair)', Ja V 434,8.

Most of the OIA comparatives[5] in *°(i)yas-* are transferred to the *a*-inflexion (see § 28.2g), with only few historical forms surviving (*seyyo* 'better' < śreyaḥ[6], *pāpiyo* 'worse' < pāpīyaḥ, *bhiyyo* 'more' < bhūyaḥ)[7]. The comparative is usually formed with the suffix *°tara-*[8] (*mahattara-*, Sn 659, *mahantatara-*, M III 170,13, *ñāṇavantatara-*, Ja V 60,14, *vaṇṇavantatara-*, D I 18,21, *sīlavantatara-*, Ja II 3,21, *balavatara-*, Mil 234,21, *divātaraṃ*, Ja III 2,7, *sāyataraṃ*, Ja VI 366,24, *pagevataraṃ*, M

---

1 See GEIGER § 100.1.

2 For Prakrit see PISCHEL § 409.

3 See GEIGER § 100.

4 For Prakrit see PISCHEL § 409 (end).

5 In Pāli the (reduplicated) positive may be used instead of the elative and the comparative (see GEIGER § 103.3): *bhaddāni-bhaddāni yānāni yojāpetvā*, D II 73,6, *etesu kataraṃ nu kho mahantaṃ*, Ja III 194,3 (for Prakrit see PISCHEL § 414 [end]).

6 An analogical form is *nīceyya-* 'inferior', M I 329,27, Sn 855, 918.

7 See GEIGER § 103. For Prakrit see PISCHEL § 414.

8 And sporadically *°ttara-* which was abstracted from *mahattara-* (*piyattara-*, Thī 375 [so read *m.c.*], *bahuttara-*, Th 937). An extended form is *lahukatarikā-*, M II 70,13.

III 145,5)[1], which was even added to old comparatives (*bhiyyatara-*, Ja IV 109,21*, *seyyatara-*, Nett 53,13, Vv-a 96,22, cf. *uttaritara-*, D I 45,20)[2] and superlatives (*pāpiṭṭhatara-*, Ja V 144,8*, Vin II 5,11[3], *seṭṭhatara-*, Ja V 148,7*, *paramatara-*, Th 518, cf. *paṭhamatara-*, Vin I 30,8)[4].

§ 39. The paradigm of the *n*-inflexion (e.g. *rāja(n)-* 'king') is composed of (**1.**) historical forms, eastern ones with split-vowel, western ones with assimilated consonants (see § 1), and (**2.**) innovations which are based (**a**) on the proportion *rājū(hi/naṃ) : rājā = pitū(hi/naṃ) : pitā*[5], (**b**) abstracted from nominal compounds (*rāja+*, *mahārāja-*) and (**c**), though only sporadically, forms of the stem *rañña-* (see § 28.2i)[6]: **1.** (nom.-voc.) *rājā*, *kamma* (also acc.), (acc.) *rājānaṃ*, (instr./abl.) *raññā*, D II 76,2, M I 82,16, *rājinā*, Ja IV 122,29*, Mhv VI 2, (gen.) *rañño*, Ud 14,1, Th 632, Thī 448,

---

[1] See GEIGER § 103. Diachronically, the adverbs *divātaraṃ*, *sāyataraṃ* and *pagevataraṃ* are probably continuations of OIA *°tarām*-forms. For Prakrit see PISCHEL § 414.

[2] On such 'double' comparatives see OBERLIES (1995: 143), for Prakrit PISCHEL § 414. On *uttari(ṃ)* (uttaram x upari) see OBERLIES (1995: 113 [s.v. uttari]).

[3] See OLDENBERG, *Kleine Schriften* p. 1166.

[4] It is also added to nouns: *bālataro*, Ja III 278,20* (so read: OBERLIES, 1995/96: 292), *malataraṃ*, Dhp 243, *vacchatara-*, D I 127,12, 148,1, *vanataraṃ*, Mil 269,1, *sappurisataro*, S V 20,7 (see GEIGER § 103.2; on such forms see also TURNER 1975: 418-420).

[5] See MICHELSON, *IF* 27 (1910) 296.

[6] See GEIGER § 92-94 and VON HINÜBER § 348-353. For Prakrit see PISCHEL § 399-404 – a voc. *rājaṃ*, Vasudevahiṇḍi 128.30, 131.9 *et passim*, is pointed out by ALSDORF, *Kleine Schriften* p. 68 – and JACOBI § 42.2.

rājino, Thī 463, Sn 299, 415, (loc.) *rājini*[1], (nom.-acc. pl.) *rājāno*, D II 209,10*, M I 86,9, Dhp 294/295, *kammāni*, Dhp 136, Sn 263, (gen.) *raññaṃ*, Ud 88,4, Ja VI 273,3*, D II 87,3 (see below), (loc.) *kammasu*, D III 156,23* (-‿x); **2a.** (instr.) *rājūhi*, Ud 41,7, M II 120,22, *rājuhi*, Ja VI 212,7*, *rājubhi*, D II 258,14*, (gen.) *rājūnaṃ*, Ud 11,3, Ja V 474,9/11, D III 64,30, Vin I 228,30 (≠ *raññaṃ*, D II 87,3), (loc.) *rājūsu*, Ja IV 76,23*, VI 294,24*, **2b.** (acc. sg.) *rājaṃ*, Vin III 222,13, Bv VI 4, (abl.) *rājato*, Ja IV 310,3*, Dhp 139, (gen.) *rājassa*, Dīp XVII 41, (voc.) *rāja*, Sn 422/423, (nom. pl.) *rājā*, (gen.) *paṭirājānaṃ*, Ja IV 472,22* (ct. *°rājūnaṃ*), **2c.** (nom. sg.) *rañño*, A II 113,21, 116,24, (loc.) *raññe*, Ud 18,8, Ja VI 330,3, D III 83,27, (instr. pl.) *raññehi*, A I 279,14[2]. The analogy of the *r*-stems (cf. 2a.) was especially effective when a *-m-* preceded *-an*[3]: *thāmunā*, Ja VI 22,16*, *brahmunā*, Ud 77,10, Th 1168, *brahmuno*, Th 182, D I 220,33, 222,2, S I 141,2, *kammunā*, Ja III 313,10*, Th 143, D III 152,5*, *kammuno*, Ja III 65,17*, Vv 1032[4] (but cf. *brahmani*, M I 2,12, ~ *satthari*). The *-u-* of *addhunā* and *addhuno* ('on / of the road'), however, is due to *saṃprasāraṇa* (see § 9.14), i.e. both are historical forms. Vocatives like

---

[1] This word is attested only in commentaries (e.g. Ud-a *ad* Ud 18,8 explaining loc. *raññe*).

[2] On this reference (Ee *raññahi*) see GEIGER's note (§ 92 note 3 [= p. 131 n. 2 of GHOSH's English translation]) and VON HINÜBER § 350. The gen. *raññassa*, Ja III 70,7*, which GEIGER (§ 92.2) cites, *can* stand for *raññ' assa*.

[3] See VON HINÜBER § 136. For Prakrit see PISCHEL § 104 and 404 (p. 284 bottom) and ALSDORF, *Kleine Schriften* p. 69 (on *kāladhammuṇā*, Vasudevahiṇḍi 75,25, 284,20 *et passim*).

[4] On the genitive *kammuno*, D I 54,2, see BECHERT, *WZKSO* 1 (1957) 74, and VON HINÜBER § 351 (cf. GEIGER § 80.2); diff. NORMAN (1990: 242-244).

nāgarāje 'king of the *nāgas*!' and *brahme* 'o brahmin'[1] have the generalised ending *-e* of – e.g. – *ise* (in the same way the vocative in *-o* [see p. 177] spread: *ayyo* 'noble one(s)' [used for sg. *and* pl.[2]] ≠ arya)[3].

Stems with *°an-* after a double consonant (< *°Cman-/van-*, also *muddha[n]-*) retain *-a-* in the weak cases[4]: (instr.) *attanā*, Dhp 165, *amhanā*, Sn 443, *kammanā*, Sn 136, (gen.) *attano*, Dhp 343, Sn 334, (loc.) *attani*, M I 138,3, Sn 666, *asmani*, Ja III 433,11*, *muddhani*, M I 168,29*, Sn 689. The *-ă-* encroached on the acc. (*attanam* 'the self', Sn 477) which, in turn, formed the basis of new stems (*jammana-* 'birth', Sn 1018, *yakana-* 'liver', D II 293,14, M I 57,17)[5]. Also, the (old) acc. in *°ānaṃ* was such a source (see § 28.2d), and the stem in *°a-* used in nominal compounds and (in the case of neuter *an*-stems) the nom. sg./pl. in *°a/ °āni*, too: *attaṃ*, *attena*, *ātume*, Pv 377, *kammena*, Ap 4,21, Ja IV 296,11*, D III 147,9*, Vv 1212, *kammāya*, Ja III 411,7*, S V 92,5, Vin V 22,31, *kammehi*, Sn 215, *kammesu*, Sn 140, (nom. sg.) *nāmam*, Sn 808, (nom./acc.) *muddhaṃ*, D I 95,13, Dhp 72, Sn 987/989.

---

1 See OBERLIES (1989/90: 168).

2 See Vin I 75,8. For Prakrit *ajjo* see PISCHEL § 372.

3 See BERGER, *WZKSO* 1 (1957) 72 n. 1, CAILLAT (1970: 17-18), ea. (1980: 51-52) and VON HINÜBER § 349.

4 For Prakrit see PISCHEL § 401 and JACOBI § 40.2.

5 For Prakrit see PISCHEL § 404 (p. 284 bottom).

	singular		plural	
	masc.	ntr.	masc.	ntr.
nom.	**(1)** *rājā* **(2c)** *rañño* – *attā*	*kamma* *kammaṃ*	**(1)** *rājāno* **(2b)** *rājā*	*kammāni*
acc.	**(1)** *rājānaṃ* **(2b)** *rājaṃ* – *attānaṃ*		**(2)** *rājāno*	
instr.-abl.	**(1)** *raññā*, *rājinā* (abl. *rājato*), **(2b)** °*rājena* – *attanā* (abl. *attato*), *kammanā*, *kammunā*		**(2a)** *rājūhi*, **(2b)** °*rājehi*, **(2c)** *raññehi*	
gen.	**(1)** *rañño*, *rājino*, **(2b)** *rājassa* – *attano*, *kammuno*		**(1)** *raññaṃ*, **(2a)** *rājūnaṃ*	
loc.	**(1)** *rājini*, **(2c)** *raññe* – *attani*, *kammani*		**(2a)** *rājūsu*	
voc.	**(1)** *rājā̆*, (°)*rāje* – *attā̆*		**(1)** *rājāno*	

Most of the other *n*-stems of OIA (incl. *puṃs*-) have been transferred to the *a*-declension (see § 28.2g), with only some historical forms being retained[1]: (nom. sg.) *pumā* 'man' (pumān), Ja VI 238,21* (C^{ks} *pumo*), Ap 42,11, Ras II 83,6, *maghavā* 'Indra', Ja IV 403,28*, V 139,17*, VI 212,13*/15*, Dhp 30 – used also as voc., S I 221,24* –, *yuvā* 'young boy',

[1] See GEIGER § 93 and VON HINÜBER § 352. For Prakrit see PISCHEL § 403 / 412.

Ja V 322,7*, Thī 139, D I 80,16, Dhp 280, Sn 420[1], *sā* 'dog' (śvā), D I 166,8, M I 77,35, S I 176,13*, (instr.) *pumunā* 'by the man', Ja VI 80,9* = 550,7*, (gen.) *poso* 'the man's' (puṃsaḥ [x po(risa)-][2]), Ja II 52,6* = III 331,8* = IV 425,27* – with corresponding 'eastern' *pose*, Ja III 262,23*[3].

§ 40. The distinction of the *r*-stems in *nomina agentis* and kinship terms has been retained[4]: (nom.) *khattā*, D I 112,29, *satthā*, *nattā*, Ja III 427,5*, (acc.) **satthāraṃ*[5], (nom./voc. pl.) *satthāro* vs. *pitā*, *pitaraṃ*, *pitaro*. The nom. sg. in *°ā* was used as vocative, the nom. pl. as acc. (*nattāro*, Ud 91,23, *pitaro*, Pv-a 17,27, *mātā-pitaro*, Thī 433 [*coni.*, Ee *°pitū*]). Also, the gen., loc. and voc. sg. and the loc. pl. are historical forms (*satthu*, *satthari*, *sattha*; *pitu*, *pitari*, *pita*, *pitusu*). The instr./abl. (*sattharā*, *pitarā*)[6], however, is analogical to the loc. (*satthari*, *pitari*)[7], while the younger form in *°ārā*[8] shows the vocalism of the acc.: *satthārā vā satthāraṃ saṅghena vā saṅghaṃ*, D I 163,8-9. The latter case formed the basis

---

1 On *yuvi(n)-*, Ja IV 106,18*, 222,23*, see VON HINÜBER § 352 (cf. GEIGER § 93.2).

2 Or is the *-o-* simply due to the preceding *p-* (see § 12.12).

3 See NORMAN (1992a: 86-88).

4 See GEIGER § 90-91 and VON HINÜBER § 344-347 (cf. BARTHOLOMAE 1916: 23-30). For Prakrit see PISCHEL § 55 / 389-392 and JACOBI § 42.1.

5 Beside *sattharaṃ*, Bv XXII 14.

6 *matyā* 'by the mother', Ja VI 16,6*, is artificially integrated into the feminine *ī*-declension (see VON HINÜBER, *IT* 10 [1982] 138 [*pace* TRENCKNER 1908: 105 n. 4]; cf. id. 1999: 156); and *petyā*, Ja V 214,5* (*qu.* Sadd 140,9-10), is formed in analogy.

7 See EDGERTON, *JAOS* 73 (1953) 117 (cf. AiGr. III p. 208).

8 See INSLER (1994: 71).

for a stem in *°āra-* (perhaps on the model of *kammāra-* : *kammāraṃ*)[1]: (instr./abl. pl.) *nattārehi*, Ud 92,2, (gen. pl.) *satthārānaṃ*, Ja I 509,3, Nidd I 146,19, 248,2, *satthāra-dassanaṃ*, Bv II 59, *satthārato*, Nidd I 93,3 (*qu.* Sadd 140,28). Other forms were based on the gen. sg. in *-u* (on *pituc-ca* see § 24)[2], which itself was elucidated; and also on the plural forms in * *°ubhi/naṃ/su* which had generalised *u* < *ṛ*[3]: (acc. sg.) *pituṃ*, Cp 223[4], (instr.) *satthunā*, Mhv XVII 12, (gen.) *satthuno*, Th 131, Sn 547, 573, *pituno*, Vin I 17,1, *satthussa*, Vin V 171,20*, Mhv IV 32, *bhātussa*, Mhv VIII 9, *dhītuyā*, S II 243,25, Vin I 140,35, III 35,26, *mātuyā*, Ap 22,25, Cp 152, Pv 122, Mhv X 80, *buddhamātussa*, Ap 541,12 (*qu.* Sadd 669,7), (nom. pl.) *bhātuno*, Thī 408, (acc.) *°pitū* (Thī 433 [see above]), (instr./abl. pl.) *mātāpitūhi*, Vin I 93,30, (gen.) *pitūnaṃ*, It 110,6[5] (and *pitunnaṃ*, Dhp-a I 161,12, which sometimes scans ⏑⏑⏑ [Pv 249 (*tri.*)][6]). Eastern Aś has the corresponding *i*-forms (Aś K *pitinā*, *bhātinā*, *bhātinaṃ*, *mātāpitisu*), while in Pāli this vowel appears only in compounds and suffix derivations (cf., however, *mātinaṃ* 'of the mother's', Ja VI 263,1* [*vait.*]): *piti+*, *(a)pitika-*, *pitito* (← pitṛ- 'father'), *bhātika-* (← bhrātṛ- 'brother'), *(a)mātika-* (side by

---

1 See GEIGER § 90.3 and BLOCH (1965: 136).

2 The nominative (!) *ātu* 'father', M I 449,1 (*bhikkhussa ātu māri bhikkhussa mātu māri*), is formed from a masculine corresponding to Skt. *attā* after *mātu* (see CPD s.v. ātu).

3 See BERGER (1955: 60) and BLOCH (1965: 137).

4 See VON HINÜBER § 344.

5 *°ūnaṃ* is the regular ending of the *u*-stems and *not* a continuation of OIA *°ṝṇām* (see EDGERTON, *JAOS* 73 [1953] 118 [*pace* PISCHEL § 58]).

6 See Sadd 797 n. 4 (cf. also VON HINÜBER § 346).

side with *satthu+*, *dhītu+*, *bhattu+*, *bhātuka-*)[1].

The vocatives *k(h)atte* (D I 128,15, M II 164,26, Ja V 220,24*, VI 492,2*), *°rāje* (etc.) show the productive *e*-suffix (see § 39 [p. 170]).

	singular	plural
nom.	*satthā* *pitā, mātā*	*satthāro* *pitaro, mātaro, bhātuno*
acc.	*satthāraṃ* *pitaraṃ, mātaraṃ (pituṃ)*	*satthāro* *pitaro, mātaro*
instr. abl.	*sattharā, satthārā, satthunā* *pitarā, mātarā*	*satthūhi, satthārehi* *pitūhi, mātūhi*
gen.	*satthu, satthuno, satthussa* *pitu, pituno, bhātussa*	*satthūnaṃ, satthārānaṃ* *pitūnaṃ, pitunnaṃ, mātūnaṃ*
loc.	*satthari* *pitari*	*satthūsu, satthāresu* *pitūsu, mātūsu*
voc.	*sattha, satthā, khatte* *pitā*	*satthāro* *pitaro, mātaro*

The voc. in *-a* (< nom. *-ā*) was the source of a new *a*-stem (starting from words used for addressing people), the nom. in *-ā* of an *ā*-stem: (nom.) *jāmāto* 'son-in-law', Ja IV 219,25, ***n(a)hāpito*** 'barber', D I 225,16, Vin I 252,17*, *sallakatto* 'surgeon', Sn 560, (acc.) *khattaṃ* 'minister', D I 112,8, M II 164,19, *n(a)hāpitaṃ*, D I 225,6, (loc.) *nahāpite*, Mhv XXIX 20, *nette* 'in the leader', Ja III 111,18*/23* = V 222,22*/27*, *sallakattaṃ*,

[1] Cf. *a-mātāpitari-saṃvaḍḍho*, Ja I 436,19* (see CPD s.v.).

M I 429,4[1], (nom. pl.) *bhattā* 'husbands', Vin IV 155,33; *(Rāhula)mātāya* 'of the mother (of Rāhula)', Ja I 62,13, *(Nanda)māte* 'o mother (of Nanda)!', A IV 65,12.

dhītā- 'daughter'[2] inflects *also* as a regular *ā*-stem: (nom. sg.) *dhītā*, Thī 46, 336 (*dhīta mhi*), D II 268,3, (acc.) *dhītaraṃ*, Ja I 207,23*, Thī 98, S I 86,8, *dhītaṃ*, Cp 118, (gen.) *dhītāya*, Pv 798, Mhv V 169, *dhītu*, Ja VI 366,10, Dhp-a I 397,6, (loc.) *dhītari*, Dhp-a I 397,7, *dhīte*, Ja III 21,28, Dhp-a III 8,12, (nom. pl.) *dhītaro*, Ja V 311,8* (acc. ibid. 19*), S I 170,27*, *dhītā*, Mhv II 18, (instr.) *dhītāhi*, Mhv VII 68, (gen.) *dhītānaṃ*, Ja III 4,7, (loc.) *dhītāsu*, Ja I 152,8. (Nom. sg.) *asakya-dhītarā* (see CPD s.v.) and (nom. pl.) *(puttā) dhītarā*, Nidd I 134,1 (so B^{p} S [Ee *putto dhītā*]), however, are formed on the base of the (old) acc. *dhītaraṃ* (see above).

§ 41. The paradigm of the *°m/va(nt)*-stems (including *maha[nt]-* 'great, tall')[3] is composed of (**a**) historical (in the plural only nom./voc. [= acc.] and gen. pl. have survived) and (**b**) newly created forms based on the acc. sg. (*°[m/v]anta-* ← *°[m/v]antaṃ*)[4]: (**a**) (sg.) *sīlavā*, *°vantaṃ*, *°vatā*, *°vato*, *°vati*, *°va* (< °van [?]), (pl.) *°vanto*, *°vataṃ*, (**b**) (sg.) *°vanto*, *°vantena*, *°vantā*[5], *°vantassa*, *°vante*/ *°vantamhi*/ *°vantasmiṃ*, *°vanta*, (pl.)

---

[1] See GEIGER § 90.4.

[2] *dhītā-* is a contraction of **dihitā-* (cf. p. 49) which goes back to *duhitā́* (see OBERLIES 1999: 39-41). For Prakrit see PISCHEL § 392.

[3] See GEIGER § 96-98 and VON HINÜBER § 359-363. For Prakrit see PISCHEL § 396 and JACOBI § 40.3.

[4] This stem (*sīlavanta-*, *mahanta-*) is used as prior member of compounds (beside we have *mahā-* and by analogy *brahā-*).

[5] This ablative ending, which is not recorded by GEIGER, seems to be used very rarely, and only in late texts: *Gaṅgā ... Himavantā pabhāvitā* '... from the Himavant ...', Ap

°vantā, *°vante*, *°vantehi*, *°vantānaṃ*, *°vantesu*, *°vantā*[1]. The nom. sg. in *°vā* is used as voc.: *āyasmā*, S II 268,24, *cakkhumā*, Ap 39,12, *Bhagavā*, S V 80,14. The feminines are derived from the weak stem (*sīlavatī*, D II 12,27).

	singular	plural
nom.	*sīlavā*, (ntr.) *ojavaṃ* *mahā*, *mahanto*	*sīlavanto*, *sīlavantā*, (ntr.) *oja-vantāni* *mahantā*, (ntr.) *mahantāni*
acc.	*sīlavantaṃ* *mahantaṃ*, *mahaṃ*[2]	*sīlavanto*, *sīlavante* *mahante*
instr.-abl.	*sīlavatā*, *sīlavantena* *mahatā*, *mahantena*	*sīlavantehi* *mahantehi*
gen.	*sīlavato*, *sīlavantassa* *mahato*, *mahantassa*	*sīlavataṃ*, *sīlavantānaṃ* *mahataṃ*, *mahantānaṃ*
loc.	*sīlavati*, *sīlavante*, *°van-tamhi*, *°vantasmiṃ* *mahati*, *mahante*	*sīlavantesu* *mahantesu*
voc.	*sīlavā̆*, *yasavanta*	*sīlavanto*, *sīlavantā*

51,15 (cf. Cāndravṛtti II 1,81 = III 3,55: ***himavato gaṅgā prabhavati***), 23,1, 343,27 (see also BECHERT 1958: 311). Cf. also BECHERT, *'Alte Veḍhas' im Pāli-Kanon. NAWG* 1988.4, p. 9-10 with n. 38 (on D II 93,31ff.: *svākkhāto* + *bhagavantā [/ °vātā / °vatena] dhammo sandiṭṭhiko* ...).

[1] For Prakrit see PISCHEL § 397.

[2] Cf. *sumahaṃ puraṃ*, Ja VI 165,20*. For Prakrit see PISCHEL § 398.

The present participle in *°a(nt)-/ °e(nt)-* inflects in the same way (e.g. gen. pl. *sataṃ*, Ja IV 292,28, 294,4* [so read[1]]), except for the nom. sg.[2] which ends in *-aṃ* (< -an)[3]; it has occasionally preserved the historical instr. pl. (*sabbhi* < sadbhiḥ)[4]. The word *araha(nt)-* 'Buddhist saint' follows either inflexion (*arahaṃ, arahā*)[5]. The paradigm of *bhava(nt)-*[6], used for addressing people, shows some contracted forms (instr. sg. *bhotā*, gen. *bhoto*, voc. *bho* – with the old *-o* < *°(v)aḥ* (cf. *āvuso* [see AiGr. III p. 258f.])[7] –, voc. pl. *bhonto* [bhavantaḥ], instr. sg. fem. *bhotiyā*, Ja VI 523,18*, voc. sg. fem. *bhoti*, Ja VI 523,7* = 19*, D II 249,8, *bhotī* [< nom.[8]], Ja III 95,13* Sn 988). On *bhante* (*pace* GEIGER 98.3) see § 22.2.

rem. (**a**) The seemingly incongruent nom. sg. masc. *vasaṃ*, Ja III 419,13* (*socayissati maṃ kantā gāme vasaṃ aninditā* [*vasantī*, ct.]) and 530,12* (... *upaṭṭhitā, tapassinā jotir ivā vane vasaṃ*

---

[1] See OBERLIES (1995/96: 272).

[2] A rare exception is acc. sg. *gacchataṃ*, Ja V 28,23* (see OBERLIES 1995a: 132).

[3] Cf. *asaṃ* < asan (Ja IV 435,21* = VI 235,31* [see OBERLIES 1995/96: 295]). But also the neuter ends in *-aṃ* (*asaṃ* < asat [Ja II 32,2*]). See GEIGER § 97.2 and LÜDERS (1954: 159 n. 1). For Prakrit see PISCHEL § 398.

[4] See GEIGER § 98.2 and VON HINÜBER § 359-363 (cf. SMITH, *Orientalia Suecana* 3 [1955] 32 n. 3).

[5] See GEIGER § 98.1. For Prakrit see PISCHEL § 398.

[6] See GEIGER § 98.3.

[7] *āvuso* is an 'eastern' word. What we expect as its final is therefore *-e* (the more so as *u* precedes; see § 4.2). On *ayyo* see p. 170.

[8] This is to avoid the opening [-]⏑⏑⏑.

[*vasantena*, ct.]) is the participle transformed into a '*ṇamul*-absolutive' (see p. 270).

	singular	plural
nom.	*bhavaṃ* (as ntr. M III 172,26) *arahaṃ, arahā*	*bhavanto, bhonto* *arahanto, arahantā*
acc.	*bhavantaṃ* *arahantaṃ*	*bhavante* *arahante*
instr.-abl.	*bhotā* *arahatā*	*bhavantehi* *arahantehi*
gen.	*bhoto* *arahato, arahantassa*	*bhavataṃ* *arahataṃ, arahantānaṃ*
loc.	– *arahante, arahantamhi*	– *arahantesu*
voc.	*bhavaṃ, bho*	*bhonto*

Only sporadically are forms of a stem in *°ata-* used in nom. sg. (*ajānato* 'ignorant', Thī 240, *icchato* 'desiring', Th 320[1], *jīvạto* 'being alive', Ja III 539,2* [(◡)-◡-]) and pl. (*ajānatā* 'ignorant fools', Th 129)[2]. The feminines are usually derived from the strong stem (*kubbantī-*); only adjectives have a feminine in *°atī-* (*sīlavatī-*, *mahatī-*) as has *sa(nt)-*

---

[1] This form is wrongly defined as *nom. pl.* by GEIGER (§ 97).

[2] See VON HINÜBER § 359 and – for Prakrit – PISCHEL § 398.

(*satī-*)[1].

Starting from the nom. sg. ntr. ending in *°m/vaṃ* (< °m/vat)[2] the *°m/va(nt)*-stems were transformed into *°m/va*-stems[3]: (acc. sg. masc.) *balavaṃ*, Vin II 1,12, *bhāṇumaṃ*, Sn 1016[4], *satīmaṃ*, Sn 212, *Himavaṃ*, Ja VI 272,4*, Ap 441,21, (gen. sg.) *Accimassa*, Dīp III 14, *iddhimassa*, As 421,4, *Bandhumassa*, D II 7,1, (nom. pl. masc.) *mutīmā*, Sn 881, (nom. sg. fem.) *kittimā*, Ja III 70,6* = VI 508,21*, *Sirimā*, Bv V 21. The same holds good for the participles: *jāno* (~ *jānaṃ*[5]), Ja III 24,2*, *dado* (~ *dadaṃ*), S I 32,14*, *passo* (~ *passaṃ*), Th 61, *anukubbassa* (~ *°kubbantassa*), Ja II 205,10*, III 108,17*. If these forms without *-nt-*[6] were created in the east of the MIA linguistic area and were taken over into Pāli by replacing the ending *-e* (as LÜDERS maintained [1954: 158-160]), the pattern *putraḥ* : *putte* // *dānam* : *dāne* may have played a role: *jāno* < **jāne* (: jānaṃ).

rem. (**b**) One of the forms without *-nt-*, viz. *visodhaye*, Dhp 281,

---

1 See GEIGER § 98 rem. 3 ([= p. 138 n. 2 of GHOSH's English translation]) and VON HINÜBER § 363.

2 *asaṃ* (asat), Ja II 32,2*, *ojavaṃ*, S I 212,30* (see GEIGER § 96 / 97). See also p. 177 n. 3.

3 See SMITH, *Orientalia Suecana* 3 (1954) 32 n. 3. For Prakrit see PISCHEL § 398.

4 Since *bhānumat-* as a designation of the 'sun' is a masculine in Sanskrit it can be assumed that the same holds true for Pāli. But it cannot be ruled out that *bhāṇumaṃ* goes back to (nom.-acc. ntr. sg.) *bhānumat*.

5 On *jānaṃ* see VON HINÜBER (1968: 44-45).

6 On such forms see GEIGER § 97.2, BERGER (1956: 110), NORMAN (1969: 137 [ad Th 61] and 1992: 168 [ad Sn 92]) and VON HINÜBER § 360 / 490.

was perhaps not 'translated' into its western equivalent, as it was regarded as an optative (see LÜDERS 1954: 159 and BERGER 1956: 110); (**c**) The part. *sampajāna-* does not belong here (*pace* LÜDERS 1954: 157-158 and NORMAN 1992: 224 [ad Sn 413]), being an haplological shortening of *samprajān<ān>ah* (see § 22.1)[1].

3.2. The pronouns

§ 42. The pronouns have marked peculiarities of inflexion, which entail a transfer to the nominal inflexion by adding the suffix *°ka-* (*amuka-*, *asuka-*). They are especially liable to wear and tear and consequently to renewal. Their inflexion, on the other hand, has preserved archaic characteristics such as the use of the dative (as genitive)[2].

(**1**) The personal pronouns show a great number of forms which are due to analogies[3] between the cases as well as between the numbers. The pro-

---

[1] Of the part. perf. act. only the nom. sg. masc. has survived: *(a)vidvā*, M I 311,7, Sn 535, 728, *bhaya-dassivā*, Dhp 31/32 (see GEIGER § 100.2).

[2] But also a 'new' dative is created: *yāya atthāya*, D I 90,19.

[3] (**a**) *tuyhaṃ* (≠ tubhyam) is formed in analogy to *mayhaṃ* (see SMITH, *MSL* 23 [1935] 272); (**b**) the nom. *mayaṃ* (vayam) takes its *m-* from the oblique cases of the singular, and the initial *t-* of the plural of the second person stems from the singular, while the *-e-* of the instr. and loc. (cf. OIA *asmābhiḥ, asmāsu*) is analogical to the corresponding forms of the third-person pronoun. It was called for by the nom./acc. *amhe*. This (as nom.) is formed according to the proportion (*amhe* <) **asme* : *asmān* = *te* : *tān* (see p. 186). Later on the ending *-ān* was replaced by *-e*, which is the general substitution in the acc. pl., and the acc. was also *amhe/asme* (see INSLER, *Die Sprache* 34 [1988/90] 141); (**c**) based on *amhe* the gen. *amhaṃ* was formed analogical to *mamaṃ*.

nouns of the first and second persons[1] have no distinction of gender. The bracketed forms of the following chart are the ones used more rarely (on which see below):

	1. person	2. person
nom.	*ahaṃ (mhi, asmi)*[2]	*t(u)vaṃ*
acc.	*maṃ, mamaṃ*[3] *(me, mayhaṃ)*	*taṃ, t(u)vaṃ (te, tavaṃ)*
instr.-abl.	*mayā, me (mamato)*	*t(v)ayā, te*
gen.	*mama(ṃ), mayha(ṃ), me (maṃ)*	*tava(ṃ), tuyha(ṃ), tumhaṃ, te (tayā)*
loc.	*mayi*	*t(v)ayi*

Individual forms: (I) nom. *mhi*, Ap 195,7, 217,4[4] (see *rem.* a. below), *asmi*, Ja V 165,27*[5], acc. *me*, Ja II 443,14*, VI 266,18*[6], *mayhaṃ*, Ja V 214,20*,

---

[1] See GEIGER § 104 and VON HINÜBER § 365-373. For Prakrit see PISCHEL § 415-422 and ALSDORF, *Kleine Schriften* p. 68 (on *ṇe* [cf. PISCHEL § 419] and *bhe* [cf. PISCHEL § 422]).

[2] On the *sandhi* variants of *ahaṃ* see CPD s.v. ahaṃ.

[3] See GEIGER § 104.1 (his examples are, however, not beyond doubt). It is possible that also *mama* is used as an accusative: *kiṃ mama paro karissati*, Thī 493, *mam eva anukampāya*, Th 623 (cf. CPD I,530b).

[4] See CPD I,501b (s.v. asampatta) and 529a l. 34-35 and BECHERT (1958: 312).

[5] See OBERLIES (1997: 11 n. 23). For Prakrit see PISCHEL § 417 and ALSDORF, *Kleine Schriften* p. 63-64.

[6] See CPD I,529b-530a.

mama, Thī 493, gen. *mayha* (see § 4.1)[1], *maṃ*, Ja IV 332,4* (*mama*, ct.), S IV 61,13[2]; (**II**) acc. *te*, M II 127,18, Ja I 225,27-28[3], *tavaṃ*, Ja V 507,25*, gen. *tuyha* (see § 4.1), *tayā*, Ja VI 288,9* (*tayā ham asmi*[4] 'I belong to you')[5]. The stems used in compounds are *maṃ*- (Ja IV 14,2*, 253,13*[6], D II 100,5, M II 123,28, S IV 315,23 [cf. CPD I,532b]) and *tvaṃ*- (*tvaṃnātho 'smi,* Ja IV 253,13*).

rem. (**a**) *mhi* (asmi) seems to have been used as pronoun as it was taken as the singular of the nom. pl. of the personal pronoun *amhe*[7]; (**b**) the opposition of the Vedic dissyllabic nominative t_u*vám* to the monosyllabic acc. *tvā́m* is continued by Pāli *tuvaṃ* vs. *taṃ*[8]; (**c**) the gen. *mama* and *tava* are the bases for the acc. *mamaṃ* and *tavaṃ* and for the abl. *mamato*[9]; (**d**) *maṃ* and *taṃ*, Sn 48,9, are not

---

[1] On *mayhaṃ* as 'agent' see BECHERT (1958: 315). On abl. *me*, Vin I 22,32* = S I 105,15*, see CPD I,530a.

[2] For Prakrit see PISCHEL § 418.

[3] See CPD s.v. akkosati.

[4] Or do we have to interpret *tayāham asmi* as /*tayi aham asmi*/? In that case the gen. *tayā* does not exist.

[5] For Prakrit see PISCHEL § 421.

[6] See OBERLIES (1995/96: 294). Ja V 90,25* (Ee *ehi maṃgiriṃ*) is to be read *eh' imaṃ giriṃ* (correct OBERLIES 1995: 154 [s.v. maṃ-] accordingly).

[7] See BECHERT (1958: 312).

[8] See VON HINÜBER § 370 and OBERLIES (1999: 46-47).

[9] *ahakaṃ* is attested only with the grammarians, *mayā*, Ja III 398,13*, IV 18,2*, and *tayā*, Vv 625 (and Thī 383), are not ablatives (*pace* CPD I,530a), but examples of an *instrumentalis comparationis*, and *amhaṃ*, Th 1045, is the regular genitive *plural*

ablatives (*pace* LÜDERS 1954: 142) but accusatives construed with √*bhī* (see also § 30.4).

	1. person	2. person
nom.	*mayaṃ, amhe (no)*	*tumhe (vo)*
acc.	*amhe, asme, no*	*tumhe, vo*
instr.-abl.	*amhehi, no (asmā[b]hi)*	*tumhehi, vo*
gen.	*amhākaṃ, asmākaṃ, amhaṃ, no (ne)*	*tumhākaṃ, tumhaṃ, vo (ve)*
loc.	*amhesu (asmā̆su)*	*tumhesu*

(I) nom. *no*, Ja VI 578,20*[1], Ap 598,15 (etc.)[2], instr. *asmāhi*, Ap 539,10[3], gen. ('eastern') *ne*, M II 73,5[4], loc. *asmāsu*, Ja V 349,11*, 352,11*, 378,20*, *asmasu*, Ja V 343,14* (= *mayi*, Ja-m 136,9), 439,11*, 352,10*/11*[5]; **(II)** nom. *vo*, Ja III 521,27*, V 391,26*, 395,4*, VI

(*pace* GEIGER § 104.1).

[1] See OBERLIES (1995a: 157 [s.v. vayaṃ]) and id. (1997: 11 n. 22).

[2] Or is this *no* a mere particle which is frequently appended to verbs (see CPD I,531b)?

[3] = Thī-a 153,3* (Ee *asmābhi*). On the instrumental *no* see BECHERT (1958: 312).

[4] See NORMAN (1969: 237).

[5] For Prakrit see PISCHEL § 419.

576,29*[1], (used as voc.[2]) Vin I 23,21/25, M I 206,9/12, Mil 19,4, acc. *vo*, Ap 584,20, Ja III 57,23*, D III 81,3, Sn 682[3], gen. ('eastern') *ve*, Sn 333 = Dhp 315, Th 653, 1004/5[4]. The stems used in compounds are *amha-** and *tumha-*[5].

> *rem.* (**a**) *amhaṃ*, Th 1045, is the regular gen. pl. (*pace* GEIGER § 104.1)[6]; (**b**) On the dual *vaṃ* see § 28.1.

(**2**) The non-personal pronouns[7] distinguish gender. The paradigm of *ta(d)-* is composed of historical and newly created forms:

---

[1] See LÜDERS (1954: 30 n. 2), OBERLIES (1995: 143) and id. (1997: 11 n. 22). For Prakrit (Vasudevahiṇḍi 88,21) see ALSDORF, *Kleine Schriften* p. 68.

[2] But see p. 69 (*rem.* f).

[3] On (the possible accusative) *tumhaṃ*, Vin IV 241,21**, see VON HINÜBER (1968: 110) and id. § 371.

[4] For Prakrit see PISCHEL § 422.

[5] See VON HINÜBER § 371.

[6] And also *amhākaṃ* and *tumhākaṃ*, Ja I 221,29, are ordinary genitives (see CPD s.v. amhāhaṃ [*pace* GEIGER § 104.1]).

[7] See GEIGER § 105-106 and VON HINÜBER § 374-378 (for Prakrit see PISCHEL § 423-425). The pronouns *so*, *sā*, *taṃ* (etc.) are "used to strengthen other pronouns", usually preceding them, and "*so* may refer also to the person contained in a verbal form: *so karohi* '(you) do!', Dhp 236, *so tato cuto amutra udapādiṃ* 'departed from there I was born again at that place', D I 13,23" (GEIGER § 106). The relative pronoun followed by a corresponding form of the 3. person personal pronoun acquires the meaning 'whoever, whichever'.

<table>
<tr><td></td><td colspan="3">singular</td><td colspan="3">plural</td></tr>
<tr><td>nom.</td><td>so (sa, se)</td><td>taṃ (se)</td><td>sā</td><td rowspan="2">te</td><td rowspan="2">tāni</td><td rowspan="2">tā (tāyo)</td></tr>
<tr><td>acc.</td><td colspan="3">taṃ</td></tr>
<tr><td>instr.</td><td colspan="2">tena</td><td rowspan="2">tāya</td><td colspan="2" rowspan="2">tehi</td><td rowspan="2">tāhi</td></tr>
<tr><td>abl.</td><td colspan="2">tamhā, tasmā</td></tr>
<tr><td>gen.</td><td colspan="2">tassa</td><td>tassā, tissā (tāya, tissāya)</td><td colspan="2">tesaṃ (tesānaṃ)</td><td>tāsaṃ (tāsā-naṃ)</td></tr>
<tr><td>loc.</td><td colspan="2">tamhi, tasmiṃ</td><td>tassaṃ (tāsaṃ), tis-saṃ (tāyaṃ)</td><td colspan="2">tesu</td><td>tāsu</td></tr>
</table>

The nom. sg. masc. *sa* – in OIA only allowed before consonants – stands beside *so*, which becomes the dominant form. The nom. sg. ntr. *taṃ* (tat) has the nominal ending *-aṃ*. The corresponding 'eastern' form of both *so* and *taṃ* is *se*[1], which is also part of *seyyathā* ~ *sayathā*, Th 412 (< Atharvaveda [Śaunaka] 17,1.20-21 / Brāhmaṇa+ *sá yáthā*)[2] – *taṃyathā*, Mil 1,13[3], seems to be a 'hyper-translation'. After the model of the fem. (*tā*) the nom. masc. *te* was used *also* for the acc. The instr. fem. sg. *tāya*

---

[1] *se* = *taṃ* is wrongly translated as *so* (*nesaṃ bhavissati uposathakammaṃ*), Vin I 102,30 (see also p. 69 n. 6). For Prakrit *se* – used *also* for the oblique cases (on such *se* in Pāli see LEUMANN, *Kleine Schriften* p. 547, and AiGr. III § 238bα *rem.*) – see PISCHEL § 423 and OBERLIES (1999: 49-50 with n. 71).

[2] See p. 13 (and PISCHEL § 423). Also BHS knows *sayyathā* (see BHSD s.v. yathāpi).

[3] See TRENCKNER (1908: 104). Cf. AMg. *taṃ-jahā* (Āyāraṅgasutta 6,11, 17,21).

(tayā) is borrowed from the nominal type *kaññāya* – as is the nom./acc. pl. *tāyo* (see § 31.4) – to avoid homonymity with the 2nd person pronoun *tayā* (tvayā). The gen. sg. *tissāya* has a blended ending (*tissā x [tā]ya*) as have some forms of the gen. pl. (*tesānaṃ*, *tāsānaṃ*; cf. *esānaṃ*, M II 154,2, *katamesānaṃ*, D I 206,5, Vin III 7,22, *sabbesānaṃ*, M III 60,24). On *tissā* (tasyāḥ) see § 7.11[1], on *tāsaṃ* (tasyām) § 3.4. The stem used in compounds is *taṃ-/ta(d)-* (Vv 1264, Th 719)[2].

(3) The stems *eta(ṃ)-* and *ya(ṃ)-* (these are the stem-forms: Vin I 57,35; Ja III 131,12*, IV 107,20*) inflect in the same way[3]. An 'eastern' nom. sg. ntr. is *ye* (D II 278,16, M II 254,24[4]) which is also part of *yebhuyyena* 'mostly, usually'. The anaphorical pronoun *ena(ṃ)-* is used only as acc. of all three genders (*enaṃ*)[5]. After the pattern of *ta(ṃ)-* : *eta(ṃ)-* a new anaphorical pronoun *na-* is created to *ena(ṃ)-* which inflects like *(e)ta(ṃ)-*[6].

rem. (**a**) Owing to dialect mixture the endings of the nom./acc. pl. were identical for masc. and neuter (*-ā*, *-āni*). This contributed to the confusion of the masc. and neuter plural forms, frequently

---

1 See also BLOCH (1965: 147) and SCHWARZSCHILD (1991: 47-49).

2 *tadaṃ*, Ud 80,13, Sn 147,10/13, 148,6/10 (cf. Sadd 627 n. 7), and *yadaṃ*, Nidd I 54,12 (cf. NORMAN 1992: 301 [ad Sn 778]), are enlargements of *ta(d)-* and *ya(d)-* after the model of *idaṃ* (see VON HINÜBER § 377).

3 See GEIGER § 107 / 110 and VON HINÜBER § 381. For Prakrit see PISCHEL § 426-427.

4 See CPD s.v. ²avitakka, rem. (cf. TRENCKNER 1908: 128 and GEIGER § 110).

5 See GEIGER § 107.2 and VON HINÜBER § 389. For Prakrit see PISCHEL § 431.

6 See SCHELLER (1967: 22 n.1 [*pace* SMITH, *Orientalia Suecana* 2 (1953) 121 n. 3]), GEIGER § 107.2, AiGr. III p. 522 / 524 and VON HINÜBER § 389 (cf. JOHANSSON, *Monde Oriental* 2 [1907/08] 89-92). For Prakrit see PISCHEL § 431.

encountered when a relative pronoun refers to a noun: *vinicchayā yāni pakappitāni*, Sn 838[1], *ratanāni .. ye ... ratanāni ... te*, Ja VI 274,9*-12*; (**b**) As *naṃ*, Ja VI 511,2*, refers to 'mother and father' it should be an acc. pl.

(4) The stem *ki(ṃ)-* of the interrogative pronoun[2] (this is also the stem-form: *kiṃjacca-*, Sn 80,13, *kiṃsīla-*, Sn 324) is not only used for the nom./acc. sg. ntr. but forms derived from it supplement the '*ka*-paradigm'[3] (*kiñ[ci desaṃ]*, Vin III 168,1 [*koci deso*, ibid. 168,5], *kismā*, *kissa*, *kimhi*, *kismiṃ*) which inflects as *ta(ṃ)-* does (and as *katara-* and *katama-* do[4]). This contributes to the mingling of the masculine and neuter forms, which is complemented by a levelling of sing. and pl. forms: *ko nu tumhe* 'Who are you?', Ja V 390,18*.

rem. (**a**) On *ke*, D III 24,19* = 25,3* (cf. GEIGER § 111.1), see LÜDERS (1954: 14-15) – diff. BERGER (1956: 98) –, on *ko-nāmo*, Vin I 93,32, VON HINÜBER § 379 (*ko°* out of *ke°*, the eastern equivalent of *kiṃ°*)[5]; (**b**) *kañcinaṃ*, Th 879, is *kañci* with added particle *naṃ* (*pace* GEIGER § 111.1); (**c**) *kati-* 'how many' has the following forms: (nom. pl. mfn.) *kati*, (instr.) *katīhi*, (gen.) *katī-*

---

[1] See LÜDERS, *Philologica Indica* 291 n. 3.

[2] See GEIGER § 111 and VON HINÜBER § 379. For Prakrit see PISCHEL § 428.

[3] On *katto* 'how?', Ja VI 213,22*, see ALSDORF, *Kleine Schriften* p. 814 n. 70.

[4] See GEIGER § 111.2 and 3. On *katamesānaṃ* see p. 186.

[5] One may think, however, of a different – and more simple – explanation: *konāmo te upajjhāyo* is a crossing of *ko te upajjhāyo* and *kiṃnāmo te upajjhāyo*. Cf. also phrases like *tvaṃ konāmo sī ti pucchi, ahaṃ Dīghapiṭṭhiko nāma sāmī ti, bhāriyā te kānāmā* (!) *ti*, Ja VI 338,10'-11', and *kānāmā te pavattinī*, Vin II 272,38.

naṃ, (loc.) *katīsu* (see GEIGER § 111.4 and CPD s.v.).

(5) In the paradigm of *ida(m)-*[1] – this is the stem form (*idappaccaya-*, D I 185,27)[2] – historical forms ([masc. sg.] *ayaṃ*, *imaṃ* – both forms also fem. –, *asmā*[3], *assa*[4], *asmiṃ*, [pl., (nom./acc.)] *ime*, *ehi*, *esaṃ*, *esu*, [fem. sg.] *assā*, [fem. pl.] *imā*, *āsaṃ*[5], [ntr.] *idaṃ*, *imāni*) are complemented by new ones based on the old acc. *imaṃ*: (masc. sg.) *imassa*[6], *imasmiṃ*, (pl.) *imehi*, *imesaṃ*, *imesu*, (fem. sg.) *imāya*, *imissā*, *imāsaṃ*, (pl.) *imāyo*, *imāhi*, *imāsaṃ*, *imāsu*, (ntr.) *imaṃ*. Since the enclitic gen. pl. *esaṃ* and *āsaṃ* – *both* used for masc. *and* fem.[7] – can lose their initial vowel in *sandhi* (*na 'saṃ*) these forms were reinforced (*esānaṃ*, *āsānaṃ*). The instability of the initial, however, remained (*'sānaṃ*)[8].

rem. On *tadaminā* see § 5.8

---

[1] See GEIGER § 108 and VON HINÜBER § 382-387; for Prakrit see PISCHEL § 429-430. Also this pronoun is frequently combined with other pronouns (see GEIGER § 108.2 and CPD s.v. ayaṃ)

[2] As to the *sandhi* see § 24 (p. 121-122).

[3] *asmā* is also used as a feminine: *asmā ratyā vivasane*, Ja VI 492,7* = 24*.

[4] On the *sandhi* variants of *assa* see CPD s.v. [1]assa.

[5] On *āsaṃ* as gen. pl. masc. see CPD I 406a (last line) and NORMAN (1991: 181 [g. 278]).

[6] This form is anticipated by *imásya*, RV 8.13.21 (see TEDESCO, *Language* 21 [1945] 138). Another form of the gen. sg. masc. is *imissa*, Ja I 333,2 (cf. GEIGER § 108.1).

[7] See VON HINÜBER § 383.

[8] See SCHELLER (1967: 22 n. 1).

<table>
<tr><th></th><th>masc. / ntr. sg.</th><th>masc. / ntr. pl.</th><th>fem. sg.</th><th>fem. pl.</th></tr>
<tr><td>nom.</td><td>ayaṃ
(ntr.) idaṃ</td><td rowspan="2">ime
(ntr.) imāni</td><td>ayaṃ</td><td rowspan="2">imā, imāyo</td></tr>
<tr><td>acc.</td><td>imaṃ
(ntr.) idaṃ, imaṃ</td><td>imaṃ</td></tr>
<tr><td>instr.</td><td>iminā[1], anena</td><td rowspan="2">imehi, ehi</td><td rowspan="2">imāyā</td><td rowspan="2">imāhi</td></tr>
<tr><td>abl.</td><td>imasmā, imamhā, asmā</td></tr>
<tr><td>gen.</td><td>imassa, assa</td><td>imesaṃ, āsaṃ, esaṃ, imesānaṃ, esānaṃ</td><td>imissā, imāya, assā(ya)</td><td>imāsaṃ, āsaṃ, imāsānaṃ</td></tr>
<tr><td>loc.</td><td>imasmiṃ, imamhi, asmiṃ</td><td>imesu, esu</td><td>imissaṃ, imissā, imāyaṃ, imāsaṃ, assaṃ</td><td>imāsu</td></tr>
</table>

(6) The singular of both masc. and fem. of the paradigm of *amu-* is a direct continuation of that of OIA *adas-*[2]. The *-u* of *asu* (nom. sg. masc.), which at Ja V 395,26*/396,4* scans ⏑- (i.e. *aso* < asau)[3], and of (nom./acc. sg.

---

[1] According to ALSDORF (1968: 33) Pāli also had an instr. *imenaṃ*: *kiṃ nu imenaṃ karissāmi*, Ja V 184,14* (so read m. c.).

[2] See GEIGER § 109 and VON HINÜBER § 388. For Prakrit see PISCHEL § 432.

[3] See CPD sv. amu, OBERLIES (1995/96: 276-277) and BLOCH, *Recueil d'Articles* p. 523 (cf. SAKAMOTO-GOTO, *Journal of Indian and Buddhist Studies* 26.2 [1978] 991).

ntr.) *aduṃ* – *amuṃ* is used beside – is due to the influence of *amu*-[1]. The plural is built up exclusively from forms of this stem, which encroached likewise on the nom. sg. masc. (*amu*).

	masc. / ntr. sg.	masc. / ntr. pl.	fem. sg.	fem. pl.
nom.	*asu*, *amu* (ntr.) *aduṃ*, *amuṃ*	*amū* (ntr. also *amūni*)	*asu*	*amū*[2]
acc.	*amuṃ* (ntr.) *aduṃ*, *amuṃ*		*amuṃ*	
instr.	*amunā*	*amūhi*	*amuyā*	*amūhi*
abl.	*amusmā*, *amumhā*			
gen.	*amussa*	*amūsaṃ*	*amussā*, *amuyā*	*amūsaṃ*[3]
loc.	*amusmiṃ*, *amumhi*	*amūsu*	*amussaṃ*, *amuyaṃ*	*amūsu*

(7) A number of adjectives are inflected, in part or wholly, according to the pronominal declension ([e.g.] loc. sg. fem. in *-assaṃ* ~ *-āya*, nom. pl. masc. in *-e* ~ *-ā*, gen. in *-esaṃ* ~ *-ānaṃ*)[4]: *añña(tara)-*[5], *(a)para-*, *itara-*,

[1] See WACKERNAGEL, *Kleine Schriften* p. 620, JOHANSSON, *IF* 3 (1894) 222 n. 4, and BERGER (1955: 18 n. 12).

[2] GEIGER (§ 109) gives also *amuyo*. But this is only a grammarian's form.

[3] The gen. *amūsānaṃ* which GEIGER cites is not attested.

[4] (Loc. sg. fem.) *uttarassaṃ disāyaṃ*, S I 148,4*, ~ *uttarāya disāya*, D I 74,23, 153,19, Ap 541,5 (cf. *uttarāyaṃ disāyaṃ*, Vasudevahiṇḍi 280,27), (nom. pl. masc.) *añ-*

uttara-, *ekacca-* and *sabba-*[1].

rem. (**a**) [2]*vissa-* is most probably (and only[2]) attested at Ja V 153,9* (*visse devā ... Tāvatiṃsā sa-indakā* [Ee *misse*]); (**b**) *tuviya-* 'your', Ja V 26,20* (cf. B[d]) *qu.* Sadd 805,2 (so read according to CPD s.vv. apa/avarādha[3]), seems likewise to be a *hapax*; (**c**) The oblique cases of *atta(n)-* are employed in sg. as reflexive pronoun of all three persons and genders and of both numbers[4]. The same holds good for the nom. and gen. of *tuma-*: *tumo*, A III 124,10, Sn 890, Vin II 186,31, *tumaṃ*, Pv 410, *tumassa*, Sn 908 (GEIGER § 107.4)[5]; (**d**) The possessive pronoun for all three persons is *sa(ka)-* 'own' (sva[ka]-): *saṃ*, Ja VI 327,20* (read *san niketaṃ*), *sena*, Ja II 22,23*, *samhā*, Ja VI 502,34*, *samhi*, D II 225,17*[6], *sāni*, M I 366,5, *sesu*, Ja V 26,4*, *sakaṃ*, Ja IV 331,7*, *sakamhā*, D I 81,25, *sake*, Ja IV 103,15*.

ñatarā, S IV 341,23, *itarā*, Dīp VI 26 (see GEIGER § 113 and OBERLIES 1997: 10).

5 There is also a fem. *i*-form in the paradigm of *añña-*: *aññissā*, M I 30,27, Vin I 15,10.

1 For Prakrit see PISCHEL § 433.

2 GEIGER's (§ 113.2) sole example, Dhp 266, does not belong here. As Gāndhārī Dhp 67 shows, we have here *vissaṃ* < veśmam (see BROUGH 1962: 191-192).

3 See also Sadd V 1426 and OBERLIES (1995a: 137).

4 See GEIGER § 112.2. For Prakrit see PISCHEL § 434.

5 On *tyamhi*, Ja V 85,9*, VI 292,21*, *tyāsu*, V 368,6*, and *dussa*, III 54,1*, see VON HINÜBER § 380 respectively § 388 (*pace* GEIGER § 107.3).

6 It is possible that Th 1211 has the loc. *s(v)amhi* (see OBERLIES 1995: 137).

3.3. The numerals

§ 43. (**1**) The numeral[1] *eka-* ‘one’ inflects as a pronominal adjective (see § 42.7)[2], i.e. (nom. pl.) *eke* ‘some’, (gen.) *ekesaṃ*, (obl. fem.) *ekissā/ekissaṃ*[3]; (**2**) Due to the loss of the dual the numeral ‘two’ (with the stems *d[u]vā-*, *d[(u)v]i-*, *d[v]e-*, *du[v]-* and *bā-*) had to be remodelled. Its inflexion is the same for all three genders[4]. The form of the nom./acc. fem. and ntr., *d(u)ve* (cf. OIA *$d_u$vé*), was transferred to the masc., the ending being identical to that of *ime*, *te*, *sabbe*[5]. The remaining cases are formed analogical to those of the numeral ‘three’ (as is the gen. of *ubha-*): *dvīhi*, *dvinnaṃ*[6], *dvīsu* (beside ‘eastern’ *duvesu*). *ubha-* has generalised the *o* of the nom. (< ubhau): nom./acc. *ubho*, instr./abl. *ubhohi*, gen. *ubhinnaṃ*, loc. *ubhosu* (cf. *ubho<hi> hatthehi*, *ubho<su> kūlesu nadiyā*, see § 28.7)[7]. *ubhaya-* inflects as an *a*-stem (it is used both in sg. and in pl. with noun

---

[1] See GEIGER § 114-117, VON HINÜBER § 390-410 and NORMAN (1994: 1-33). For Prakrit see PISCHEL § 435-451.

[2] *ekā*, Ja VI 412,15*, does not attest a nominal inflexion: *Pañcālā ca Videhā ca ubho ekā bhavantu te* means ‘they should come to terms’.

[3] In the feminine plural *ekaccā-* complements *ekā-* (see Sadd 284,33): *ekā*, D I 181,1, ~ *ekaccāsu*, Vin II 65,2.
On the ‘eastern’ nom. sg. ntr. *eke* see NORMAN (1991: 69) and cf. CPD II,577b.

[4] The western Aśoka inscriptions keep the inflexion of masc. and fem. apart (G *dvo morā*, *dve cikichā*).

[5] Only the late Apadāna uses the loc. *duve* (443,1/3).

[6] On Ja V 387,15* see OBERLIES (1995/96: 298).

[7] On *vubho*, Ja VI 509,24*, see § 25 (p. 125-126).

and verb in plural). It is contaminated with *dvi-* to *dubhaya-*[1]; (**3**) The numeral *ti-* 'three' (with the stems *ti-* and *te-*) distinguishes in the nom./acc. all three[2], and in the genitive two, genders; both these genitives were modelled after *catunnaṃ* and *channaṃ*[3], the fem. one receiving its geminate *-ss-* from (nom./acc.) *tisso*: nom./acc. masc. *tayo* (trayaḥ), fem. *tisso* (tisraḥ), ntr. *tīṇi* (trīṇi), gen. masc./ntr. *tiṇṇaṃ*, fem. *tissannaṃ* (← *tisanaṃ < tisṛṇām). The instr./abl. and loc., identical for all genders, show the inflexion of an *i*-stem (with *-ī-* in accord with *tīṇi*): *tīhi*, *tīsu*. The gen. also has a double ending (*tiṇṇannaṃ*, Vin I 162,36, Mil 309,8), by analogy with *pañcannaṃ*, *channaṃ*, *sattannaṃ*[4]. --- *rem. ti*, S II 135,3, Vin IV 119,23, resembling Vedic *trī́*[5], is probably due to a haplology of endings (*dve vā t<īṇ>i vā udaka-phusitāni*)[6]; (**4**) 'Four' (*catu[r]-*)[7] has two forms for nom. *and* acc. masc. (owing to case confusion and after the model of fem.); also the other cases are historical forms whose compensatory lengthened *-ū-* conforms to the vocalism of 'three': (nom./acc.) *cattāro*, *caturo*, (instr./abl.) *catūhi*, *catubbhi*, (gen.) *catunnaṃ* (with a standardized ending

---

1 See Sadd V 1451.

2 Thī 518, however, uses *tīṇi* for the feminine gender: *sakhiyo tīṇī* (so read) *janiyo* (see NORMAN 1971: 178-179).

3 As was *bahunnaṃ* (see p. 20 n. 7).

4 See BARTHOLOMAE (1916: 6 n. 2 / 21).

5 VON HINÜBER § 393 even sees in *tī* the direct continuation of Vedic *trī́* (cf. AiGr. III § 177 a *rem.*).

6 See CAILLAT, *Sanskrit and World Culture*, Berlin 1986, 372 n. 56.

7 The stems used in compounds are *catu(r)-* and *cātu(r)-*. Is the latter which is also to be found in Prakrit (see PISCHEL § 78 and JACOBI § 14) abstracted from *vṛddhi* derivations? Cf. *temāsa-* 'three months (of the rainy season)', M I 438,10.

°nnaṃ [≠ °r̥ṇām][1]), *catūsu* (*°ūsu*, S I 43,2*). The fem. has as nom.-acc. and gen. the historical forms (*catasso*, *catassannaṃ* [< *catasanaṃ : tissannaṃ]), whereas the remaining cases are supplied by the masc. (as is the rare acc. *caturo* [Ja VI 38,2*]). The nom./acc. ntr. is a historical form, too (*cattāri*); (**5-10**) The numerals 'five' through 'ten' continue the old forms; but the instr. has the ending *-ahi*, while the gen. has *-annaṃ* by analogy (sporadically *-anna*: *pañcanna*, Sn 964 [with Nidd I 482,22*], *dasanna*, Ja V 448,16*) and 'six' has *ch-* (with *cha[t]-* as stem) as its initial (see § 13 [p. 71])[2]: (nom.-acc.) *pañca*, (instr.-abl.) *pañcahi*, (gen.) *pañcannaṃ*, (loc.) *pañcasu* (etc.). Archaic forms like *aṭṭhāhi* (aṣṭābhiḥ)[3] and *dasabhi* (daśabhiḥ) are rarely encountered (Ja I 414,5* = III 207,14*, Vin I 38,22).

---

[1] See BARTHOLOMAE (1916: 6 n. 2).

[2] 'Eastern' ²*sa-* seems to stand beside 'western' *cha-* (see VON HINÜBER § 399; but cf. TIEKEN, *WZKS* 31 [1987] 200). On *chaḷa-* 'six', Ja VI 238,32* (B[d]), see p. 5 n.3 and 197 n. 4.

[3] In compounds the final of *aṭṭha-* may be lengthened: *aṭṭhākhuraṃ*, Ja I 163,4* = 10* (so read).

	dva- (masc. / fem. / ntr.)	*ti- / te-*	*catu(r)-*	(5-10)
nom. acc.	*d(u)ve*	(masc.) *tayo* (fem.) *tisso* (ntr.) *tīṇi*	(masc.) *cattāro*, *caturo* (fem.) *catasso* (ntr.) *cattāri*	*pañca* (etc.)
instr.-abl.	*dvīhi*	*tīhi*	*catŭ̄hi*, *catubbhi*	*pañcahi* (etc.) *aṭṭhāhi*, *dasabhi*
gen.	*d(u)vinnaṃ*	(masc. / ntr.) *tiṇṇaṃ* (fem.) *tissannaṃ*	(masc. / ntr.) *catunnaṃ* (fem.) *catassannaṃ*	*pañcanna(ṃ)* (etc.)
loc.	*dvīsu*	*tīsu*	*catŭ̄su*	*pañcasu* (etc.)

(11-18) The numerals 'eleven' through 'eighteen' have a by-form *°rasa-*, which probably originated in 'twelve' and 'seventeen' ([*dvādasa-*/] *bārasa-*[1] < dvādaśa- / *sattarasa-* < saptadaśa-) by dental dissimilation (see p. 88) to then spread by analogy[2]: *ekādasa- / (°rasa-)*, *pañcadasa-*, *soḷasa-*

---

[1] Though permitted by the Saddanīti *ekārasa-* is not attested in the Theravāda canon, and *bārasa-* 'twelve' quoted by this grammar has completely disappeared from the canonical texts (see VON HINÜBER § 400; cf. NORMAN, *IIJ* 34 [1991] 205).

[2] See BERGER, *MSS* 47 (1986) 31.

/ *°rasa-*, *aṭṭhādasa-* / *°rasa-*. 'Thirteen' (*terasa-/telasa-* < *trayadaśa-[1]) also has a form with *-ḷ-* < -ḍ- (*[aḍḍha]teḷasa-*), as has 'forty' (*cattāḷīsa-*), while 'fourteen' (*catuddasa-*) also shows also abnormal loss of *-t-* (*cuddasa-*) and the genuine MIA forms of 'fifteen' are *paṇṇarasa-* and *pannarasa-* (see § 16.3); (**19/29** [etc.]) 'Nineteen' is *ekūnavīsati-* (only Ap 174,22 has *ūnavīsa-*), 'twenty-nine' *ekūnatimsa-* (only Ja III 138,20* and Ap 181,18 have *ūnatiṃsa-*), (etc.); (**20/30**) As in Epic Sanskrit 'twenty' took over the ending of 'thirty' (and sometimes also *vice versa*): *vīsati-*, *vīsa-*, *vīsā-*, *tiṃsa-*, *tīsā-*, *chattiṃsati-* (viṃśati-, triṃśat-)[2]; (**21-28/31-38**) *°vīsa-* (*bāvīsa-*, Kvu 138,21, *paṇṇuvīsa-*, Ja III 138,20*) and *°vīsati-*, *tiṃsa-* and (sporadically) *tiṃsati-* are the bases of the numerals '21-28' and '31-38' ('33' with analogical levelling: *tettiṃsa-* < **tetthiṃsa-* < trayastriṃśat-); (**40**) *cattārīsa-* has by-forms with *-l-* and *-ḷ-* (see also above); compounded with other numerals, it is sometimes shortened to *(°)tālīsa-* (→ *tālīsa-*, Ap 103,13, 234,14 [*uddāna*]); (**50**) *paṇṇāsa-* 'fifty' (beside *paññāsa-*) shows the same development of *-ñc-* as 'fifteen'; (**60**) The initial of *saṭṭhi-* contrasts with that of *cha(ṭ)-* 'six'. *dvaṭṭhi-* 'sixty-two', D I 54,4, is the 'eastern' form corresponding to 'western' *dvāsaṭṭhi-*, S IV 286,24[3]; (**72**) Historical *bāsattati-* (Vin I 100,11*) is superseded first by *dvāsattati-* and then by *dvesattati-*; (**84**) *cūḷāsīti-* ~ *cullāsīti-* (*colāsīti- [with analogical *-ā-*, cf. *caturāśīti-*, Mahābhārata 1,2.96] < ca<t>uraśīti-) is the 'eastern' form corresponding to 'western' *caturāsīti-*. The other numerals continue the OIA forms.

The numerals 'one' through 'eighteen' are used as adjectives, unless they inflect as neuters (sg.) in analogy with *vīsaṃ* (< *viṃśat). The nume-

---

[1] First it develops to **trayidasa-* (cf. Aś *traidasa-*). On Pkt. *terasa-* see PISCHEL § 119.

[2] See OBERLIES (1997: 10 with n. 21).

[3] See NORMAN (1994: 82-83).

rals 'nineteen' and upwards are neuter or feminine substantives in *-aṃ* or *-ā* and *-ti* respectively[1]. When connected with substantives, they may be used appositionally in the same case as the substantive, or else the qualified substantive may be put in the genitive plural. Often, however, the numerals are not inflected at all. Finally, a determinative compound may be formed[2].

The ordinals[3] continue – *mutandis mutatis* – the OIA ones (on *dutīya-* and *tatīya-* see § 7.8a)[4]. The higher numbers (except for '60th') may be formed by adding °*ma-* to the cardinal: *vīsa-*, *vīsatima-* (viṃśa-, viṃśatitama-), *saṭṭhitama-*. They are all inflected as *a*-stems. Their feminine is always in *-ā*, while those in *-ī* are used to denote dates (*aṭṭhamī-* '8th day', *cātuddasī-* '14th day' [see CDIAL 4606], *pañcadasī-* '15th

---

1 For Prakrit see PISCHEL § 445 / 447.

2 In texts like the Dīpavaṃsa a numeral (as well as *ubho*) as the first member of a compound can retain its case ending (see TSUCHIDA, *StII* 13/14 [1987] 306 n. 30): *tīṇi-vassamhi nigrodho catuvassamhi bhātaro, chavassamhi pabbajito mahindo* ... 'When (Aśoka had) completed three years, (the story of) Nigrodha happened, after the fourth year (he put his) brothers (to death), after his sixth year Mahinda ... received the Pabbajjā ordination', Dīp VII 31-32 (OLDENBERG's transl.).

3 See GEIGER § 118, VON HINÜBER § 411 and NORMAN (1994: 33-47). For Prakrit see PISCHEL § 449.

The acc. of the ordinals is used to form temporal adverbs: *paṭhamaṃ* 'the first time', *dutiyaṃ* 'the second time' (see GEIGER § 119.3).

4 Sporadically the ordinal number is used instead of the cardinal number: *pañcamehi bandhanehi* 'with five bonds', S IV 201,22, 202,9 (see GEIGER § 118.4 and OBERLIES 1997: 10-11). On *chaḷa-* (see above, p. 5 n. 3) see also OBERLIES (1995: 134).

Noteworthy are compounds of ordinal numbers with *atta(n)-*: *attaduttiya-* 'oneself with one companion', D II 147,21, *attacatuttha-* 'oneself with three others', M I 393,21.

day')[1].

There are other numeral derivatives[2]: (**a**) multiplicative adverbs ([*saki(ṃ)* 'once',] *dvikkhattuṃ* 'twice', *tikkhattuṃ* 'thrice')[3], (**b**) adverbs with the suffixes *-dā*, *-dhā* and *-so* (*ekadā* 'once', *dvidhā* 'in two parts', *sattadhā* 'in seven parts', *anekaso* 'repeatedly'[4]), (**c**) numeral adjectives with the 'suffixes' *°guṇa-* and *°vidha-* (*catugguṇa-* 'fourfold', *aṭṭhaguṇa* 'eightfold', *ekavidha-* 'single-fold'). To denote fractional sense *aḍḍha-* is added to the next higher ordinal: *aḍḍhatiya-* 'two and a half'[5], *aḍḍhuḍḍha-* 'three and a half'[6].

---

1 See OBERLIES (1996: 113).

2 See GEIGER § 119. For Prakrit see PISCHEL § 450-451.

3 *aṭṭhārasa-kkhattuṃ* shows 'tmesis' at Ap 92,23: *aṭṭhārasañ ca khattuṃ so*.

Also *vāra-* can be used to form multiplicatives: *ekavāraṃ* 'once', *dve vāre* 'twice', *tayo vāre* 'thrice' (see GEIGER § 119.3).

4 The adverbial suffix *-so* is added to numerals in a distributive sense (see GEIGER § 119.3). Quite often it is added also to nouns and adjectives (see NORMAN 1992: 204 [ad Sn 288]).

5 On this word see § 22.1.

6 See AiGr. III § 178d *rem.* (p. 349).

If *aḍḍha-* is added to a cardinal the whole compound denotes *half of* the numeral: *dasaddha-* (sic) 'five', Th 1244 (see GEIGER § 119.2; for Prakrit see PISCHEL § 450).

3.4. The Verb

§ 44. Compared with the verb system of OIA, that of Pāli has undergone extensive reorganisation. The dual has been completely lost, and the medium survives only in some forms. Its function has been partly taken over by the causative (*bhikkhunī ... bahuṃ lasunaṃ harāpesi* 'The nun brought much garlic', Vin IV 258,14), and passives in °*iyati* are sporadically used as such: *([upa/pariy/sam]ādiyati* 'clings to; controls; takes, grasps'[1], *vediyati* 'feels'[2], *sādiyati* 'takes pleasure in'[3]; cf. *uttariyati* 'boils over', *ruccati* 'indulges in')[4]. The system of tenses[5] has been simplified: it comprises the present, the future (and conditional) and a combined preterite consisting of imperfect, aorist and perfect[6]. The subjunctive and the precative are missing from the moods (cf., however, § 46.2 rem.)[7]. Of derived present stems only the causative, the passive and the denominative

---

[1] *pariyādiyeyyaṃ*, Vin I 25,2, *samādiya*, Bv II 117, *samādiyāhi*, Thī 249, *samādiyassu*, Vv 1216 (see GEIGER § 136.4).

[2] A I 141,6, M I 59,12, Vin III 37,25 (see GEIGER § 136.4).

[3] D I 166,4, Vin II 294,20, III 29,18.

[4] See GEIGER § 136.4, 175.1, VON HINÜBER § 415 and SAKAMOTO-GOTO (1993); cf. NORMAN (1992a: 14-15 n. 6) and BHSG § 37.23. For Prakrit see PISCHEL § 550.

On passives used as actives (*annaṃ ... / taṃ khajjare bhuñjare piyyare ca*, Ja IV 380,13*, *parihāyati*, Cp 16) see DE VREESE, *JAOS* 81 (1961) 20 (cf. OBERLIES 1995: 131 [s.v. khajjati] and CPD s.v. abhi-bhūyati). For Prakrit see PISCHEL § 550.

[5] Pāli had a kind of 'aspect' system comparable to that of Vedic Sanskrit (see BECHERT 1958a, 1995).

[6] See BLOCH (1965: 225).

[7] See VON HINÜBER § 413 (cf. PISCHEL, *ZvS* 23 [1877] 424-425, GEIGER § 123, BLOCH 1965: 221 and NORMAN, Traces of the Subjunctive in Middle Indo-Aryan, in: *Facets of Indian Culture. Gustav Roth Felicitation Volume*. Patna 1998, 97-108).

are productive categories, while the desiderative and the intensive[1] have been preserved only in a few historical forms: *jigucchati* 'is disgusted' (jugupsate [see § 7.11]), *tikicchati* 'cures' (cikitsati, see p. 88), *sussūsati* 'wishes to hear' (śuśrūṣate)[2], *lālappati* 'talks much' (lālapyate), *jaṅgamati* 'visits' (jaṅgamyate [:: *(anu)caṅkamati* 'walks up and down' < (*)caṅkramati ← caṅkramīti ~ caṅkramyate])[3].

The focus of the verbal conjugation is no longer the root but the present stem, i.e. the 3sg. of the indicative without the ending *-ti*[4]. All *regular* verb forms are based on it; forms that are not so constructed are chiefly historical relics. According to its stem-final, two 'conjugations' can be distinguished. In one type (the more numerous) the present stem ends in *-a* (the OIA present classes I, VI and IV, the latter as a rule with characteri-

---

1 See GEIGER § 184 (*desid.*) and 185 (*intens.*) and VON HINÜBER § 417. For Prakrit see PISCHEL § 555 (*desid.*) and 556 (*intens.*).

2 On *sussūyati*, M III 221,8, which GEIGER § 184 n. 3 regards as a corruption, see BHSG § 40.1.

3 (Desid.) *jigīsati* ~ *jigiṃsati* 'wishes to win' (see § 3.5), *jighacchati* 'is hungry', *titikkhati* 'bears, endures', *dicchati* 'wishes to give' (*dicchare*, Ja IV 65,21* = S I 18,27*), *vavakkhati* 'wishes to call', (intens.) *kākacchati* 'snores', Ja I 318,2, Mil 85,22 (*krākrathyate), *dhamadhamāyati* 'blows strongly', Mil 117,21, *lolup(p)ati* 'is greedy' (in: *lolupa-* 'greedy' and *loluppa-* 'greediness'; see OBERLIES 1996: 100 n. 55). *daddaḷhati*/*daddallati* 'blazes' seems to be an onomatopoetic remodelling of (Skt.) *jājvalyate* and not its direct continuation (*pace* GEIGER § 41.2; see also VON HINÜBER § 167 and BROUGH 1962: 186). On *siṃsati* (GEIGER § 184) see p. 23 n. 1, on *momuha-* 'bewildered' see p. 91 n. 4.

4 See LEUMANN (1940: 206 [= *Kleine Schriften* p. 304]), EDGERTON (1954: 78) and VON HINÜBER § 418.

stic -*CCa*- < -Cya-[1]); in the other, it ends in a long vowel, most commonly -*e* (see § 45), fairly often -*ā*, rarely -*ī* or -*o*[2]. This 'second' conjugation comprises the old athematic presents now made uniform by suppressing alternations, this as a consequence of generalising a frequent form (*eti* ... *enti* 'he goes / they go'[3], *brūhi* .. *brūmi, brūti* 'say! / I say / he says'[4], *jahāmi* ... *jahanti* 'I leave / they leave', *suṇomi* ... *suṇoma* 'I hear / we hear'); or which were thematicised, i.e. transferred to the 'first' conjugation[5] – a process based on a form constantly used (thus all verbs of class VII and √*bandh*[6] were thematicised forming a group with *muñcati*, etc.[7]):

---

[1] **miyati* out of (OIA) *mriyate* 'dies' is remodelled after [2]*jīyati* 'grows old' (< jīryati) to yield (Pāli) *mīyati* (see p. 49 n. 3). Forms of these present stems lists GEIGER § 137. Present stems of the old fourth and sixth class and newly built stems with characteristic -*āya*- (on which see below) are given by GEIGER § 134, 136 and 138. For Prakrit see PISCHEL § 472-484 (old class I), 485-486 (old class VI) and 487-489 (old class IV).

[2] See EDGERTON, *JAOS* 73 (1953) 117, and id. (1954). For Prakrit see also JACOBI § 51-55.

[3] Ind. pr. *emi*, *esi*, *eti*, *ema*, *etha*, *enti*; imp. 2sg. *ehi*, 3sg. *etu*, 2pl. *etha*; opt. 2sg. *eyyāsi*, 3sg. *eyya* (see GEIGER § 140.3 and – for Prakrit – PISCHEL § 493). On *adhīyati* 'he studies' ~ *adhiyanti* 'they study' see CPD s.v. adhīyati and OBERLIES (1993/94: 162 n. 74).

[4] See GEIGER § 141.2 (*brūmetu*, D I 95,19, is a scribal error for *brūtu me* 'he should say to me'; see OBERLIES 1995: 130). For Prakrit – it has generalised *be(mi)* < **bravimi* ← *bravīmi* – see PISCHEL § 494, ALSDORF, *Kleine Schriften* p. 64, and BHAYANI, *Sambodhi* 7 (1978/79) 116.

[5] The thematic vowel *a* of this conjugation preserves the individuality of both root and termination.

[6] See GEIGER § 146.4. For Prakrit see PISCHEL § 513.

[7] See GEIGER § 144. For Prakrit see PISCHEL § 506-507.

(cl. II) *hanti* 'he beats' → *hananti* 'they beat' (→ 3sg. *hanati*[1]), [1]*seti* 'he lies' (śete) → *senti* 'they lie'[2],
(cl. III) *jahāmi* 'I leave' → *jaha(n)ti* 'he leaves / they leave, *dadhāmi* 'I put' → *da(d)ha[n]ti* 'he puts / they put' (see p. 90-91)[3],
(cl. V) see below[4],
(cl. VII) *chindanti* 'they cut' → *chindati* 'he cuts',
(cl. VIII) *kubbanti* 'they make' (kurvanti) → *kubbati* 'he makes'[5],
(cl. IX) *gaṇhanti* 'they take' (gṛhṇanti[6]) → *gaṇhati* 'he takes'[7].

---

[1] See GEIGER § 140.1 and EDGERTON (1954: 80).

[2] Cf. *adāmi* 'I eat', Ja VI 365,23*/24* (see CPD s.v. adeti and OBERLIES 1995/96: 286-287), *āsati* 'sits' (on *āsetha*, Ja V 222,16*, see GEIGER § 129 and VON HINÜBER § 435), *duhati* 'milks', *ravati* 'cries', *rudati/rodati* 'weeps', *lehati* 'licks', *(as)sasati* 'inhales', *sāsati* 'orders', *supati/soppati* 'sleeps'. On the old 2nd class and its continuation in Pāli see GEIGER § 140-141 (on *atthi* see below), for Prakrit see PISCHEL § 492-499. For *veti*, Th 497, allegedly '= vetti' (GEIGER § 140.1), read (')*vedi* (see NORMAN 1969: 201 [ad loc.]).

[3] On the verbs of the OIA class III (√ghrā, √gṛ [/ jāgṛ], √dā, √dhā, √hu) in Pāli see below (cf. GEIGER § 142-143; for Prakrit see PISCHEL § 500-501). A haplologically shortened imperative of *jahāti* is *jahi* 'leave' (<*jahi*<*hi*>), Ja V 92,9* (see OBERLIES 1995a: 135).

[4] See GEIGER § 147-148. For Prakrit see PISCHEL § 502-505.

[5] See GEIGER § 149(b). For Prakrit see PISCHEL § 508-509.

[6] This starting-point was favoured by the proportion *-āmi* : *-ati* : *-anti*: *jānāmi* → *jānati* (jānāti) ← *jānanti*.

[7] See GEIGER § 146 (for Prakrit see PISCHEL § 505 [*√stṝ*], 510-512). Cf. *jānati* 'knows', *(ajjho/apa/avat)tharati* 'spreads, covers', (√stṝ), *punanti* 'they clean' (on *phunanti*, Ja VI 108,11*, see OBERLIES 1995/96: 300), *lunanti* 'they cut', Mil 33,2 (see GEIGER § 145-146). On *manthati* 'churns' < manthati (≠ mathnāti 'robs') see OBERLIES, *OLZ* 94 (1999) 392.

Or alternatively, a new stem was extracted from such forms as (3sg.) *jūhati* 'he sacrifices' (on *jūhati* see § 3.4) and *jaggati* 'lies awake' from (OIA) 3pl. *juhvati* and *jāgrati*[1].

Verbs of the old 5th class[2] were often transferred to the 9th class (a tendency already present in the Vedic language): *ocināti* 'gathers', *vicināti* 'examines' ([°]cinoti), *pāpuṇāti* 'attains, reaches' (prāpnoti), *sakkuṇāti* 'is able' (śaknoti)[3], *suṇāti* 'hears' (śṛṇoti)[4]. Thus the *(n)o*-present, which disturbs the verbal system of *a*- and *e*-presents, was gradually superseded by the *(n)ā*-present which fitted in better. And even the small difference in vocalism (*°asi / °ati* :: *°āsi / °āti*) was finally levelled: *gaṇhati* 'grasps', (imp.) *pāpuṇa* 'attain!' (Thī 432), *suṇa* 'hear!' (Thī 404), (opt.) *kiṇe* 'he may buy' (Ja V 375,26*), *pāpuṇe* 'he will reach' (Ja I 275,18*, Dhp 138, Sn 324), *(°)mine* 'I shall create' (Ap 29,26), 'he will measure' (Ja V

---

1 See GEIGER § 142.3-4 (cf. OBERLIES 1997: 14).

2 *munāti*, Dhp 269, probably based on √*mnā* (see Sadd V 1695), is used to 'explain' the word *muni-* (see OBERLIES 1999: 42). This accounts for its *u*-vowel (cf. VON HINÜBER § 157).

3 On *sakkati* (Ja I 290,23) see GEIGER § 148.c (Th 533 [Ee ... *sakkati deva-devo*], however, should be corrected to *maññām' ahaṃ Sakka'si deva-devo* [see NORMAN 1969: 207]). For Prakrit (*sakkaṇomi, sakkuṇomi, sakkai, sakkei*) see PISCHEL § 505.

4 See GEIGER § 147 / 148 (*pāpuṇāti* and *sakkuṇāti*) and OBERLIES (1999: 36-37).

stanati 'moans' (different from √*stan* 'to thunder' [see NARTEN. *Kleine Schriften* I,407]) and (Epic Skt.) *stuvate* 'praises' must have been crossed with a class IX verb to yield [1]*thuṇāti / thunāti* 'moans' (*anutthunāmi*, Ja V 479,10*, *anutthunaṃ*, Ja III 114,6*, *anutthuṇāti*, Sn 827) and [2]*thuṇāti/ thunāti* 'praises' (*thunanti*, Sn 884, *anutthuṇanti*, Sn 901). But I do not know what this second verb is (*bhaṇati / bhaṇāti / bhaṇanti*?). GEIGER's explanation (§ 149) fails to convince. For Pkt. see PISCHEL § 494 (for *bhaṇāi* ibid. § 514).

468,18*), *suṇe* 'I may hear' (Ja IV 240,29*). A number of verbs were analogically transformed into presents of the *ya*-class[1]: ²*ghāyati* 'smells' ([jighrāti] :: *sāyati*[2] 'tastes' [svādate] / *khāyati** 'eats' [khādati]), *n(a)hāyati/sināyati*[3] 'bathes' (:: [pass.] *snāyate), *yāyati* 'goes, walks' ([*yāti*[4]] :: *ṭhāyati* 'stands', see p. 214), *vāyati* 'blows' ([*vāti*[5]] :: *vāyu-* 'wind'). Other athematic verbs were supplemented or replaced by new creations based (e.g.) on the imperative (*[ā]deti* / *°dheti* ← *dehi* / *dhehi* 'give!'/ 'put!') or aorist (*ghasati* 'eats, devours' ← ghásat, *pāheti* 'sends' ← *pāhesi* [√hi])[6].

The possible contraction of *-aya-* > *-e-* and *-ava-* > *-o-* (see § 11.4 and 12.4) led to various doublets: *jeti* ~ *jayati* 'wins', *ḍemāna-* 'flying' (Ja II 443,10* [so read with Bᵈ]) ~ *ḍayamāna-* (Ja IV 347,26*), *hoti* ~ *bhavati* 'is' (see § 44.2). And in line with that model, even primary *-e-* could be resolved into *-aya-*: *acceti* (atyeti) → *accayanti* (≠ atiyanti) 'they pass by', Th 145, S I 109,1* (*accayeyya*, Sn 781)[7], *etu* → *ayantu* (≠ yantu) 'let them

---

[1] See GEIGER § 138.

[2] On this verb see BERGER (1956: 105).

[3] Ind. pr. *n(a)hāyati*, Vin II 122,27, IV 118,16, imp. 2sg. *nhāya*, Vin III 110,15, 3sg. *nahāyatu*, Vin I 280,8, opt. *n(a)hāyeyya*, Vin IV 119,4**, S I 90,19, inf. *n(a)hāyituṃ*, Vin I 47,8, II 122,29, IV 118,9, aor. *sināyi*, Ap 204,10, inf. *sināyituṃ*, M I 39,6 (see GEIGER § 140.2).

[4] On Pāli *yāti* 'goes' see GEIGER § 140.2.

[5] On Pāli *vāti* 'blows' see GEIGER § 140.2.

[6] See BLOCH (1965: 226), GEIGER § 33 n. 2 (= p. 79 n. 3 in GHOSH's English translation) and CPD s.v. ²a *rem.* c. *pāhesi* seems to have influenced *pahiṇati* because later texts have forms of *pāhiṇati* (see WACKERNAGEL, *Kleine Schriften* p. 170).

[7] See GEIGER § 140.3.

go', Ja IV 447,4* (so read)[1], [1]*seti* (śete) → *saya(ti)* 'lies', Ja II 53,16*, Th 888, Vin I 57,30, S I 110,26* (*saye*, It 120,10*, *sayetha*, Th 501)[2]. All this lent the verbal system its variegated appearance.

The old forms were, however, preserved to a great extent: (class II) *abhithom'ahaṃ* 'I praise', Ap 423,13 (°staumi, see § 46.1), *sinâhi* 'bathe!' (snāhi), (class III) *jahāti* 'gives up'[3], (class V) *suṇomi* 'I hear', *pappoti* 'reaches', *sakkoti* 'is able'[4], (class VII has left no traces), (class IX) *kiṇāti* 'buys', *gaṇhāti* 'takes, grasps'[5], *jānāsi/jānāti* 'you know / he knows'[6], *jināti* 'deprives'[7], *(o)punāti* 'winnows' (see § 12.8), *(°ni[m])mināti*

---

[1] Cf. (the old imperative) *ayāma* 'let us go', D II 81,14 v.l. (see CPD s.v.). See also p. 220 n. 3.

[2] See GEIGER § 140.4.

[3] *jahāsi*, Ja III 295,20*, *(pa)jahāti*, Ja III 523,18*, Sn 1, 506, 589, 789.

[4] *pappomi*, Ap 496,24, *pappoti*, Th 35, 292, Dhp 27, Sn 584, *pappotha*, Ap 596,17, *papponti*, Ja III 256,18*, *pappontu*, Th 603, *sakkoma*, Sn 597, Vin I 31,9, *sakkonti*, Vin I 31,7, *suṇomi*, Ja IV 443,22*, *suṇoma*, Sn 350, 1110, *suṇohi*, D I 62,20, Sn 273, *suṇotha*, Sn 997. For Prakrit see PISCHEL § 503 (√*śru*), § 504 ([*pra+*]√*āp*) and § 505 (√*śak*).

[5] *(pag)gaṇhāsi*, S I 141,14*, Dhp-a III 57,4, *(°)gaṇhāti*, Vin IV 324,30, *(°)gaṇhātu*, Ja I 495,2*, Sn 479, Vin II 192,15 (see GEIGER § 146). On *(ug)gahāyati* see p. 8. Though an *e*-verb *gaheti* is not attested (see OBERLIES, *ZDMG* 147 [197] 534) some forms of (e.g.) *anu(g)gaṇhāti* appear as if derived from it (see CPD s.v.).

[6] *jānāsi*, Sn 504, *jānāti*, Sn 276, S I 103,23. The stem *jānā-* is generalised: (2pl. pres.) *jānātha*, Thī 346, (2sg. imp.) *jānāhi*, Thī 59, D I 88,22 (Ja VI 365,26*, however, read *vijānahi* [*vait.*]), (3sg. imp.) *jānātu*, It 28,9, 29,10 (see GEIGER § 145).

[7] On this verb see OBERLIES (1995: 135 [s.v. jāpeti]) and id., *OLZ* 94 (1999) 390-392.

'builds'[1]. And especially verbs like **(1)** *atthi* 'exists', **(2)** *bhavati* 'is', **(3)** *karoti* 'does, makes', **(4)** *dadāti* 'gives', *dadhāti* 'puts', **(5)** *tiṭṭhati* 'stands' retained their old inflexion (beside numerous neo-forms):

(1) After the pattern *°āma : °āmase, °anti : °ante* a medium of *atthi* is formed based on 1pl. *asma*, *amha* 'we are' – themselves analogical to *asmi* 'I am' (and its by-form *amhi*) and probably due to the abl. endings *-smā* and *-mhā* also with *-ā* as final – and 3pl. *santi* 'they are': (1pl.) *smase*, Sn 595, *amhase*, *amhāse*, Ja III 309,27*, VI 553,14*[2], D II 275,11* (*āgat' amhāse*), (3pl.) *sante*, Sn 868. The 1st persons tend to join the preceding word, which led to the loss of the initial *a-*: *mana mhi upakūḷito* 'I am scorched a bit', Ja I 405,16*, *sītibhūta mhi* 'I have become calmed', Thī 76 = 101, *ummagga-patipanna mhi* 'I have entered upon a wrong path', Thī 94, *sītibhūta mha* 'we have become calmed', Thī 66, *avāgata mha* 'we are far away from', Ja V 82,23*[3]. *atthi*, which never lost its *a-*, and univerbated *natthi* 'does not exist' (< nâsti)[4] are used as petrified forms also with a plural subject[5]: *ye sattā saññino atthi* 'those beings

---

[1] See CPD s.v. abhi-nimmināti and OBERLIES (1995a: 142).

[2] See ALSDORF, *Kleine Schriften* p. 321.

[3] See SCHELLER (1967: 12 n. 4) and – for Prakrit – PISCHEL § 85 (end) and 96. On the use of the *verbum substantivum* in conjunction with the verbal adjective see LÜDERS (1954: 31 n. 2). For Prakrit see ALSDORF, *Kleine Schriften* p. 63, and BHAYANI, *Sambodhi* 7 (1978/79) 115.

[4] See SCHELLER (1967: 32 n. 2).

[5] See GEIGER § 141 and EDGERTON, *JAOS* 57 (1937) 18. For Pkt. see PISCHEL § 515. *atthi* and *santi* can be combined with another verb in the same clause (see also OBERLIES 1995: 108 [s.v. atthi]): *atthi bhikkhu ummattako sarati pi uposathaṃ na pi sarati* 'There is one monk [who] remembers ...', Vin I 123,5-6, *santi sattā appara-*

which have consciousness ... ', Ap 4,13 (cf. Pv 541: *siyā nu sattā*), *natthi khandhādisā dukkhā* 'there is no misery (pl.) like that of the *skandhas*', Dhp 202, *na sasassa tilā atthi na muggā nāpi taṇḍulā* 'the hare has no sesamum nor beans nor grains of rice', Ja III 55,4* (= *na santi mudgā na tilā na taṇḍulā ... śaśasya ...*, Jāt-m 31,19*)[1]. Except for the 3sg. *atthu* the imperative is preserved in only a few forms: (2sg.) *(a)hi*, Ja VI 193,8*[2], (2pl.) *attha* (D I 192,30 = 195,13), (3pl.) *santu*, Ja VI 483,1* (Ee *nassantu*; read *no santu*[3]). The optative has two paradigms, one with the stem *ass-*[4], the other with *siy-* (see p. 3). On *siyuṃ* 'they might be' (with *siyaṃsu*, M II 239,4, according to a proportion like *siyā : siyaṃsu* = *addasā : addasaṃsu*) see § 47.[5]

---

jakkhajātikā assavanatā dhammassa parihāyanti 'There are beings, (almost) free from passions by nature, who will not be released because they do not hear the Doctrine', D II 38,15 = Vin I 5,25-26 (note the abl. *assavanatā*, see § 31.1). For Prakrit see Pischel § 417 – with reference to *Petersburger Wörterbuch* s.v. [1]as p. 535 – and ALSDORF, *Kleine Schriften* p. 64 n. 1.

[1] For Prakrit see PISCHEL § 417 and 498, for Aśokan Prakrit see SEN, *Syntactic Studies of Indo-Aryan Languages*. Tokyo 1995, 353.

[2] See OBERLIES (1995: 111).

[3] See ALSDORF, *Kleine Schriften* p. 286.

[4] This stem is the outcome of (OIA) *syā(t)* influenced by the commoner strong forms of the present stem with initial *a-* like *asmi* and *asti* (see OBERLIES 1999: 45 [*pace* GEIGER § 141.1]).

[5] On *atthi* see CPD s.v. atthi, GEIGER § 141 and VON HINÜBER § 456. For Prakrit see PISCHEL § 498 and JACOBI § 72.

	indicative	imperative	optative
1sg.	*asmi, amhi, mhi*		*siyaṃ*[1], *assaṃ*
2sg.	*asi*	*(a)hi*	*siyā, assa(si)*
3sg.	*atthi*	*atthu*	*siyā, assa*
1pl.	*asmā̆, amhā̆, amha-si* (p. 9), *mha* (med.) *smase, amhā̆se*		*assāma*
2pl.	*attha*	*attha*	*assatha*
3pl.	*santi* (med.) *sante*	*santu*	*siyuṃ, siyaṃsu, as-su(ṃ)*

(2) *bhava(ti)* 'is, becomes' has this uncontracted form with *bh- and* uncontracted *-ava-* (only the Ap knows *bhonti* 'they are', 596,13[2]) – only this stem is used in the optative (on *hup/veyya* see p. 80) – and a form with initial *h- and* contracted *-o-* < *-ava-* (see § 14.15 rem. b IV [p. 91])[3]. In

---

[1] On Ja V 216,3* see OLDENBERG, *Kleine Schriften* p. 1088 n. 1.

[2] And it is also only the Apadāna (321,18) which uses (aor. 1sg.) *bhosiṃ*. Only the participle *bhava(nt)-* used as term of address shows *-o-* < -ava- (see p. 177).

BOLLÉE, *Kuṇālajātaka*. London 1970, 38, reads Ja V 433,9* as *kicce jate 'natt-hacarāni bhonti*. Even if this would be the actual reading (cf., however, CPD s.v. anatthacara) it would be only one of the pecularities of the Kuṇālajātaka which is markedly different from all other Jātakas. On *bhavati*, Ja VI 228,16*, which FRANKE (*BB* 22 [1897] 289) wanted to correct to +*bhoti* see OBERLIES (1993/94: 160 n. 61).

[3] See GEIGER § 131.2. For Prakrit see PISCHEL § 475-476.

some compounds these two forms are contaminated: *anubhoti* 'experiences', *saṃbhoti* 'arises'. *(abhi)saṃbhuṇāti* 'reaches' took over the 'ending' from its synonym *pāpuṇāti* (: prāpnoti)[1].

	indicative	imperative	optative
1sg.	*bhavāmi, homi*		*bhaveyyaṃ*
2sg.	*bhavasi, hosi*	*bhava, bhavāhi, hohi*[2] (med.) *bhavassu*	*bhaveyyāsi*
3sg.	*bhavati, hoti*	*bhavatu, hotu*	*bhave, bhaveyya*
1pl.	*bhavāma, homa* (med.) *bhavāmase* (used also as imp.)		
2pl.	*bhavatha, hotha*	*bhavătha, hotha*	*bhavetha*
3pl.	*bhavanti, honti*	*bhavantu, hontu*	*bhaveyyuṃ*

---

1 See WACKERNAGEL, *Kleine Schriften* p. 418 n. 1; cf. CPD s.v. abhisambhavati (*pace* GEIGER § 131.2)

2 *hehi*, Bv II 9 (see GEIGER § 131.2), is a wrong reading of the old PTS edition. The new one has *hehiti* 'it will be'.

(3) The indicative present *karoti/kurute* 'does, makes' (and its opt. *kuyirā* ~ *kuriyā*[1] < kuryāt) is retained and has influenced other parts of the paradigm[2]: *karoti* .... *karonti*, (imp.) *karohi* ... *karontu*[3], (opt.) *kariyā* ~ *kayirā*[4], (ind.) *kuruse, kurute*, (imp.) *kuru, kurutu, kurutaṃ*[5]. The 3pl. (OIA) *kurvanti* (→ **kurvati*) was the base of the present (3sg.) *kubbati* and its optative (3sg.) *kubbetha*, Sn 702, 719[6]. It was sanskritisized to *krubbati*[7] under the influence of (OIA) *kriyate*. The 1sg. *kummi* 'I do', Ja II 435,19*, VI 499,16*, goes back to (Epic) Skt. *kurmi*, which itself is based on (1pl.) *kurmaḥ*. From the (OIA) future *kariṣyati* 'will do, will make' a new stem *kar-* was abstracted[8] (cf. *dakkha[ti]* 'sees' < drakṣya[ti] 'will see'[9]). It

---

1 *kuriyā*, Ja VI 206,12* = 209,15', 298,6* (C[k], cf. C[s] at 298,12'), *kuyirā*, Ja VI 298,6* as *qu.* Sadd 514,29* (see VON HINÜBER § 150, 453).

2 See GEIGER § 149. For Prakrit see PISCHEL § 508-509.

3 *karomi* and *karoma* are used as imperatives (cf. M III 179,27, Vin II 295,5) – as they are in Epic Sanskrit.

4 See SMITH *apud* BLOCH, *Recueil d'Articles* p. 135 n. 1, and VON HINÜBER § 453. On *kayiraṃ*, Dhp 313 = S I 49,10*, see § 4.6.

5 Ja IV 309,3* (= *karotu*, Jāt-m 112,19*), VI 288,23* (with CS *kurutaṃ bhavaṃ* ⏓⏓-⏑- [see ALSDORF, *Kleine Schriften* p. 399 n. 33]).

6 On opt. 3sg. *kubbaye*, Sn 943-944, see VON HINÜBER § 451 (diff. GEIGER § 149b and NORMAN 1992: 348).

7 This is a frequent reading of South Asian mss. (VON HINÜBER, *Journal of the Siam Society* 71 [1983] 87-88).

8 See HOFFMANN, *Aufsätze zur Indoiranistik* II,586-587 n. 24 (*pace* GEIGER § 149c).

9 See GEIGER § 136.3 and PED s.v. See also p. 245 n. 3 and 248 n. 2. Cf. *dassati* 'gives (/ gave)', Ja I 279,14, < dāsyati (or is it a future used as preterite?).

served as the base of an imperative ([2sg.] *kara, karassu*) and an optative ([1sg.] *kareyyāmi, kareyyaṃ, kareyy'ahaṃ*, Cp 218, [3pl.] *kareyyuṃ*, [all persons[1]] *kare*).

	indicative	imperative	optative
1sg.	*karomi* *kummi*	*karomi*	*kareyyāmi, °a(ṃ),* *kareyy'ahaṃ, kare*
2sg.	*karosi* *kuruse* *kubbasi*	*karohi* *kuru* *kara, karassu*	*kareyyāsi, kare* *kariyā, kayirāsi*
3sg.	*karoti* *kurute* *kubbati*	*karotu*, (med.) *ka-rotha* *kurutu, kurutaṃ*	*kareyya, kare* *kariyā(tha), kayirā̆* *kuriyā, kuyirā* *kubbetha*
1pl.	*karoma, ka-rom(h)ase*	*karoma*	*kareyyāma*
2pl.	*karotha*	*karotha*	*kareyyātha* *kayirātha*
3pl.	*karonti* *kubbanti*	*karontu*	*kareyyuṃ, kayi-ruṃ, kare*

---

[1] (1sg.) Ja II 138,13* (*karomi*, ct.), IV 240,30* ≠ 241,9*, (2sg.) Ja IV 223,6* (*[mā] kareyyāsi*, ct.), V 116,26* (*[mā] kari*, 118,12'), 448,24* (*[mā] kari*, ct.), (3sg.) Ja I 443,10* (*kareyya*, ct.), III 105,22* (*kareyya*, ct.), Dhp 42 = Ud 39,15*-16* (*kareyya*, Ud-a) ≠ Dhp 43, (3pl.) Ja I 289,30* = V 435,17* (*kareyyuṃ*, 437,17' [cf. 435,20* and Mil 205,12]). On this form see VON HINÜBER § 425 / 453.

rem. ad 3: **(a)** *ku/ariy°*, *ku/ayir°* is always dissyllabic except at Ja V 435,20* (*sabbā ca itthī kayiruṃ nu* [so Be; Ee *kareyyuṃ no*] *pāpaṃ* 'and all women commit sin[s]' --⏑--/⏑⏑-⏑--); **(b)** Syntagmata out of *karoti* and a noun in the accusative can take their object in the accusative (so-called 'compound verbs'[1]): *imaṃ dīpaṃ ārakkhaṃ sugato kari* 'the Blessed guarded this island', Dīp I 28, *ekaccaṃ bhikkhuṃ pavayha-pavayha kāraṇaṃ karonti* 'they punished this monk ....', M I 442,26 ≠ 444,21, *kumbhaṃ pi añjaliṃ kariyā* 'he will greet the pot, too', Ja VI 298,6* (Ee *kumbhaṃ pañjaliṃ kariyā*), *pakkhehi taṃ pañjalikaṃ karomi* 'with my wings I pay homage to you', Ja III 174,26* = 175,14*, *bhariyaṃ katvā padakkiṇaṃ* 'having honoured his wife ... ', Ja VI 525,3*, *amhākaṃ rājānaṃ paribhavaṃ karontassa* ' .... of him who abuses our king ...', Ja VI 164,2 (... *rājānaṃ paribhāsantassa*, B[d]), *ṣabbāmitte raṇaṃ katvā* 'having fought against all enemies ...', Ja II 91,6*, *paññāya tittaṃ purisaṃ taṇhā na kurute vasaṃ* 'thirst does not have control over a man who ...', Ja IV 172,24*, *dhammaṃ sajjhāyaṃ karoti* 'he studies the doctrine', A III 22,15, *ludd(h)ā dhanaṃ saṃnicayaṃ karonti* 'Being greedy, they stored wealth', Th 776 = M II 72,28*, *chabbaggiyā bhikkhū bahuṃ lohabhaṇḍaṃ kaṃsabhaṇḍaṃ saṃnicayaṃ karonti* 'the group of six monks stored a lot of iron and copper ware', Vin II 135,11-12, *Bhagavā ... ca gattāni sītaṃ karissati* 'the Exalted one will cool his limbs', Ud 83,14 = D II 129,2 *maṃ ca sotthiṃ karissati* 'and he will rescue me', Ja III 430,30*, *bhātaraṃ sotthiṃ katvāna* 'having rescued his brother', Ja II 91,7* (cf. ... *bhariyāya-m-akāsi sotthiṃ*, Ja III 349,9*).

---

1 See CPD s.vv. *adinna*, *'kata* (III,84a *rem.*) and *karoti* (1.c.VII), VON HINÜBER (1968: 71-73) and WIJESEKERA, *Syntax of Cases in the Pāli Nikāyas*. Kelaniya 1993, p. 43.

(4) Beside (a) *dadāti* 'gives'[1] and (b) *da(d)hāti* 'puts' (see § 14.15 rem. b, I [p. 90]) Pāli has a number of new stems[2]: **(a) 1.** *dada-* (extracted from *dadāmi*), the base of (e.g.) the optative *dadeyyaṃ* (*dadeyyāsi*, *dade[yya]* ...), **2.** *de-* (see p. 204), **3.** *dajja-* (abstracted from the optative *dajjaṃ* < dadyām, as *haññati* ← hanyāt[3]), **4.** (only) 1sg. *dammi*, Ja IV 257,15*, and 1pl. *damma*, Ja V 317,24* (analogical to *kummi*, see above [3])[4]; **(b) 1.** *daha-* (also in: *saddahati* 'believes'[5]), **2.** *dhe-*.

---

[1] The present-stem *dadā-* was generalised: (2pl. imp.) *dadātha*, Vv 742 (*dadātha vittā* [⏑]-⏑--).

[2] See CAILLAT, *IF* 88 (1983) 317. On *nipadāmase*, Ja III 120,24* (*dāmase*, ct.), see PED s.v. (diff. [?] Sadd V 1494).

[3] See FRANKE, *Kleine Schriften* p. 283, and CAILLAT, *BEI* 9 (1991) 9-13.

[4] See GEIGER § 143. On *(°)ādiyati* see p. 199.

[5] GEIGER (§ 123) pointed out that *saddahāsi*, Ja I 426,8*, VI 245,17*, is no 'subjunctive' (cf. FRANKE, *Ostasiatische Zeitschrift* 6 [1917/18] 295) but the historical form of the 2sg. (*śraddadhāsi*).

	dadā-	*de-*	*daha-*	*dhe-*
ind. pres.	*dadati*, *dadāma*, *dadanti*, (med.) *dadāmase*[1] (also used as imp.)	*demi ... denti*	*dahāmi .... dahanti*	*(samā)dhe-mi, dheti*
imp.	*dada / dadāhi, ... dadantu*	*(dehi) ... dentu*	*(sad)daha, odahassu*	*(dhehi), vid-hentu*
opt.	(1sg.) *dadey-yaṃ*, (2sg.) *da-deyyāsi*, (3sg) *dadeyya, dade*, (1pl.) *dadeyyā-ma*, (2pl.) *dadeyyātha*, (3pl.) *dadeyyuṃ*	(1sg.) *deyyaṃ*	*daheyya(ṃ), daheyyuṃ*, (med.) *sad-dahetha, vidahe*	*saddheyya*

(5) *tiṭṭha(ti)* 'stands' has the present stems **1.** *ṭhā-* (see § 45), **2.** *ṭhāyāmi*, Th 888 (analogical to neighbouring *sayāmi* 'I lie' and influenced by *ṭhāyi[n]-* 'standing, being in a state of' < sthāyin-), **3.** *ṭhaha-* (analogical to *dahati*) and **4.** *ṭhe-* (see § 45).

---

[1] Ja III 131,15*, V 317,23*/25*.

§ 45. Not only were old athematic verbs transferred to the 'first conjugation' (see § 44) but also 'thematic' ones were transformed into root-presents[1], i.e. *ā*- and *e*-verbs of the 'second conjugation', either by analogy (*°[t]ṭhāti* 'stands' :: *yāti* 'goes'[2], *[upa]gāti* 'sings' < *gāyati* 'sings'[3], *akkhāti* 'preaches' :: [2/3sg. aor.] *akkhā* 'you/he preached') or by 'shortening' (<*bi*>*bhemi* 'I fear', S I 111,2* [see § 11 *rem.* c][4], *vi*<*ja*>*hāmi* 'I abandon [= I spit out]', Ja VI 78,15*, <*da*>*dāmi* 'I give', Pv 60 [as read by Pv-a], Cp 17 [as read by the Siamese edition, see Ee p. 2 n. 14]).

Many more verbs, however, were transferred to the *e*-class[5]. For the most part this transference started from the verbal adjective in *°ita*-[6]: *uṭṭheti* 'stands up' (← *uṭṭhita*-), *phuseti* 'touchs' (← *phusita*-), Thī 6, ^{2}*seti* 'binds' (← *sita*-), Ja IV 11,20*[7]. These *e*-verbs are often distinguished from *e*-causatives by their *a*-vocalism (*bhajehi* 'pay honour!', Ja III 148,13*, ~

---

1 See CPD I,550a, s.v. *aññāti* (for Epic Sanskrit see NARTEN, *Kleine Schriften* I,84-85). On 'root optatives' see SMITH, *Analecta rhythmica* (Studia Orientalia XIX:7, Helsinki 1954), p. 10 n. 2, and OBERLIES (1996: 113).

2 See OBERLIES (1999: 37).

3 See § 6.8. It is that this contraction was influenced by a word such as *gāthā*- (cf. *ekaṃ me gāhi gāthakaṃ* 'Sing for me [just] one little song!', Ja III 507,25*).

There is no *trāti* 'protects' in Pāli (*pace* GEIGER § 138), and *tāyati* is the old present (see WACKERNAGEL, *Kleine Schriften* p. 423 n. 1).

4 Is *vihemi*, Ja V 154,19*, a wrong reading instead of *bibhemi* as is (probably) *vibheti*, Ja V 509,21* (see PED s.vv. vibheti / viheti^{2})?

5 See GEIGER § 139.2 and VON HINÜBER § 447 (on *akkhehi*, Ja VI 318,20*, see, however, CPD s.vv. ^{2}akkha / akkhāti).

6 On this kind of present-stem formation see below § 56 rem. b.

7 See OBERLIES (1989/90: 181-183).

bhājeti 'distributes', *vadeti* 'tells', Ja IV 61,19*, ~ *vādeti* 'plays [an instrument]'[1]), though causatives were also used instead of the simple verbs, i.e. as 'common' *e*-verbs (then their causative is formed with *-āpaya-* / *-āpe-*, see § 52).

---

[1] Cf. *na maṃ tapati ātapo ātappā tapayanti maṃ* 'It is not the heat of the sun which torments me: The afflictions torment me', Ja III 447,23* (~ *na ātapo tapayati antakā tāpayanti mām*, Mvu III 186,2*). The regular causative of *tapati* is *tāpayati*. On *puneti* (= *punāti*), Th 533, see Sadd V 1617.

§ 46. The endings[1] of the **(1)** *indicative present* and the *future* (for the use of 1sg. *-aṃ* in the future see p. 244[2]) are (sg.) *-mi*, *-si*[3], *-ti*[4], (pl.) *-ma*, *-tha*, *-nti* (the secondary ending *-ma* has replaced primary **-mo*)[5]; the 1sg. of the indicative has a by-form *-ā̆haṃ* (*rocāhaṃ* 'I find pleasure in', Ja V

---

1 See chart on p. 226.

2 GEIGER gives just one example for a 1sg. ind. pres. in *-aṃ* (for Prakrit see ALSDORF, *Kleine Schriften* p. 58-59, BHAYANI, *Sambodhi* 7 [1978/79] 114, and BALBIR, in: *Dialectes dans les littératures indo-aryennes* [édité par COLETTE CAILLAT]. Paris 1989, 509): *gacchaṃ*, Thī 306, however, is the 1sg. of the future of *gacchati* (see VON HINÜBER § 420). *jānaṃ*, which NORMAN (1991: 181-182) claims to be a 1sg., is likely to be a 'frozen' participle (see VON HINÜBER, l.c.).

On Prakrit *-ami* (a remodelling of *-āmi* after *-asi* and *-ati*) – unknown to Pāli – see PISCHEL § 454 and BALBIR, in: *Dialectes dans les littératures indo-aryennes* (édité par COLETTE CAILLAT). Paris 1989, 514.

3 On *kāmehi* 'you desire', Ja V 295,15*, ~ *kāmesi*, Mahāvastu II 481,12, see LÜDERS (1954: 85 n. 4) and OBERLIES (1996: 116).

4 In analogy with *-āmi* (and after the model of the old *nā*-class [*pacināsi*, Ja III 22,2*]) 2sg. and 3sg. sometimes also have *-āsi* and *-āti* (see GEIGER § 123 and VON HINÜBER § 413; cf. SMITH 1950: 34, CAILLAT, *IF* 75 [1970] 302-303, and OBERLIES 1993/94: 167 with n. 113): *kim-atthiko tāta khaṇāsi khāsuṃ* (-⏑--), Ja IV 46,10*, *kiṃ gijjha paridevāsi* (⏑⏑--), Ja III 331,2*, *sādhu paṭibhaṇāsi me* (⏑-⏑-), Ja III 405,8*, *bhaṇāti* ... (-⏑-), Ja VI 360,8* (so read [see Sadd V 1647 pointing to Ja III 405,8*]), *yā-y-aññaṃ anusāsāti* (⏑---), Ja I 429,27*, *sace hi so sujjhati yo hanāti* (-⏑--), Ja VI 210,32* (cf. Sadd 398 n. e and CAILLAT, *BEI* 10 [1992] 100-101). Such forms were considered to be remains of the old subjunctive (see also p. 222). On Pkt. *bhaṇāsi* / *bhaṇādi* (etc.) see PISCHEL § 514.

5 See GEIGER § 122.1 and VON HINÜBER § 422. For Prakrit see JACOBI § 56 and PISCHEL § 453-456 (on 1pl. *-mo* / *-mu* see ibid. § 455, ALSDORF, *Kleine Schriften* p. 59-60 and BHAYANI, *Sambodhi* 7 [1978/79] 115).

178,7* [Āryā][1], *anuyācahaṃ* 'I requested', Cp 243, *upaṭṭhahaṃ* 'I look after', Ja V 90,9*[2], *palāyahaṃ* 'I run away', Ja II 340,9*, *ramahaṃ* 'I take pleasure in', Ja V 112,31* [C^k], *virocahaṃ* 'I shine forth', *saṃpaṭivijjhahaṃ* 'I pierce', Thī 149[3], Ap 298,9, *anusāsahaṃ* 'I instruct', Ja IV 428,2*[4] ≠ V 348,16* [B^d])[5], the first pl. one in *-masi* (*amhasi* 'we are', Ja IV 296,22*, VI 553,14* [so read], *okandāmasi* 'we cry out', Ja VI 555,1*[6], on opt. *viharemasi* '... were we to dwell', Thī 375, see p. 225 n. 1)[7]. The corresponding *ātmanepada* endings of the singular are *-e*[8], *-se*, *-te* (~ *-sī* / *-tī* [see § 8.4]), while of the plural only[9] *-nte* is preserved (on *-mase*[10] see

---

1 See ALSDORF (1968: 31).

2 See VON HINÜBER (1994: 159).

3 So read also at Ap 375,28 (*pace* Ap Ee p. VIII [!]).

4 So read (see SMITH, *BSL* 33 [1932] 169).

5 See SMITH, *BSL* 33 (1932) 169-172, CPD I,528b (2Aε), PISANI (1952: 287), BECHERT (1958: 312) and VON HINÜBER § 421. Cf. *icchāmahaṃ* 'I wish', Vin I 32,38.

6 C^ks read *°damasi*; quoted as *ukkantāmasi*, Sadd 842,10, *okk °*, ibid. 511,18, 628,8.

7 Though this ending is only very sporadically used, it seems to live on in New Indo-Aryan and Dardic languages (see BLOCH 1965: 235, TURNER 1975: 289-299, and OBERLIES, *Historische Grammatik des Hindi*. Reinbek 1998, 37 n. 44).

8 Cf. *ottape*, S I 154,33* (so read [see CPD s.v. anottāpi(n); cf., however, CPD s.v. ottapati]). Vasudevahiṇḍi has a 1sg. *ātm.* in *-ahe* (ALSDORF, *Kleine Schriften* p. 59).

9 As far as I can see *maññivho* 'you boast', Ja III 311,26*, is used as an indicative pure and simple (on 2pl. *-vhe* – an indicative ending taught by the Pāli grammarians – see VON HINÜBER § 423).

10 A pure indicative value of this ending is postulated by GEIGER (§ 122.2) for *abhinandāmase* 'we are pleased', Vv 156, and *tappāmase* 'we are tired', Vv 153. But also

below, 2.; cf. opt. 1pl. in *-emase*)[1]. The last one has a by-form *-are* (see p. 8 n. 6)[2] – known from Aś G RE XIII (*anuvatare*)[3] – which is used for the future and aorist as well (see § 48-49)[4].

---

ohadāmase, Ja II 355,7*, is a statement pure and simple without any 'imperative' nuance. The same seems to hold good for *jahāmase*, Ja VI 550,24*, 553,17*, *panudāmase*, Ja VI 491,19*, and *bhavāmase*, Ja VI 567,10*, Th 1128. And this ending is used also in the future tense (*lacchāmase*, Vv 320, *sikkhissāmase*, Sn 814).

The Vasudevahiṇḍi uses *-mahe* as 1sg. (see ALSDORF, *Kleine Schriften* p. 59).

1 See GEIGER § 122.2 and VON HINÜBER § 423-425. For Prakrit see PISCHEL § 457-458 (for 1st sg. ind. prs. *ātm.* in *-e* see also BHAYANI, *Sambodhi* 7 [1978/79] 115).

2 *udicc[h]are* 'they see', Vin I 25,28 (see CPD s.v. udikkhati.), *upapajjare* 'they are reborn', Dhp 307, *uppajjare* 'they rise (again)', Th 337, *khādare* 'they eat (= hurt)', Ja II 223,14*, *jāyare* 'they are born', Ja IV 53,23*, S I 34,16*, *jīyare* '(the eyes) lose (their sight)', Ja VI 528,5*, *ñāyare* 'they are known / called', Ap 27,8, *miyyare* 'they die', Sn 575, *bujjhare* 'they understand', Thī 453, *labhare* 'they obtain', S I 110,32*, *nisīdare* 'they sit down', Ap 352,17, *socare* 'they grieve', Dhp 225, Sn 445, *pamuccare* 'they are / will be released', Thī 242, *vuccare* 'they are called', Ja I 129,22*, *sūyare* 'they are heard', Ja VI 528,30*, *haññare* 'they are killed', S I 76,22, (fut.) *karissare* 'they will make', Ja III 398,29*, VI 490,29*, *bhavissare* 'they will become', Ja III 207,9*, VI 505,14*, *vasissare* 'they will dwell', Th 962.

3 Prakrit grammarians give *°ire* for the 3pl. *ātmanepada* – an ending not attested in literature (see PISCHEL § 458 and LEUMANN, *Morphologische Neuerungen im altindischen Verbalsystem*. Amsterdam 1952, p. 10).

4 See GEIGER § 122.2, BECHERT (1958: 313) and VON HINÜBER § 425.

(2) The *imperative* endings[1] (sg.) *-mi*, (pl.) *-ma* and *-tha* (with lengthened stem vowel *-ātha*, Ja III 427,11*, V 302,24, Sn 385, 692[2]) are transferred from the indicative[3]; its 2sg. has -ø (i.e. the pure stem vowel) and after long/lengthened vowels *-hi* (*jīvāhi* 'may you live!', Sn 1029)[4] – borrowed from OIA athematic *ā*-roots –, its 3sg. *-tu* (and *-ātu* [Ja IV 309,12*/16*, 310,12*/23*] in analogy with *-āhi*[5], which on the other hand was transformed into *-ahi* [*vijānahi*, Ja VI 365,26* (thus read)]) and its 3pl. *-ntu*. The final *-a* of these endings may be lengthened by *pluti* (see § 6.3b): *mā pabbajā* 'do not go forth', Ja V 184,25* (Āryā), *nikkhanaṃ* 'bury!' (see § 4.6). The rare 1pl. in *-mu*[6] (*pappomu* 'may we attain', Ja V 57,19*; frequently attested in 1pl. opt. *-emu*, see below) is a remodelling of regular *-ma* (see above) after *-tu* and *-s(s)u*[7]. The *ātmanepada* endings, which are frequently used, are (sg.) *-ssu*[8] (by *saṃprasāraṇa* < -sva; 3sg. *-tu* gives rise

---

1 See GEIGER § 124-126 and VON HINÜBER § 426-434. For Prakrit see PISCHEL § 467-471, JACOBI § 57 and SCHWARZSCHILD (1991: 146-152).

2 See Geiger § 123.

3 See GEIGER § 125 and VON HINÜBER § 426, 429-430. The remodelling of the old imperative ending (1sg.) *-āni* into *-āmi* can be seen in (1sg. imp.) *(handa dāni) apāyāmi* 'let me go away', Ja VI 183,16* (≠ *apemi*) which corresponds to OIA *apāyāni* (see BLOCH, *BSL* 37 [1936] 50, and VON HINÜBER § 426).

4 See GEIGER § 125.

5 See CAILLAT (1970: 26-27) and VON HINÜBER § 428 (cf. CAILLAT, *IF* 75 [1970] 302-303).

6 In Prakrit *-mo* and *-mu* are used as 1sg. (see ALSDORF, *Kleine Schriften* p. 60).

7 See VON HINÜBER § 429.

8 Even *e*-verbs and causatives have *-assu*: *desassu*, M I 169,3*. There is not a single example of a 2sg. imperative in *-essu* in the whole canon (the Chaṭṭha Saṅgāyana

to analogical *-su* [*bhikkhasu* 'beg!', Th 1118, *avekkhas<s>u* 'look down!', Vin I 6,1*, *nudasu* 'push back!', Ja IV 443,24*[1], *bhuñjas<s>u* 'enjoy!', Ja II 445,28* = III 327,26*][2]), *-taṃ*[3] (with its historical *sandhi* variant *[vaḍḍha]tām [eva]* 'it should indeed grow', Ja III 209,9*, see § 26), (pl.) *-mase*, *-vho* and *-ntaṃ*[4]. The ending of the 1pl. *-mase*[5] is an indicative ending

---

CD-ROM gives only *ramessu*, Dhp 371, instead of which the PTS edition reads *bhamassu*).

1 See OBERLIES (1995/96: 287).

2 See BERGER (1955: 61 n. 122) and VON HINÜBER § 431. Prakrit has *-asu* as well as *-āsu* (see ALSDORF, *Kleine Schriften* p. 60 n. 2). The latter has its *-ā-* either due to the influence of the parallel form in *-āhi* or due to compensatory lengthening.

3 *acchataṃ*, Ja VI 506,8* (*acchatu*, ct.), *khamyataṃ*, Ja IV 36,6* (*khamyatu*, ct.), *labhataṃ*, D II 150,13, *āniyyataṃ*, D II 245,21, *āhariyyataṃ*, D II 245,7 (so read; see CPD s.v. āhariyyati). For this imperative passive see below (p. 222).

4 See GEIGER § 126. Another 3pl. is *-ruṃ* which is only rarely attested: *āhaññaruṃ*, Ja IV 395,18*, *visīyaruṃ* 'let [pieces of flesh] come off', Th 312 (on the form see VON HINÜBER § 425, on the meaning OBERLIES, *OLZ* 94 [1999] 389).

5 *icchāmase*, Pv 526, *ujjhāpayāmase*, S I 209,14*, *karomase*, Ap 33,13, D II 288,1* (v.l. *°masi*), Ja II 258,21*, VI 163,26*, *gacchāmase*, Ja V 78,11*, 200,21*, *ajjhagamāmase*, Ja VI 442,12* / 14*, *gaṇhāmase*, Ja VI 182,13*, 441,5*, *papatāmase*, Ja VI 441,20*, *ghātayāmase*, Ja VI 491,10*, *(°)carāmase*, Sn 32, S I 210,21*, Ap 339,19, *jānāmase*, Pv 649 = Vv 1267, *ojināmase*, Ja VI 222,3*, *dadāmase*, Ja III 131,15*, *duhāmase*, Ja V 105,25*, *(°)nayāmase*, Ja VI 222,2*, Pv 257 (so read; E *nīyāmase*), *saṃnāhayāmase*, Ja VI 221,33*, *(°)patāmase*, Ja IV 361,27*, Pv 789, *posiyāmase*, Ja VI 509,25* (read *posayāmase*? B[d] *posissāmase*), *bhakkhayāmase*, Ja III 198,23*, *bhaṇāmase*, S I 209,28*, *bhavāmase*, Sn 32, *yāmase*, Pv 609 = Vv 1227, *yamāmase*, Ja III 488,11* = Th 275 = Dhp 6 = M III 154,12*, *saṃyamāmase*, S I 209,27* (see GEIGER § 133), *(°)ramāmase*, Ja II 268,9*, S I 131,2* ≠ Thī 139, 370 = 371 (*ehi ramāmase* [m.c. *-ĕ*] is comparable to *ehi ... vajemase*, Ja II 268,2*, on which

which was fashioned out of (1pl. ind.) *-masi* (see above, p. 218) on the analogy of *-(n)ti : -(n)te*[1]. The ending *-vho* of the 2pl.[2] seems to be a 'hyper-Pālism' for eastern **-vhe* < **-hvaṃ* < *-dhvam*[3]. In the 3sg. passive, more recent *(haññа)tu* 'let him be killed' supersedes older *(āharīya)taṃ* 'let it be brought'[4].

> *rem.* It has been surmised that the imperative endings *-āhi* / *-ātu* / *-ātha*, attested also with Aśoka, are remains of a historic subjunctive (see also NORMAN, Traces of the Subjunctive in Middle Indo-Aryan, in: *Facets of Indian Culture. Gustav Roth Felicitation Volume*. Patna 1998, 97-108). More probably, however, this *-ā-* is due to paradigmatic levelling (see SMITH 1950: 34 and CAILLAT, *IF* 75 [1970] 302-303). See also p. 217 n. 4.

---

see p. 225 n. 1), *ramayāmase*, Vv 169 (*handa ... ramayāmase*), *labhāmase*, Ja II 440,16*, V 254,32*, Pv 429, 434, *vasāmase*, Ja II 418,10*, VI 515,27* = 516,10* = 517,19* (v.l. L[k] *vasemhase*, see p. 225 n. 1), *vāyāmase*, Ja VI 35,14*, *vijahāmase*, Ja III 430,17*, *vidhamāmase*, Ja III 261,12* (so read), *sārayāmase*, S I 197,16*, *sobhayāmase*, Ap 25,31, *hanāmase*, Ja IV 345,6*. On optatives in *-emase* see p. 225 with n. 1.

[1] See GEIGER § 122.2 / 126, BERGER, *MSS* 11 (1957) 111, and VON HINÜBER § 433.

[2] *passavho* 'see!', Sn 998, *pucchavho* 'ask!', Sn 1030, *bhajavho* 'resort to!', Ja I 472,16*, *nivattavho* 'turn back!', Ja II 358,7*, *manta(ya)vho* 'converse with!', D I 122,14, Ja II 107,18*/19*, IV 438,21*, *kappayavho* 'make!', Sn 283, *paridevayavho* 'mourn!', Ja IV 439,7* (see also GEIGER § 126).

[3] See BERGER, *MSS* 11 (1957) 112 n.5, and VON HINÜBER § 434. On *pamodathavho*, Ja IV 162,26*, with its double ending as univerbation of /*pamodatha vo*/ (so ibid. 22* B[d] [Ee *modathavho*]) adjusted to the imperative ending *-vho* see VON HINÜBER § 434 (cf. FRANKE, *Kleine Schriften* p. 283, GEIGER § 126 and OBERLIES 1995/96: 293).

[4] See VON HINÜBER § 432.

(3) The *optative* has two sets of suffixes – one with generalised *-e-* (based on OIA 3sg. *-et*), one with *-eyyă̄-* (a contamination of the OIA thematic and athematic endings, starting from 1sg./3pl. *-eyam/-eyuḥ*, see § 14.9)[1] –, and two sets of endings, (a) the old optative endings (the *-ā[≠]* of the athematic ones, supported by that of the second set of endings [*-eyyāmi* ... *-eyyāma*], was retained except for the 3sg. [see below]) and (b) those of the indicative present (with substitution of secondary *-ta* by primary *-tha*): (1sg.) *-eyyaṃ*[2], *-eyyāmi*, *-e*, (2sg.) *-eyya*, *-eyyāsi*, *-esi*, (3sg.) *-eyya*, *-eyyāti*, *-e*[3], (1pl.) *-eyyāma*, *-emu*[4], (2pl.) *-eyyātha*[5], (3pl.) *-eyyu(ṃ)*[6]. The medium[7]

---

1 For Prakrit see PISCHEL § 91 / 122 / 459 (*-ejjā ~ -ijjā*).

2 Prakrit has also a 1sg. in *-jjaṃ* not noted by PISCHEL (see ALSDORF, *Kleine Schriften* p. 59).

3 A rather strange form is 3sg. *apace* 'he should honour', A IV 245,6*, Ap 581,19 (see CPD s.vv. ²apaca, apacāyati).

4 Not attested is expected *-*ema* < (OIA) *-ema* – at least not in canonical texts (Sn 898 *sikkhema* must be a wrong reading [cf. VON HINÜBER, *MSS* 36 (1977) 47 n. 23], and *ujjhema*, Ja VI 138,14*/16*, is an indicative [VON HINÜBER 1994: 145 *pace* CPD s.v. ujjhati]) – though it is found in Aśokan Prakrit (see VON HINÜBER § 438; ibid. § 442 on *hañchema*, Ja II 418,11*). On *ujjheti* see MANU LEUMANN, *Kleine Schriften* p. 342-347, and HAEBLER, *MSS* 16 (1964) 23-24.

5 Also *-etha* is not to be found in canonical texts (see VON HINÜBER § 438). Cf., however, CPD s.v. abhisajati (!).

6 See GEIGER § 129 and VON HINÜBER § 435-436. For Prakrit see PISCHEL § 459-466 and JACOBI § 58.

7 See GEIGER § 129 and VON HINÜBER § 443-444.

has (2sg.) *-etho*, *-etha*, *-eyyātho*[1], (3sg.) *-etha*[2], (1pl.) *-emase*[3]. The 2sg. active in *-esi*[4] is an analogical formation: *-esi* : *-e* = *-eyyāsi* : *-eyya*[5]. This latter ending goes back to **-eyyā* whose final *-ā* was shortened according to § 4.4. The 1pl. act. in *-emu*[6] is due to the blending of optative **-ema* (see

---

1 On *(labh)etho*, Sn 833 (~ *labhetha*, Pv 546, *dadetha*, 551, *passetha*, ibid.; cf. *āgac-cheyyātho*, D I 90,19, *manasi-kareyyātho*, ibid. 20) see VON HINÜBER § 443.

2 Instead of expected *-(e)ta* < *-(e)ta* / *-(ī)ta* (see GEIGER § 129 [see ibid. on *āsetha*, Ja V 222,16*, used as 3pl.] and VON HINÜBER § 444). (Athematic) *-īta* is used instead of (thematic) *-eta* already in the Brāhmaṇas, and the Mahābhārata (but not the Rāmāyaṇa [!]) has quite a lot of instances.

3 On *-emhase* and *-emahe* see below, p. 225 n. 1.

4 *adesi*, Ja V 31,25*, 496,20*, *anumaññesi*, Ja V 343,2* (so read [see CPD s.v. anumaññati]), *avhayesi*, V 220,22*, VI 274,12*, *āharesi*, VI 267,22*, *udikkhesi*, VI 299,5* *pariharesi*, IV 210,22*, *pucchesi*, V 201,3*, *maññesi*, Ja VI 343,33*, *vajjesi*, Pv 345, 469, +*vasesi*, Ja VI 175,12* (cf. *passesi*, Ja II 150,5* [opt. or *e*-verb?]). Is it too bold to see in *āvesi*, Ja IV 406,24* C[ks] (Ee with B[ds] *ṭhapehi*), the 2sg. optative of *āveti* ~ *āpeti* (< *appeti* < arpayati)? The "context demands imp. 2sg. 'put, place'" (CPD s.v. āvesi)! Cf. also OBERLIES (1995/96: 295).

5 See FRANKE, *Kleine Schriften* p. 282, ALSDORF, *Kleine Schriften* p. 388 n. 24, CAILLAT (1970: 25), ea. (1980: 53), VON HINÜBER (1994: 128) and id. § 439 (cf. CPD s.v. avhāyati, NORMAN 1992: 373 [ad Sn 1064], and VON HINÜBER, *MSS* 36 [1977] 43).

6 *upāsemu*, Ja VI 222,14*, *(vi)jānemu*, Ja V 44,25*, VI 13,14*, S I 34,11*, Sn 76, 599, 999, Vv 1210, 1270, *taremu*, Ja IV 164,2*, *dakkhemu*, Ja IV 462,8* = 463,2*, Dhp-a III 217,19* v.l. (Ee *dakkhema*), *dademu*, Ja VI 317,16*, *dālemu*, Th 1146, *passemu*, Ja VI 525,13*, *viharemu*, Ja II 33,25*, VI 221,19*, Vin I 25,19, *sakkuṇemu*, Ja V 24,26*, Pv 246. On *vāsayemu*, Ja VI 288,11*, see ALSDORF, *Kleine Schriften* p. 399 n. 33.

p. 223 n. 4) and imperative *-mu* (see p. 220), and the 1pl. mid. in *-emase*[1] seems to have originated in a similar way[2]. Corresponding to the analytical form in *-ăhaṃ* of the indicative (see p. 217-218), the optative has (1sg.) *-eyyăhaṃ* (M I 487,13, Ja IV 241,19*[3]) and (2sg. med.) *-eyyāhe* (D II 267,11*). *bhavehaṃ* 'I might be', Ap 458,26, has this form with the alternative optative suffix *-e-*[4] (the beginning of this optative is signalled by [e.g.] *jahe ahaṃ* 'I should give up', Ja III 14,15*)[5].

---

[1] *samācaremase*, Vv 981, *mahemase*, Vv 800 (*pūjāmase*, ct.), *vajemase*, Ja II 268,2* (*gamissāma*, ct.), *(°)vademase*, Ja III 335,11*, D III 197,22* (v.l. *vademhase*; ~ Āṭānāṭikasūtra [Ed. H. HOFFMANN 47b4] *vadanti*), *sādhayemase*, Ja II 236,19*. *viharemasi* (see GEIGER § 129) stands (m.c.) for *viharemase* in the *vait.* Thī 375: *yadi viharemasi kānanantare* (⏑⏑⏑⏑-⏑⏑|-⏑-⏑-).

If *saremhase*, Thī 383 (an odd *vaitālīya*-pāda: *api dūragatā saremhase* [⏑⏑-⏑⏑-⏑-⏑-]), should not be accepted as the correct reading (cf. GEIGER § 122 and VON HINÜBER § 433) it is not to be emended to *saramhase* (thus NORMAN 1971: 141) – this would be an aorist which definitely does not fit the context – but to *saremase* (with mss. PS) or *sarāmase* (with sec. hand of ms. B). Apart from this form (and *vademhase*, D III 197,22* v.l. [see above]) an optative in *-emhase* is only once attested – at least to the best of my knowledge – with *vasemhase*, the reading of ms. L^k at Ja VI 515,27* = 516,10* = 517,19* (Ee *vasāmase*). On +*vaṇem(h)ase*, Ja II 137,28*, see p. 240 n. 2. The 'inorganic' *-h-* (cf. *tuṇhīra-* ~ *tūṇī-* 'quiver') of these forms reminds of that of *gaṇhāmhase* and *karomhase* (VON HINÜBER § 433 and id., *JPTS* 10 [1985] 11). *maññemahe (mayaṃ)* [(--)⏑-⏑-], Ap 546,24 (v.l. *maññāmase* [see BECHERT 1958: 313, cf. VON HINÜBER § 444]) seems to be a blending of Pāli *-emase* and Skt. *-emahi*.

[2] See VON HINÜBER § 438 / 444.

[3] Cf. *miyyāhaṃ*, Ja VI 498,20* (*mareyyaṃ ahaṃ*, ct.). See Sadd V 1691.

[4] Cf. *ālabhehaṃ*, Aśoka Sep I.

[5] See BLOCH, *Recueil d'Articles* p. 135-148, CPD I,528b (cf. *Epilegomena* 21* [s.v. *analyt.*] and 28*-29* [s.v. *opt.*]) and VON HINÜBER § 441.

(4) The endings of the *preterite* are those of the tenses which merged into it (see § 48).

<table>
<tr><th></th><th>Indicative</th><th>Imperative</th><th>Optative</th></tr>
<tr><td rowspan="2">1sg.</td><td colspan="2">-mi
-ăhaṃ (future -aṃ)</td><td rowspan="2">-eyyaṃ, -eyyāmi, -e, -ey-yăhaṃ, -ehaṃ</td></tr>
<tr><td>(med.) -e</td><td>–</td></tr>
<tr><td>2sg.</td><td>-si
(med.) -se, -sī</td><td>-ø, -hi
(med.) -s<s>u</td><td>-eyya, -eyyāsi, -e, -esi
(med.) -etho, -etha, -eyyā-tho</td></tr>
<tr><td>3sg.</td><td>-ti
(med.) -te, -tī</td><td>-tu
(med.) -taṃ</td><td>-eyya, -eyyāti, -e
(med.) -etha</td></tr>
<tr><td>1pl.</td><td colspan="2">-ma
-masi -mu
(med.) -mase</td><td>-eyyāma, -emu
(med.) -em(h)ase</td></tr>
<tr><td>2pl.</td><td>-tha</td><td>-tha
(med.) -vho</td><td>-eyyātha</td></tr>
<tr><td>3pl.</td><td>-nti
(mid.) -nte</td><td>-ntu
(med.) -ntaṃ</td><td>-eyyu(m)</td></tr>
</table>

§ 47. The regular optative of both 'conjugations' is that in *-e(yya)-* (see § 46.3)[1]. But some historical forms of the optative of athematic verbs were preserved: *siyā/assa* 'it may be' (see p. 3), *dajjaṃ* 'I should give', Vin I 148,25 (*dajjāhaṃ*), Ja VI 515,19*[2], *dajjāsi* 'you should give', Ja VI 251,26*, *dajjā* '(if) he were to give', Th 468, D II 267,10*, Dhp 224, S I 57,32*, *kuriyā* 'he might do', Ja VI 206,12*, ~ (2/3sg.) *kayirā*, Ja II 42,8*, V 112,27*, Th 152, Dhp 53, Sn 728 ≠ 1051, *(°)jāniyā̆* 'he certainly knows', Th 85, Sn 713 (with *-ī̆-* from optatives like *kayirā*), *jāniyāma* 'we should know', Sn 873[3], *(vi)jaññaṃ* 'I should know', Sn 482, *jaññāsi* 'you should know', Ja VI 194,11*[4], *(anu)jaññā* 'he would know', Ja II 42,12*, V 63,8*, VI 36,14*, Th 10, Dhp 157, Sn 116, 394, 397-398 (probably analogical to *dajjā*[5]). And these relics were the pattern for new 'athematic' optatives (*vajj°* [← vadati] 'might say', Ja V 221,21*, VI 19,4*, 82,6*, 526,35*, 551,14*, Thī 307-308, Sn 859, 971)[6].

Sporadically the suffix *-e(yya)-* was added to the optative stem in *°(i)y-*: *anuppadajjeyyāsi* 'you should hand over', D III 61,10, *anupadajjeyya* 'he should hand over', Vin III 259,13** = 36, *anupadajjeyyāma* 'we should hand over', Vin III 259,11** = 35, *dajjeyyātha* 'you should give',

---

1 See CPD, *Epilegomena* 28*-29* (s.v. *opt.*), GEIGER § 127-130 and VON HINÜBER § 435-445.

2 Here *dajjaṃ* is used as preterite 'I gave' (see NORMAN 1991: 179), a usage of the optative known from Epic Sanskrit (cf. EDGERTON, *JAOS* 57 [1937] 32-33, and KATRE, *NIA* 1 [1938] 536).

3 Cf. *jāniyāmase*, M II 143,11*.

4 On this optative see VON HINÜBER § 11.

5 See GEIGER § 145 and VON HINÜBER § 11.

6 See GEIGER § 143(d) and VON HINÜBER § 440.

Vin I 232,7, *pakampiye* 'he will bend', Ja VI 295,9* (C^k), *maddiye* 'he shall crush', Cp 271, *haññe* 'he should kill', A IV 254,17*[1]. And often imperative endings were attached: *dajjehi* 'may you give!', Vin III 217,4. On the analytic optative see § 46.3 (end).

§ 48. The preterite replaced the (OIA) aorist, imperfect and perfect, supplemented by the verbal adjective (with/without *hoti*) used as *verbum finitum* (see § 56 rem. a). The core of this tense is the (OIA) aorist; historical forms of the imperfect and perfect were integrated into its paradigms (or transformed into aorists [*āhaṃsu* 'they said' ← *āha* 'he said'[2], *[a]vedi* 'he knew' ← *veda* 'he knows'][3]): (imperfect[4]) *kasaṃ*, Thī 112, *amaññaṃ* 'I thought', Ja V 215,6*, *pavapaṃ* 'I sowed', Thī 112, *adadaṃ* 'I gave', Vv 622, *adadā* 'you gave', Ja V 161,8*, VI 571,20*, *abravī* 'he

---

[1] See CPD s.vv. asnāti / anuppadeti (with references to *asmiye*, Ja V 397,29* – cf. LÜDERS [1954: 132] –, and *paṭikiriyemu*, Ja IV 384,13* [C^ks (Ee *paṭikaremu*)]), SMITH, *Retractationes rhythmicae* (Studia Orientalia XVI:5, Helsinki 1951), p. 4, CAILLAT, *ABORI* 72/73 (1991/92) 637-645, and ea. *BEI* 9 (1991) 11.

These forms may well be belong to the Vedic °*yet*-optative (on which see LEONID KULIKOV, The Vedic *-yet*-optative. A formation not yet recorded in Sanskrit grammars. *Proceedings of the Second International Vedic Workshop* [Kyoto 1999]. Forthcoming).

[2] See GEIGER § 171.

[3] See INSLER (1994: 77). Most probably also the nom. sg. of *vedi(n)-* 'knowing', viz. *vedi* (see § 34), was integrated into this aorist paradigm (see WACKERNAGEL, *Kleine Schriften* p. 159 n. 1). A 'typical' aorist ending was added to *avedi* yielding *avedesi*, Ja III 420,29* (so read with B^d). On *avedi* 'she showed', Ja IV 35,3*, see CPD s.v.

[4] See GEIGER § 161 (a) and VON HINÜBER § 479. For Prakrit see PISCHEL § 515.

said'[1], *āsi* 'he was'[2], *apucchasi* 'you asked', Sn 1050[3] (with primary ending[4]), (perfect[5]) *āsa* 'he was', D III 155,9*[6], *āsu(ṃ)* 'they were', *āha* 'he said', *āhu* 'they said'[7], *jagāma* 'he has gone', Ja VI 203,2*[8], *babhūva* 'it arose , Ja VI 282,22*[9], *jahuṃ* 'they have given up', Ja III 19,23*[10], *vidahū* 'they have appointed', Ja VI 284,16*[11], *vidū/vidu(ṃ)* 'they know/knew'[12]
Of the OIA aorist types five have survived (**5** only in traces), of which two

---

[1] (3sg.) *abravī*, Th 430, Thī 366, Sn 355, *abravi*, Sn 986, *abruvi*, Ja III 62,20*, and – as analogical forms – (1sg.) *abruviṃ*, Ap 497,26, Cp 202, (3pl.) *abravuṃ*, Ap 46,16, Ja V 112,30*, Th 720.

[2] See BLOCH, *Recueil d'Articles* p. 275-276 (particularly on *āsimha*, Ap 595,3), and VON HINÜBER § 479. For individual forms see CPD s.v. atthi (I,114a).

[3] This form is used as the last word of a *jagatī* ([-]⏑-⏑x).

[4] See CPD s.v. and s.v. ²a- rem. c. where reference is made to *asiñcati* 'he sprinkled', Vv-a 307,12' (cf. GEIGER § 161 and VON HINÜBER, *MSS* 36 [1977] 42).

[5] See GEIGER § 171 and VON HINÜBER § 480. For Prakrit see PISCHEL § 518.

[6] See SMITH *apud* BLOCH, *Recueil d'Articles* 276 n. 1, and CPD I,553b (s.v. ¹atthi).

[7] See GEIGER § 171.

[8] On traces of the perfect of *(ā)gacchati* see VON HINÜBER § 480 and id. (1994: 173-176). Sometimes aorist and perfect seem to have been blended (see p. 233 n. 1).

[9] See BECHERT (1955: 26 n. 66).

[10] See WACKERNAGEL, *Kleine Schriften* p. 158.

[11] See OBERLIES (1996: 116); cf. id., *ZDMG* 147 (1997) 535 with n. 11.

[12] See GEIGER § 171 and PED s.v. vindati.

(**3** and **4**) are productive[1]: (**1**) The root-aorist (*akā, [ajjh]agaṃ, aṭṭhā, adaṃ, adassaṃ, amarā, ahuṃ*)[2], (**2**) the thematic (asigmatic) aorist (*akaram, agamaṃ, acchida, addasaṃ, a(b)bhidā̆, avoca, ahuvā̆*), (**3**) the *s(iṣ)*-aorist (*akāsi, aññāsi, addakkhi*[3], *alattha, ahāsi, pāyāsi, pahāsi, ajesi, pāhesi, assosi*[4]), (**4**) the *iṣ*-aorist (*akarī, akkamī, agami, āgañchi, aggahī, acāri*), (**5**) and the reduplicated aorist (*avoca, ajjhapatto, udapatto, apatt[h]ā / pāpatt[h]ā* < [adhy/ud/pra]apaptat [rebuilt from **°pattā* after *patto* < prāptaḥ])[5].

---

1 See Geiger § 158-170 (type 1: § 160; type 2: § 161-162; type 3: § 163-165; type 4: § 166-170) and von Hinüber § 481-488. For Prakrit see Pischel § 516 and Alsdorf, *Kleine Schriften* p. 60.

2 On *ahuṃ* see below, p.232, on *assu(ṃ)*, Ja III 541,10*, 542,1*, see CPD s.v. (*pace* Geiger § 160), on *pāvā*, Sn 782, 888, see Norman (1992: 302) and cf. Sadd 322 n. 9, 389 n. 1, Sadd V 1603 and CPD s.v. ²avati.

3 On (1sg.) *asakkhiṃ*, Th 88, *(a)sakkhissaṃ*, A I 139,1, M III 179,28, (3sg.) *(a)sakkhi*, D I 96,10, Vin I 10,6, (1pl.) *sakkhimha*, D II 155,2 (← [fut.] *sakkh°* x asākṣīt [√sah]) see Oberlies (1996: 114-115 [*pace* Geiger § 164 and170]).

4 *hoti* forms its aorist in the same manner: (1sg.) *ahosiṃ*, Th 620, (2sg.) *hosi*, Ja II 200,14, (3sg.) *ahosi*, Vin I 23,7, Sn 835, (1pl.) *ahumha*, Ja I 362,19*, Thī 305, 520 (as well as *ahumhase*, Ap 482,7, and *ahosimha*, Ja IV 253,25), *ahesuṃ*, D II 5,7 (on this form see § 11.8). Due to various analogies (see BHSG § 32.28) we find also (1g.) *ahuṃ* (see p. 232), (1pl.) *ahesumha*, M I 265,1, (3pl.) *ahiṃsu*, Ap 144,5, 155,16, 194,1, 412,2 (see Ee of Ap II, preface p. VIII, and Bechert 1958: 314), Ja I 54,5 (v.l. *°ahaṃsu*), *(pātur)ahaṃsu*, Ja I 11,2, Ap 412,2, *(adhi)bhaṃsu*, S IV 185,31, *pātubhaviṃsu*, Ap 442,12 (see Bechert 1958: 314). For *ajjhabhī / anvabhī* and *bhaviṃ / bhaviṃsu* see below, p. 236

5 See Kern, *Verspreide Geschriften* II.2 ('s-Gravenhage 1913), p. 274, id. Toev. I,67, Norman (1992: 387 [ad Sn 1134]) and von Hinüber, *MSS* 32 (1974) 65-72 (= 1994: 52-61), id. (1994: 174) and id. § 482 (*pace* Geiger § 159.III). Cf. Oberlies (1993/94: 163 n. 87).

(1) root-aorist:

– *karoti* 'does, makes': (1sg.) *akaṃ*, Ap 172,6, Ja V 160,1* (*akariṃ*, ct.) – built from *akā* after the pattern *adā* : *adaṃ* –, (2sg.) *akā*, Ja V 184,5* (*mā* ... *akā*), 317,15*...19*, (3sg.) *akā*, Ap 394,18, Ja III 12,9* (*akari*, ct.), IV 293,2* (*akāsi*, ct.), V 29,2* (*akāsi*, ct.), 184,5* (*mā* ... *akā*).[1]

– *gacchati* 'goes': (1sg.) *(°)ajjhagaṃ*, Ja VI 180,3* (*ajjhagāhaṃ*), Th 405, Thī 67, S I 103,10, *adhigaṃ*, Thī 122 (without augment!), (2sg.) *āgā*, Sn 841, (3sg.) *agā*, Sn 538, *ajjhagā*, Sn 204, *āgā*, Ja III 165,7*, (3pl.) *ajjhagū*, Ja I 256,7*, Sn 330, *āgu*, D II 258,8*, *āguṃ*, Ja VI 568,4*. The paradigm is supplemented by (1pl.) *āgamhā̆*, Sn 570,597 (type **3**).[2]

– *tiṭṭhati* 'stands': (3sg.) *aṭṭhā*, It 86,3*, Sn 429. This aorist has been enlarged with the endings of type **3** and **4**: (1sg.) *aṭṭhāsiṃ*, Thī 73, (3sg.) *aṭṭhāsi*, Vin II 195,25, (3pl.) *aṭṭhaṃsu*, D II 84,28.[3]

– *dadāti* 'gives': (1sg.) *adaṃ*, Ja III 411,10*, Ap 513,24, 514,9, Cp 24, (on 2sg. *ado*, Ja IV 14,1* = V 161,12*, VI 482,23*, see below p. 239), (3sg.) *adā*, Ja III 231,20*, Sn 303, (1pl. *adamha*, Ja II 71,4*, Vin II 291,11, and 2pl. *adattha*, Ja II 166,21, Vin II 291,11, are taken over from aorist type **3**), (3pl.) *aduṃ*, Ap 573,24.

– (*passati* ~) **dassati* 'sees': (1sg.) *adassaṃ* Sn 837, (analog.) *adassiṃ*, Cp 12 (so read), (3sg. [analogical]) *adassī*, Sn 934. Here belong – as in Vedic Sanskrit[4] – forms of the old *s*-aorist (*adrāk*): (1sg.) *addaṃ*, Ja III 380,6* / 18* (see BLOCH 1965: 228), (3sg.) *addā̆*, Th 986 ≠ S IV

---

[1] On *ahaṃ* 'I brought', Ja VI 563,5* – and *ahaṃsu* 'they brought', Ja V 200,6* – as aorist(s) of *harati* see ALSDORF, *Kleine Schriften* p. 323, and VON HINÜBER § 484.

[2] (3sg.) *āga*, D II 258,20*, is formed to *āgu* after the pattern *āhu* : *āha* (see GEIGER § 160.1 / 4.).

[3] The present *ṭhahati* forms an aorist of type 4: (1sg.) *adhiṭṭhahiṃ*, Cp 305, (3sg.) *adhiṭṭhahi*, Th 1131. See GEIGER § 160.2, 163.1 and 167.

[4] See NARTEN, *Die sigmatischen Aoriste im Veda*. Wiesbaden 1964, 147.

207,16*, Ja III 139,2* (cf. OBERLIES 1993/94: 164), VI 125,5*.[1]
– *bhavati* / *hoti* 'is': (1sg.) *ahuṃ*, Ja III 411,5*, Th 316, Ap 300,19 – formed analogical to *adaṃ* – , (2sg.) *ahu*, Thī 57, 190, (3sg.) *ahu*, Ja IV 122,11*, Dhp 228, Sn 139, (1pl. [!]) *ahuṃ*, Thī 225, (3pl.) *ahū*, Ja IV 34,15* (mss. *ahu*), D II 256,8*, Dīp V 39 – also an analogical formation (after °*gū* etc.).
– *miyyati* 'dies': *amarā*, Ja III 389,18*, Th 779.[2]

(**2**) the thematic (asigmatic) aorist:
– *karoti* 'does, makes': (1sg.) *akaraṃ*, Ja III 206,21*, IV 116,19*, (2sg.) *akarā̆*, Ja I 431,1*, III 160,22*, (3sg.) *akaraṃ*, Ja IV 241,1* (*akariṃ*, ct.), V 70,17*[3], *akarā*, Ja IV 417,8*, (1pl.) *akarāma*, M I 93,15 = II 214,27, (3pl.) *akaruṃ*, Ja IV 116,26* (*kariṃsu*, ct.), V 353,5* (*akaṃsu*, ct.), VI 156,25* (*kariṃsu*, ct.), D II 256,4*, Mhv III 30, 33, *karuṃ*, Dīp VI 11. Here belong also (1pl.) *akaramha*, M I 93,16 = II 214,28 ≠ 31, *akaramhase*, Ja III 26,18* (*akarimha*, ct.) = *akaramhasa*, Dhp-a I 145,6* (see MATSUMARA, *JIBS* 32 [1983] 545).[4]
– *gacchati* 'goes': (1sg.) *agamaṃ*, Th 258, 259, (2sg.) *āgamā*, Ja III 344,22*, Sn 834, (3sg.) *agamā*, Sn 408, *āgamā*, Ja III 128,3*, (3pl.) *agamuṃ*, Sn 290, Cp 106, *āgamuṃ*, Ja V 172,27*. Here belongs (1pl.)

---

[1] See GEIGER § 162.3 and HOFFMANN, *Aufsätze zur Indoiranistik* I,147.

[2] Vedic *marati* is not an ind. pr. (*pace* GEIGER § 137 / 161 and WACKERNAGEL, *Kleine Schriften* p. 157) but the subj. of the root aorist (see TEDESCO, *Language* 20 [1944] 212). And also canonical Pāli has only *mīya-* / *miyya-* as present stems.

[3] Cf. FAUSBÖLL ad loc.

[4] See GEIGER § 162.1 (who wrongly maintains that Vedic *ákaram* – a root aorist – is an imperfect).

agamamha, Sn 349 (see NORMAN 1992: 213)[1].

– *chindati* 'cuts': (3sg.) *acchidā*, Sn 357, *acchidda*, Dhp 351, (3pl.) *acchiduṃ*, S I 35,14 (v.l. [1sg.] *acchidaṃ*).

– (*passati* ~) **dassati* 'sees': (1sg.) *addasaṃ* (*adraśam [with *-ra-* from the *s*-aorist]), Ja V 41,21*, Th 315, Thī 48,97 (*addasāmi*, Th 1253, Thī 135, S I 168,18*, *addasā*, Ja V 42,10*, Thī 218), (2sg.) *addasā̆*, D II 130,20, M III 179,19, Ja V 42,1*, (3sg.) *addasā̆*, Ja III 139,2*, V 47,27*, Sn 358, 409, (1pl.) *addasāma*, Ja II 355,17* (*adassāma*, M II 140,13), (2pl.) *addasā̆tha*, M II 108,32, Ja V 55,23* (the *-ā-* is in analogy to aorist forms of *dā-* and *ṭhā-*), (3pl.) *addasuṃ*, A II 52,30*, Ja VI 544,7*, D II 256,7*, *addaṃsu*, Ud 70,26. This aorist has been enlarged with the endings of type **3** and **4**: (1sg.) *addasāsiṃ*, Ja V 165,23*, Th 287, Sn 937, (2sg.) *addasāsi*, Thī 309, (3sg.) *addasāsi*, Ja V 158,16*, (3pl.) *addasaṃsu*, Ud 39,25, Ja V 173,5* (so read), Vin I 8,34, *addasāsuṃ*, D II 16,6, M I 153,23, Vin II 190,24, *addasiṃsu*, D II 274,3* (see GEIGER § 165).[2]

– *bhindati* 'splits': *abhida* (⏑⏑-), D II 107,5*, Ja III 29,17* – and with *-bbh-* on the pattern of *acchidā* (see § 20 *rem.* b [p. 112]) – *abbhidā*, Ja I 247,29*, II 163,25*.[3]

– (*)*vatti* 'speaks' has two sets of forms, one with *-o-* (i.e. the reduplicated aorist) and one with (analogical) *-a-*: (1sg.) *avocaṃ*, Thī 124, *avacaṃ*, Thī 429, Dhp-a III 194,17, (2sg.) *(a)voca*, Dhp 133, *avaca*, Thī 109, 415,

---

[1] On *ajjhagamā*, Ja II 285,23* = Vin III 147,22* (read +*ajjhagāmā*) as a crossing of aor. *ajjhagamā* and pf. *jagāma* see OBERLIES (1996: 114) who compares +*ajjhagāmuṃ*, S I 12,13*, and +*ajjhagāmāsi*, Ja V 171,8* / 12*, with the same long root vowel.

[2] On *addassāsiṃ*, Ap 20,9, and *addassa*, Nd I 327,6 (*ad* Sn 910 [*addasā*]) see SAKAMOTO-GOTO, in: *Dialectes dans les littératures indo-aryennes* (édité par COLETTE CAILLAT). Paris 1989, 407.

[3] On S V 263,4* see CPD s.v. abhindi, on Ja III 190,3* see Sadd V 1666 and OBERLIES (1995a: 128)

Vin IV 223,12, (3sg.) *avoca*, Th 870, Thī 494, *avaca*, Ja I 294,21, (1pl.) *avocumhā*, M II 28, 91, III 15,8, (2pl.) *avocuttha*, Mil 9,11, *avacuttha*, Vin II 297,10, (3pl.) *avocuṃ*, M II 147,29, Sn 691, *avacuṃ*, Ja V 260,4*.[1]
– *bhavati / hoti* 'is': (1sg.) *ahuvā*, S I 36,2*, (2sg.) *ahuvā*, S I 36,9*, (3sg.) *ahuvā*, Ja II 106,1*, III 131,11* (1./3sg. also *ahuvāsi*, Vv 1196, Ja VI 521,21*), (1pl.) *ahuvāma*, M I 93,13, II 214,24 (/ *ahuvamha*, M I 93,14, II 214,25, *ahuvamhase*, Ja III 26,18* = Dhp-a I 145,6*), (2pl.) *ahuvattha*, D II 147,16, M I 445,26, S IV 112,6.[2]

(**3**) the *s(iṣ)*-aorist:

– *karoti* 'does, makes': (1sg.) *akāsiṃ*, Ja V 86,20*, Th 219, 626, Thī 74, D III 257,2, (2sg.) *akāsi*, Ja III 349,9*, IV 398,9*, Th 1207, Thī 244, (3sg.) *akāsi*, Ja IV 383,28* = 385,9*, V 51,30*, VI 117,12*, Sn 343, 537, (1pl.) *akamha*, Ja III 47,4*, (2pl.) *akattha*, Ud 51,14*, Ja IV 443,10*, Vin I 89,2, Vv 1258, Pv 74, (3pl.) *akaṃsu*, Ap 72,3, Ja IV 385,14*-15*, VI 106,3*, 119,14*, Thī 119, Sn 882, Vin I 129,2, *akāsuṃ*, Mhv XXXI 99 v.l. (see Geiger § 159).

– *jānāti* 'knows': (1sg.) *(abbh)aññāsiṃ*, M III 208,30,Vin III 5,23, (2sg.) *uññāsi*, Ja V 63,1*-25*, (3sg.) *ñāsi*, Sn 471 (without augment!), *aññāsi*, Vin I 18,13, Sn 540, (3pl.) *abbhaññāsuṃ*, S IV 11,30, *abbhaññaṃsu*, D II 150,31 – *aññiṃsu*, Ud 44,7, is a type (**4**) form, as is (1pl.) *ñāsiṃha*, Ja V 307,21*.

– (*passati* ~) **dassati* 'sees': (1sg.) *(ad)dakkhiṃ*, Th 510, Thī 147, D II 287,17*, Sn 938, *adakkhiṃ*, S IV 207,16* (so read), (2sg.) *addakkhi*, Ja III 189,23*, VI 544,5*, Sn 841, (3sg.) *addakkhi*, Th 986, S I 117,3*, Sn 208, *adakkhi*, Ja VI 354,26* (so read m.c.), (3pl.) *addakkhuṃ*, Ja IV 351,23*, D II 256,6*, S I 23,11*, *addakkhu*, A II 52,28*, Ja V 412,1*.

---

[1] See GEIGER § 162.4.

[2] See GEIGER § 162.2. *Pace* GEIGER l.c. *ahuvā* might be directly equated with Vedic *abhuvat* (see EDGERTON, *JAOS* 57 [1937] 32, BHSG § 32.109 and PISANI 1952: 287).

– *labhati* 'gets, obtains': *alattha* (Ja IV 310,3*, M II 49,8, S IV 302,9, Sn 110,22) – a remodelled continuation of (3sg.) *alabdha* – was the base for an active paradigm: (1sg.) *alatthaṃ*, Th 747, D II 268,6, (2sg.) *alattha*, S I 114,14, (1pl.) *alatthamha*, M II 63,1, (3pl.) *alatthuṃ*, D II 274,22*, *alatthaṃsu*, S I 48,34.[1] In the same manner (1sg.) *asayitthaṃ*, A I 136,29, and *alabhitthaṃ*, Th 217, developed from *asayittha* and **alabhittha* (see GEIGER § 161.2).

– *harati* 'takes': (1sg.) *°hāsiṃ*, Th 66, 513, 903, (3sg.) *ahāsi* Ja III 85,12* (read m.c. *pāhāsi*), V 204,23*, Dhp 3, 4, Sn 469, 470 (on *ahaṃ* and *ahaṃsu* – instead of which Th 925 has *[vi]hiṃsu* – see p. 231 n.1).

(**4**) the *iṣ*-aorist:

– *karoti* 'does, makes': The aorist *akarī* is a new formation, based on the ind. pres. *karati* (see p. 210): (1sg.) *akariṃ*, Dhp-a I 31,21*, *kariṃ*, Ja V 205,1* (mss. *kari*), (2sg.) *(a)kari*, Ja IV 4,20* (*akari*), V 71,13* (*kari*), VI 84,11* (... *kari* ... *akari*), (3sg.) *(a)kari*, Ja V 231,6, *akarī*, D II 157,13*, Ja V 9,29*, VI 20,18*, (2. pl.) *karittha*, Ja I 90,1, 263,5, 492,23, III 167,26, (3pl.) *kariṃsu*, Ja II 352,8, III 6,2, Dhp-a I 102,23.

– *kamati* 'walks, steps': (1sg.) *pakkāmiṃ*, Th 34, (3sg.) *pakkāmi*, Vin I 8,10, (1pl.) *upasaṃkamimha*, S IV 97,8, (3pl.) *atikamiṃsu*, D II 130,14, *abhikkāmuṃ*, D II 256,15*, *pakkāmu(ṃ)*, Ja V 151,9* (see OBERLIES 1995/96: 278), Sn 1010, *upakkamuṃ*, Ja V 18,9*, (3sg. mid.) *abhikkamatha*, Ja V 340,15*.

– *gacchati* 'goes': (1sg.) *(°)agamiṃ*, Th 9, (2sg.) *agami*, Sn 339, (3sg.) *agami*, D II 264,9, (1pl.) *agamimha*, S I 202,33*, (2pl.) *agamittha*, Dhp-a III 22,7, (3pl.) *agamiṃsu*, Ja II 416,23'; (1sg.) *(°)gañchiṃ*, Vv 829 v.l. (Ee *gacchiṃ*), Ja III 85,11*, V 166,23*, Cp 335, (3sg.) *āgañchi*, Sn 979, *upagañchi*, D I 1,19, II 99,2, Cp 203, (3pl.) *abbhugañchuṃ*, S I 24,20, *upagañchuṃ*, D II 99,1, *gañchīsu* (cad. of odd śloka pāda), Ap 563,18.

– *gaṇhāti* 'grasps': (1sg.) *aggahiṃ*, Th 97, (2sg.) *(anug)gahi*, Th 334,

[1] See GEIGER § 161.2. On *laddhā*, Ja III 138,21*, see p. 265 (*pace* GEIGER § 159.III).

gahī, Ja V 371,18*, (3sg.) *aggahī*, Ja V 91,4*, *paṭiggahi*, Th 565.
– *carati* 'moves about': (1sg.) *(a)cāri(ṃ)*, Th 423, Thī 79, (3sg.) *acāri*, Dhp 326, Sn 354, *ānucāri*, Ja I 188,10*, *avācari*, Ja V 444,5* = 27*, (3pl.) *acārisuṃ*, Sn 284, *ācariṃsu*, Ja VI 589,9*.

(5) the reduplicated aorist[1]:
– On *avoca(ṃ)* see above, thematic (asigmatic) aorist (2), p. 233.
– *patati* 'falls': *ajjhapattaṃ*, Sn 1134, *ajjhapattā*, Ja II 60,10*, 450,27*, III 296,2*, V 158,6*, 197,30*, VI 566,30*, *udapattā*, Ja III 484,22* (read prob. *udapattāsi*[2]), V 71,11* (cf. OBERLIES 1993/94: 162 n. 78), 255,17*, *apatt[h]ā / pāpatt[h]ā*, Ja V 255,20*, VI 16,29*.

Beside historical forms, which were partly analogically rebuilt (*adāsi* 'he gave'[3], *adamha* 'we gave' [≠ adāt, adāma][4], *ajjhabhī* 'you over-powered', It 76,6*, *anvabhī* 'he suffered', D III 147,10* = 149,2* [≠ °bhūt][5], *akkocchi* 'he abused', Ja III 212,6* = Dhp 3 [≠ ākrukṣat][6], *pāvekkhi* 'he entered', Ja III 460,2* [≠ prāvikṣat], *ārukkhi* ~ *abhirucchi* 'he mounted' [≠ ārukṣat], *apattha* 'it flew' [≠ apaptat])[7], the aorist has new formations based on the present stem: Those of the 'first conjugation' (see

---

1 On the text of Ee – the aorist was taken as a verbal adjective and altered to agree with the subject – see VON HINÜBER (1994: 52-61 / 174).

2 See VON HINÜBER (1994: 61).

3 Cf. (1pl.) *adāsimha*, Thī 518.

4 See GEIGER § 163.

5 See CPD s.vv. adhibhavati / anubhavati, EDGERTON, *ABORI* 23 (1942) 126, and BHSG § 32.28.

6 *Pace* GEIGER § 164.

7 See VON HINÜBER § 481 / 484.

p. 200-201) built an aorist of the fourth type (1sg. *pucchi* 'I asked', Bv II 38, 1pl. *apucchiṃha* 'we asked', Sn 875, 3sg. *ajāni* 'he learned', Sn 536, 1sg. *[°]bhaviṃ* 'I was', Ap 503,20, 512,11, Ja II 336,19*, 3pl. *[°]bhaviṃsu* 'they were', Ja I 228,3, Dhp-a IV 15,5, Mil 291,24[1], 1sg. *caṅkamiṃ* 'I paced up and down', Th 272, 3pl. *sussūsiṃsu* 'they wished to hear', Vin I 10,8)[2], those of the 'second' one of the third type (*kathesi* 'he told [the story]', *pūjesi* 'he honoured', *adhibhosi[ṃ]* 'I overcame', Ap 545,8[3], *māresi* 'he killed')[4].

The endings of the preterite are basically those of the OIA *a-/s-/(s)iṣ-* and root-aorist (see VON HINÜBER § 486-488):

---

[1] Very strange is (3pl. [!]) *jāyetha*, Ja V 72,2*, instead of *jāyiṃsu* (so ct. 74,10' [see WACKERNAGEL, *Kleine Schriften* p. 163]).

[2] GEIGER's § 167-169 give a lot of examples.

[3] Only the Apadāna knows *bho(n)ti* and – consequently – *bhosiṃ* (321,18). See p. 208 with n. 2.

[4] See EDGERTON (1954: 79-80) and VON HINÜBER § 418. Many examples can be found in GEIGER § 165.2.

	(1)	**(2)**	**(3)**	**(4)**
1sg.	*adaṃ* *ahuṃ*	*agamaṃ*	*akāsiṃ*	*agamis(s)aṃ,* *agamiṃ*
2sg.	*ado* *ahŭ̄*	*agamā* *āsado*	*akāsi*	*agami* (med.) *patisevit-* *tho*
3sg.	*adā* *ahŭ̄*	*agamā* (med.) *abhāsa-* *tha*	*akāsi* (med.) *alattha*[1]	*agami* (med.) *sandittha*
1pl.	*adamha* *ahumha,* *ahuṃ* (!) (med.) *adamha-* *se, agamhase,* *ahumhase*[2]	*agamamha* (med.) *akaram-* *hase, dadamha-* *se*	*akamha*	*agamimha* (med.) *agamim-* *hase*
2pl.	*adattha*	*agamat(t)ha*	*akattha*	*agamittha*
3pl.	*aduṃ* *ahū*	*agamuṃ* (med./pass.) *abajjhare, am-* *aññaruṃ*[3]	*akāsuṃ, akaṃ-* *su*	*agamisuṃ, aga-* *miṃsu, agamuṃ* (see 2)

---

[1] On this aorist see Sadd V 1220 (s.v.) and VON HINÜBER § 261.

[2] *agamhase*, Ap 243,9, 473,6, 583,6, *adamhase*, Ap 185,21, Pv 395, *ahumhase*, Ap 482,7.

[3] *abajjhare*, Ja I 428,1*, *amaññaruṃ*, Ja III 488,2* (see GEIGER § 159.II and BLOCH 1965: 229). On the ending *-ruṃ* see LEUMANN, *Morphologische Neuerungen im altindischen Verbalsystem*. Amsterdam 1952, 10.

(1/2) Attested 2sg. *ado* 'you gave' (instead of expected **adā* < adāḥ), Ja IV 14,1* = V 161,12*, VI 482,23*, has the ending of the 2sg. of type **2**[1], *accasaro* 'you transgressed (all the rules)', Ja IV 6,10*, *kudho* 'you were angry', Ja IV 385,16* (so read [Ee *kuddho*])[2], *āsado* 'you have attained', Ja I 414,6* = III 207,15*, M I 326,35, Vin II 195,28*, *pamādo* (see § 2), (< [2sg. imp.] -aḥ). The ending *-ā* (*agamā* < agamaḥ) is an adjustment to the 3sg. *-ā*[3] which has its ending (*agamā* ≠ agamat) analogical to that of other aorist types. 1/2pl. *adamha* 'we gave', *adattha* 'you gave' and *agamamha* 'we went', *agama(t)tha* 'you went' (instead of **adāma*, **adāta*, **agamāma*, **agamata*) have the endings of type **4** (with the *a*-vowel of types **1/2**)[4].

The 3pl. of **(2)** in *-uṃ* (≠ OIA *-an*) is in analogy to **(1)** and **(3)**, for which see § 4.5; the 1pl. med. of **(1/2/4)** in *-mhase* (*akaramhase* 'we ma-

---

1 See GEIGER § 161 (b).

2 See OBERLIES (1996: 114).

3 3sg. med. ends in *-tha*: *samakampatha* 'it quaked', Ja VI 570,12*, *samapajjatha* 'it turned into, appeared', Ja V 71,30*, *upapajjatha* 'it arose', Th 30, *apūratha* 'it became full', Ja IV 441,1*, *abhassatha* 'it fell', Sn 449, *abhāsatha* 'he said', Sn 30, *nivattatha* 'he returned', Ja IV 443,6*, *vindatha* 'he acquired', Thī 420 (cf. [pass.] *khīyatha* 'it perished = dried up', Cp 323, *aḍayhatha* 'it is / will be burnt', Ja V 252,29*, *ahīratha* 'it is / will be taken away', Ja V 253,2* [on the last two forms see OBERLIES 1996: 115]).

4 See OLDENBERG, *Kleine Schriften* p. 1168 (cf. GEIGER § 159.II). For 2pl. in *-tha* see GEIGER § 162.3.

de', *ahuvamhase* 'we were'[1], *agamimhase* 'we went'[2]) is formed to *-mase* (see § 46.1/2 [cf. p. 218-219 n. 10]) after the pattern (aor.) *-mha* : (ind.) *-ma* (i.e. *-mhase* : *-mase* = *-mha* : *-ma*).

(3) 1sg. *akāsiṃ* (≠ akārṣam) is analogical to 2/3sg. *akāsi* 'you / he made', which have their ending (*-i* < -īḥ, -īt) according to the rhythmic rule (see § 4.4); 2pl. *akattha* 'you made, you did' and (4) *agamittha* 'you went'[3] have *-ttha* instead of expected *-*ṭṭha* (< -ṣṭa)[4], as has (4) 3sg. med. *-ittha*[5] as well as 2sg. med. *-ittho* (← -iṣṭhāḥ[6]). On the ending of *akāsuṃ* 'they made' see § 4.5 (*assosuṃ*).

(4) 1sg. *agamiṃ* 'I went' seems to be built on 3sg. *agami* 'he went'

---

1 *akaramhase*, Ja III 26,18*, *dadamhase*, Ja III 47,3* (*dadimha*, ct.) = Pv 804, *(mā ...) pamadamhase*, Ja III 131,16*, *ahuvamhase*, Ja III 26,18*.

2 *āsādimhase*, D III 10,11 / 26, *agamimhase*, Pv 143, *cajimhase*, Ap 594,7 v.l. (Ee *cajimha no*), (*na c)chādimhase*, Pv 80, *mā ... pajahimhase*, Ja VI 182,14*, *paribhāsimhase*, Pv 396, *pātayimhase*, Ap 472,28 (so read), *nimimhase*, Ja II 369,17*, *avasimhase*, Ja IV 98,14*.

Since the context of Ja II 137,28* excludes an aorist, *vaṇimhase* (cf. *icchāma*, ct.) must be regarded as a wrong reading for *vaṇem(h)ase* (on which see p. 225 n. 1 [diff. PED s.v. vaṇeti]).

3 Cf. *pucchittha*, Mhv XVII 33, *jīyittha*, Ja I 468,2*, *ruccittha*, Vin III 175,22 = Dhp-a I 13,23, *sandittha*, D II 129,33, *paṭivedayittha*, Ja V 32,19*, (pass.) *adissittha*, Th 170, *dīyittha*, S I 58,9, *sūyittha*, Dhp-a I 16,3.

4 This is also the case in Prakrit (see PISCHEL § 517) where *-itthă* is used also for 2pl. and 3pl.

5 See GEIGER § 159.IV. For Prakrit see PISCHEL § 517, BHAYANI, *Sambodhi* 7 (1978/79) 115, and BALBIR, in: *Dialectes dans les littératures indo-aryennes* (édité par COLETTE CAILLAT). Paris 1989, 507-508.

6 Cf. *patisevittho*, Ja IV 222,9*, *pucchittho*, D II 284,2, *amaññittho*, M III 247,6, Th 280, *vihaññittho*, Th 385. On this ending see BLOCH (1965: 229).

after the pattern of *akāsiṃ* 'I made' : *akāsi* 'he made'[1]. The historical ending *-isaṃ* (of the old *iṣ*-aorist) is – due to the mutual influence of aorist and future (see § 49) – often replaced by *-issaṃ*[2] (though sometimes only secondarily: *musāvadaṃ abhāsissaṃ* [⏑-⏑-] 'I spoke [the oath] falsely', Pv 33 as read by Pv-a [see § 18.7]): *agacchisaṃ* 'I went', Th 258, *apaccisaṃ* 'I was cooked', Thī 436, *abhuñjisaṃ* 'I ate', Th 1056, *atimaññisaṃ* 'I despised', Pv 40[3], *nikkhamissaṃ* 'I went out', Ja IV 330,27* (*nikkhamiṃ*, ct.), *adhigacchissaṃ* 'I obtained', Sn 446, *sandhāvissaṃ* 'I wandered through', Dhp 153, *nandissaṃ* 'I rejoiced', S I 176,12*, *pavissaṃ* 'I entered', Ja IV 330,19*, *(a)pucchissaṃ* 'I asked', Sn 1116, Ap 563,17, *(a)maññis(s)aṃ* 'I thought', Th 342, 424, 765, M III 247,2, Ap 547,17, *vandissaṃ* 'I worshipped', Th 480, 621, Ap 334,4. 3pl. *(agam)uṃ* – comparatively rare in old texts (Sn 290, 302 = 306, 415, 1014, Ja V 112,30*, VI 156,25*)[4] – has taken over the ending of type **3**.

---

1 See Oldenberg, *Kleine Schriften* p. 1170. GEIGER (§ 159.IV), however, regards *-iṃ* as the direct continuation of Vedic *(akram)īm*.

2 See GEIGER § 159 (IV), OLDENBERG, *Kleine Schriften* p. 1169-1170, SMITH (1952: 182), BECHERT (1958: 314), id. (1961: 16-17 with n. 2), NORMAN (1969: 141 [ad Th 78]) and VON HINÜBER § 465 / 484 (for Prakrit see PISCHEL § 516 and ALSDORF, *Kleine Schriften* p. 60-61). CPD I,130a (cf. ibid. I,344a line 20) calls such forms *future(s) in præterito* (cf. OBERLIES 1996: 114 n. 131).

Cf. (3pl.) *ājāniyā hasissiṃsu* 'the thoroughbreds whinnied', Ja VI 581,20* (*hasiṃsu*, ct.); see OBERLIES (1996: 114 n. 131).

3 Cf. CPD s.v. atimaññati.

4 See OLDENBERG, *Kleine Schriften* p. 1170, and INSLER (1994: 86).

The augment *a*-[1] is prefixed when (**a**) the aorist would be monosyllabic without it (*adā*). And it is used (at least in the language of the canon) with (**b**) all disyllabic aorists except for continuations of the *iṣ*-aorist (type **4**) where it is facultative (*[a]labhi*). It is facultative also with (**c**) polysyllabic aorists, (generally[2]) apart from those which were enlarged within Pāli (*agamāsi*[3]) or which continue old imperfects or thematic aorists (*abhāsattha*)[4].

---

[1] Sometimes the augment is 'misplaced' or even added in a wrong way (see CPD s.vv. ²a [*rem.* a/b] / ajjha and OBERLIES 1997: 12; cf. BHSG § 32.2): *a-paribrūhayi*, Ja V 361,16*, *pacc-a-niyyāhi*, D II 22,16, *ajjh-a-bhāseyya*, Ja V 351,3*. This happens rather often with *pāpuṇāti* which was regarded as a verb on its own: *a-pāpuṇiṃ*, Ap 59,6, 64,24, 371,30.

mā is used in Pāli not only with unaugmented, but also with augmented aorists (and also with other verb forms; see PED s.v. mā and cf. CPD s.v. ²a-; cf. BHSG § 42).

Occasionally even finite verb forms are compounded with the negative prefix *a(n)*- (see CPD s.vv. ³a- [7.], anūpaneyya, apatthave, BHSD s.v. a-, an-, NORMAN 1992: 309 [ad Sn 799] and OBERLIES 1995: 106 [s.v. ³a-(7)]): *(accharāsaṃghātamattaṃ pi cetosantiṃ) an-ajjhagaṃ* 'Not (even for the duration of a snap of the fingers) have I obtained (peace of mind)', Th 405 (*na labhiṃ*, ct.). For Prakrit see PISCHEL § 464 (*asiyā* = *na syāt*).

[2] Cf. (1sg.) *pivāsiṃ*, Ud 42,14, (3sg.) *viramāsi*, Thī 397.

[3] (3sg.) *agamāsi*, Th 490, (3pl.) *agamaṃsu*, Vv 1157, Ja V 54,14*, Dhp-a I 64,2. Likewise (1sg.) *ahuvāsi*, Vv 1196, (2sg.) *avacāsi*, Vv 648, (3sg.) *avacāsi*, Th 14, (3sg.) *avocāsi*, Sn 680, 685, (3sg.) *ahuvāsi*, Ja VI 521,21* (so read), *avacāsi*, Ja VI 525,14*.

[4] See WACKERNAGEL, *Kleine Schriften* p. 155-171 (**a.** ibid. 156, **b.** ibid. 157-162, **c.** ibid. 162-170), GEIGER § 158 and VON HINÜBER § 485 (cf. CPD s.v. ²a-).

Beside these forms Pāli has (though rarely) an *e*-preterite[1]: (2sg.) *bhuñje* 'you ate', Ja III 144,24* (with v.l. *bhuñji*), *udassaye* 'you raised up', Ja V 26,13* (*ussāpesi*, ct. [so read][2]), *nibbāpaye* 'you extinguished', Ja III 157,8* = IV 61,28* = Pv 379, (3sg.) *anusāse* 'he instructed', Ja VI 291,13*, *apakkame* 'he went away', S I 124,7*, *nicchare* 'issued forth', Ap 320,5, *nijjhāpaye* 'he made (me) reflect', Ja IV 87,2*, *upanāmaye* 'he gave', Ja IV 408,7* (BeCeSe *°ayi*). This form is (in the last resort) an optative used as a preterite[3], and only the Buddhāpadāna uses this ending (-*e* < -eḥ / -et) for 1sg.[4]: *abhivādaye* 'I saluted', Ap 1,10 (so B^{p} [Ee *°vādayiṃ*]; see CPD s.v. abhivādeti), *āhane* 'I have beaten (the drum)', Ap 5,25, *āhare* 'I offered', Ap 1,12, *māpaye* 'I built', Ap 1,13.

---

1 See CPD I,261b (s.v. *apakkamati*), I,375b (s.v. abhisajati), I,558 (s.vv. *anusāsati* and *apakkamati*) and I,560a (s.v. *abhiropeti*) and VON HINÜBER § 445 (cf. SMITH, *BSL* 33 [1932] 171, VON HINÜBER, *MSS* 36 [1977] 39-48, and NORMAN 1991: 179 and 1992: 231 [ad Sn 448]). For Prakrit (*care*, *udāhare*, *pucche*) see PISCHEL § 466.

2 (Other than CPD I,559 l. 1-2) CPD II,402a (s.v.) sees in *udassaye* a "pot. 2 sg.".

3 On this usage of the optative (well known from the Sanskrit Epics [KATRE, *BDCRI* 1 (1939/40) 8-13]) see OBERLIES (1997: 15). For Prakrit see PISCHEL § 466 / 515, ALSDORF, *Kleine Schriften* p. 61-63, BALBIR, in: *Dialectes dans les littératures indo-aryennes* (édité par COLETTE CAILLAT). Paris 1989, 509-510, and OBERLIES, l.c.

4 See BECHERT (1958: 313).

§ 49. Historical forms of the future[1] and new formations based on the present-stem (*incl.* the passive stem [*kariyissati*, Vin I 107,19][2]) stand side by side[3]. Both have the endings of the indicative present[4] (the medium is attested in the forms *-se*, *-te*, *-mase* and *-are*, see § 46.1), the 1sg. has *-aṃ* in addition to *-āmi* (see also § 46 [p. 217]). The close relationship of future and aorist, which gave rise to future stems such as *kassa-* /*kāsa-* 'will make' or *hassa-* 'will take'[5] (*kārṣy- / *hārṣy- < [a]kārṣ- x

---

[1] *dakkhaṃ*, Th 1099, *dakkhasi*, S I 116,11*, *dakkhisi*, Ja VI 497,15*, Thī 232, *dakkhiti*, Sn 909, *bhokkhaṃ*, Ja IV 127,20*, *mokkhasi*, S I 111,29* = Vin I 21,18*, *mokkhanti*, Dhp 37 (with passive meaning), *vakkhāmi*, Ja I 346,2', *vakkhati*, M III 207,23, S I 142,32, *vakkhāma*, M III 207,23, S IV 72,9, *vakkhanti*, Vin II 1,21, *pavekkhāmi*, Ja III 86,5*, *sakkhati*, Sn 319, *sakkhinti*, Sn 28 (on *sagghasi* see § 16.9), *checchaṃ*, Ja III 500,23*, *checchati*, Th 761, Dhp 350, *pacchati*, A IV 362,10 (so read against Ee *pajjati*), *bhecchati*, A I 8,4 (v.l. *bhijjissati* [!]), *bhejjati* (see § 16.9), *lacchati*, Ja II 258,18*, S I 114,19, *lacchāma*, Ja IV 292,21*, *lacchāmase*, Vv 320, *vacchāmi*, Ja VI 523,11*, *vacchaṃ*, Thī 414, 425, *vacchasi*, Ja VI 172,19*. This *-cch-* was regarded as future suffix and hence generalised (*rucchiti*, Ja V 366,13* [so read with C^{ks} ibid. 18'], VI 80,13* ≠ 550,11*, *uparucchanti*, Ja VI 551,30*, *avasucchati*, Ja VI 80,14* = 550,20*). The future *rucchi°* then gave rise to an aorist *rucchi* (Ja IV 285,24* = V 182,10* ~ VI 152,17* [so read (see BECHERT 1961: 19 and OBERLIES 1995/96: 282)]). For historical *seṭ*-futures see GEIGER § 154.

[2] See GEIGER § 155.3 and VON HINÜBER § 463. For Prakrit see PISCHEL § 549.

[3] See GEIGER § 150-156 and VON HINÜBER § 463-475 (cf. CPD, *Epilegomena* 25* [s.v. *fut.*], SMITH 1952: 169-183, and BLOCH 1965: 227-228). For Prakrit see PISCHEL § 520-534 and JACOBI § 59.

[4] Note *viharissāmu*, Ja IV 440,22*. It seems to be the sole example of this ending in the future tense (for Prakrit see PISCHEL § 530 [*dāhāmu*]).

[5] Cf. *kassāmi*, Th 1138-1139, Pv 554, *kassaṃ*, Th 381, Pv 250 v.l., S I 179,8, *kāsaṃ*, Ja IV 286,21*.... 287,15* (Āryā), VI 36,20* (B^{d} *kassaṃ* = Sadd 514,18), *kassāma*, Ap 185,19, D II 288,2*, *vihassaṃ*, Th 1091, *vihassati*, S I 157,1* = 21* (see CAIL-

karişy- / [a]hārṣ- x harişy-)[1] and which led to the use of *-issaṃ* as a preterite ending (see p. 241), points to the fact that this ending is taken from the aorist. As a terminational element, the future ending was subject to lenition[2] (see § 18.7): *karis<s>āmi* 'I shall make', Ja III 161,14*, Ap 72,31, *khīyis<s>anti* 'they will be abandoned', Ja V 392,4*, *caris<s>āmi* 'I shall wander', Ja III 381,21*, IV 487,12*, *dakkhisāma* 'we shall see', Ja III 99,7*[3], *passis<s>āmi* 'I shall see', Pv 528, *phusis<s>aṃ* 'he will realise', Th 386[4], *phusis<s>ati* 'he will touch', Sn 693, *bhavis<s>ati* 'there will be', Sn 691-694, Pv 575, *muccis<s>ati* 'he will be released', Ja VI 449,3*[5], *parirakkhis<s>āmi* 'I shall guard', Ja IV 480,11*, *sikkhis<s>āmase* 'we shall train ourselves', Sn 814. And this *-s-* could be further weakened to *-h-* (primarily after a long vowel and in verbs which

---

LAT, *ABORI* 68/69 [1977/78] 103), *vihessati*, Th 257 = D II 121,1* (see GEIGER § 153.1), *vihissāmi*, Thī 181 ~ 121 (cf. NORMAN 1971: 87, 96), *āhissaṃ*, Ja VI 523,7* (see SMITH 1952: 179 and VON HINÜBER § 470).

1 See SCHULZE, *Kleine Schriften* p. 102, THIEME, *Kleine Schriften* p. 909, VON HINÜBER § 469 and OBERLIES (1999: 38).

2 See TURNER (1975: 297 / 325) and OBERLIES (1996: 115-116). The editions often have the unmetrical *ss*-form.

3 The same contamination of '*aniṭ*-' and '*seṭ*-' future is (e.g.) *pavakkhissaṃ*, Cp 2, and *sakkhissati* 'he will be able', Vin III 19,33, Dhp-a III 80,7, 176,4 (see GEIGER § 152, SMITH 1952: 180 and BLOCH 1965: 227). See also p. 246 n. 3 and 248 n. 2.

On *dakkhisaṃ* 'I saw', Thī 84 (= *dakkhasi*, Ap 576,8), see BECHERT (1958: 314), NORMAN (1971: 80 [ad loc.]), SAKAMOTO-GOTO, in: *Dialectes dans les littératures indo-aryennes* [édité par COLETTE CAILLAT]. Paris 1989, 405, and OBERLIES (1996: 115).

4 SMITH's attempt to restore the wording of this *āryā* (Sadd IV, 8.5.09 [3]) is certainly wrong.

5 See OBERLIES (1993/94: 168 n. 122).

are frequently used[1]): *padāhisi* 'you will give' (pradāsyasi), Thī 303, *anubhohisi* 'you will experience', Thī 510, *parinibbāhisi* 'you will be quenched', Th 415, *vihāhisi* 'you will live', Dhp 379, Ja I 298,26* (~ *hāhasi*, Ja III 172,26*), *hehisi* 'you will be', Th 1142, *hehiti* 'it will be', Thī 249, 250, 288, Bv II 9, *hohisi* 'you will be', Th 382, D II 144,20, Pv 9, *hohiti* 'it will be', Th 1137, Thī 465[2], *ehisi* 'you will come', Ja V 480,4*, VI 386,6* (B^{ds}), Thī 166, *ehiti* 'he will come', Ja II 153,18*, VI 579,11*, Pv 155, *ehinti* 'they will come', Ja I 209,16*, *kāhiti* 'he will make' (*kārṣyati), Ja VI 497,2*, *kāhinti* 'they will treat (you)', Thī 509 (Ee against mss. *khāhinti* ['they will eat = devour']) – with normalisation of the ending *kāhasi* 'you will do' (Thī 57), *kāhati* 'he will do' (Ja III 99,15*, VI 449,3*, D III 185,6*) and *kāhanti* 'they will do' (Ja II 130,6*, VI 436,29*, 510,3*)[3]. A future of the Apabhraṃśa type *-esai* is attested in a few forms: *taresino* 'of one who will cross (a river)', Ja III 230,21*[4],

---

1 See SCHWARZSCHILD (1991: 1-5). On the endings see above, § 7.12. ALSDORF, *Kleine Schriften* p. 61, pointed out that the archaic language of the Vasudevahiṇḍi knows future forms with *-ī-* due to compensatory lengthening (*ghattīhaṃ*, 51,22, *bhuñjīhaṃ*, 22,28, *pucchīhāmo*, 89,21, *dacchīhāmo*, 138,7) and that "the 'missing link' between *-issaṃ* and *-īhaṃ* is supplied by the Mahānisīha, where futures in *-īsaṃ* occur, e.g. *vimuccīsaṃ sujjhīsaṃ*" (l.c. n. 1). Diff. on the *h*-future BERGER (1955:79).

2 The twofold future of *bhavati* is conditioned by the development *hessati* < bhaviṣyati on the one hand (*hessaṃ*, Ja III 224,3*, Th 1100, Pv 62, *hessāmi*, Thī 460, *hessati*, Ja III 279,16*, *hessāma*, Bv II 72, *hessatha*, S IV 179,24, *hessanti*, Ja VI 524,10*), and the influence of the vocalism of the present *hoti* on the other.

palehiti, Th 307, is to be cancelled from GEIGER's list of *h*-futures (§ 150). We have to read *palāyati* 'it flees' (see BERGER, *MSS* ²4 [1961] 34-35 n. 10).

3 A 'double' future is *panudahissāmi* 'I shall push', Ja VI 508,2* (so read with all mss. which however have *-he-*), Th 27 = 233 (see ALSDORF, *Kleine Schriften* p. 302).

4 See also NORMAN (1969: 205 [ad Th 527]) and id. (1992: 373 [ad Sn 1064])

bhāsesamānā 'who wants to speak', Ja V 404,6*[1].

rem. **(a)** On the futures *(°)hañch(āmi)* 'I shall beat', M I 171,12* [= Vin I 8,26*, see below], Ja IV 102,9*[2], and (1-3sg.) *gañchāmi / gañchisi / gañchiti* 'shall / will go', Ja V 183,27*, 304,14*/19*, S I 186,3* (S^{1-3}), Sn 665, M I 392,17[3], *gañchittha*, Ja V 191,21*[4] (< *han$_{t}$sy[āmi] / *gan$_{t}$sy[āmi]) see § 18.4[5]. The former is sporadically handed down as *(°)hañh-* (D II 72,6[6], Vin I 8,26*[7]) and

---

1 See Smith (1952: 172), Sadd V 1415, Caillat (1970: 15-16), Norman (1969: 205 [ad Th 527] and 1992: 177 [ad Sn 147]) and Oberlies (1996: 116).

2 This stem even serves as base for an optative: *hañchema*, Ja II 418,11* (*hanissāma*, ct.).

3 Ee has here *(abbhug)gañchīti* (cf. Trenckner 1908: 125). The parallels S IV 323,13 and A IV 80,27 have in Ee *abbhuggacchissati* which Trenckner (1908: 125 n. 1) and CPD (s.v. abbhuggacchati) correct into *°gañchiti* (Trenckner's ms. of Saṃyuttanikāya, however, reads *abbhuggacchati*; see Trenckner l.c.).

4 Diff. on this word Berger, *MSS* ^{2}4 (1961) 39 n. 13 (on Berger's explanation of all these forms see below, p. 248 n. 4).

5 See Trenckner (1908: 125-127), Sadd 181 n. 1 and 463 n. d/f, Smith (1952: 180), Bechert (1961: 20 / 27), von Hinüber § 474, Norman (1969: 123 [ad Th 14]), id. (1992: 270 [ad Sn 665]) and – for Prakrit – Pischel § 523 and Alsdorf, *Kleine Schriften* p. 218 (cf. van Nooten, *JAOS* 90 [1970] 159).

6 Ee reads *āhañhi 'me* which can be interpreted as sandhi of /*āhañhiṃ ime*/ (see p. 117). And this *āhañhiṃ* would be the regular *saṃprasāraṇa*-form of **āhan-t-syam* (cf. von Hinüber § 474).

7 Trenckner proposes to correct Ee *āhañhi* to *āhañchaṃ* (1908: 127 n. 1). Cf. Oldenberg, *Kleine Schriften* p. 1174.

(°)haṅkh-[1] (A II 40,10 = S IV 104,26, M I 10,12), the latter often as *gacchi-* and *gaccha-*[2]: *(°)gacchisi* (< *gan̥syasi [with *sampra-sāraṇa*, see § 7.12]), Th 356 (Th-a *gañchisi*),[3] *gaccham*, Ja III 136,5*, VI 230,27*, 507,31* = 508,6*, Thī 306, 426, *(°)gacchasi*, A IV 301,17, Ap 276,24 (v.l. *gañchasi*), Ja VI 416,16*, 543,16*, Th 1213, *gacchati*, Ja V 302, 12*, VI 500,4*, *gacchāma*, Ja VI 457,25*, *gacchanti*, Ja IV 184,11*, VI 516,20*[4]; (**b**) Only sporadically is a periphrastic future attested[5]: *gantā* 'he will go', Ja IV 273,17*, V 267,19*, 270,12*[6], *āgantā* 'he will come', Ja II 420,3*

---

[1] For *haṅkh-* we have to postulate a pre-form **haṅ-k-ṣ(yati)* out of **han-t-syati* (see GEIGER § 153.2). Or was *paṭihanti* blended with another verb which had a *-kkh-* future? For *kkh*-futures in Prakrit see PISCHEL § 521.

[2] The relationship of the futures *gacchati* and *gacchissati* is the same as between *dakkhati* / *sakkhati* and *dakkhissati* / *sakkhissati* (see BLOCH 1965: 227). See also p. 245 n. 3 and 246 n. 3.

[3] This form is not haplologically shortened (NORMAN 1969: 123 [ad Th 14] *pace* GEIGER § 65.2). But haplology *can* account for *gacchiss' (ādāya)* 'you will go' (< *gacchissasi*), Ja VI 543,20* (which TRENCKNER 1908: 126 corrects to *gañchis' ādāya*), and *sakkhī* 'you will be able' (**sakkhihi*), Ja V 116,5* (cf. ALSDORF, *Kleine Schriften* p. 314, and OBERLIES 1996: 116 n. 137). Or did *-*ihi* develop to *-ī* (cf. *dhītā-* < **dihitā-* [see p. 175 n. 2])?

[4] This was made possible as the indicative present can be used instead of the future if the speaker is not very particular with the employment of tenses (see BERGER, *MSS* ²4 [1961] 29-41, who, however, explains *gañch°* as a misspelling of *gacch°* [cf. VON HINÜBER 1994: 128]). And some languages even do without a future tense as (e.g.) Indo-European (see BEEKES, *Comparative Indo-European Linguistics: An Introduction*. Amsterdam 1995, 226).

[5] See GEIGER § 172, CPD s.v. āganta(r) and VON HINÜBER § 475.

[6] Here *gantā* is used as nom. pl.: *ye ... hanti ... channā gantā te nirayaṃ adho* (*gantā-ro*, ct.).

(so read), It 95,10 (*anā°*), *āgantāro* 'they will come', A II 159,36, It 4,18*, M II 130,16*, Sn 754, *pucchitāro* 'they will ask', Sn 140,6 (cf. *bhavitaṃ* [ə: *bhavitā*] *te mahabbayaṃ* 'you will be terrified', Ja VI 507,12*[1]; see also p. 268); (**c**) The future can be used in the sense of an (hortative) optative: *bhaṇa khippaṃ yan te kīrihiti* 'say quickly, what may be done for you', Thī 424 (so read against Ee *karihiti* [see SMITH 1952: 177 n. 2])[2].

	ss-future	*h*-future	*CCh*-future	*ñch*-future
1sg.	(a) *karissāmi, karissaṃ* (b) *kassāmi, kassaṃ, kāsaṃ*	*kāhāmi*	*lacchāmi, lacchaṃ*	*gañchāmi, gañchaṃ, āhañchiṃ*
2sg.	(a) *karissasi*	*padāhisi, vihāhisi*	*lacchasi*	*gañchisi*
3sg.	(a) *karissati* (b) *vihassati*	*kāhiti, kāhati*	*lacchati*	*gañchiti**
1pl.	(a) *karissāma* (b) *kassāma*	*kāhāma*	*lacchāma*	*gañchāma**
2pl.	(a) *karissatha*	*kāhitha*, kāhatha*	*lacchatha*	*gañchitha**
3pl.	(a) *karissanti*	*kāhinti, kāhanti*	*lacchanti*	*gañchinti**

---

1 See FRANKE, *Literarisches Zentralblatt* 1917, col. 1157, and NORMAN (1991: 177).

2 See SEN, *Syntactic Studies of Indo-Aryan Languages*. Tokyo 1995, 357-360.

§ 50. The conditional[1], used as *modus irrealis* (see also p. 257-258), is formed from the (almost exclusively[2]) augmented future stem by adding the endings of the second aorist (3sg *-issa* < *-issā* according to § 4.4); only the 3pl. has *-aṃsu*: (1sg.) *abhavissaṃ* 'I were', Ja I 470,15[3], (2sg.) *abhavissa*, Ja III 30,6, (3sg.) *agamissa* 'he would go', M I 342,16, *abhavissa*, Ja III 335,11*, Vin I 13,38, (1pl.) *alabhissāma* 'we would get', Ja III 35,10, (3pl.) *abhavissaṃsu*, Vin I 13,31. Of the medium only the 3sg. in *-tha* is attested (*okkamissatha* 'it would have climbed down', D II 63,3, *āpajjissatha* 'it would have attained', D II 63,13).

§ 51. Denominatives (in the broad sense) are formed from 'nouns' (**a**) without[4] or (**b**) with suffix *-ya-* (**1.** without [and *-(a)ya-* > *-e-*], **2.** with lengthening of the preceding vowel[5] [with a causative in *-āpaya-* /

---

1 See GEIGER § 157 and VON HINÜBER § 476 (cf. CPD, *Epilegomena* 22* [s.v. *cond(it).*]). In Prakrit the present participle – and (as in Pāli, too) the optative – has taken over the function of the conditional which is no longer used (see also p. 257-258).

2 Cf. *uppajjissa*, Dhp-a III 137,19, *karissa* ... *labhissa*, Dhp-a II 39,20, *pāpuṇissa*, Dhp-a III 131,18.

3 On *agacchaṃ*, Th 1098, see NORMAN (1969: 273) and VON HINÜBER § 476.

4 It seems preferable to put it like that and not to speak of the suffix *a* as GEIGER § 188.1 does (see also PISCHEL § 491).

5 On the rhythmic rule – avoidance of the succession of three or more short syllables – which governs this lengthening (in OIA) see INSLER, in: *Papers in honor of Robert S.P. Beekes*. Amsterdam – Atlanta 1997, 103-110.

-āpe-, see § 52[1]]) or (**c**) *-ĭya-*[2]: (**a**) *(o)kaḍḍhati* 'drags (away)' (← *[o]kaḍḍha-*)[3], *laggati* 'sticks to' (← *lagga-* < lagna-)[4], *(saṃpa)vedhati* 'trembles' (← *vidhita-* < viddha- x vyathita-)[5], *sukkhati* 'is dried up' (← *sukkha-* < śuṣka-), *nighaññati* 'strikes down' (**nighañña-* [cf. *attaghañña-*, Dhp 164])[6], *paripañhati* 'puts a question' (← [pari]praśna-), *sajjhāyati* 'studies' (← svādhyāya-), *nāvati* 'rejects' (← hnāva-)[7], (**b**) **1.** *patthayati* 'request', *maggayati* 'seeks' (Thī 384), *theneti* 'steals', *daṇḍeti* 'punishes' (Mil 186,8), *baleti* 'strengthens' (Ja III 225,14*), *saṃgāmeti* 'fights', *sajjeti* 'prepares' (← *sajja-* 'ready' < sajya- 'placed on the bow-string'), *sukheti* 'makes happy', *pihāyati* (~ *pihayati*) 'desires' (← *pihā-* 'desire' < spṛhā-)[8], *mettāyati* 'is benevolent towards' (← *mettā-*, see § 31 rem.), *tapassati* 'undergoes austerities', Dhp-a I 53,3 (tapasyati), *namassati* 'pays honour to' (namasyati), **2.** *cirāyati* 'delays' (← cira-), *pacalāyati* 'nods', Th 200 (← *pacala-*), *mahāyati* 'worships', Ja IV 236,2* (← *maha-*), *rahāyati* 'wishes to be alone' (← *raha-* < rahas-), *saddāyati* 'makes a

---

1 GEIGER (§ 187.2) is certainly not right to attribute a non-causal meaning to a number of *āpaya*-denominatives.

2 See GEIGER § 186-189. For Prakrit see PISCHEL § 490-491 and 557-559.

3 See TEDESCO, *JAOS* 85 (1965) 374-377 (cf. also VON HINÜBER § 493).

4 See OBERLIES (1993: 140 [s.v. *laei*]) and BHSG 28.19 (*pace* GEIGER § 136.2).

5 On the formation of denominatives from verbal adjectives see BLOCH (1965: 236 / 267), TURNER (1975: 416-417) and OBERLIES (1996: 97 with n. 37). Cf. id (1989/90: 183), CPD s.v. kaḍḍhati and VON HINÜBER § 493.

6 See OBERLIES (1996: 103).

7 On this word see § 15.1.

8 See OBERLIES (1996: 121).

sound', Ud 61,6-7 (← śabda-), *mamāyati* 'is attached to, cherishes', Th 1150 (← [gen.] *mama*)[1], (**c**) *aṭṭīyati* 'is worried' (← *aṭṭa*-), *paṭiseniyati* 'fights against', Sn 390 (← *paṭisenā*-), *vivādiyati* 'quarrels' (← *vivāda*-), *balīyati* 'overcomes' (← *bala*-), *rasīyati* 'delights in' (← *rasa*-).

§ 52. Pāli has causatives (see § 44) formed with the suffix *-aya-/-e-* from the root (*chedeti* 'causes to cut off', *sāveti* 'causes to be heard, declares') or – though rarely – from the present stem[2] (*nacceti* 'causes to dance', *laggeti* 'makes stick', *tīreti* 'accomplishes' [← **tīrati* < tīryate[3]]). The causative-stem may show a vowel grade different from its base (CVCC- and [C]V̄C-bases usually remain): 1. *CaC*-roots generally have *ā*-vocalism as against *-a-* of the simplex (*pāteti* vs. *patati*); only *Can/m*-bases often do not have vowel alternation (*gameti* 'causes to go', *janeti* 'produces'; *nikkhāmeti* 'drives out' vs. *kamati* 'walks' [< krāmati][4]); 2. *Ci/eC*- and *Cu/oC*-bases have *e*- and *o*-vocalism (*deseti* 'points out', *codeti* 'urges') and 3. *Cĭ/ŭ*-bases result in *Cāy/v*- (*bhāyayati* 'frightens'[5], *cāveti* 'drives away, disturbs'). Sometimes the vowel grade varies rhythmically: *namayati* 'bends' vs. *paṇāmeti* 'dismisses'[6]. (Mostly) added to *Cā*-bases –

---

1 On *harāyati* see p. 13 (67).

2 See GEIGER § 178-182 and VON HINÜBER § 489. For Prakrit see PISCHEL § 490 and 551-554 and JACOBI § 65 / 70.

3 See EDGERTON, *Language* 22 (1946) 96 n. 7.

4 See CAILLAT, *IF* 88 (1983) 316. *apakkamanti* 'they depart', Ja III 457,5*, scans ⏑– – –⏑, thus hiding the old present stem *°kāmanti*.

5 Ja III 99,14* (*°te*), 210,3* (so read: OBERLIES 1993/94: 164).

6 See BLOCH (1965: 226) and CAILLAT, *IF* 88 (1983) 315.

which sometimes shorten their radical vowel[1] – is the suffix *-paya-/-pe*: *jāpeti* 'causes to be deprived' (jyāpayati)[2], *ñāpeti* 'explains' (jñāpayati), *yāpeti* 'keeps himself alive' (yāpayati)[3], *nijjhapayati* 'has someone pardoned' (nidhyāpayati; see § 5.4), *vijjhāpeti* 'extinguishes' (**vikṣāpayati*)[4], *voropeti* 'deprives (someone) of (something)' (avaropayati [√ruh]). This suffix was abstracted and added to any verb stem to form causatives (very frequently to present stems): *laggāpeti* 'makes stick' (based on *laggati*). If the base itself was a causative, the derivation had a 'double causative' meaning[5]: *ṭhapāpeti* 'orders to be erected' (based on *ṭhapeti* 'erects'), *bhāyāpeti* 'orders to frighten', *ropāpeti* 'causes to be planted' (based on *ropeti* 'plants'). *chedāpeti* 'has cut' and *gāhāpeti* 'causes to seize', two of the few instances where derivation and base seem to have identical meanings, are blends of *chindāpayati* and *gaṇhāpeti* (based on *chindati* 'cuts off' and *gaṇhati* 'seizes') and (the old causatives) *chedayati* and *gāheti* (see EDGERTON, *Language* 22 [1946] 99 with n. 10).

rem. (**a**) *labbheti* 'procures' (≠ Skt. *lambhayati*), Vin IV 5,38*, Dhp-a III 213,10,[6] stands for **lābheti* (cf. § 3.3) which is formed analogical to *labhati*; (**b**) *nayati* has a caus. *ānāpeti* 'causes to be

---

[1] See GEIGER § 180, for Prakrit PISCHEL § 551. See LEUMANN (1940: 226-227 [= *Kleine Schriften* p. 319-320]) on different explanations of this process.

[2] It does not belong to *jayati* (see OBERLIES, *OLZ* 94 [1999] 391 *pace* GEIGER § 180.2).

[3] See BHSG s.v. yāpayati and OBERLIES, *OLZ* 93 (1998) 105.

[4] See TEDESCO, *OLZ* 35 (1932) 526.

[5] See EDGERTON, *Language* 22 (1948) 94-101.

[6] See PED s.v. labhati.

brought'[1], i.e. *naya-* is regarded as a causative stem (see LEUMANN 1940: 226 [= *Kleine Schriften* p. 319]); (**c**) (part.) *bhojaṃ*, Ja VI 207,4*, is used instead of the causative[2]: *bhojaṃ ... dhūma-sikhiṃ patāpavaṃ* (*bhojento*, ct.); (**d**) on the causative used instead of the medium see p. 199.

§ 53. The opposition of active and passive[3] is shown not by the endings – the passive, too, has active endings (apart from frequent *-are* [p. 219]; on the imp. see § 46.2) –, but by the stems[4]: *bajjhati* 'is bound' vs. *bandhati* 'binds', *parihīrati* 'is carried' (see § 8.6) vs. *pariharati* 'carries about', *harīyati* 'is carried' vs. *harati* 'carries'. Historical forms are preserved to a great extent ([C]V/V̄C-bases have [C]VCC-passive stems[5]), partly (**a**) remodelled after the present stem, or due to (**b**) rhythmical exigencies: *paññāyati* 'is known, is perceived' (prajñāyate), *gayhati* 'is caught' (gṛhyate), Vin I 88,35, *dīyati/diyyati* 'is given'[6] (dīyate, see §

---

1 It is often written *āṇāpeti* due to the semantically similar *āṇāpeti* 'orders'.

2 There is – as far as I can see – not one instance of a nom. sg. masc. of a caus. participle in *-eṃ*.

3 See GEIGER § 175-177 and VON HINÜBER § 458-460. For Prakrit see PISCHEL § 535-548 and JACOBI § 64.

4 See BLOCH (1965: 225).

5 LEUMANN (1940: 235-236 [= *Kleine Schriften* p. 325-326]).

6 Pāli has the suffix *-(i)yya-* (on which see VON HINÜBER § 213; cf. PISCHEL § 91, 535) – as far as I can see – preponderantly in verb stems ending in *ī* (including that which developed in the passive from OIA *ā*) and – by extension – in *ū*: *niyyati*, Sn 580, *diyyati*, Thī 467, *pahiyyati*, S IV 31,3, *suyyati*, Ja IV 141,20*.

TURNER maintained that *-īya-* "may possibly represent the eastern dialect element in Pāli" and *-iyya-* "the western, since in Prākrit, where this suffix has been largely extended and is regularly added to the present stems to form the passive ....

14.9), [1]*jīyati* 'is deprived' (jīyate), *vuccati* 'is called' (ucyate), *vuppati* 'is sown' (upyate, see § 25), *ḍayhati* 'is burnt' (dahyate, see § 14.6, 22.3)[1], (**a**) *kariyati/kayirati* 'is made' (kṛiyate x karoti), *hāyati* 'is abandoned, diminishes', Ja IV 108,26*, Sn 817 (:: *jahāti*), *muñceyya* 'he may be released' (:: *muñcati*), Dhp 127, (**b**) *karīyati* 'is made' (see § 8.3d)[2]. Additionally, new passive stems are formed with the suffix *-ī̆ya-* (a contamination of *-[i]ya-* and *-īya-* [from *(d)īya(ti)*, etc.][3]) which is added to the present stem, especially to that in *-e-*: *pucchīyati* 'is asked' (← *pucchati*), *harīyate* 'is carried away' (← *harati*), M III 148,14[4], *([sam]anu)yuñjiyati* 'is examined' (← *yuñjati*), A V 156,5, Vin I 86,29, *posiyati* 'is brought up' (← *poseti*), Ja III 289,7* (*posiyāmase*), *bhājiyati* 'is distributed', Ud 48,24 (← *bhājeti* [see p. 216])[5]. Sometimes this suffix is added to passive stems (to form 'double' passives)[6]: *anupalabbhiyamāna-* 'not to be found', A I 174,11, S III 112,6, Nidd I 122,27, *uppacciyati* 'becomes dry' (ut-√pac), *uppajjiyati* 'is procured' (ut-√pad), *paricchijjiyamānaṃ* 'being clearly marked off',

---

there seems to have been a somewhat similar division: Mahārāṣṭrī and Ardhamāgadhī had *-ijja-* (e.g. *dijjai*); Śaurasenī and Māgadhī had *-īa-* (e.g. *dīadi*)" (1975: 200). Cf. also VON HINÜBER § 213. On *-īya-* ~ *-iyya-* see § 3.3.

1 On *patāyante/i*, Ja III 283,16*, D III 201,17*, possibly < °tāyante, see PED s.v. (with lit.).

2 On [2]*kīrati* (*kiyirati < kiriyate < kriyate), Th 143, Thī 424 (so read; Ee *karati*), *anubhīrati*, M III 123,20 (obviously corrected to *°hīra°* by CPD) and *(°)hīrati* (*hiyirati < hiriyate < hriyate), Th 453, M III 188,28, 189,7, Sn 205, see § 8.6.

3 See LEUMANN (1940: 233-234 [= *Kleine Schriften* p. 324-325]).

4 See GEIGER § 176.1.

5 See GEIGER § 176.2.

6 Or is this just another example of *-CCiy-* < *-Cy-* (see § 21)?

Dhp-a I 22,1, 35,15[1]. Only a few traces of the 3sg. aorist passive in *-i* are preserved[2]: *udapādi* 'was born', Ja III 29,5*, V 162,2, M I 31,34, *abhedi* 'was destroyed', Ud 93,12*, *nirodhi* 'was extinguished', ibid., *samatāni* 'was stretched out', D III 85,11[3]. But new passive aorists are formed from passive stems: *chijjiṃsu* 'they were cut', *haññiṃsu* 'they were killed'[4].

rem. On passives used as actives see above, p. 199 n. 4.

3.5. The *verbum infinitum*

§ 54. The present/future participle (see p. 177) is formed by adding *°nt-*[5] (fem. *°ntī-* [p. 178]) to the present/future stem (*kubba[nt]-* and *sa[nt]-* are as historical forms one of the very few exceptions)[6]: *kara(nt)-* / *kubba(nt)-* 'making, doing', *tiṭṭha(nt)-* 'standing', *jāna(nt)-* 'knowing', (fut.) *marissaṃ*[7] 'who is dying' , (pass.) *khajja(nt)-* 'being eaten'. Frequently it is thematicised (see § 28.2d): *karonta-* 'making, doing', *santa-*

---

[1] See CPD s.vv. and GEIGER § 176.3 (cf. OBERLIES, *WZKS* 34 [1990] 84 n. 21 and BHSG § 37.21).

[2] See GEIGER § 177 and VON HINÜBER § 462.

[3] Cf. *āpādi* which, however, is used as a medium (see VON HINÜBER § 462). For Prakrit see BALBIR, in: *Dialectes dans les littératures indo-aryennes* (édité par COLETTE CAILLAT). Paris 1989, 518-519.

[4] See GEIGER § 168 and VON HINÜBER § 462. For Prakrit see PISCHEL § 549.

[5] On forms without *-nt-* see p. 179.

[6] See GEIGER § 190 and VON HINÜBER § 490. For Prakrit see PISCHEL § 560.

[7] See GEIGER § 193. For Prakrit see PISCHEL § 560.

'being; good', *sayanta-* 'lying', *hananta-* 'killing'. As the medium was no longer used as a living category and the passive had active endings (see p. 254), the suffixes *°māna-* and *°āna-* – though often concealed by the first one – became true alternatives[1]: *caramāna-* 'walking', *jāgaramāna-* 'being awake', *kubb(am)āna-* 'making, doing'[2], (pass.) *vuccamāna-* 'being called', *apekkhāna-* 'longing for', Ja V 340,1*, *avhayāna-* 'invoking', Ja IV 247,23*, *āsasāna-* 'hoping, desiring', *iriyāna-* 'behaving', Sn 947, *esāna-* 'seeking', Thī 283, Sn 592, *ghasāna-* 'eating', Vin II 201,25*[3], *(yācana)jīvāna-* 'living', Ja III 353,20*[4], *bhuñjāna-* 'enjoying', Ja II 262,28*, S I 5,5* (Ee both times *bhuñjamāna-*), *vadāna-* 'saying', Sn 898, *bhikkhayāna-* 'begging', Ap 115,7, *kāmayāna-* 'desiring', Sn 767, *jigiṃsāna-* 'wishing to acquire', D II 267,6*, *anupādiyāna-* 'not grasping', Sn 915, *paripucchiyāna-* 'asking', Sn 696 (see NORMAN 1992: 281)[5].

rem. Pāli shows the incipient use of the present participle as conditional (i.e. to denote the *irrealis*)[6]: *adhammaṃ sārathi kayirā maṃ ce tvaṃ nikhaṇaṃ vane* 'you would do wrong, charioteer, if you

---

1 See GEIGER § 191-192, VON HINÜBER § 491 and NORMAN (1992: 174 [ad Sn 131]). For Prakrit where *°āṇa-* is used only rarely see PISCHEL § 561-563.

2 Pāli has *āsīna-* 'sitting' (Ja III 95,17*, Dhp 227, D II 212,21*) as has OIA and Sanskrit.

3 See CPD s.v. *asaṃkharāna*.

4 See YAJIMA, *CASS Studies* 5 (1980) 180 n. 6.

5 See GEIGER § 192, NORMAN (1992: 174 [ad Sn 131]) and OBERLIES (1996: 117). On *aṅhamāna-* 'eating' < *aśnamāna- (Sn 239-240) see GEIGER § 191 and LÜDERS (1954: 132).

6 See OBERLIES 1991 (cf. VON HINÜBER § 476 and NORMAN 1991: 174 [also on *vidhamaṃ*, Ja VI 490,7*]).

would bury me in the forest', Ja VI 12,31*[1] (see also p. 29).

§ 55. The *participium necessitatis* is formed with the suffixes *°(i)tabba-* (°[i]tavya-, see § 16.4)[2], *°anīya-/aṇīya-* (with its variants *°aniya-/°aṇiya-*[3] and *°aneyya-/°aṇeyya-* [see § 7.8, 11.10])[4], *°teyya-*, *°tayya-/°tāya-*, *°ya-* and *°a-*[5]. Beside numerous historical forms of the two first-named gerundives (*gantabba-*, *ñātabba-*, *labhanīya-*, *dassaneyya-*) there are many based on the present stem (*pucchitabba-*, *hotabba-*, *sāretabba-*, *bhijjitabba-*, *avissāsaniya-*, *avedaniya-*, *asakkuṇeyya-*). The suffixes *°teyya-* and *°tayya-/°tāya-* are (probably) blendings of *°tabba-* and *°aneyya-* or *°ayya-* (**[a]kayya-* < [a]kārya- etc.) respectively[6]: *ñāteyya-* 'to be known', S I 61,26, *daṭṭheyya-* 'to be seen', M III 131,18, S I 61,27, *patteyya-* 'to be reached', S I 61,27 = IV 93,7[7] (pra-√āp), *laddheyya-* 'to be obtained', Ja VI 225,28*, Pv 681, *ñātayya-* 'to be known' (√jñā), *a(t)tasitāya-* 'where one ought not to fear', S III 57,27 (√tras), *alajjitāya-*

---

[1] Cf. *sv'assa gomayacuṇṇāni +abhimanthaṃ* (so C[k] [see CPD s.v. abhimanthati]) *tiṇāni ca / viparītāya saññāya nāsakkhi sañjaletave*, Ja VI 371,13*-14*. For Prakrit see OBERLIES (1991: 122 n. 2).

[2] Sometimes this suffix is enlarged with *°ka-* (*khāditabbaka-*, Dhp-a III 137,9).

[3] E.g. *anumodaniyaṃ* (⏑⏑-⏑⏑-), Ap 394,18 (cf. HENDRIKSEN, *Syntax of the infinite verb-forms in Pāli*. Copenhagen 1944, 13 n. 1).

[4] These forms are often used as nouns: *karaṇīya-* 'task, duty', *khādanīya-* 'solid food', *yāpanīya-* 'subsistence', *mohaneyya-* 'enchantment'.

[5] See GEIGER § 199-203 and VON HINÜBER § 495-496 (cf. CPD, *Epilegomena* p. 25* [s.v. *ger.*]). For Prakrit see PISCHEL § 570-572.

[6] See GEIGER § 203, Sadd V 1548 (s.v. patteyya) and VON HINÜBER § 496.

[7] So read.

'of what one is not to be ashamed', Dhp 316 (√lajj), *ghātetāya-* 'to be killed', M I 231,2 ≠ II 122,1, *pabbājetāya-* 'to be banished', M I 231,3 ≠ II 122,2. The suffix (OIA) *°ya-* lost its clarity due to the (usual) assimilation of *-y-* to the preceding consonant (and the possibility of simplifying the resultant geminate [*-ekh-* < *-ekkh-*], see § 3.2b) and has consequently survived only in historical forms[1]: *(a)kāriya-* '[not] to be done', It 18,17* = Dhp 176 ([a]kārya-), *(a)garahiya-* '(not) blamable', S I 240,2*, *gārayha-* 'blameworthy', Sn 141[2], *suppahāya-* 'easy to abandon', Sn 772, *(a)labbha-* '(un)attainable'[3], *(a)kicca-* '[not] to be done', Ja III 131,10*, Th 167, Dhp 276 ([a]kṛtya-), *akkheyya-* 'not to be destroyed' (akṣeya-)[4], *keyya-* 'to be bought', Ja VI 180,27* (kreya-), *deyya-* 'to be given', D I 87,10, Sn 982 (deya-), *viññeyya-* 'to be known', D I 245,17, Vin I 184,20 (vijñeya-), *(a)bhabba-* '(un)able' ([a]bhavya-), *pāsaṃsa-* 'to be praised' (see § 6.4), *(a)sekha-* '(not) in need of further training' (*[a]śaikṣya-)[5]. The suffix *°a-* was added to present stems to form (quasi-)gerundives (type OIA *sukara-*, *duṣkara-*): *dukkara-* 'difficult to be done', *sulabha-* 'easy to be obtained', *dupposa-* 'difficult to nourish'[6], *a/sutappaya-* 'not / easy to be satiated', *duddamaya-* 'hard to be tamed', Th 5, *dummocaya-* 'difficult to be released', Dhp-a IV 56,18, *du/suviññāpaya-* 'difficult / easy to be taught', S I

---

1 See GEIGER § 202.

2 On *aggarayha-*, Ja VI 200,28*, see CPD s.v.

3 *alabbhanīya-* 'unattainable', A III 54,8, and *alabbhaneyya-* '= prec.', A III 56,28* ≠ Ja III 205,9*, have got their *-bbh-* from this word (see CPD s.v. and GEIGER § 201).

4 See KATRE, *Calcutta Oriental Journal* 1 (1934) 172-173.

5 See CPD s.v. asekha.

6 See OBERLIES (1996: 109-110 n. 116).

138,6[1]. Some isolated forms as *asantuleyya-* 'not payable by' (*asaṃtulya-) seem to be analogical to (e.g.) *(a)deyya-* ([a]deya-).

rem. A few gerundives are used as action nouns: *bhejja-* 'breaking', Vin III 47,2 (see NORMAN 1993: 73).

§ 56. As the verbal adjective[2] is preserved largely in historical forms, it has become the most frequent irregular form of the verb system (especially in the 'first conjugation'), very often unconnected with the present stem[3]: *(sam)atta-* 'taken, gasped' (*[sam]ādadāti*)[4], *bhūta-* 'become, produced' (*bhavati/hoti*), *laddha-* 'received' (*labhati*), *pakka-* 'baked, ripe' (*pacati*), *(paṭi)mukka-* 'tied to / released' (*muñcati*)[5], *jāta-* 'born' (*jāyati*), *iṭṭha-* 'desired' (*icchati*), *sitta-* 'sprinkled' (*siñcati*), *kata-* 'made, done' (*karoti*), *(añ)ñāta-* '(not) known' (*jānāti*), *(°)ñatta-* 'reputation', M I 318,29 (*ñāpeti*)[6]. Only the derived verbs have a consistent form in *°ita-*[7] (as

---

[1] See AiGr. II,1 § 76b rem. (p. 178-179), FRANKE, *WZKM* 15 (1901) 403, and CPD s.v. atappaya (cf. FALK, *Festschrift Dieter Schlingloff*. Reinbek 1996, 40-42).

[2] See GEIGER § 194-197 and VON HINÜBER § 492. For Prakrit see PISCHEL § 564-567.

[3] See JACOBI § 67-69 and EDGERTON (1954: 79).

[4] On this verbal adjective, which was replaced by *ādinna-*, see CAILLAT, *BEI* 7/8 (1989/90) 34-38 (see also SMITH 1952: 170 [on M I 388,19: ***kukkuravataṃ dīgharattaṃ samattaṃ samādiṇṇaṃ***]).

[5] On such *kk*-verbal adjectives (especially in Prakrit) see VON HINÜBER § 493.

[6] Sometimes the verbal adjective is adjusted to the present stem (see SAKAMOTO-GOTO, *MSS* 44 [1985] 183-184): ***luta-*** 'cut off', Ja VI 25,9* (~ ***lūna-***, Thī 107) :: ***lunāti*** (see OBERLIES 1995a: 156), ***avakanta-*** 'cut off' (< °kṛtta-) :: ***°kantati***. ***abhiranta-*** 'fond of' (≠ abhirata-), however, is formed in analogy with ***kanta-***.

[7] See SMITH (1950: 14).

have some underived ones too, such as *carati* or *khādati*): *kārita*- 'made to do' (*kāreti*), *kathita*- 'said, spoken' (*katheti*), *jighacchita*- 'hungry' (*jighacchati*). Following this pattern 'new' verbal adjectives were derived from present stems[1]: *āharita*- 'brought' (*āharati*), *supita*- 'slept' (*supati*). Thus two verbal adjectives often appear side by side: [2]*puṭṭha-/pucchita*- 'asked' (*pucchati*), *(pa)muñcita-/pamutta*-, 'set free' (*muñcati*)[2]. And after this pattern – and after 'historical' groups such as *paññatta*- :: *paññāpeti* 'arranges, provides' – 'short' forms of verbal adjectives originated: *patta*- 'fallen' (*patati*)[3], *nijjhatta*- 'made to understand' (*nijjhapayati* ~ *nijjhāpeti*)[4], *paṭiyatta*- 'dressed' (*paṭiyādeti*)[5]. Sporadically the suffix °*ta*- is substituted by °*na*-: *dinna*- 'given' (: datta-)[6]. On the other hand, *milāta*- 'withered' and *luta*- 'cut off' replaced (OIA) *mlāna*- and *lūna*- (see § 9.8).

rem. (**a**) The verbal adjective of transitive verbs – except for that

---

1 Sometimes (unintelligible) aorist forms were transformed into verbal adjectives: *anvagataṃ* < *anugaṃ* < anvagāt (see OBERLIES, *WZKS* 34 [1990] 101), *ajjhapatto* < **ajjhapattā* < adhyapaptat (see p. 236 with n. 1). Cf. *samajano* 'has arisen' ← (3sg. pret.) **samajanā* (Ja III 488,1* = M III 154,1*), see SCHMITHAUSEN, *WZKSO* 14 (1970) 92 n. 157.

2 GEIGER § 196 gives a lot examples.

3 See p. 115 (§ 22.2 *rem.*).

4 Cf. BHSD s.v. nidhyapta.

5 See CPD I,438b.

6 See also OBERLIES (1995a: 162 [s.v. sīta-]). For Prakrit see ALSDORF, *Kleine Schriften* p. 64.

Very rare are new '*aniṭ*-forms': *(paccā/pari)bhaṭṭha*- 'spoken', Ja II 48,5, VI 187,20, Vv 993 (*subhāsitā ... gāthāyo, nijjhatto mhi subhaṭṭena* [!]). See TEDESCO, *JAOS* 85 (1965) 377, and Sadd V 1647.

of verbs meaning 'to drink', 'to eat'[1], 'to give birth to' (*devī dhītaraṃ vijātā*, S I 86,6) and of (e.g.) *abhirūḷha-* 'having mounted', *avagata-* 'having understood', ³*patta-* 'having reached'[2] – is used in the passive[3], while that of intransitive verbs is used as a rule in the active sense (exceptions are rare and generally late: *diṭṭho ahaṃ dhammavaraṃ* 'I have seen ...', Ap 41,27, *yo avahato* 'who has stolen ...', Vin III 64,10)[4]; **(b)** The verbal adjective, especially that in *°ita-*, was the base for the formation of new present stems (see § 45, 51a); **(c)** Some causatives with full grade vowel have verbal adjectives with zero grade vowel: *cudita-* ~ *codita-* 'urged' (*codeti* 'urges'), *rusita-* 'annoyed' (*roseti* 'annoys')[5]; **(d)** The combination of verbal adjective and auxiliary verb serves as 'plusquamperfect' and as a *futurum exactum*: *patto abhavissaṃ* 'I would have attained', Ja I 470,15, *gato bhavissati* 'he would be gone', Ja II 214,4[6].

---

1 Cf. CPD s.v. ²asita (2).

2 See GEIGER § 173.2.

3 Quite often the verbal adjective is used in the sense of an action noun (see BLOCH 1965: 274 and RENOU, *Grammaire Sanscrite* § 153c): *akkuṭṭha-* 'reviling', *gata-* 'going', Ja I 295,8*, *rodita-* 'weeping', Ja III 214,12*, *hata-* 'killing', Th 180 (see NORMAN 1969: 129 [ad Th 36], 1971: 116 [ad Thī 261], 1992: 210 [ad Sn 331]).

4 See HENDRIKSEN, *Syntax of the infinite verb-forms in Pāli*. Copenhagen 1944, 27 (and 166 [*addition*]) and BECHERT, *MSS* 10 (1957) 57 (cf. HENDRIKSEN, *Acta Orientalia* 20 [1948] 81-82, and BECHERT 1958: 313). For Prakrit see JACOBI § 82, GHATAGE, *ABORI* 21 (1939/40) 85-86, CHANDRA, *Proceedings of the All-India Oriental Conference* (Thirtieth Session). Poona 1982, 334-335, and BHAYANI (1998: 8-9).

5 Cf. CPD s.v. appaṭisaṃvidita.

6 On such periphrases see GEIGER § 173-174. For Prakrit see PISCHEL § 519 and JACOBI § 113.

By adding the suffix °*va(nt)*- to a verbal adjective an active participle is formed[1]: *bhuttava(nt)*- 'having eaten', *vusitava(nt)*- 'having spent', *(as)sutava(nt)*- '(not) having heard, with(out) learning' (inflected according to § 41). The suffix °*āvi(n)*-, a continuation of Vedic °*āvín*- ([see p. 8 *pace* GEIGER § 198.3), has the same function: *anikīḷitāvi(n)*- 'who has not yet enjoyed sensual pleasures in full', *assutāvi(n)*- 'not having heard, without learning, *katāvi(n)*- 'having done', *(vi)jitāvi(n)*- 'having conquered', *bhuttāvi(n)*- 'having eaten' (inflected according to § 34)[2].

§ 57. The most usual infinitive suffix is °*(i)tuṃ*[3]. In historical forms it is added to the root (*[vi]ketuṃ*, *sotuṃ*), in new formations to the present stem (*pappotuṃ*, *pucchituṃ*, *tikicchituṃ*, *sajjhāyituṃ*, *phassetu[ṃ]*, Sn 393, [pass.] *pamuccituṃ*, Th 253)[4]. Sometimes it is enlarged by the particle *-ye*[5] (with sporadic dropping of *-ṃ*): *kātuṃ-ye* 'to do', Thī 418 (so read),

---

[1] See GEIGER § 96.1 / 198.2 and VON HINÜBER § 494. For Prakrit see PISCHEL § 569. On *ādinnava(nt)*-, Mhv VII 42, see GEIGER § 198.2 and CPD s.v.

[2] See GEIGER § 198.3, VON HINÜBER § 494 and OBERLIES, *OLZ* 94 (1999) 392. For Prakrit see METTE, *IT* 11 (1983) 130, BALBIR, in: *Dialectes dans les littératures indo-aryennes* (édité par COLETTE CAILLAT). Paris 1989, 518, and BHAYANI (1998: 6-8).

[3] See GEIGER § 204-206 and VON HINÜBER § 497. For Prakrit see PISCHEL § 573-580 (cf. BLOCH 1965: 250 and SCHWARZSCHILD 1991: 22-27).

[4] As in Sanskrit, the infinitive loses its final *-ṃ* when compounded with the word *kāma*-: *jīvitu-kāma*-, Dhp 123, *daṭṭhu-kāma*-, Sn 685 (see GEIGER § 207).

[5] On this particle, comparable to Prakrit *-je* (see SCHWARZSCHILD 1991: 104-110 and OBERLIES 1993: 78 [s.v. *-je*]), see NORMAN (1971: 154-155). Such forms, i.e. °*uṃ-je*, are used in Prakrit as absolutives (see BHAYANI, *Sambodhi* 7 [1978/79] 115; cf. PISCHEL § 576).

gaṇetuye 'to count', Bv IV 28, *jānituṃ-ye* 'to know', Ja IV 463,9*[1], *maritu-ye* 'to die', Thī 426, *hetu-ye* 'to become' (bhavitum), Bv II 9. The suffix *°tave* (< °tavái) is inherited from Vedic Sanskrit (see p. 8). Historical forms served as models for new ones: *kātave* 'to do', Ja V 318,17*, Cp 318, Vv 738, *(anuk)kamitave* 'to walk (after)', S I 24,8* (so read [see CPD s.v. anukkamati]), *gantave* 'to go', Ja IV 221,26*, Thī 332, *dātave* 'to give', Ja IV 434,12*, Sn 286, Cp 129, 132, *padātave* 'to take', Ja I 190,3* (*padātave ti +pādātave* [see C^{v}] *sandhivasena ākāralopo veditabbo, gahetuṃ ti attho*, ct.[2]), *dharetave* 'to hold', Ap 422,15, *netave* 'to lead', Dhp 180, S I 107,24*, *(pa)muttave* 'to let free', Ja IV 337,25*, *yācitave* 'to beg', Ja IV 452,18*, *(saṃpa)yātave* 'to proceed', Sn 834, *vattave* 'to speak', Ja III 309,9* = S I 205,2*, *(pa)hātave* 'to abandon', Th 186, Dhp 34, Sn 817, *nidhetave* 'to lay down', Ja III 17,6*, *rajetave* 'to colour', Th 1155, *lapetave* 'to talk', Ud 21,14*. Another rare suffix is *°tāye* of unknown origin[3]: *khāditāye*, Ja V 33,7*, *jagghitāye*, Ja III 226,10*, *dakkhitāye*, D II 254,7* = S I 26,25*, *pucchitāye*, Ja V 137,6*. And the acc. and dat. of *a*-stems were used as infinitives (see § 28.3): *niyyāhi abhidassanaṃ* 'go out in order to see ...', Ja VI 193,22*, 533,3* = 18*[4], *na ca mayaṃ labhāma bhagavantaṃ dassanāya* 'and we did not get an opportunity to

---

[1] Cf. VON HINÜBER § 497.

[2] Cf. Sadd 613,14: *pa-ādātave ti chedo* (see also Sadd V 1552 l. 1-2).

[3] See SAKAMOTO-GOTO, in: *Dialectes dans les littératures indo-aryennes* (édité par COLETTE CAILLAT). Paris 1989, 399-400.

The final *-ye* looks much like the enlarging particle of the infinitives *kātuṃ-ye*, *maritu-ye* (see above); we are left with *khāditā-* (etc.) which, however, defies analysis.

[4] See OBERLIES (1996: 117).

see the Blessed One', Vin I 253,11-12[1].

§ 58. The absolutive shows a similar variety of formations: **(1)** *°(i)tvā̆* (see § 5.2d), **(2)** *°(i)tvāna(ṃ)*, **(3)** *°(t)tu(ṃ)* (< *°tvu < °tva, see § 5.2d, 9.14[2]), **(4)** *°tūna*, **(5)** *°(i)yā̆* (roots in short vowels insert a *-t-* before the suffix *°yā̆* and the resulting cluster is assimilated to *-ccā̆*), **(6)** *°(i)yāna(ṃ)*, **(7)** *°eyya*, **(8)** *°aṃ*[3]. (All) these suffixes *can* be added to the present stem:

(1) *ñatvā*, *jānitvā* (both) 'having known', *gantvā* 'having gone' (with *-n-* analogical to inf. *gantum*[4]), *samāhatvā* 'having carried together', Ja V

---

[1] On *etase*, Thī 291 (*éta*[*ve*] x [*jivá*]*se*), see VON HINÜBER § 497 (cf. KERN, *Bijdrage tot de verklaring van eenige woorden in Pāli-geschriften voorkomende*, in: *Verspreide Geschriften II.2*, p. 304, and BLOCH 1965: 250), on *āsāduṃ*, Ja V 154,19*, see GEIGER § 65.2 and OBERLIES (1996: 117), and on *saṭṭhuṃ*, Ja VI 185,14*, see VON HINÜBER § 497.

[2] See also BECHERT (1955: 16 n. 36). The inscriptions of Aśoka (*ālabhitu*, RE I Jaugaḍa) show that the absolutive in *°tu* belongs to the 'eastern' language (see BLOCH, *Recueil d'Articles* p. 404, and VON HINÜBER 1982: 134).

[3] See GEIGER § 209-210 **(1/2)**, 211 **(4)**, 212-213 **(5)**, 214 **(6)** and VON HINÜBER § 498-499. For Prakrit see PISCHEL § 581-594 (**1.** § 582, **2.** § 583, **4.** § 584-586, **5.** § 589-591, **6.** § 592), BHAYANI, *Sambodhi* 7 (1978/79) 115 **(2.)**, and SCHWARZSCHILD (1991: 37-41). (*Pace* PISCHEL § 583) also JM knows absolutives in *-ttāṇaṃ* (see ALSDORF, *Kleine Schriften* p. 69, BHAYANI, *Sambodhi* 7 [1978/79] 115, BALBIR, in: *Dialectes dans les littératures indo-aryennes* (édité par COLETTE CAILLAT). Paris 1989, 507-508).

[4] See GEIGER § 209.

32,18*[1], *(a)laddhā̆* '(not) having received', Sn 306, Ja III 138,21*[2], S I 126,24* = 32*[3], *piṭṭhā* 'having pounded', Ja III 425,19* (piṣṭvā); *katva* 'having made', Ja VI 299,31*, *karitva* 'having made', Vv 409[4], *chetva* 'having cut', Sn 535, Ap 24,5 (Ee *chetvā*, v.l. *chettu*), *daditvā* 'having given', Th 532, *siñcitva* 'having baled out', Sn 771[5], **(2)** *katvāna* 'having made', It 12,12*, Ja V 49,11*, *akkamitvāna* 'having stepped upon', Bv II 52, Cp 93, *gahetvāna* 'having seized', Sn 309, *cavitvāna* 'having fallen from', Ap 395,13, *chetvāna* 'having cut', Dhp 346, *daditvāna* 'having given', Cp 92, *bhutvāna* 'having eaten', Th 23[6], *bhetvāna* 'having broken', Th 753, *hutvāna* 'having become', Sn 281[7], *(a)laddhāna* '(without) having attained', Ja V 465,5*, M II 72,26*, *yajitvānaṃ* 'having sacrificed', Ja VI 136,25* (Ee *°tvāna*)[8], **(3)** *daṭṭhu* 'having seen', Ja V 249,7*, 250,27*, Sn 424, 681[9], *abhihaṭṭhuṃ* 'having brought', M I 222,3, **(4)** *kātūna* 'having

---

1 See OBERLIES (1995a: 160).

2 The explanation of VON HINÜBER, in: *Buddhism in Ceylon and Studies on Religious Syncretism in Buddhist Countries* (ed. by H. BECHERT). Göttingen 1978, 50 n. 9, is, however, contradicted by NORMAN (1994: 115-116).

3 Cf. CPD s.v. aladdhā.

4 See ALSDORF (1968: 84).

5 See SMITH (1950: 36), SAKAMOTO-GOTO (1988: 108 n. 13/16), INSLER (1994: 73-74), OBERLIES (1995/96: 272 / 276) and id. (1996: 118).

6 The *-o-* of *bhotvā*, Th 800 = S IV 74,7*, seems to be due to the vocalism of *bhojana-*.

7 *vavakkhitvāna*, D II 262,8*, seems to belong to *avekkhati* (ava-√īkṣ).

8 See OBERLIES (1996: 118).

9 On *daṭṭhu* (and *da/iṭṭhā*) see SAKAMOTO-GOTO, in: *Dialectes dans les littératures indo-aryennes* (édité par COLETTE CAILLAT). Paris 1989, 400-404, 410 (cf. ea. 1988:

made', Vin III 96,32, 170,25, *apakīritūna* 'having thrown away', Thī 447 (so read [see Ee p. 244]), *paritātūna* 'having saved', Ja V 71,3*, *āpucchitūna* 'having asked leave', Thī 426, *hātūna* 'having brought', Ja IV 280,17*, *chaḍḍūna* 'having thrown away', Thī 469, *voḍhūna* 'having drawn', Thī 441 (so read [see Ee p. 243]), **(5)** *āmanta* 'bidding farewell' (āmantrya)[1], *acchejja* 'having removed', S I 127,3*, *kacca* 'having done' ([*]kṛtya), Thī-a 147,19, Ap 533,15 v.l. (Ee *katva*), *sakkacca(ṃ)* 'respectfully' (satkṛtya), Ja IV 310,23*, D II 356,1, Th 1054, *sacca* 'having remembered' (smṛtya), Ja II 134,1*[2], *pecca* 'having died', Ja VI 288,25* (so read)[3] ~ *peccaṃ* (see § 4.5), *dajjā* 'having given' (← *dadāti*), Pv 324, *kariya* 'having made' (← *karoti*)[4], Ja VI 291,16*, Thī 402, D III 153,17*, *cariya* 'having undertaken', D III 153,17*, *dakkhiya* 'having seen' (← *dakkhati*), Thī 381-382, *jāniyā* 'having recognized', Ja IV 112,7*[5], *āliṅgiyā* 'having embraced', Ja IV 441,9*, *orundhiyā* 'having locked up', Ja IV 480,12*, *khādiyā*, 'having eaten' Ja V 464,6*, (enlarged with *-ka-*) *gayhaka* 'having grasped', Ja III 361,2* (*gahetvā*, ct.)[6], **(6)** *uttariyāna* 'having descended', Ja IV 441,8*, V 204,9*, *paribhuñjiyāna* 'having enjoyed', Ja V 505,28*, *parivisiyāna* 'having waited upon', Pv 253, *samekkhiyānaṃ*

---

107 n. 13, CPD s.vv. adaṭṭhā/adiṭṭhā, Sadd V 1587 [s.v. ²passa] and VON HINÜBER § 498).

[1] See NORMAN (1991: 179) and DE JONG, *IIJ* 21 (1979) 298.

[2] See TEDESCO, *JAOS* 77 (1957) 47-48.

[3] This absol. is construed with *tayī* as if a loc. of a verbal adjective (*tayi gate*, ct. [see ALSDORF, *Kleine Schriften* p. 399 n. 33]).

[4] It always scans -⏑.

[5] See SAKAMOTO-GOTO, *WZKS* 28 (1984) 54-55 n. 43.

[6] See OBERLIES (1996: 118).

'looking', Ja VI 309,10*, D III 25,1, *khādiyānaṃ* 'having eaten', Ja V 24,4*, *posiyānaṃ* 'having nourished', Ja VI 150,24*[1], *anumodiyānaṃ* 'having approved', Ja V 143,9*, (**7**) *oceyya* 'having collected', Ja IV 440,16* (see p. 62 n. 2), *tuleyya* 'having regarded', Ja III 357,18*, *vineyya* 'having removed', Sn 21, 58, *viceyya* 'having considered', Sn 517 (vicīya)[2], (**8**) *jīvagāhaṃ (gahetvāna)* 'having captured alive'[3], Ja V 310,20*, *samācāraṃ* 'having performed', Th 727, *sampassaṃ* 'having seen', A III 43,22*, *samphusaṃ* 'having come in contact', Ja VI 236,1*, *saṃsaraṃ* 'being reborn', Ja VI 226,17* (for the two last instances see below), (enlarged with *-ka-*) *udarāvadehakaṃ* 'having filled their belly', Th 935, *avagaṇḍa-kārakaṃ* 'so as to fill the cheeks (with food)', Vin IV 196,11*, *ālumpakārakaṃ* 'breaking off into morsels', D III 85,26.

rem. (**a**) The Pāli tradition wrongly interpreted (unrecognized) absolutives in *[*]°ttā*[4] (< °tvā) as periphrastic futures in *°tā*: *abhijānām' ahaṃ ... dakkhiṇena passena sato sampajāno niddaṃ okkamitā*[5], M I 249,36[6]; (**b**) A few nouns are abstracted from

---

[1] See ALSDORF (1968: 47).

[2] *-eyya* seems to be a metrical variant of *-īya* which seems to have originated under the influence of the optative and the *participium necessitatis* (NORMAN [1990: 222] wrongly derives *viceyya* from *vicarya* – is this an error for *vicārya*?]).

[3] On this phrase see FORSSMAN, *StII* 13/14 (1987) 69-76.

[4] We have only a few instances of an absolutive in *-ttā* (see p. 269).

[5] *abhijānāti* is systematically construed with the absolutive (s. PIND, *Bauddhavidyāsudhākaraḥ. Studies in Honour of Heinz Bechert on the Occasion of His 65th Birthday*. Swisttal-Odendorf 1997, 535 n. 63).

[6] See CPD s.vv. atimaññati / okkamitā, VON HINÜBER § 475, id., *IT* 10 (1982) 135-137, and NORMAN (1992: 156 [ad Sn 69] and 252 [ad Sn 537]).

absolutives: *asañcicca-* (←*asañcicca*), *upanidhā-* (← *upanidhāya*)[1].

The most common suffix (*°tvā* [**1**]), which is not only added to verbs without prefix (as *°[i]yā̆*[2] is not confined to verbs with prefix), seems to be a Sanskritisation of genuine *°ttā* (< °tvā; see § 1)[3] which is preserved only very sporadically and then mostly remodelled (*bhuttā*, Ja V 465,6*[4], *[a]-diṭṭhā* [(a)dṛṣṭvā], Ja V 215,28*, 218,18*, 220,2*, *hiṃsitaṃ* [hiṃsitvā], Ja IV 142,14*, *kattaṃ* [see § 4.6])[5]. This transformation of *°ttā* into *°tvā* affected **dissa* (dṛśya[6]): *disvā*, *adisva*, Ja III 161,14*[7], V 53,22*, *disvāna(ṃ)*, Ja VI 143,8* (Ee *disvāna*). The suffix *°tūna* (**4**) seems to be based on **tū̆*, which resulted from a blending of (absol.) *°tvā* and (inf.) *°tuṃ*[8] and

---

1 See CPD, *Epilegomena* p. 20* (s.v. *abstr.*) and VON HINÜBER (1994: 160). Cf. also *ajaddhuka-* 'abstention from eating' / *ajaddhumārikā-* 'death by starvation' (← jagdhvā [?]), M I 245,13 (see LEUMANN, *Kleine Schriften* p. 546).

2 *°(i)yā* is either a continuation of Vedic *°yā* (cf. AiGr. II 2 § 635b) or a contamination of *°ya* and *°tvā*.

3 Also an absolutive in *°tā* seems to be attested: *paccuggatā*, Ja VI 557,20* (see VON HINÜBER § 498 and NORMAN 1992: 156 [ad Sn 69]).

4 See Sadd V 1660.

5 See also NORMAN (1992a: 92-94).

6 This absolutive is attested in Epic Sanskrit (Mbh 1,218.22, 7,76.21, 78.46, R 1,29.16, 47.11).

7 See OBERLIES (1995/96: 276).

8 Unknown to Pāli is the usage of the infinitive as absolutive and *vice versa* (for Prakrit see PISCHEL § 576-577, 579, 585, 588, 590 and OBERLIES 1993: 131 n. 147), unless *abhihaṭṭhuṃ* (see p. 266) is an example.

was enlarged by *-na(ṃ)* in analogy with *°tvāna(ṃ)*, as was the abs. in *°(i)yă* (**5, 6**)[1]. The absolutive in *°aṃ*[2] (**8**) is of two-fold origin: a) the Vedic *ṇamul*-absolutive (of the form *preverb-root*[full or lengthened grade]-*aṃ*[3]), b) nom. sg. masc. of the present pariciples in *-aṃ* used as absolutive (see p. 177-178).

---

1 See SAKAMOTO-GOTO (1988: 94-95) and ea. (1991: 18-19).

2 See CPD, *Epilegomena* 20* (s.v. *abs.*) and NORMAN (1969: 125-126, 1971: 65-66, 1992: 299-300).

3 See WHITNEY, *Sanskrit Grammar* § 995b, and RENOU, *Grammaire Sanscrite* § 105d.

4. Literature

ALSDORF 1968	LUDWIG ALSDORF. *Die Āryā-Strophen des Pali-Kanons*. Wiesbaden: Franz Steiner, 1968 (AWLM 1967.4).
BARTHOLOMAE 1916	CHRISTIAN BARTHOLOMAE. *Ausgleichserscheinungen bei den Zahlwörtern zwei, drei und vier im Mittelindischen*. Heidelberg 1916 (*Sitzungsberichte der Heidelberger Akademie der Wissenschaften*. Phil.-hist. Klasse, Jahrgang 1916, 5. Abhandlung).
BECHERT 1955	HEINZ BECHERT. Vokalkürzung vor Sandhikonsonant. *MSS* 6 (1955) 7-26.
BECHERT 1958	– Grammatisches aus dem Apadānabuch. *ZDMG* 108 (1955) 308-316.
BECHERT 1958a	– Über den Gebrauch der indikatischen Tempora im Pāli. *MSS* ²3 (1958) 55-72.
BECHERT 1961	– Das Cullasutasomajātakam. *MSS* ²4 (1961) 13-28.
BECHERT 1980	– Allgemeine Bemerkungen zum Thema "Die Sprache der ältesten buddhistischen Überlieferung". In: *Die Sprache der ältesten buddhistischen Überlieferung* (ed. by H. BECHERT). Abhandlungen der Akademie der Wissenschaften in Göttingen. Phil.-hist. Klasse. Dritte Folge, Nr. 117. Göttingen 1980, 24-34 (English translation: *Buddhist Studies Review* 8 [1991] 3-19).
BECHERT 1995	– Zur Kontroverse um die Aoristformen im Pāli. In: *Sauhṛdayamaṅgalam. Studies in Honour of* SIEGFRIED LIENHARD *on his 70th Birthday*.

Stockholm 1995, 27-35.

BERGER 1955 HERMANN BERGER. *Zwei Probleme der mittelindischen Lautlehre*. München: Kitzinger, 1955.

BERGER 1955a — *Kauṭalya* ist älter als *Kauṭilya*, *MSS* 6 (1955) 27-29.

BERGER 1956 – Review of LÜDERS 1954. *GGA* 210 (1956) 96-111.

BHAYANI 1997 HARIVALLABH C. BHAYANI. *Some Topics in the Development of OIA, MIA, NIA*. Ahmedabad: L.D. Institute of Indology, 1997 (L.D. Series 118).

BHAYANI 1998 – *Indological Studies. Literary and Performing Arts, Prakrit and Apabhraṃśa Studies*. Ahmedabad: Parshva Publication, 1998.

BLOCH 1965 JULES BLOCH. *Indo-Aryan. From the Vedas to Modern Times*. Paris: Adrien-Maisonneuve, 1965 (English translation of *L'Indo-Aryen*. Paris 1934).

BROUGH 1962 JOHN BROUGH. *The Gāndhārī Dharmapada. Edited with an introduction and commentary*. London: Oxford University Press, 1962.

CAILLAT 1970 COLETTE CAILLAT. *Pour une nouvelle grammaire du Pāli*. Torino 1970 (Istituto di Indologia della Università d Torino. Conferenze IV).

CAILLAT 1980 – La langue primitive du bouddhisme. In: *Die Sprache der ältesten buddhistischen Überlieferung* (ed. by H. BECHERT). Abhandlungen der Akademie der Wissenschaften in Göttingen. Phil.-hist. Klasse. Dritte Folge, Nr. 117. Göttingen 1980, 43-60.

CAILLAT 1994 – Doublets désinentiels en moyen indo-aryen.

In: *Bopp-Symposium 1992 der Humboldt-Universität zu Berlin* (ed. by R. Sternemann). Heidelberg 1994, 39-52.

CAILLAT 1997 – Vedic and Early Middle Indo-Aryan. In: *Inside the texts – beyond the texts* (ed. by M. Witzel). Cambridge 1997, 15-32.

EDGERTON 1954 FRANKLIN EDGERTON. The Middle Indic Verb System. In: *Asiatica. Festschrift Friedrich Weller*. Leipzig 1954, 78-81.

GEIGER (1916) WILHELM GEIGER. *Pāli. Literatur und Sprache.* Strassburg: Karl J. Trübner, 1916 (= Grundriss der Indo-Arischen Philologie und Altertumskunde I/7).

GEIGER 1994 WILHELM GEIGER. *A Pāli Grammar*. Translated into English by BATAKRISHNA GHOSH, revised and edited by K.R. NORMAN. Oxford: The Pali Text Society, 1994.

VON HINÜBER (2001) OSKAR VON HINÜBER. *Das ältere Mittelindisch im Überblick*. Wien: Verlag der Österreichischen Akademie der Wissenschaften, 2001 (Second revised edition).

VON HINÜBER 1968 – *Studien zur Kasussyntax des Pāli, besonders des Vinaya-Piṭaka*. München: Kitzinger, 1968.

VON HINÜBER 1982 – Pāli as an artificial language. *IT* 10 (1982) 133-140.

VON HINÜBER 1994 – *Selected Papers on Pāli Studies*. Oxford: The Pali Text Society, 1994.

VON HINÜBER 1999 – Pāli: How do we see it eighty years after Geiger's grammar? In: *Wilhelm Geiger and the Study of the History and Culture of Sri Lanka* (ed. by ULRICH EVERDING and ASANGA TILAKARAT-

NE). Colombo: Goethe Institute and Postgraduate Institute of Pali and Buddhist Studies, 1999, 148-158.

INSLER 1994 — STANLEY INSLER. Rhythmic Effects in Pali Morphology. *Die Sprache* 36 (1994) 70-93.

JACOBI (1886) — HERMANN JACOBI. *Ausgewählte Erzählungen in Mâhârâshṭrî. Zur Einführung in das Studium des Prâkṛit*. Leipzig: Verlag von S. Hirzel, 1886.

LEUMANN 1940 — MANU LEUMANN. Zur Stammbildung der Verben im Indischen. *IF* 57 (1940) 205-238 (= *Kleine Schriften* p. 303-328).

LÜDERS 1954 — HEINRICH LÜDERS. *Beobachtungen über die Sprache des buddhistischen Urkanons*. Berlin 1954 (Abhandlungen der Deutschen Akademie der Wissenschaften zu Berlin. Klasse für Sprachen, Literatur und Kunst. Jahrgang 1952, Nr. 10).

NORMAN 1969 — KENNETH ROY NORMAN. *The Elder's Verses I: Theragāthā. Translated with an introduction and notes*. London: The Pali Text Society, 1969.

NORMAN 1971 — *– The Elder's Verses II: Therīgāthā. Translated with an introduction and notes*. London: The Pali Text Society, 1971.

NORMAN 1990 — *– Collected Papers. Volume I.* Oxford: The Pali Text Society, 1990.

NORMAN 1991 — *– Collected Papers. Volume II.* Oxford: The Pali Text Society, 1991.

NORMAN 1992 — *– The Group of Discourses (Sutta-Nipāta)*. Volume II. Oxford: The Pali Text Society, 1992.

NORMAN 1992a — *– Collected Papers. Volume III.* Oxford: The Pali Text Society, 1992.

NORMAN 1993 – *Collected Papers. Volume IV.* Oxford: The Pali Text Society, 1994.

NORMAN 1994 – *Collected Papers. Volume V.* Oxford: The Pali Text Society, 1994.

OBERLIES 1989/90 THOMAS OBERLIES. Miscellanea Palica (I). *BEI* 7/8 (1989/90) 157-184.

OBERLIES 1991 – Die Verwendung des Part. Präs. als Konditional im Pali. *IIJ* 34 (1991) 121-122.

OBERLIES 1992 – Eine Dissimilationsregel in den Aśoka-Inschriften: Ein kleiner Beitrag zur Sprachgeographie Indiens. *WZKS* 36 (1992) 19-22.

OBERLIES 1993 – *Āvaśyaka-Studien: Glossar ausgewählter Wörter zu E. LEUMANNs 'Die Āvaśyaka-Erzählungen'.* Stuttgart: Franz Steiner, 1993 (Alt- und Neu-Indische Studien 45,2).

OBERLIES 1993/94 – Der Text der Jātaka-Gāthās in Fausbølls Ausgabe (Stand und Aufgaben der Jātaka-Forschung I – Teil 1). *BEI* 11/12 (1993/94) 147-170.

OBERLIES 1995 – Beiträge zur Pali-Lexikographie (Miscellanea Palica II). *IIJ* 38 (1995) 105-147.

OBERLIES 1995a – Beiträge zum Pali-Lexikon (Miscellanea Palica III). *HS* 108 (1995) 127-164.

OBERLIES 1995b – Die Wurzel *gad* im Mittelindischen. *HS* 108 (1995) 190-191.

OBERLIES 1995/96 – Der Text der Jātaka-Gāthās in Fausbølls Ausgabe [II] (Stand und Aufgaben der Jātaka-Forschung I – Teil 2). *BEI* 13/14 (1995/96) 269-305.

OBERLIES 1996 – Stray remarks on Pali phonology, morphology, and vocabulary (Miscellanea Palica V). *MSS* 56 (1996) 91-130.

OBERLIES 1997 – Pali, Pāṇini and 'popular' Sanskrit (Miscellanea Palica VI). *JPTS* 23 (1997) 1-26.

OBERLIES 1999 – Middle Indo-Aryan and (the) Vedic (Dialects). (Miscellanea Palica VII). *HS* 112 (1999) 39-57.

OBERLIES 1999a – *ca* 'when, if', *ce(d)* 'and' – worlds upside-down? In: *Vidyopāsanā. Studies in Honour of Harivallabh C. Bhayani*. Mumbai – Ahmedabad 1999, 169-172.

PERNIOLA 1997 VITO PERNIOLA. *Pali Grammar*. Oxford: The Pali Text Society, 1997.

PISANI 1952 VITTORE PISANI. Noterelle Pāli. *Rendiconti del Istituto Lombardo dei scienze e lettere. Classe di lettere*. Vol. 85 (1952) 279-288.

PISCHEL (1900) RICHARD PISCHEL. *Gammatik der Prakrit-Sprachen*. Strassburg: Karl J. Trübner, 1900 (= Grundriss der Indo-Arischen Philologie und Altertumskunde I/8).

SAKAMOTO-GOTO 1987/88
JUNKO SAKAMOTO-GOTO. *ū* vor dem Wurzelanlaut *h* im Mittelindischen. *IT* 14 (1987/88) 353-382.

SAKAMOTO-GOTO 1988 – Die mittelindische Lautentwicklung von *v* in Konsonantengruppen mit Verschlußlaut bzw. Zischlaut. *IIJ* 31 (1988) 87-109.

SAKAMOTO-GOTO 1991 – Mittelindische Absolutivbildung auf *-tvā/*-tvāna(m)* und verwandte Probleme der Lautentwicklung. In: *Middle Indo-Aryan and Jaina Studies* (ed. by C. Caillat). Leiden 1991, 10-21.

SAKAMOTO-GOTO 1993 – Zu mittelindischen Verben aus medialen Kausativa. *Jain Studies in Honour of Jozef Deleu* (ed. by R. Smet and K. Watanabe). Tokyo 1993,

261-314.

SCHELLER 1967 — MEINRAD SCHELLER. Das mittelindische Enklitikum *se*. *ZvS* 81 (1967) 1-53.

SCHWARZSCHILD 1991 — LUISE ANNA SCHWARZSCHILD. *Collected Articles of LA Schwarzschild on Indo-Aryan 1953-1979*. Compiled by ROYCE WILES. Canberra: Faculty of Asian Studies, 1991.

SMITH 1950 — HELMER SMITH. Les deux prosodies du vers bouddhique. *Vetenskapssamfundets i Lund Arsberättelse* 1949-1950,I (p. 1-43).

SMITH 1952 — – Le futur moyen Indien et ses rythmes. *JAs* 1952, 169-183.

TRENCKNER 1908 — VILHELM TRENCKNER. Critical and philological notes to the first chapter (*bāhirakathā*) of the Milinda-Pañha (= Pali Miscellany). *JPTS* 1908, 102-151.

TRENCKNER (no date) — – *Radices Linguae Pālicae*. Copenhagen (a copy of the hand-written manuscript was made available to me by courtesy of Professor Dr. A. Wezler).

TURNER 1960 — RALPH L. TURNER. *Some Problems of Sound Change in Indo-Aryan*. Poona: University of Poona, 1960 (P.D. Gune Memorial Lectures 1).

TURNER 1975 — – *Collected Papers 1912-1973* (ed. by J. BROUGH). London: Oxford University Press, 1975.

WARDER 1967 — A.K. WARDER. *Pali Metre. A Contribution to the History of Indian Literature*. London: The Pali Text Society, 1967.

5. Abbreviations and sigla

The abbreviations of texts are those of the *Critical Pāli Dictionary*. The following abbreviations and signs have been employed:

V	any vowel
C	any consonant
N	any nasal
S	any sibilant
T	tenues
≠	word initial/final position
+	seam of preverb/verb, stem/suffix or a compound
ə:	*id est*
:	instead of, a substitute for
::	analogical to
~	side by side with
x	blended with
<	developed from
≮	not developed from
←	based on
†	*vox nihil*
aup.	Aupacchandasaka
jag.	Jagatī
tri.	Triṣṭubh
vait.	Vaitālīya
AMg.	Ardhamāgadhī
Aś(oka)	Edict of King Aśoka
Aśoka PE	Pillar Edict of King Aśoka
Aśoka RE	Rock Edict of King Aśoka

Aśoka Sep	Separate Edict of King Aśoka
Ee	Pali Text Society Edition of Pāli texts
JM.	Jaina Māhārāṣṭrī
MIA	Middle Indo-Aryan
OIA	Old Indo-Aryan
Pā	Pāli
PII	Proto-Indo-Iranian
PIE	Proto-Indo-European
Pkt.	Prakrit
Skt.	Sanskrit

GEIGER	= GEIGER 1916 (see also GEIGER 1994).
VON HINÜBER	= VON HINÜBER 2001.
JACOBI	= JACOBI 1886.
PISCHEL	= PISCHEL 1900.
AiGr.	= *Altindische Grammatik* of JAKOB WACKERNAGEL / ALBERT DEBRUNNER.
BHSD	F. EDGERTON. *Buddhist Hybrid Sanskrit Dictionary*. New Haven 1953 (Reprint: New Delhi: Motilal Banarsidass, 1977).
BHSG	F. EDGERTON. *Buddhist Hybrid Sanskrit Grammar*. New Haven 1953 (Reprint: New Delhi: Motilal Banarsidass, 1977).
CDIAL	R. L. TURNER. *A Comparative Dictionary of the Indo-Aryan Languages*. London 1968.
CPD	*A Critical Pāli Dictionary*. By V. TRENCKNER, D. ANDERSEN, H. SMITH *et al.* Copenhagen 1924ff.
EWAia	M. MAYRHOFER. *Etymologisches Wörterbuch des Altindoarischen*. Heidelberg 1986-1996.
KERN, *Toev.*	H. KERN. *Toevogselen op 't woordenboek van Childers*. Amsterdam 1916.

Kl. Sch.	*Kleine Schriften* (of the 'Glasenapp-Stiftung')
PED	*Pali-English Dictionary*. Edited by T.W. RHYS DAVIDS and W. STEDE. London 1921-1925 (Reprint: New Delhi: Munshiram Manoharlal, 1994).
Sadd	*Saddanīti. La Grammaire Palie d'Aggavaṃsa*. Texte établie par HELMER SMITH. Lund 1928-1966.
Sadd IV	– Tables, 1e Partie: Textes cités, Sūtras, Racines, Morphèmes, Système Grammatical et Métrique. Lund 1949.
Sadd V	– Tables, 2me Partie: Vocabulaire (*Index Verborum*). Lund 1954.

ABORI	Annals of the Bhandarkar Oriental Research Institute
AWLM	Akademie der Wissenschaften und der Literatur, Mainz (Abhandlungen der geistes- und sozialwissenschaftlichen Klasse)
AO	Acta Orientalia
BEI	Bulletin d'Études Indiennes
BB	Betzenbergers Beiträge
BSL	Bulletin de la Société de Linguistique
HS	Historische Sprachforschung
IF	Indogermanische Forschungen
IHQ	Indian Historical Quaterly
IIJ	Indo-Iranian Journal
IT	Indologica Taurinensia
JAOS	Journal of the American Oriental Society
JAs	Journal Asiatique
JBORS	Journal of the Bihar Oriental Research Society
JIBS	Journal of Indian and Buddhist Studies
JOIB	Journal of the Oriental Institute Baroda
JPTS	Journal of the Pali Text Society

MSL	Mémoires de la Société de Linguistique
MSS	Münchener Studien zur Sprachwissenschaft
NIA	New Indian Antiquary
StII	Studien zur Indologie und Iranistik
VIJ	Vishveshvaranand Indological Journal
WZKS	Wiener Zeitschrift für die Kunde Südasiens
ZII	Zeitschrift für Indologie und Iranistik
ZvS	Zeitschrift für Vergleichende Sprachforschung

6. Indices and concordances

6.1. Index rerum

→ aspiration, assimilation, contraction, degemination, dissimilation, elision, palatalisation, syncope, vowels of Pāli

only single consonants § 15.1
→ aspiration
y
as glide and *sandhi* consonant § 25
*y^h p. 93 n. 4

6.2. Index verborum

a(n)-	p. 242 n. 1
aṃsi- ~ °aṃsa-	§ 3.5
(a)kataññū-	§ 10.7
akammaneyya-	p. 62 n. 2
akalu-	p. 79 n. 4
(a)kāriya-	p. 259
(a)kicca-	p. 39, 259
akilāsu-	p. 79 n. 3
(a)kutūhala-	p. 51 n. 4
akuppa- ➜ *a(saṃ)kuppa-*	
(a)kusīta-	§ 14.4
akkuṭṭha-	p. 262 n. 3
akkula-pakkulika-	p. 122
akkocchi	p. 106, 236
akkhacchinna-	p. 123
akkhaṇa(vedhin)-	p. 9, § 5.4
akkhāti	§ 45
akkheyya-	p. 61, 258
(a)garahiya-	p. 259
agaru- ~ agalu-	p. 79 n. 4
aggañña-	p. 58 n. 6
aggahesuṃ ➜ *gaṇhāti*	
aggi-	
aggīhi, aggīsu	§ 8.3c
(ag)gini-	§ 7.13a, 21, 27
(aggi)parijita-	p. 76 n. 5
aggi-m-āsīna-	§ 25a
aggihutta-	§ 9.10
(agg')upaṭṭhāka-	§ 6.8
aggha-	§ 17
agghiya-	§ 7.13a
agyāgāra-	p. 102
agha-m-miga-	p. 123
aṅgaṇa- ➜ *(an)aṅgaṇa-*	
(aṅgāra)kāsu-	§ 3.4
aṅgulicchinna-	p. 123
accayanti ➜ *acceti*	
accasaro (2sg. pret.)	p. 239
accāyika-	p. 60 n. 6, 120
accāsana-	p. 120
accāhita-	p. 120
Accima	p. 179
accugamma	p. 122
accupatī	§ 22.1
acceka-	§ 11.5
acceti	p. 204
(3pl.) *accayanti*	p. 204
accodara-	§ 12.11
accharā-	§ 18.1, 28.2a
acchi-	p. 89 n. 8
acchera-	§ 11.5, 16.2, 22.3
ajakara-	§ 14.4
ajati	p. 9
ajaddhuka-	p. 269 n. 1
ajaddhumārikā-	p. 269 n. 1
ajānata-	p. 178
(a)jimha-	§ 18.3
ajja	p. 54, 97
ajjaṇho ~ ajjuṇho	p. 54 n. 7
ajjatagge	p. 126

6.3. Index locorum

6.4. Concordance to GEIGER's and VON HINÜBER's grammars

	GEIGER	VON HINÜBER
§ 2	(§ 29)	(§ 154)
§ 3.1	§ 2.1	§ 107
§ 3.2	§ 5-8	§ 108-110
§ 3.3	§ 6.1-2	§ 109-110
§ 3.4	§ 6.3	§ 111-112
§ 3.5	§ 6.3	§ 111
§ 4.1-4	§ 66.2	§ 168-169
§ 4.5-6	§ 66.2	§ 113
§ 5	§ 16-17	cf. § 158
§ 5.3	§ 12	§ 122-124
§ 5.10	§ 24, 31.1	§ 153-154
§ 6	–	–
§ 6.4	§ 24, 33	cf. § 160
§ 6.6	§ 3	§ 116
§ 6.7-9	§ 27	§ 142, 145
§ 7	–	–
§ 7.2b	§ 32.2, 33.2	–
§ 7.3	§ 12	§ 122-124
§ 7.4-5	§ 15.1-2	cf. § 114
§ 7.8	§ 19.1, 23, 32.2	§ 159
§ 7.9	§ 16c, 17d	§ 158
§ 7.11	§ 18.2	§ 157
§ 7.12	§ 25 (cf. 19.1)	§ 129-133
§ 7.13-14	§ 29-30	§ 152-154
§ 8	–	§ 118-119
§ 8.3a	§ 32.1, 33	–
§ 8.3c	§ 10.1	–
§ 8.3e	§ 6.3	§ 112
§ 8.4	cf. § 32	§ 416

§ 8.5	–	§ 118-119
§ 8.6	cf. § 27.6-7	§ 148
§ 9	–	–
§ 9.2b	§ 33.2	–
§ 9.3	§ 12	§ 122-124
§ 9.4	§ 14	§ 127
§ 9.5-7	§ 15.3-4	cf. § 114
§ 9.9-10	§ 15.3-4	–
§ 9.11-13	§ 16a/b, 17a, 18.1, 19.2	§ 157-158
§ 9.14	cf. § 25.2	§ 134
§ 9.15	§ 31.2	§ 154-155
§ 10	–	–
§ 10.5-6	§ 28	§ 282
§ 11	–	–
§ 11.1-2	§ 15	§ 116
§ 11.3	§ 10.2	§ 114
§ 11.4	§ 26.1	§ 138
§ 11.5-6	§ 27.5	§ 146-147
§ 11.9	§ 9	§ 157
§ 11.14	§ 3	§ 116
§ 12	–	–
§ 12.1-2	§ 15	§ 116
§ 12.3	§ 10.2	§ 114
§ 12.4	§ 26.2	§ 138
§ 12.5	§ 27.8	§ 145
§ 12.6	§ 66.2	§ 169
§ 12.7	§ 28	§ 139
§ 12.9	§ 25.2	§ 134
§ 12.16	§ 3	§ 116
§ 13	§ 2.2, 3, 35, 38.6	§ 202, 219
§ 14.1	§ 40.1a, 62.1	§ 185
§ 14.2	§ 38	§ 177-178
§ 14.3	§ 36	§ 177

§ 14.4	§ 39	§ 179
§ 14.5	§ 42.1-2	§ 195
§ 14.6	§ 42.3	–
§ 14.7	§ 42.5	§ 203-206
§ 14.8	§ 46	§ 214
§ 14.9	–	§ 213, 216
§ 14.10	§ 44-45	§ 217-218
§ 14.14	§ 47.1	§ 181-182
§ 14.16	§ 33.1	§ 281
§ 15.1	§ 49.2-51.2	§ 162, 227, 243, 246
§ 15.2	§ 64.2	§ 229
§ 15.3	§ 50.2	§ 244
§ 16.1	§ 51-55	§ 225-226, 247-248
§ 16.2	§ 51.1	§ 228
§ 16.3	cf. § 48	§ 250-251
§ 16.4	§ 52-54	§ 226
§ 16.5	§ 64.1	§ 256
§ 16.8	§ 64	§ 251, 256
§ 16.9	§ 61.1	§ 167
§ 17	§ 58-59	§ 260-261
§ 18.1	§ 57	§ 237-238
§ 18.2	§ 56	§ 232-234
§ 18.3	§ 49.1	§ 245
§ 18.4	§ 50	§ 239-244
§ 18.5	§ 51.5	§ 284-285
§ 18.6	§ 53.3, 54.6, 59.3	§ 245, 252-255
§ 19	§ 40.2, 60.2, 62.2	§ 186
§ 20	§ 55, 57, 62.2	§ 237, 249, 280
§ 21	–	§ 156
§ 22.1	§ 65.2	–
§ 22.2	§ 20	–
§ 22.3	§ 47.2, 49, 65.1	cf. § 245
§ 23	§ 66-74	§ 262-268

§ 24	§ 66.2, 74.3	–
§ 25	§ 72-73	§ 271-277
§ 26	cf. § 71.2b	§ 269
§ 27	§ 66.1	§ 278
§ 28-29	§ 75-77	§ 286-295
§ 28.2	§ 75	§ 289-291
§ 30	§ 78-80	§ 296-324
§ 31	§ 81	§ 333-336
§ 32	§ 82-83, 85	§ 325-332
§ 33	§ 84	–
§ 34	§ 95	§ 354-358
§ 35	§ 87.2, 100.2	–
§ 36	§ 86, 87.1	§ 337-341
§ 37	§ 88	§ 324
§ 38	§ 89, 99-101	§ 343
§ 39	§ 92-94	§ 348-353
§ 40	§ 90-91	§ 344-347
§ 41	§ 96-98	§ 359-363
§ 42.1	§ 104	§ 365-373
§ 42.2	§ 105-106	§ 374-378
§ 42.3	§ 107, 110	§ 381, 389
§ 42.4	§ 111	§ 379
§ 42.5	§ 108	§ 382-387.
§ 42.6	§ 109	§ 388
§ 42.7	§ 113	–
§ 43	§ 114-119	§ 390-411
§ 44	§ 120	§ 412-418
§ 44.1	§ 141.1	§ 456
§ 44.2	§ 131.2	§ 457
§ 44.3	§ 149	§ 450-453
§ 44.4	§ 142.2, 143	§ 454-455
§ 44.5	§ 132	–
§ 45	§ 139.2	§ 447

§ 46.1	§ 121-122	§ 419-425
§ 46.2	§ 124-126	§ 426-434
§ 46.3	§ 127-129	§ 435-445
§ 47	§ 127-129	§ 435-445
§ 48	§ 158-171	§ 477-488
§ 48.1 (root aorist)	§ 159 (I), 160	§ 482.1, 486
§ 48.2 (them. aorist)	§ 159 (II), 161-162	§ 482.2
§ 48.3 (*s[iṣ]*-aorist)	§ 159 (III), 163-165	§ 482.3
§ 48.4 (*iṣ*-aorist)	§ 159 (IV), 166-169	§ 482.4
§ 48.5 (redupl. aorist)	–	§ 482.5
§ 48.6 (augment)	§ 158	§ 485
§ 48.7 (*e*-preterite)	–	§ 445
§ 49	§ 150-156	§ 463-475
§ 50	§ 157	§ 476
§ 51	§ 186-189	cf. § 417
§ 52	§ 178-183	§ 489 (cf. § 415)
§ 53	§ 175-177	§ 458-462
§ 54	§ 190-193	§ 490-491
§ 55	§ 199-203	§ 495-496
§ 56	§ 194-198	§ 492-494
§ 57	§ 204-207	§ 497
§ 58	§ 208-214	§ 498-499

6.5. Concordance to PISCHEL's *Grammatik der Prakrit-Sprachen*

The above concordance of GEIGER's *Pāli. Literatur und Sprache* and VON HINÜBER's *Das ältere Mittelindisch im Überblick* (2001) and the present Pāli grammar on the one hand and the following concordance to PISCHEL's *Grammatik der Prakrit-Sprachen* on the other may render this grammar helpful for Prakrit studies, too – hopefully all the more as a short summary of the contents and a number of *addenda et corrigenda* have been added to each paragraph of PISCHEL's grammar (indicated by an arrow [➔]).

	paragraph / page of the present grammar

☞ *Prakrit*

PISCHEL § 6 (Prakrit and Vedic Sanskrit)	**p. 6-14**
PISCHEL § 7 (Prakrit and the language[s] of Aśoka's edicts)	**p. 1-3**

☞ *The sound system of Prakrit*

PISCHEL § 45	**§ 2 / 13**

☞ *Vowels*

PISCHEL § 47 (the development of [OIA] *ṛ*)	**§ 5.3, 7.3, 9.3**
➔ See BERGER (1955: 19-65) and WERBA, *WZKS* 36 (1992) 13 n. 9.	
PISCHEL § 49 ([MIA] *a* < [OIA] *ṛ*)	**§ 5.3**
PISCHEL § 50 ([MIA] *i* < [OIA] *ṛ*)	**§ 7.3**
PISCHEL § 51 ([MIA] *u* < [OIA] *ṛ*)	**§ 9.3**
PISCHEL § 52-53 ([MIA] *V* < [OIA] *ṛ*)	**§ 5 *rem.* a (p. 33-34)**
PISCHEL § 55 ([MIA] *i/u* < [OIA] *ṛ* in kinship nouns in *ṛ*)	**§ 40 (p. 173)**
PISCHEL § 56 ([MIA] *≠ri-* < [OIA] *≠ṛ-*)	**p. 56 n. 5**

➔ Words showing *≠ri-* < *≠ṛ-* are Sanskritisms (see BERGER 1955: 38)[1].

PISCHEL § 57 ([MIA] *≠a-/i-/u-* < [OIA] *≠ṛ-*) **§ 5.3, 7.3, 9.3**

➔ (a) On *mahesi-* (re-compounded < /*mahā* + *isi-*/) 'great sage' see **p. 62 n. 6** and **120**.

➔ (b) *ujju-* < **uju-* (< ṛju-) :: *ajjava-* (< ārjava-), see SMITH (1950: 13) and BERGER (1955: 51 n. 99).

PISCHEL § 58 ([MIA] *-ī-* / *-ū-* < [OIA] *-ṝ-*; [MIA] *-iCC-* / *-uCC-* < [OIA] *-īr-* / *-ūr-* < **-ṝ-*) **p. 56 n. 2**

➔ (a) *tūha-* < [OIA] **tūrtha-* < [PIE] **tṛh₂th₂ó-* (see OBERLIES 1999: 41 with n. 31).

PISCHEL § 59 ([MIA] *-ili-* < [OIA] *-ḷ-*) **§ 9.4**

PISCHEL § 60 ([MIA] *e* < [OIA] *ai*) **§ 11.2**

PISCHEL § 61a ([MIA] *o* < [OIA] *au*) **§ 12.2**

PISCHEL § 62-66 (compensatory lengthening of vowels) **§ 3.4**

PISCHEL § 67 (degemination and lenition of [MIA *-ḍh-* <] MIA *-ṭṭh-* < [OIA] -ṣṭ-) **p. 101 n. 10**

PISCHEL § 68 (*sandhi* [MIA] *-ām eva / avi* ← [OIA] *-am eva / api* [see also § 349]) **§ 26**

PISCHEL § 69-70 (lengthening of vowels at morpheme boundaries) **§ 6.3a, 8.3a**

PISCHEL § 71 (lengthening of final vowels: voc., imp., exclamations) **§ 6.3b, 8.3b 10.3a**

PISCHEL § 72 (lengthening of final vowels: nom. sg.) **§ 32.2**

PISCHEL § 73 (lengthening of final vowels in the ind. pres. and the *ya*-absol.) **§ 8.4, 58.5**

PISCHEL § 74 ([MIA] *-VNC-* < [OIA] *VCC*) **§ 3.5**

PISCHEL § 75 (final long vowel beside short vowel plus *anusvāra* [*-ā* ~ *-am*]) **§ 4.6**

PISCHEL § 76 (*metath. quant.*: long vowel instead of short vowel plus *anusvāra*)

---

[1] LÜDERS, *Brüchstücke der Kalpanāmaṇḍitikā des Kumāralāta*. Leipzig 1926, 45, opines that (Pāli) *sammiñjeti* 'to bend back the arm' goes back to (*)*saṃriñjayati* ~ *samṛñjayati* (on this word see also OLDENBERG, *Kl. Sch.* p. 1172, and OBERLIES 1995: 139).

§ 3.4, 6.3d, 8.3e

PISCHEL § 77 ([unetymological] long vowel in preverbs) **§ 6.3c, 10.3c, 12.11**

➜ On *ajjhovavanna-* see OBERLIES (1993: 14 [s.v.])

PISCHEL § 78 (strengthening of vowels) **p. 68 n. 5, § 11.14, 12.16**

➜ On *uluga-* (ulūka-) see **p. 55 n. 2**.

PISCHEL § 79-82 (Pkt. *-i- / -u-* < [OIA] *-ī- / -ū-*) **§ 7.8, 9.8**

➜ (§ 80) *kulala-* 'a particular bird' < *kurara-* (and *not* < *kulāla-*): CHARPENTIER, *Paccekabuddhageschichten*. Upsala 1908, 7 n. 1.

➜ (§ 82) On the continuations of **dvitya-* and **tritya-* see **p. 41 n. 4**.

PISCHEL § 83-84 (law of *mora*) **§ 3.2**

➜ (PISCHEL § 84) On *sindhava-* (≠ saindhava-) see **p. 44-45 (§ 7 *rem.*a)**.

PISCHEL § 85 (*-ĕ≠ / -ŏ≠*) **§ 11 *rem.* a, 12 *rem.* a**

PISCHEL § 86 (*metath. quant.*: [MIA] *VNC* < [OIA] *V̄rC*)

PISCHEL § 87 ([MIA] *V̄C* < [OIA] *V̆CC[C]*) **§ 3.2b, 5.2, 8.2, 10.2**

PISCHEL § 88 (preverb *ā* before √*khyā* / √*jñā* and other roots) **cf. p. 101 n. 5**

PISCHEL § 89 ([MIA] *V̄C* < [OIA] *V̄NC[C]*) **cf. p. 55 n. 3**

PISCHEL § 90-91 (*metath. quant.*: [MIA] *VCC* < [OIA] *V̄C*) **§ 3.3**

PISCHEL § 92-96 (treatment of word-finals before enclitics and of the initial consonant of these enclitics) **cf. p. 93 n. 2, 122**

PISCHEL § 97 (shortening of long vowels at the seam of compounds) **§ 5.2c, 7.2b 9.2b**

PISCHEL § 98 (shortening of the long *ī* of *śrī-* and *hrī-*) **§ 36 *rem.* (p. 164)**

PISCHEL § 99

– short *-i-* and *-u-* in the obl. pl. cases of the *i-/ī-* and *u-/ū*-inflexion **§ 32.9, 36.7**

– short *-i-* (and *-u-*) in the nom. and acc. pl. of the fem. *ī-* and *ū*-stems **§ 36.1**

– abl. sg. in *-ao* of the *a*-stems **§ 30.4**

PISCHEL § 101-103 ([MIA] *i* < [OIA] *a*) **§ 7.9, 7.11**

➜ (§ 103) On *candimā-* see **p. 45**.

➜ (§ 103) On *kiha* (katha<m> x ki[m-]) see OBERLIES (1993: 56 [s.v. *kiha*]).

PISCHEL § 104 ([MIA] *u* < [OIA] *a*) **§ 9.11**

➔ *śusāṇa-* < **svusāna-* < *smaśāna-* see **§ 9.14**.

PISCHEL § 105 ([MIA] *ŭ*-stems < [OIA] *ā̆*-stems) **§ 10.7 (cf. p. 135 n. 5)**

➔ (a) *ajjū-* / *ajjuā-* 'mother-in-law' < *āryā-* :: *śvaśrū-* / **śvaśrukā-* (see CHARPENTIER, *IF* 32 [1913] 98 n. 1).

➔ (b) *ghiṃsu-* ← **ghṛṃsu-* ~ (RV) *ghraṃsá-* (see CAILLAT, *ABORI* 68 [1987] 551-557 and CHARPENTIER ad *Utt.* II 8; diff. BHAYANI 1997: 9-10)

PISCHEL § 107 ([MIA] *e* < [OIA] *a*) **§ 11.9**

➔ (a) On *ettha* (see also PISCHEL § 119 / 121) see **§ 11 *rem.* b**.

➔ (b) On *sejjā-* < **sajjā-* x *sei* (śayyā- x śete) see OBERLIES (1993: 166).

➔ (c) On *heṭṭhā* see **§ 11.3**.

➔ (d) On *helli* / *hale* / *halā* see OBERLIES (1993: 167 [s.v. halā]).

PISCHEL § 108-109 ([MIA] *i* < [OIA] *ā*) –

➔ (b) On 1pl. °*imo* (see also PISCHEL § 455) see OBERLIES (1999: 46).

➔ (c) (°*metta-* <) °*mitta-* (≠ °mātra-) has received its *-i-* from *mia-* (mita-): EMENEAU, *Sanskrit Studies of M.B. Emeneau*. Berkeley 1988, 197.

PISCHEL § 110 ([MIA] *ī* < [OIA] *ā*) –

➔ On °*mīṇa-* ≠ °*māna-* (see also PISCHEL § 138) see OBERLIES (1999: 46).

PISCHEL § 111 ([MIA] *-uCC-* < [OIA] *-āCC-*) **cf. § 9.12**

PISCHEL § 112 ([MIA] *-eC-* / *-oC-* ~ [OIA] *-ā̆C[C]-*) **§ 11.9, 12.14**

PISCHEL § 113-114 ([MIA] *-a≠* / *-aṃ≠* < [OIA] *-ā≠*) **§ 4.6**

PISCHEL § 117 (*u__u* < *i__u*) **§ 9.13**

➔ *īsattha-* < *iṣvastra-* 'science of arms' (see OBERLIES 1997:13).

PISCHEL § 118 (*ṇu-* < *ni-*; °*uka-* ~ °*ika-* [e.g. *geruya-* ~ *geria-* < *gairika-*]) **cf. p. 43 n. 3**

PISCHEL § 119 (*-e-* < *-i-* followed by a cerebral that closes the syllable) **§ 11.3**

➔ On *geddha-* see **§ 11.14**.

PISCHEL § 120 (individual words: *uṭṭhubhati*) **p. 90-91**

PISCHEL § 121-122 (*e* ~ *ī* in words like *erisa-*, *kerisa-*)

➔ On *erisa-* see **§ 11 *rem.* b**.

PISCHEL § 123 ([MIA] *a* < [OIA] *u*) **§ 5.7-9**

➔ *taraccha-*: Already in Vedic *tarákṣu-* and *tarákṣa-* stand side by side (see OBERLIES, *MSS* 53 [1992] 122).

PISCHEL § 124 ([MIA] *i* < [OIA] *u*) **§ 7.10-11**
PISCHEL § 125 (*ŏ* < *u* followed by a cerebral that closes the syllable) **§ 12.3**
PISCHEL § 126 (individual words) –

➜ *uvvīḍha-* / *uvvūḍha-* < udvṛḍha- (see WACKERNAGEL, *Kleine Schriften* p. 414-416)

PISCHEL § 127 ([MIA] *-ŏCC-* < [OIA] *-ūCC-*) **cf. § 12.10-11**
PISCHEL § 128 ([MIA] *i* < [OIA] *e*) **§ 7.6**
PISCHEL § 129 ([MIA] *a* < [OIA] *e*) **cf. p. 32 n. 8**
PISCHEL § 130 (individual words) –

➜ On *aṇṇaṇṇa-* / *annanna-* (cf. also PISCHEL § 353) see **§ 16.9** ***rem.*** **c** (cf. AiGr. III § 241b *rem.* [p. 492]).

PISCHEL § 131 (split vowels [*anaptyxis*]) **§ 1 (p. 2), 21**
– metrical value **§ 2**
– VC_VC < $\bar{V}CC$ (e.g. *āyariya-* 'teacher' < *ācārya-*) **§ 3.2**
PISCHEL § 132 / 140 (split vowel *a*) **§ 5.10**
PISCHEL § 133-137 / 140 (split vowel *i*) **§ 7.13**
PISCHEL § 138 (split vowel *ī*) –

➜ *ī* never functions as *svarabhakti* vowel: passivs in *°īa-* are new formations (with the suffix *°īya-* < *°iyya-*) based on the present stem, the *part. nec.* in *°aṇīa-* is a continuation of OIA *°anīya-*, participles in *°mīna-* show a suffix that is different from OIA *°māna-* (see above *rem.* on PISCHEL § 110) and *accharīa-* is formed out of *acchari(y)a-* after the model of *°ī(y)a*-derivations (< *°īka-* [see **§ 1 (p. 3)** of the present grammar]).

PISCHEL § 139 (split vowel *u*) **§ 9.15**
PISCHEL § 141-145 (loss of initial vowels) **§ 27**

➜ (PISCHEL § 144) On *eṇhiṃ* (< *iyaṇhi* < **iyā* [< idā(nīm)] + *aṇhi* [loc. sg. of *ahan-* 'day']) see KATRE, in: *A Volume of Eastern and Indian Studies presented to Professor F. W. Thomas*. Bombay 1939, 141.

PISCHEL § 147 (inflexion of *itthī-* / *thī-* < *strī-*) **§ 7.14, 36** ***rem.***
PISCHEL § 148 (syncope) **§ 22.2**

➜ On the (alleged) syncopation of vowels see OBERLIES (1997: 13-14).

PISCHEL § 149 ([haplological] loss of syllables) **§ 22.1**

PISCHEL § 150 (loss of initial and final syllables) –

PISCHEL § 151-155 (*saṃprasāraṇa* and *-e-* < *-aya-* / *-o-* < *-ava-*) **§ 7.12, 9.14 11.4, 12.4**

→ On *thīṇa-* / *ṭhīṇa-* (≠ styāna- [*pace* PISCHEL § 151 end]) see **p. 50 (§ 8 *rem.* a).**

→ (PISCHEL § 151) Add: *āiṇṇa-* 'thoroughbred' < **ājanya-* (cf. Pāli *ājañña-*) ~ *ājāneya-* (LEUMANN apud HÜTTEMANN, *Jñāta-Erzählungen* p. 11 n.).

→ (PISCHEL § 153) *ettiya-* ← *iyattaka-* x *e[tad]-* (see WACKERNAGEL, *Kleine Schriften* p. 156 and CDIAL 1589).

PISCHEL § 156-175 (vocalic *sandhi*) **§ 23**

PISCHEL § 176 ([MIA] *-era-* < [OIA] *-arya-*) **§ 22.3**

→ On *pora-* see GHOSAL, *VIJ* 5 (1967) 38-41.

PISCHEL § 177 (assimilation of neighbouring vowels) **§ 5.8-9, 7.9-10, 9.11-13**

PISCHEL § 178-183 (final *anusvāra* and *anunāsika*) **p. 17-18 n. 6, 121 (*rem.*) § 4.1**

☞ *Consonants* (see also PISCHEL § 45)

PISCHEL § 184-185 (development of initial consonants) **§ 13, 15**

PISCHEL § 186-187 (development of middle consonants) **§ 14.2-3**

PISCHEL § 188 (development of inter-vocalic aspirate consonants) **§ 14.15 *rem.* b**

PISCHEL § 194 / 197 (gemination of consonants [*VCC* < *VC*]) **cf. § 3.3 (and p. 60 n. 5)**

→ (PISCHEL § 197) *tatto, katto, jatto, aṇṇatto* are formed analogical to *matto* < *mattaḥ* (see AiGr. III § 219dγ [p. 445]).

PISCHEL § 195 (assimilation of consonants *and* insertion of an anaptyctic vowel) **§ 21**

PISCHEL § 196 (treatment of consonant clusters at the seam of compounds) **§ 20**

PISCHEL § 198 ([MIA] *-d[h]-* < [OIA] *-t[h]*) **§ 16.9**

PISCHEL § 199 ([MIA] *-v-* < [OIA] *-p-*) **p. 76-77 n. 6, 79 n. 4**

PISCHEL § 200 ([MIA] *-h-* < [OIA] *-ph-*) –

PISCHEL § 201 ([MIA] *-v-* < [OIA] *-b-*) **§ 13 *rem.* g (and p. 73 n. 6)**

PISCHEL § 201-204 (development of *tenues* into *mediae*) **§ 14.2**

PISCHEL § 205-209 ([MIA] aspirates < [OIA] non-aspirates) **§ 14.1, 14.15**

→ *kacchabha-* is formed out of *kaccha[pa]-* (< *kassapa-* x *maccha-*) and the 'animal-suffix' *°bha-* (*pace* PISCHEL § 208).

PISCHEL § 210 ('nasal- and semivowel-aspirates') **§ 15.1 (and p. 93 n. 4)**

→ *pamhusai* is a blending of *pra-√mṛṣ* and *pra-√smṛ* (see OBERLIES 1993: 109 [s.v. pamhaṭṭha-]).

PISCHEL § 211 ([≠]*ch-* < [≠]*S-*) **§ 13**

PISCHEL § 212 ('jumping' of the aspiration) –

→ On *dhūyā-* 'daughter' see OBERLIES (1999: 39-41).

PISCHEL § 213-214 (de-aspiration) **§ 19**

PISCHEL § 215-216 ([MIA] dentals instead of [OIA] palatals and *vice versa*) **§ 14.14b (p. 88), 15.4 *rem.* a**

PISCHEL § 218-219 ([MIA] cerebrals instead of [OIA] dentals, often after original *r*) **§ 1 (p. 1-3), 14.5, 16.5**

PISCHEL § 220 (non-cerebralisation of [*r*___]*t*) **§ 1 (p. 1-2)**

PISCHEL § 221 ([MIA] (≠)*ḍha-* < [OIA] (≠)*tha-*) –

→ On (*ḍh* <) *ṭh*___*t* < *th*___*t*-dissimilations see **§ 14.14b** (e.g. *kaṭhita-* **[p. 87]**).

PISCHEL § 222 ([MIA] (≠)*ḍa-* < [OIA] (≠)*da-*) **§ 14.6**

PISCHEL § 223 ([MIA] (≠)*ḍha-* < [OIA] (≠)*dha-*) –

→ On *āḍhatta-* and *āḍhiya-* see OBERLIES (1993: 29 / 30 [s.vv]).

PISCHEL § 224 ([MIA] *ṇ* < [OIA] *n*) **§ 14.7**

PISCHEL § 227-229 (development of OIA sibilants) **§ 13**

PISCHEL § 230 ([MIA] continuations of [OIA] *k*) –

→ *thova-* < stoka- x *theva-* (see CHARPENTIER, *Monde Oriental* 13 [1919] 11 n. 4; cf. id. *ad* Utt. XXXII 100).

PISCHEL § 231 ([MIA] *-va-* / *-ma-* < [OIA] *-ga-*) **§ 14.2 (p. 78 n. 1)**

→ *agaḍa-* < *gaḍ(ḍ)a-* (< *garta-* / *°karta-* [CDIAL 3967]) x *avaḍa-* (< *avaṭa-* [CDIAL 774]): See OBERLIES, *IIJ* 37 (1994) 344.

PISCHEL § 233 (development of *cha*) **cf. p. 97, § 16.1 rem.**

PISCHEL § 234 ([MIA] *√aṅg* ← [OIA] *√añj*) **p. 70 n. 1**

PISCHEL § 235 ([°]*sirai* < [°]sṛjati) –

→ Not only *√sṛ* and *√sṛj* are involved in the formation of (°) *sirai* but also *√śri* (see SCHWARZSCHILD 1991: 142-143).

PISCHEL § 236 ([MIA] (≠)*y*- < [OIA] (≠)*j*-; -V∅V- < -*VjV*-) **p. 94 n. 3**

PISCHEL § 238 ([MIA] -*VḍV*- / -*VḷV*- < [OIA] -*VṭV*-) **§ 13 (p. 72)**

PISCHEL § 239 ([MIA] -*VḍhV*- / -*VhV*- < [OIA] -*VṭhV*-) –

PISCHEL § 240 ([MIA] -*VḷV*- < [OIA] -*VḍV*-) **§ 13**

PISCHEL § 241 ([MIA] -*VrV*- < [OIA] -*VḍV*-) **cf. p. 72 n. 3**

PISCHEL § 242 ([OIA] *ḍh* remains unaltered in MIA; *ḷha* [written *lha*] < *ḍha < [OIA] *ṣṭa*) –

PISCHEL § 243 ([MIA] *veḷu*- < [OIA] *veṇu*-) **§ 13 *rem.* e**

PISCHEL § 244 ([MIA] -*l*- / -*ḷ*- < [OIA] -*t*- / -*d*-) **p. 71-72 with n. 4, 88**

➜ On °*līvaṇa*- < °*dīpana*- see OBERLIES (1995b: 191).

PISCHEL § 245 ([MIA] -*r*- < [OIA] -*t*- / -*d*-) **§ 14.14b.2 (p. 88 with n. 6)**

➜ On the 'dental' pronounciation of *r* see **p. 89**.

PISCHEL § 246 ([(alleged) MIA] -*v*- < [OIA] -*t*- / -*d*-) –

PISCHEL § 247 (*limba*- < *nimba*-) **§ 14.14b2**

PISCHEL § 248 ([MIA] -*m*- < [*]-*v*- < [OIA] -*p*-) **§ 14.14b.2 (p. 89)**

➜ On *viḍima*- (see also PISCHEL § 103) see OBERLIES, *OLZ* 93 (1998) 107.

➜ *kuṇima*- < **kuṇiva*- < *kuṇapa*- (due to *n*__*m* < *n*__*v*-assimilation).

PISCHEL § 249 (*pāraddhi*- 'hunting' < prārabdhi-) –

PISCHEL § 250 ([MIA] (≠)*m*- < [OIA] (≠)*b*-) –

➜ On *māhaṇa*- see MAYRHOFER, *WZKS* 36 (1994) 169-171.

PISCHEL § 251 ([MIA] (≠)*v*- < [OIA] (≠)*m*-) **§ 14.14b.1 (p. 87)**

PISCHEL § 252 ([MIA] ≠*j*- < [OIA] ≠y-; [MIA] -*jj*- < [OIA] -*y*-) **§ 1 (p. 4), 14.9**

PISCHEL § 254 ([MIA] -*va*- < [OIA] -*ya*- in the vicinity of palatals) **§ 14.8**

➜ *pajjava*- < paryaya- (see BERGER 1955: 54).

PISCHEL § 255 (*laṭṭhi*- < *yaṣṭi*-) **§ 14.12**

PISCHEL § 256-259 (*r* ~ *l*) **§ 14.10**

PISCHEL § 260 ([MIA] ≠*ṇ*- / ≠*n*- < [OIA] ≠*l*-) **§ 14.14b.1 (p. 86)**

PISCHEL § 261 ([MIA] -*m*- < [OIA] -*v*-) **p. 87 with n. 4, 89 with n. 4**
cf. p. 100 n. 2

PISCHEL § 262-264 ([MIA] -*h*- < [OIA] -*S*-) **§ 18.7 (and p. 109 n. 6)**

PISCHEL § 265 ([MIA] -*v*- < [OIA] -*s*/*ṣ*- in numerals) –

PISCHEL § 266 ([MIA] aspirated media < [OIA] *h* [e.g. *idha* < iha]) **§ 14.15 *rem.* d**

➜ On the passives *dubbhai*, *vubbhai*, *libbhai* (etc.) – formed after the pattern *x* : *duddha-* = *labbhai* : *laddha-* – see JACOBI, *Kleine Schriften* p. 115, BERGER, *MSS* 19 (1966) 73, and OBERLIES (1993: 152 [s.v. *virubbhai*]).

PISCHEL § 267 ([MIA] *-NCh-* < [OIA] *-Nh-*) **cf. § 18.5 (and p. 108 n. 8)**

➜ See GHOSAL, *JOIB* 13 (1963/64) 214-219.

PISCHEL § 268-272 (assimilation of consonant clusters: general rules) **§ 15-18**

PISCHEL § 273 ([MIA] *-ṇṇa-* < [OIA] *-ñca-*) **§ 16.3 (cf. p. 2 n. 3)**

PISCHEL § 275 ([MIA] *-nd-* < [OIA] *-nt-*) **cf. § 16.9**

PISCHEL § 276 ([MIA] *-CC-* < [OIA] *-CN-*; [MIA] [*ṇ*]*ṇ-* / [*n*]*n-* < [OIA] [≠]*jñ-*) **§ 16.1 (p. 96); p. 2 n. 3, § 16.3**

PISCHEL § 277 (development of [OIA] *-Cm-*) **§ 16.6**

PISCHEL § 278 (assimilation of clusters consisting of different nasals) **§ 16.4**

PISCHEL § 279 (assimilation of consonant clusters containing a semi-vowel) **§ 16.4**

PISCHEL § 280 (assimilation of clusters consisting of dental and *y*) **§ 16.1 (p. 96)**

PISCHEL § 281 (non-palatalisation of [OIA] *-ty-* [> (MIA) *-tt-*]) **p. 96 n. 5, 97**

➜ On *tacca-* 'truth' (see also PISCHEL § 299) see **p. 97 n. 2.**

➜ On *pattijjai* (see also PISCHEL § 487) see SMITH (1950: 181) and CPD s.v. *apara(p)pattiya* (cf. also present grammar **p. 97**).

PISCHEL § 282 (development of *Ny*-clusters) **§ 16.1 (p. 97)**

PISCHEL § 284 (development of [OIA] *-ry-*) **p. 96 n. 6**

PISCHEL § 285 ([MIA] *-ll-* < **-ly-* < [OIA] *-ry-*) **§ 16.4**

PISCHEL § 286 (development of [OIA] *-ly-* / *-vy-*; MIA forms with *-pp-*) **§ 16.4**

➜ On *vāhippai* as an analogical *pp*-passive of *vyāharati* see OBERLIES (1993: 148).

PISCHEL § 287-288 (development of [OIA] clusters with *-r-*) **§ 16.4, 16.7**

PISCHEL § 289-290 ([MIA] *-ṭṭ[h]-* < [OIA] *-rt[h]-*) **§ 16.5**

PISCHEL § 291 ([MIA] *-ḍḍ[h]-* < [OIA] *-rd[h]-*) **§ 16.5**

PISCHEL § 292 ([MIA] *-ṭṭ-* < [OIA] *-tr-*)

PISCHEL § 293 (development of *-tra* of adverbs) **§ 16.9 *rem.* a (2)**

PISCHEL § 294 ([MIA] *-ḍḍ-* < [OIA] *-dr-*) **cf. § 16.7**

PISCHEL § 295 ([MIA] *-mbir-*, *-mbil-* / *-mb-* < **-mbr-* / *-mbl-* < [OIA] *-mr-* / *-ml-*)

§ 18.5
PISCHEL § 296 (development of [OIA] clusters with *-l-*) § 16.4
PISCHEL § 297-298 (development of [OIA] clusters with *-v-*) § 16.4
PISCHEL § 299 ([MIA] *-cc[h]-* < [OIA] *-t[h]v-* / [MIA] *-jj[h]-* < [OIA] *-d[h]v-*) **cf. p. 94 n. 3**
PISCHEL § 300 ([MIA] *-pp-* < [OIA] *-tv-* / [MIA] *-bb[h]-* < [OIA] *-d[h]v-*) § 18.6
PISCHEL § 301-311 ([MIA] *-TTh-* < [OIA] *-ST[h]-* [not always at the seam of 'compound']) § 15.2 (√*sthā*), 16.2
PISCHEL § 312 (development of *-śn-*, *-śm-*, *-[k]ṣṇ-*, *-[k]ṣm-*) § 17, 18.4
➔ On *-ṣṇ-* > *ṭṭh-* see JACOBI, *Kleine Schriften* p. 106-110 (see also the present grammar **§ 18.5**).
PISCHEL § 313-314 (development of *[-]sn-*, *-sm-* and *-ṣm-*) § 18.4
PISCHEL § 315 (development of clusters consisting of sibilant and semi-vowel) § 16.4
PISCHEL § 318 / 320-321 ([MIA] *-cch-* < [OIA] *-kṣ-*) § 18.2
PISCHEL § 319 / 320-321 ([MIA] *-kkh-* < [OIA] *-kṣ-*) § 18.2
PISCHEL § 322 (*chaṇa-* 'festival' / *khaṇa-* 'moment' < *kṣaṇa-*) § 18.2
PISCHEL § 323 ([MIA] *-V̄h-* < [OIA] *-V̄kṣ-* [*aṇuppehā* < °prekṣā]) **cf. § 3.2b**
PISCHEL § 324 (Māgadhī *-sk-* < [OIA] *-kṣ-*) –
PISCHEL § 325 ([MIA] *culla-* < [OIA] *kṣulla-*) § 16.7
PISCHEL § 326 ([MIA] *[j]jh-* < [OIA] *[-]kṣ-*) § 18.2
PISCHEL § 327 ([MIA] *-cch-* < [OIA] *-ts-*) § 18.1
PISCHEL § 327[a] ([MIA] *ū+S-* < [OIA] *ut+S-*) § 10.5, 20
PISCHEL § 328 ([MIA] *[c]ch-* < [OIA] *[-]ps-*) § 18.1
PISCHEL § 329 ([MIA] *-k+k-* / *-kkh-* < [OIA] *-ḥk[h]-* [and *duha-* ~ *dukkha-*] / [MIA] *-V̄+s-* < [OIA] *-Vḥ+s-*) § 14.13, 20
PISCHEL § 330 ([MIA] *-Nh-* / *-lh-* < [OIA] *-hN-* / *-hl-*) § 18.3
PISCHEL § 331 ([MIA] *-yh-* / *-jjh-* < [OIA] *-hy-*) § 18.3
PISCHEL § 332 ([MIA] *-bbh-* < [OIA] *-hv-*) § 18.6
PISCHEL § 333 (spontaneous cerebralisation) § 14.5 *rem.*
PISCHEL § 334 (development of clusters of more than two consonants) § 17
PISCHEL § 335 (loss of initial [OIA] consonants) **cf. p. 55 n. 4, 129 n. 1**

PISCHEL § 336-337 (prothesis of *y-* [> *j-*] and *v-* [> *p-* / *m-*]) **§ 25 (p. 125)**
PISCHEL § 338 (prothesis of *h-*) **§ 14.1 *rem.* b**
PISCHEL § 339 (development of [OIA] final consonants) **§ 4.1**
PISCHEL § 340-341 (development of consonants at the seam of compounds and before enclitics) **§ 24**
PISCHEL § 342-347 ([MIA] *-o* / *-e* < [OIA] *-aḥ* [< /*-ar*/]) **§ 1 (p. 1-2), 4.2, 30.1**
PISCHEL § 348 ([MIA] *-ṃ≠* < [OIA] *-n≠* / *-m≠*) **§ 4.1**
PISCHEL § 349 (preservation of *-m≠* before enclitics) **§ 26**
PISCHEL § 350 (loss of [MIA] *-ṃ≠*) **§ 4.1**
PISCHEL § 353 (*sandhi* consonants) **§ 5**
PISCHEL § 354 (syllabic metathesis) **§ 22.3**

☞ noun inflexion

PISCHEL § 355-359 (development of [OIA] consonant stems; gender) **p. 139 (*rem.* a/b), § 28.2**
PISCHEL § 360 (loss of the dual) **§ 28.1**

➔ Cf. CHARPENTIER *ad* Utt XXIII 88: '*Kesī-Goyamao* (*scil.* of Utt XXIII 88) ... is certainly identical with Sct. *Keśi-Gautamayoḥ*. PISCHEL § 360 &c. categorically denies that there exist any traces of the dual in the middle Indian dialects, but such are undeniably met with, although they certainly are very rare. It would probably be imprudent to deny that, for instance, *āṇāpāṇū* (PISCHEL § 105) is to be explained as anything else but Sct. *ānaprāṇau*' (see also NORMAN 1991: 115-117 and YAMAZAKI, *JIBS* XXVIII.1 [1979] 148-149).

PISCHEL § 361 (*dativus finalis*) **§ 28.3**

☞ *a*-inflexion

PISCHEL § 363-373 **§ 29-30**

➔ Stem used as case form: CHANDRA, *Sambodhi* 4 (1975/76) 34-35. **p. 136-137 n. 8**

➔ On the °*aṃ*-ablative (not recorded by PISCHEL) see ALSDORF, *Kleine Schriften* p. 66-68. **§ 30.4**

➔ (see also PISCHEL § 375) *ajjo* and other 'short' vocatives – like *avvo, tāo* and (fem.) *ammo* – have their *-o* from forms like *bho* and *āuso* (see OBERLIES 1993: 13 [s.v. ajjo], DUNDAS, *IT* 8/9 [1980/81] 163-167, and CAILLAT, *IF* 71 [1966] 308). **cf. § 12.14**

☞ *ā*-inflexion

PISCHEL § 374-376 **§ 29, 31**

➔ The nom. sg. may also end in *-a* (see BALBIR, in: *Dialectes dans les littératures indo-aryennes* [édité par COLETTE CAILLAT]. Paris 1989, 512).

➔ Often the nom. in *-ā* is used instead of the acc. in *-aṃ* (see E. LEUMANN, *Kleine Schriften* p. 498 n.1, CHANDRA, *Sambodhi* 4 [1975/76] 35, and id., *Proceedings of the All-India Oriental Conference*. Thirty-first Session. Poona 1984, 379).

➔ Cf. ALSDORF, *Kleine Schriften* p. 66: "It is unnecessary to have recourse to the Brāhmaṇa form *mālāyai* for the explanation of Pkt. *mālāe*" (*pace* PISCHEL § 375) which can be derived from (old MIA ['Pāli']) *mālāya*.

see p. 161-162 n. 10

➔ On voc. sg. *ammo* see above *ad* PISCHEL § 363-373.

➔ (§ 376) Not only in verses does the nom.-acc. pl. in *-u* occur, but also in prose: (nom. pl.) Vasudevahiṇḍi 6,21, (acc. pl.) ibid. 5,3, 11,9, 13,12, 28.10 (see CHANDRA, *Tulsī Prajñā* 2 [1976] 41-42).

☞ *i-/u*-inflexion

PISCHEL § 377-382 **§ 29, 32**

➔ (§ 379) On the instr. sg. in *-īṇa(ṃ)* and *-ūṇa(ṃ)* (cf. PISCHEL p. 264 l. 2-8 and 285 l. 32-33) see CHANDRA, *Sambodhi* 4 (1975/76) 35, id. *Proceedings of the All-India Oriental Conference*. Thirty-first Session. Poona 1984, 379-380, UPADHYE, *Dhūrtākhyāna of Haribhadra Sūri*. Bombay 1944, p. 52 = *Papers*, Mysore 1983, 152 (only once attested in Vasudevahiṇḍi [*bhattūṇa*, 35.8], but quite often in Paumacariya [*sādhūṇaṃ*, 63.22, *vāūṇa*, 65.41]).

➔ On the instr. *mahāmuṇī* and the loc. *bhikkhū* see CHARPENTIER ad Utt XXIII 12 and XI,15 respectively.

☞ (masc.) *ī-/ū*-inflexion
PISCHEL § 383 **§ 35**

☞ *ī-/ū*-inflexion
PISCHEL § 384-388 **§ 29, 36**

→ The nom. sg. the *ī*-stems may also end in *-i* (see CHANDRA, *Sambodhi* 4 [1975/76] 35, and BALBIR, in: *Dialectes dans les littératures indo-aryennes* [édité par COLETTE CAILLAT]. Paris 1989, 512). **§ 36.1**

→ Often the nom. in *-ī* is used instead of the acc. in *-iṃ* (see CHANDRA, *Sambodhi* 4 [1975/76] 35, and id. *Proceedings of the All-India Oriental Conference*. Thirty-first Session. Poona 1984, 379).

→ Also Pkt. knows an obl. sg. in *-ie* (cf. e.g. *khantie*, Utt III,13).

☞ inflexion of kinship terms in *°a(r)-*
PISCHEL § 389-392 **§ 40**

→ *piya(r)-* 'father' has a *cas. obl.* in *-āe* (see BALBIR, in: *Dialectes dans les littératures indo-aryennes* [édité par COLETTE CAILLAT]. Paris 1989, 516-518).

☞ inflexion of diphthongal stems
PISCHEL § 393-394 **§ 37**

☞ inflexion of stems in *°([m/v]an)t-*
PISCHEL § 395-398 **§ 29, 38b, 41**

☞ inflexion of *rā(y)a-* 'king'
PISCHEL § 399-400 **§ 39**

→ *rā(y)a-* has a *cas. obl.* in *-āe* (see BALBIR, in: *Dialectes dans les littératures indo-aryennes* [édité par COLETTE CAILLAT]. Paris 1989, 516-518).

☞ inflexion of *°CCa(n)*-stems
PISCHEL § 401-402 **§ 39 (p. 170-171)**

☞ inflexion of (OIA) *maghavan(t)-*, *panthā-*, *yuvan-* and *śvan-*
PISCHEL § 403 **§ 39 (p. 171-172)**

☞ ntr. *an*-stems > ntr. / masc. *a*-stems
PISCHEL § 404 **§ 28.2a (p. 131-132)**

☞ inflexion of stems in *°(m/v)in-*
PISCHEL § 405-406 **§ 34**

☞ inflexion of *s*-stems
PISCHEL § 407-411 **§ 38b**

☞ inflexion of *puṃs-*
PISCHEL § 412 **§ 39 (p. 171-172)**

☞ inflexion of other consonantal stems
PISCHEL § 413 **§ 38**

☞ comparatives and superlatives
PISCHEL § 414 **§ 38 (p. 167-168)**

☞ pronouns
PISCHEL § 415-419 (personal pronoun of the 1st person sg.) **§ 42.1 (p. 180-184)**

→ On Māgadhī *ahake* see MICHELSON, *IF* 23 (1908/09) 129-130.

→ *me* is used as acc. sg. also in JM (see ALSDORF, *Kleine Schriften* p. 68).

p. 181

→ *ṇaṃ*, recorded by PISCHEL § 415 as taught by the grammarians, is attested at Vasudevahiṇḍi 122.25 (see CHANDRA, *Tulsī Prajñā* 5 [1979] 14).

→ The instr. *mayā* – the most usual form in the Vasudevahiṇḍi and attested also in JACOBI's *Ausgewählte Erzählungen* (10,1) – is not recorded by PISCHEL § 418 (see ALSDORF, *Kleine Schriften* p. 68).

→ (ALSDORF, *Kleine Schriften* p. 68, CHANDRA, *Tulsī Prajñā* 2 [1976] 42 / 5 [1979] 14, and id. *A Critical Study of the Paumacariyaṁ*. Vaishali 1970, p.

565) JM has a gen. *amha(m)* and loc. *mai / mae* (PISCHEL § 415 / 418 only for Śaurasenī [*mai*] and the grammarians [*amha / mae*]) and *mamamhi* (wanting in PISCHEL).

→ Līlavaī 461 (Ed. by A N. UPADHYE, Bombay 1966, Singhi Jain Series XXXI)) has a nom. pl. *amhi*.

PISCHEL § 420-422 (personal pronoun of the 2nd person sg.) **§ 42.1 (p. 180-184)**

→ *te* is used as acc. sg. also in JM (see ALSDORF, *Kleine Schriften* p. 68).

p. 182

→ *tumhe* as acc. sg., *tujjhe* as nom. and acc. pl. and *tumhesu* as loc. pl. – noted by PISCHEL § 420 / 421 as only taught by Prakrit grammarians – is to be found in Vasudevahiṇḍi (see CHANDRA, *Tulsī Prajñā* 2 [1976] 42 / 5 [1979] 15).

→ (§ 422) *bhe* : *tubbhe* = *mhe* (not recorded by PISCHEL, l.c.) : *tumhe* (see ALSDORF, *Kleine Schriften* p. 68-69; cf. also CHANDRA, *Tulsī Prajñā* 2 [1976] 42).

PISCHEL § 423-425 (non-personal pronoun) **§ 42.2 (p. 184-186)**

→ (PISCHEL § 423) On *se* (formed to *so* after the pattern of *me* and *te*) see OBERLIES (1999: 49). The Vasedevahiṇḍi uses it as a gen. pl. (see CHANDRA, *Tulsī Prajñā* 5 [1979] 15).

→ (PISCHEL § 423 / 425) *siṃ* and *tīi* (noted by PISCHEL as only taught by Prakrit grammarians) are to be found in Vasudevahiṇḍi (see CHANDRA, *Tulsī Prajñā* 2 [1976] 42-43 / 5 [1979] 15).

→ (PISCHEL § 425) Vasedevahiṇḍi 191.14 *et passim* uses an abl. *tao* which PISCHEL records as only taught by the grammarians (see CHANDRA, *Tulsī Prajñā* 5 [1979] 14).

→ (PISCHEL § 425) *tāhe / yāhe* < *tarhi / yarhi* (see AiGr. III § 219dß).

→ (PISCHEL § 425) *tā* < *tat* (see BLOCH, *Recueil d'articles* 177 n. 3, and OBERLIES 1993: 85 [s.v.]).

PISCHEL § 426 (inflexion of *eta[ṃ]-*) **§ 42.3 (p. 186-187)**

→ Nom. sg. fem. *esa* is actually attested (see CHANDRA, *Tulsī Prajñā* 2 [1976] 43).

→ *ettāhe* < *etarhi* (see NORMAN, *JRAS* 1995, p. 317; completely different KATRE, in: *A Volume of Eastern and Indian Studies presented to Professor F.*

W. Thomas. Bombay 1939, 141).

PISCHEL § 427 (inflexion of *ya[ṃ]-*) **§ 42.3 (p. 186-187)**

➜ *jā* < *yat* (see OBERLIES 1993: 76 [s.v.]).

PISCHEL § 428 (interrogative pronoun) **§ 42.4 (p. 187)**

➜ On *kavaṇa-* in the Paumacariya see CHANDRA, *A Critical Study of the Paumacariyaṁ*. Vaishali 1970, p. 568.

PISCHEL § 429-430 (inflexion of *ida[ṃ]-*) **§ 42.5 (p. 188-189)**

➜ (PISCHEL § 429 end) *ajjho* / *ajjhā* is based on **ayyaṃ* (see HENDRIKSEN, *BSOAS* 20 [1957] 330)

PISCHEL § 431 (inflexion of *ena-* / MIA *ṇa-*) **§ 42.3 (p. 186)**

➜ The pronoun *iṇa-* is a dissimilated form of *ima-* (see LEUMANN, *Kleine Schriften* p. 490-504).

➜ Acc. pl. *ṇe* is attested at Vasudevahiṇḍi 16.26 and 21.10 (see CHANDRA, *Tulsī Prajñā* 2 [1976] 42), instr. pl. fem. ibid. 188.3 (see CHANDRA, *Tulsī Prajñā* 5 [1979] 14).

➜ On *ṇhe* (*ṇe* [see above] x *bhe*) – not recorded by PISCHEL – see OBERLIES, *OLZ* 93 (1998) 107.

PISCHEL § 432 (inflexion of *adas-*) **§ 42.6 (p. 189-190)**

PISCHEL § 433 (inflexion of other pronouns) **§ 42.7 (p. 190-192)**

PISCHEL § 434 (pronominal derivations)

☞ numerals

PISCHEL § 435-444 (the cardinals 1-19) **§ 43 (p. 192-196)**

PISCHEL § 445 (the cardinals 19-59) **§ 43 (p. 196)**

➜ Add *teyāla-* '43' (see Utt XXXIV 20).

PISCHEL § 446 (the cardinals 60-99) **§ 43 (p. 196)**

PISCHEL § 447 (construction of the cardinals 19-99 with nouns) **§ 43 (p. 196-197)**

PISCHEL § 448 (the cardinals 100 and above) –

PISCHEL § 449 (the ordinals) **§ 43 (p. 197)**

PISCHEL § 450 (*ardha* + ordinal / cardinal) **§ 43 (p. 198 with n. 6)**

PISCHEL § 451 (multiplicative adverbs etc.) **§ 43 (p. 198)**

☞ the verb

PISCHEL § 452 (the verb) **§ 44 (p. 199-201)**

PISCHEL § 453-456 (ind. pres. *parasmaipada*) **§ 46.1**

➜ (PISCHEL § 454) The 1sg. of the ind. pres. ends also in *-aṃ* (see ALSDORF, *Kleine Schriften* p. 58-59, and DELEU/SCHUBRING, *Studien zum Mahānisīha. Kapitel 1-5*. Hamburg 1963, 12). **cf. p. 217 n. 2**

➜ (PISCHEL § 454 / 455) On the 1sg. in *-amhi* see also UPADHYE, *Līlavaī. A Romantic Kāvya in Māhārāṣṭrī Prākrit of Koūhala*. Bombay 1966 (Singhi Jain Series XXXI), p. 75, On 1pl. in *-imo* (see also PISCHEL § 108) see OBERLIES (1999: 46).

➜ (PISCHEL § 454) Apabhraṃśa 1sg. *-aũ* goes back to *-ămi* (see OBERLIES, *Historische Grammatik des Hindi*. Reinbek 1998, 37 n. 42).

➜ (PISCHEL § 455) The 1pl. is often used as 1sg. (see ALSDORF, *Kleine Schriften* p. 59-60; on the 1sg. in *-āmo* / *-imo* see also UPADHYE, *Līlavaī. A Romantic Kāvya in Māhārāṣṭrī Prākrit of Koūhala*. Bombay 1966 [Singhi Jain Series XXXI], p. 75, and CHANDRA, *A Critical Study of the Paumacariyaṁ*. Vaishali 1970, p. 568-569).

PISCHEL § 457-458 (ind. pres. *ātmanepada*) **§ 46.1**

➜ (PISCHEL § 457) Vasudevahiṇḍi has a 1sg. in *-ahe* (ALSDORF, *Kleine Schriften* p. 59).

➜ (PISCHEL § 457) On *vaṇe* (< **maṇe* < *manye*) see ALSDORF, *Kleine Schriften* p. 64-65.

PISCHEL § 459-465 (optative) **§ 46.3**

➜ Add to § 460: The 1sg. of the opt. *parasm.* ends also in *-jjaṃ* (see ALSDORF, *Kleine Schriften* p. 59).

PISCHEL § 466 (precative) **cf. p. 199**

➜ On the *e*-'preterite' (*care*, *pahaṇe*, *udāhare*, *pucche*) see **p. 243**.

➜ On the 'preterite' in *-īa* see OBERLIES (1997: 15).

➜ On (aor.) *acche*, *abbhe* see WACKERNAGEL, *Kleine Schriften* p. 157 n. 1.

PISCHEL § 467-471 (imperative) **§ 46.2**

PISCHEL § 472 (*e*-verbs) **§ 45**

PISCHEL § 473-484 ([OIA] present class I) **§ 44 (p. 200)**

PISCHEL § 474 (*dei* 'gives') **p. 204, 213**
PISCHEL § 475-476 (*bhavati* 'is, becomes') **p. 208-209**
PISCHEL § 483 (*ṭhāi* / *ṭhāyati*) **p. 214-215**

→ (PISCHEL § 473) *jiṇai* does not belong to √*ji* but to √*jyā* (see OBERLIES, *OLZ* 94 [1999] 390-392).

→ (PISCHEL § 474) *lei* < *lahai* (labhate) :: *dei* (see TEDESCO, *JAOS* 43 [1923] 366).

→ (PISCHEL § 482) *dhovai* 'washes' < *dhāvai* x *dhoya-* (dhāvati x dhauta-): OBERLIES (1993: 95 [s.v. dhovaṇa-]).

PISCHEL § 485-486 ([OIA] present class VI) **§ 44 (p. 200)**
PISCHEL § 487-489 ([OIA] present class IV) **§ 44 (p. 200-201)**
PISCHEL § 489 (transfer of present classes: IV → I / VI) **§ 45**
PISCHEL § 489 (√*man*) **cf. p. 203 n. 2**

→ (PISCHEL § 488; cf. ibid. § 197) *laggai* is based on the verbal adjective *lagga-* (< lagna-): OBERLIES (1993: 140 [s.v. laei]). **§ 51a**

→ (PISCHEL § 489) On *(ā)vindhai* see OBERLIES (1993: 34), On *uvvihai* (< *ud-vṛhati*) see WACKERNAGEL, *Kl. Sch.* p. 415.

PISCHEL § 490 ([OIA] present class X, denominatives, causatives) **§ 51-52**
PISCHEL § 491 (denomin. without suffix) **§ 51**
PISCHEL § 492-499 ([OIA] present class II) **§ 44 (p. 201 / 205)**
PISCHEL § 492-499 (transfer of present classes: II → I / IV / VI) **p. 202**
PISCHEL § 493 (√*i*) **p. 201 / 204**
PISCHEL § 498 (√*as*) **p. 206-208**

→ On *āikkhai* see OBERLIES (1993: 28 [s.v. *aikkhiya-*]). **cf. p. 42 n. 6**

PISCHEL § 500-501 ([OIA] present class III [√*dhā*, √*bhī*] and its transfer) **p. 202 / 205**
PISCHEL § 500 (√*dhā*) **p. 213-214**
PISCHEL § 502-505 (transfer of present class V → IX / I) **p. 203 / 205**
PISCHEL § 503 (√*śru*) **p. 203 / 205 with n. 4**
PISCHEL § 504 ([*pra*+]√*āp*) **p. 205 with n. 4**
PISCHEL § 505 (√*takṣ*, √*śak*, √*stṝ*, √*stagh*) **p. 205**
PISCHEL § 506-507 (transfer of present class VII → I) **p. 202**

PISCHEL § 508-509 (√*kṛ*) **p. 210-212**
PISCHEL § 510-512 ([OIA] present class IX and its transfer → I) **p. 205-206**
PISCHEL § 513 (√*bandh*) **p. 201**
PISCHEL § 514 (*bhaṇāsi*, *bhaṇādi*, *bhaṇādu*, *bhaṇādha*, *bhaṇāhi*) **cf. p. 203 n. 4**
PISCHEL § 515 ([OIA] imperfect) **p. 228-229**
PISCHEL § 516-517 ([OIA] aorist) **§ 48 (p. 229-241)**

→ Not only in AMg. did aorist forms survive but also in (archaic) JM. (see ALSDORF, *Kleine Schriften* p. 60-62, and BALBIR, in: *Dialectes dans les littératures indo-aryennes* [édité par COLETTE CAILLAT]. Paris 1989, 508).

PISCHEL § 518 ([OIA] perfect) **p. 229**
PISCHEL § 519 (plusquamperfect) **cf. p. 262**
PISCHEL § 520-534 (future) **§ 49**
Pischel § 535-549 (passive) **§ 53**
PISCHEL § 549 (future passive) **p. 244**

→ On analogically formed passives like *sippai*, *libbhai*, *suvvai* (etc.) see JACOBI, *Kleine Schriften* p. 110-117, OBERLIES (1993: 152 [s.v. *virubbhai*]) and BHAYANI (1997: 37-45).

PISCHEL § 550 (passive used as active) **p. 199 n. 4**

→ Also JM knows this usage: *logo ... samaṇa-samīvam uvagammai*, Vasudevahiṇḍi 85.12-13

PISCHEL § 551-554 (causative) **§ 52**
PISCHEL § 552 (causative in *-ve-*) **p. 253**
PISCHEL § 555 (desiderative) **p. 200**
PISCHEL § 556 (intensive) **p. 200**
PISCHEL § 557-559 (denominative) **§ 51**

→ (PISCHEL § 557) On *appiṇai* see OBERLIES (1993: 22 with n. 18/19)

☞ the *verbum infinitum*

PISCHEL § 560 (present participle) **§ 54**

→ The present participle is used as conditional, i.e. to denote the *irrealis* (see ALSDORF, *Kleine Schriften* p. 66-67 n. 1) **§ 55 rem.**

→ In Prakrit the present participle can be used as agent noun (see BHAYANI 1998: 9).

PISCHEL § 561-563 (part. in *°[m]āṇa-*) **§ 54 (p. 257)**

PISCHEL § 564-569 (verbal adjective) **§ 56**

→ (PISCHEL § 566) A lot of verbal adjectives in *-CC-* (*-kk-*, *-gg-*, *-ṇṇ-*) are formed by analogy (see BHAYANI, *Bhāratīya Vidyā* 19 [1959] 111-115 = 1997: 46-65).

PISCHEL § 570-572 (*participium necessitatis*) **§ 55**

PISCHEL § 573-580 (infinitive) **§ 57**

PISCHEL § 581-594 (absolutive) **§ 58**

PISCHEL § 595-602 (suffixes [partly unknown to OIA / Skt.])

PISCHEL § 595 ('*l[l]*-suffixes' [cf. TESSITORI, *ZDMG* 68 (1914) 573]) **cf. p. 94 n. 3**

PISCHEL § 597 (*°tta[ṇa]-*) **p. 9 with n. 1**

PISCHEL § 602 (*°ima-*) **§ 7.8b (p. 40 with n. 3 and p. 41)**

PISCHEL § 603 (compounds) **p. 122-123**

Last additions

p. 5 n. 5 Is also *araṇa-* (in: *araṇa+vihāri[n]-*) a re-borrowing from Tamil *araṇa-* < Skt. *śaraṇa-* 'shelter'? Cf. TEDESCO, *JAOS* 74 (1954) 181; on the loss of ≠*ś-* of Sanskrit words borrowed into Dravidian see LÜDERS, *Philologica Indica* p. 178 n. 1.

On Dravidian loan-words in Pāli texts see also the contributions of M. D'ONZA CHIODO / E. PANATTONI in *Ludwik Sternbach Felicitation Volume*. Vol. II. Lucknow 1981, 811-818, and in *Bandhu: Scritti in onore di Carlo Della Casa*. Vol. I. Turin 1997, 109-115.

The Pāli vocabulary is comparatively poor in Deśī words (cf. *uddhana-* [see p. 32 n. 1], *sāhuḷa-* 'coarse cloth', M I 509,22 [~ *sāhulī-*, Deśīnāmamālā VIII 52], *siṅga-* 'the young of an animal', Ja V 92,21* [~ *siṅgaya-*, Deśīnāmamālā VIII 31]; on *tuvaṭṭeti* see VON HINÜBER, *JPTS* 26 [2000] 71-75). See also p. 34 (*rem.* d).

p. 6 PIE **keu̯d*^{h} 'to hide, to veil' (see *Lexikon der indogermanischen Verben*. Wiesbaden 1998, 319), not attested in Vedic and Sanskrit, survives in Pāli (*o-/pali)guṇṭhita-* 'veiled' (see OBERLIES 1993: 12-13).

p. 8 (3) On the prominence of the aorist see WITZEL, in: *Dialectes dans les littératures indo-aryennes* (édité par COLETTE CAILLAT). Paris 1989, 215-216 (§ 9.5).

p. 8 n. 6 The ending *-are* soon became obsolet and was replaced by *-anti*: (Cf.) +*saṃvijjare*, Ja VI 205,11*, +*āyācare*, VI 211,4* (so read with metre against *saṃvijjanti* and *āyācanti* in all mss.). See VON HINÜBER 2001: § 425 (with reference to ALSDORF, *Kleine Schriften* p. 801 / 804).

p. 10 l. 3 Cancel *āsīvisa-* (see e.g. Mahābhārata 2,59.3: *āśīviṣāḥ*).

p. 11 l. 3 Add: *kuhiṃ* 'where?', a blending of (RV) *kúha* and (MIA) *kahiṃ* (see AiGr. III p. 564).

p. 12 l. 1 Add: *thaneti* 'thunders' (RV+ *stanáyati*). See NARTEN, *Kleine Schriften* p. 403 n. 20.

p. 12 l. 3 LEUMANN, *Maitreya-samiti*. Straßburg 1919, p. 192, compares (Pāli) *dhīti(ma[nt])-* with RV+ *dhīti-* 'devotion'.

p. 12 l. 12 Can we compare monosyllabic *va* 'like' (see p. 129) to RV+ *va* 'like'? See also FRANKE, *Pāli und Sanskrit*. Strassburg 1902, 151.

p. 13 It is probable that *sāha(ssa)*, Ja VI 80,7*, goes back to Vedic *sāhná-* 'lasting [only] one day' (see WILHELM SCHULZE, *Kleine Schriften – Nachträge*. Göttingen 1966, p. 823 n. 7). And *samjambharim (karoti)* may reflect the Vedic intensive *jarbhari- / jarbhr°* (see KONOW / ANDERSON, *JPTS* 1909, 42).

As for Vedic-Pāli-isoglosses cf. also *sādṛśa-* (Śāṅkhāyana-Śrautasūtra IV 21,2) and Pāli *sādisa-* (with the *-ā-* of *tādṛś[a]-* [see AiGr. III § 218b *rem.*]).

Did Pāli *sevati* preserve the Vedic meaning 'to stick to, to rub' of √*sev* (cf. *mūlaṃ mūlena saṃsaṭṭhaṃ, sākhā sākhā nisevare*, Ja II 106,6*)? See CPD I, p. 515 and 561 (s.v. asevanā).

p. 19 l. 3 It is possible that *(a)hatthapāsa-* corresponds to (Skt.) *(a)hastapāśa-* (see DE JONG, *BSOAS* 49 [1986] 591).

p. 23 l. 4 Cf. *balya-* 'foolishness', Dhp 63, ~ *bāliya-*, Ja II 220,11*.

p. 23 l. 7 On *suriya-* (sūrya-) vs. *dibba-* (divya-) see AiGr. I § 181a *rem.* (p. 201) pointing out the retention of Vedic $-_iy-$ (and $-_uv-$).

p. 23 n. 3 On *sampavaṅka-* see also W. B. BOLLÉE, in: *Essays of Professor Jagdish Chandra Jain*. New Delhi 1994, 68-69.

p. 28 l. 1 Add: (nom. sg.) *nikkhamanā*, Ja II 208,17*, ~ *(abhi)nikkhamanaṃ*, D II 51,15.

p. 30 n. 4 On *tathatā-* see also BHSD (s.v.).

p. 32 l. 5 On the palatal colouring of *h* see also VON HINÜBER § 223.

p. 36 (5) On *°āgāra-* → *āgāra-* see VON HINÜBER, *Kratylos* 29 (1984) 168.

p. 43 l. 1 *tissā* (< tasyāḥ) might also show the influence of *kissā* (see PISCHEL § 103 and BLOCH 1965: 147).

p. 44 l. 1 The *Critical Pāli Dictionary* emends (Ee) *abbhihāsi*, Ja V 169,23*, to *abbhahāsi*.

(Cf. p. 246) "That the *ya*-present (type *púṣyati* 'to thrive') has no **-iti* for *-yati* (**pus[s]iti*), would first be due to the influence of the other *a*-classes" (TEDESCO, *JAOS* 65 [1945] 159 n. 29).

p. 45 l. 3 Add: *agghi-* ~ *agghiya-* ~ *agghika-* (on these words see LEUMANN, *Maitreya-samiti*. Straßburg 1919, p. 221).

p. 51 l. 3 Add: *(samaṇa)kuttaka-* 'wearing (only) the dress of an ascetic = pretending to be an ascetic' (see PED s.v. kuttaka).

p. 73 l. 8 Cf. *mālāguḷa(parikkhittā)*, Vin III 139,34, vs. *mālāguṇa(parikkhittā)*, A V 264,18, M I 286,21 (in parallel passages).

p. 73 n. 6 Add: *savara-* 'savage' (*śabara-*), Vin I 168,23.

p. 77 n. 5 Add: *sāḷikā-* 'Maina bird', Ja VI 421,3*, 422,30*, vs. *sāḷiyā-*, Ja VI 425,25*.

p. 79 Add *pātu(r)-* (< *prādúḥ*) to § 14.4 (see FORSSMAN, in: *Anusantatyai. Festschrift für Johanna Narten*. Dettelbach: Röll, 2000, 39-54).

p. 83 If the real ending of the absolutive was *-ttā* (see p. 269) the explanation of *lāyitvā* becomes difficult.

p. 94 n. 3 Add: *sītāluka-*, Vin I 288,16.

p. 98 On *pannarasa- / paṇṇarasa-* (§ 16.3) see also BERGER, *MSS* 47 (1986) 33.

p. 99 l. 12 It is possible that *l* is 'stronger' than the palatals and the sibilants (*semha-* would then not go back to *śleṣman-* but to *śreṣman-* [see WERBA, *Verba Indoarica*. Wien 1997, 246]).

p. 103 l. 9 On non-assimilated (°)*anv-V°* (< [°]*ann-V-*) see VON HINÜBER § 254.

p. 114 n. 1 On *pavi<si>ssāmi* (< *praviśiṣyāmi), Cp 122, Ja II 68,20 (GEIGER § 65.2) see also Sadd V 1583 (s.v. pavisati).

p. 119 l. 4 This is – of course – a purely *synchronic* description of this *sandhi* which is based on the OIA *kṣaipra-sandhi* (i.e. *app eva* < *apy eva*).

p. 125 l. 1 Cf. *sa-inda-*, D II 261,18*, 274,9*.

p. 128 l. 5 See *nantaka-* beside *anantaka-* 'rag' (cf. Pkt. *aṇantaya-*[see LEUMANN, *Kleine Schriften* p. 546]). On the Pāli word and its meaning see LÜDERS, *Kleine Schriften* p. 457-458.

p. 129 l. 3-4 *tí* for *íti* is to be found already in the Śatapatha-Brāhmaṇa (XI 6,1.3ff.), and also *pi* for *ápi* is proven by *katipayá-* (Śatapatha-Brāhmaṇa IV 3,4.19, Kāṭhaka XX 1 [: 18.12]) out of *káti* + *<á>pi*.

p. 137 l. 12 *Syncretism* is to be taken in a broad sense.

p. 139 l. 5 Add: *aṅgārino ... dumā ... accimanto / dumāni phullāni ...*, Th 527-528.

p. 164 l. 13 On *gonaṃ* < Vedic *gónām* see AiGr. I p. XXVI (= *Introduction générale* p. 11), ibid. III p. 227, and FRANKE, *Pāli und Sanskrit*. Strassburg 1902, 152.

p. 175 l. 6 (Refer back to p. 173 l. 9) The genitive *dhītu* gave rise to an amplified *dhītuyā*.

p. 177 n. 3 On the nom. sg. masc. of the present participle in *-aṃ* see also *anāyūhaṃ*, S I 1,15, *jīvaṃ*, Sn 427, *tiṭṭhaṃ* 'standing', Ja III 95,17* (so read against Ee *ṭhitaṃ* [see LÜDERS, *Philologica Indica* p. 105 n. 2]), *paccessaṃ*, Vin I 255,24, and *marissaṃ*, Ja III 214,11*.

It is possible that the mysterious *sassar iva* of Ud 79,26* should be corrected (with the *pi-pāṭha* of the Paramatthadīpanī) to *asassa-r-iva* which goes back to */asat+sat/* (as the parallel Divyāvadāna 534,23* actually reads). See OLDENBERG, *Kleine Schriften* p. 976 n. 1. On the sandhi *-ss-* < */-ts-/* see § 20, On *°r-iva* (instead of the expected *°d-iva*) see § 25 (p. 125).

p. 188 n. 6 On (Pāli) *imassa* ~ RV *imásya* see also FRANKE, *Pāli und Sanskrit*. Strassburg 1902, 152.

p. 189 GEIGER's 'dat.-gen.' fem. sg. *imissāya* is a *vox nihil*: Read Ud 68,4 – the sole reference – *imissā yeva* against Ee *imissāy' eva* (see VON HINÜBER § 387).

p. 194 l. 2 The fem. nom. *catasso* was the base for the curious instr. *catassohi*, Ap 553,9 (see VON HINÜBER § 398).

p. 203 l. 11 Add: *dade* 'I would give', Cp 27.

p. 208 l. 5 On the lengthening of the final *a* of *asma* and *amha* under the influence of the ablative endings *-smā* and *-mhā* cf. SMITH's remarks on the doublet *asmi* : *asmi-ṃ* 'I am' (1950: 5).

p. 214 l. 18 Also for GEIGER (§ 132.4) and BHSG § 28.42 *ṭhahati* is 'doubtless analogical to ... *dahati* = *dadhāti*'.

p. 216 Other *e*-verbs are (e.g.) *apanudeti*, *gantheti*, *bhakkheti* and – with resolved *-e-* (see p. 204) – *naccayanti* ('they dance', Sn 682).

p. 217-218 On 1sg. in *-ăhaṃ* cf. also the aorist *ahos' ahaṃ*, Rasavāhinī (see CPD s.v. iṇadāsī). Likewise *anuyācahaṃ* is considered a 1sg. *aorist* (i.e. < *anuyāciṃ ahaṃ* [for the sandhi see p. 117]) by CPD I 557b (s.v. anuyācati).

p. 248 n. 3 Is it the case that also *abhinivissatha* (*pāpāni parivajjetha kalyāṇe abhinivissatha* 'shun the evil ones, keep to the lovely ones', Cp 127) is haplologically shortened (< *abhinivi<si>ssatha*)? On the metre of the line quoted see CPD s.v. abhinivisati. On the use of the future as *adhortativus* see OBERLIES, *A Grammar of Epic Sanskrit* (forthcoming), § 6.2.9.

p. 257 l. 6 The CPD (s.v. *anāsasāna*) ventures to see in (*an*)*āsasāna*- a 'part. aor.'!

p. 261 l. 5 Add: *uttiṇṇa*- ~ *otarita*-, Ja I 171,17* (in the same line [!]).

p. 261 n. 1 On *anvagāt* → *anvagaṃ* see VON HINÜBER, *Kratylos* 29 (1984) 167.

p. 261 n. 6 With °*bhaṭṭha*- 'spoken' cf. *bhāṣṭa*-, Mahābhārata 3,126.28, and *abhibhāṣṭum*, ibid. 3,250.2 (see also LÜDERS, *Brüchstücke der Kalpanāmaṇḍitikā des Kumāralātā*. Leipzig 1926, 38).

p. 262 l. 5-7 Add: *adhivuttho 'mhi bhattaṃ* 'I accepted the invitation to eat [here]', Vin I 232,25, *sammuṭṭha*- 'one who has forgotten', Vin IV 4,5.

p. 268 / 270 It is quite possible that the incongruent participles *obhāsayaṃ*, A I 215,8* = IV 254,26* (*cando ca suriyo ca ... obhāsayaṃ anupariyanti* ...) and *virājayaṃ*, A II 12,22*, are (used as) *ṇamul*-absolutives. And do 'frozen' participles like *jānaṃ* (see p. 217 n. 2) belong here?

Gundelfingen (Hochschwarzwald), 18th of March 2001